England against the papacy, 1858–1861

To Gabrielle and Eliot

England against the papacy 1858–1861
Tories, Liberals, and the Overthrow of Papal Temporal Power during the Italian Risorgimento

C.T. McINTIRE

Cambridge University Press
Cambridge
London   New York   New Rochelle
Melbourne   Sydney

Published by the Press Syndicate of the University of Cambridge
The Pitt Building, Trumpington Street, Cambridge CB2 1RP
32 East 57th Street, New York, NY 10022, U.S.A.
296 Beaconsfield Parade, Middle Park, Melbourne 3206, Australia

© Cambridge University Press 1983

First published 1983

Printed in Great Britain at the University Press, Cambridge

Library of Congress catalogue card number: 82-9405

British Library cataloguing in publication data
McIntire, C.T.
England against the papacy, 1858–1861.
1. Papacy – History – 19th century
2. Great Britain – Politics and government –
19th century
I. Title
262'.132 BX1386
ISBN 0 521 24237 1

DA
47.9
.P34
M36
1983

SE

Contents

		page
	Acknowledgments	ix
	Maps	xii
	Introduction	1
1	**'English Liberties' and 'The Government of Priests'**	13
	The coming crisis	13
	England: reform and rearrange the Papal States	17
	The papacy: maintain the temporal power	22
	England turns against the papal temporal power	29
2	**Odo Russell and the network of English–papal relations**	40
	English society in Rome	40
	Odo Russell, the Whig: a two-way diplomatic medium	46
	The Mediterranean fleet and the papal trade	57
3	**Tories, the pope, and peace**	66
	Tory–papal *rapprochement*	66
	Naples, the papacy and England	70
	Queen Victoria's heir in Rome	73
	Parliament and the question of the foreign troops	79
4	**Tories, the pope, and war**	88
	The Cowley mission and the pope	88
	The proposed congress	93
	The war: English and papal neutrality	101
	The parliamentary election: Tories and papal influence	106
5	**Liberals and the revolution in the Romagna**	114
	'Let the Italians govern their own affairs'	114
	Villafranca and the confederation	123
	The papacy: first restoration, then reform	129

6	**Liberals, the congress and the Romagna**	140
	Another proposed congress and the pope	140
	England: 'non-intervention' and annexation	147
	Two rival strategies	152
7	**Liberals and the annexation of the Romagna**	163
	England's push for annexation	163
	The faithful and the papal army	169
	Annexation, not vicariat	175
8	**Liberals and the annexation of the Marches and Umbria**	189
	Next the Marches and Umbria	189
	Anticipating Garibaldi in the Papal States	192
	Peter's Pence and the Irish Brigade	200
	The conquest of the Marches and Umbria	204
	The annexation of the Marches and Umbria	212
	Conclusion	222
	Select Bibliography	228
	Index	241

Acknowledgments

A study of English–papal relations pertinent to the end of the papal monarchy in Italy necessitates research in personal and public archives in several countries. In the process, I have benefited greatly from the advice and knowledge of many people. I wish to express my deep gratitude to all those who gave me their help. There are some I would like to mention in particular: in England, Noel Blakiston, Denis Mack Smith, Derek Beales, Harry Hearder, Owen Chadwick, Maurice Cowling, Robert Blake, George Kitson Clark, E.E.Y. Hales, Cosmo Russell, Robert Williams, and especially Herbert Butterfield; in Rome, Emilia Morelli, Renato Mori, Charles Burns, and Robert Graham; in the United States, Marian Swann Miller, Ivan Scott, Otakar Odlozilik, and Edward Peters. I owe particular gratitude to Mary Carolyn Kennedy McIntire, and to my parents. I especially give my thanks to Lynn M. Case.

For the use of certain private papers, I thank the following persons, and give acknowledgment: to His Holiness Pope Paul VI for material in the Archivio Segreto Vaticano in Rome; to the gracious permission of Her Majesty Queen Elizabeth II for material in the Royal Archives, Windsor Castle; to the Earl of Derby for the Derby papers which I read in Oxford; to Viscount FitzHarris for the Malmesbury papers in Winchester; to the Earl of Mountbatten for the Broadlands papers of Lord Palmerston which I read in London; and to the Duc de Gramont for the Papiers Gramont microfilms in Paris.

I wish to give my thanks to the community in which I work, my colleagues and co-workers in the Institute for Christian Studies, Toronto. I reserve my most special thanks for my wife, Rebekah Smick-McIntire, and my children, Gabrielle and Eliot, who daily give me their love and support.

I remember the people of northern Ireland for whom some of the conflicts studied in this work are a living reality, and I wish them shalom.

I also note that 1982 is the year in which the pope, John Paul II, came to England, the Anglican–Roman Catholic International Commission issued the *Final Report*, the British representative to the Vatican was elevated to the rank of full Ambassador, and the pope created a Nunziature in London.

CTM, September 1982

A note on the footnotes and abbreviations

The footnotes which refer to archives provide data, including classifying numbers and letters, which indicate specific documents. The data are arranged in the following order where appropriate:
for official despatches: author; recipient; where written; date; despatch number; archive; subarchive, section, or year; volume and page or folio.
for private letters: author; recipient; where written; date; collection of personal papers; archive; section; volume and page or folio.

Abbreviations

AMAE, CP	France. Archives du Ministère des Affaires Etrangères. Correspondance Politique.
AMAE, MD	France. Archives du Ministère des Affaires Etrangères. Mémoires et Documents.
ANParigi	Papal States (The Vatican). Archivio della Nunziatura di Parigi.
ANVienna	Papal States (The Vatican). Archivio della Nunziatura di Vienna.
ASdS	Papal States (The Vatican). Archivio Segreto del Segretario di Stato.
ASMAE	Piedmont-Sardinia. Archivio Storico del Ministero degli Affari Esteri.
ASV	Papal States (The Vatican). Archivio Segreto Vaticano.
FO	Great Britain. Foreign Office.
HHSA PA	Austria. Haus-, Hof-, und Staatsarchivs. Politische Akten des Ministeriums des Aussen.
PRO	Great Britain. Public Record Office.
RA	Great Britain. Royal Archives, Windsor Castle.

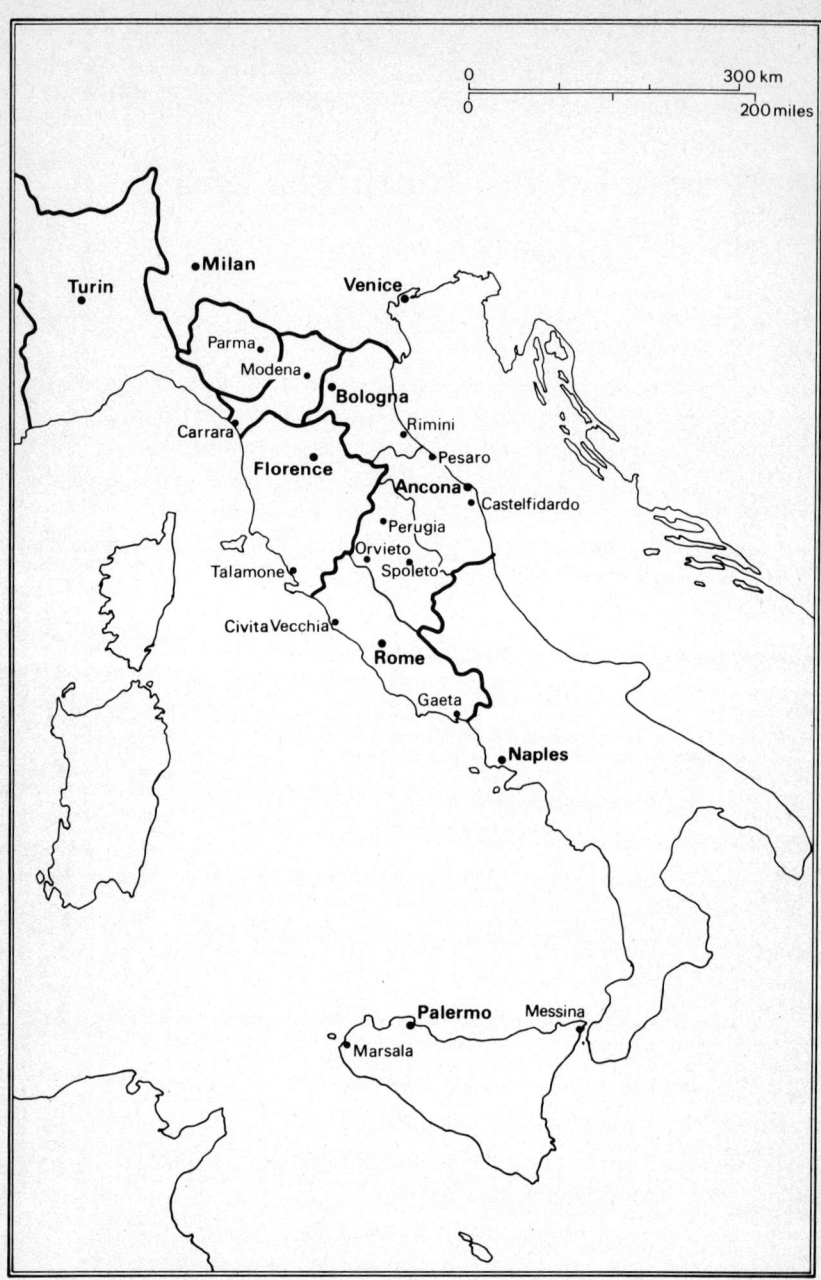

Map 1 Italy: cities and towns

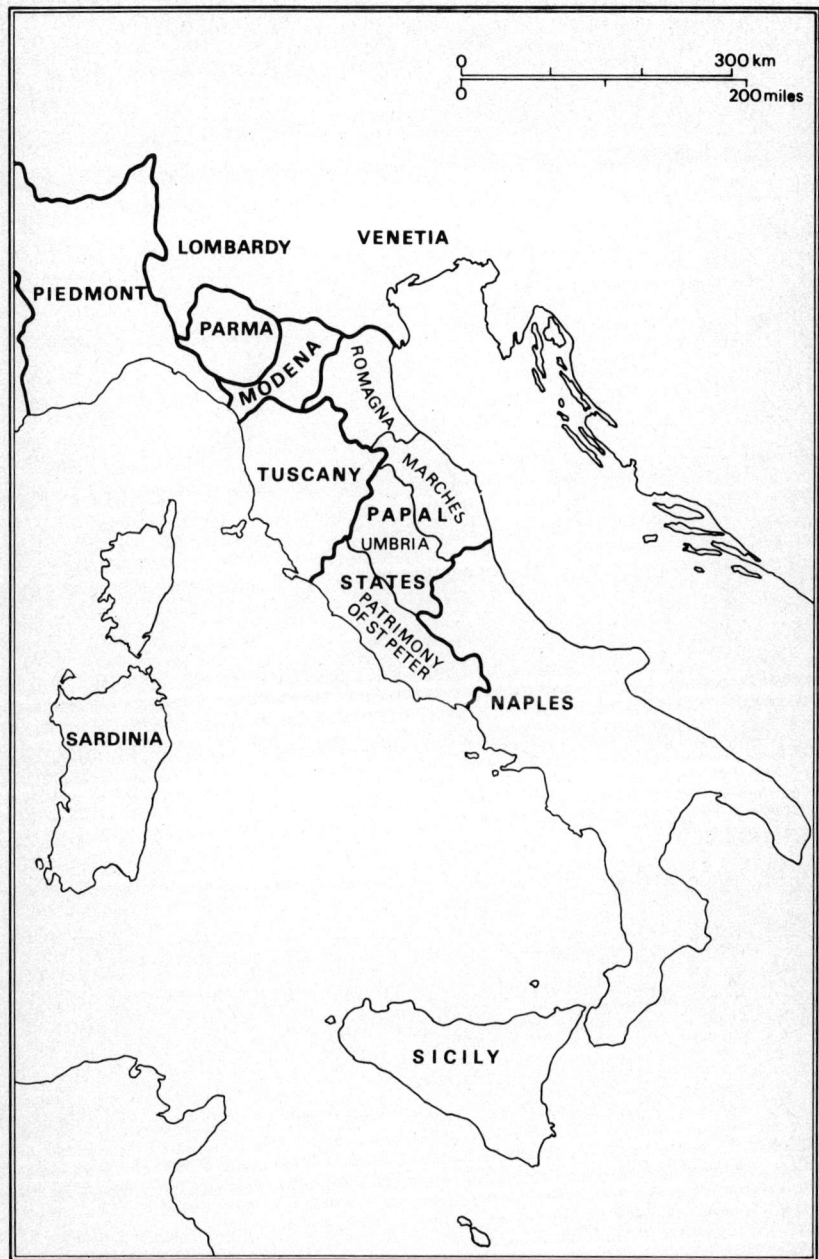

Map 2 Italy: December 1858

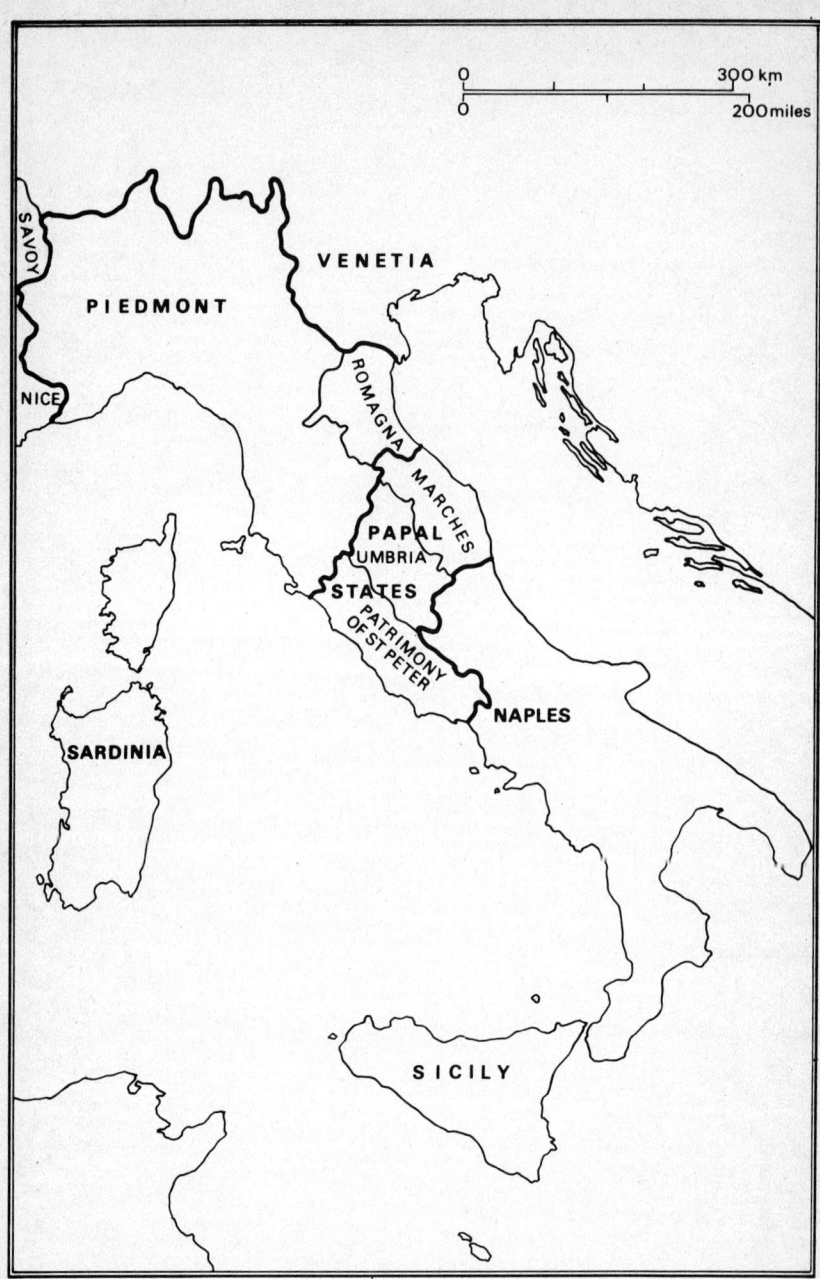

Map 3 Italy: after March 1860

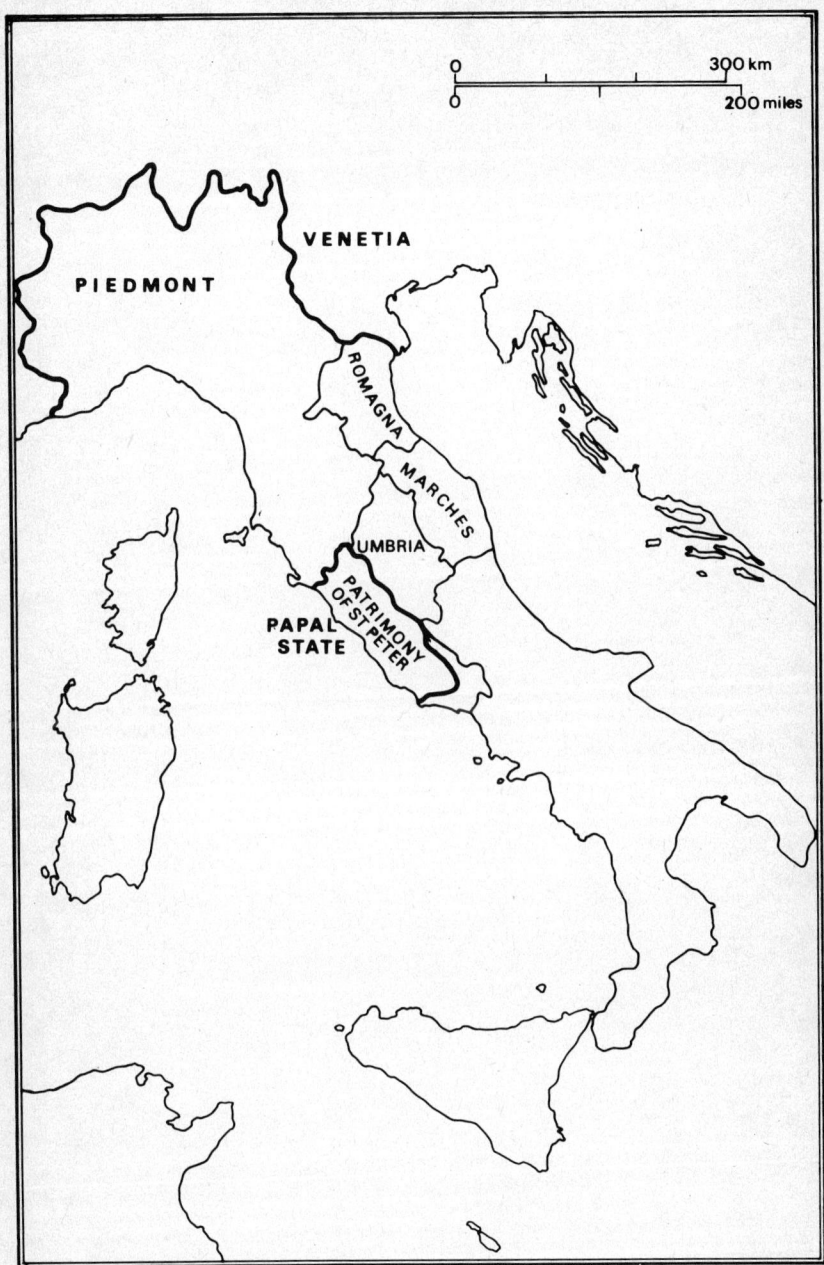

Map 4 Italy: after October 1860

Introduction

'The Papal Question is the Gordian knot of Italian politics, and its solution is indispensable to any permanent settlement of the Peninsula.'
Edinburgh Review (1860)

'One thing is quite certain, and that is, that no possible settlement of the vexed affairs of Italy can take place while the temporal dominions of the Pontiff stand in its midst, a moral plague spot, at once contagious and infectious.'
Illustrated London News (1860)

For eleven hundred years before 1858 the popes of Rome were monarchs. Like other monarchs in the latter centuries of that epoch, they ruled over specific peoples and a definite territory. They promulgated laws, dispensed justice and collected taxes; they maintained an army, kept prisons and engaged in diplomacy. Unlike other monarchs, they governed as the Vicar of Christ on earth and head of the universal church. They called their state, the States of the Church, the Papal States. Their political rule was the papal temporal power. 'God' and Caesar were one.

Between 1858 and 1861, Pope Pius IX lost most of his people, his territory and his taxes. By means of war and revolution in Italy, and diplomatic power and intrigue in Europe, the papal monarchy was overthrown in most of the central Italian peninsula, first in the Romagna in June 1859, then in the Marches and Umbria in September 1860. The Kingdom of Piedmont-Sardinia annexed the Romagna in March 1860, and the Marches and Umbria in November 1860. The pope was left with only Rome and the surrounding area. In March 1861, the greatly expanded Piedmont reconstituted itself as the Kingdom of Italy with Victor Emmanuel as king. The pope and the king, and everyone else, waited for the finale which came during the Franco-Prussian war in 1870 when the Italian army took control of the papal city of Rome. Pius IX lived on in the Vatican and its gardens while Victor Emmanuel ruled all Italy from Rome.[1]

[1] A splendid, short documentary history of Italy which covers these events is Denis Mack Smith, ed., *The making of Italy, 1796–1870* (New York: Harper and Row, 1968). Then see Denis Mack Smith, *Victor Emanuel, Cavour, and the Risorgimento* (London and New York: Oxford, 1971) esp. ch. 1.

Introduction

The Papal States dated at least from the 750s when King Pippin of the Franks granted Pope Stephan II extensive territory which the Franks had taken from the Lombards. With the authority of both the Lombards and Byzantium broken in Italy, the popes became the effective political authority in the region. The pope and the Frankish king regarded the act as a restoration of the 'donation of Constantine' from the fifth century. Even before the 750s, the popes exercised semi-political authority in landed estates known since the sixth century as the patrimony of St Peter.[2]

By December 1858, the popes were the longest-reigning monarchs in Europe. The Papal States encompassed four areas known as the Romagna, the Marches, Umbria and Lazio, and occupied the middle third of the Italian peninsula extending from the Po valley in the north nearly down to Naples in the south. It was one of the largest of several separate political entities in Italy, along with the Kingdom of Piedmont-Sardinia, the Kingdom of Two Sicilies, the duchies of Tuscany, Parma and Modena, and the Austrian provinces of Lombardy and Venetia. Rome was the seat of government as well as of the Catholic Church, and, because of its association with the caesars, the arts and the popes, perhaps the most historically compelling city in Europe. Bologna, Ravenna, Ancona and Perugia were other papal cities possessing significance and attraction of their own. Pope Pius IX was political ruler over more than three million subjects, including almost two hundred thousand in Rome itself. Simultaneously, he was spiritual ruler over perhaps two hundred million Catholics in the world, who, especially at this time, grew increasingly to regard him as their father, and to care deeply what happened to the papal monarchy.[3] The papal temporal power was not an inconsiderable thing.

In the European context the most effective and most consistent opposition to the papal monarchy came from England. During 1858 to 1861, two consecutive British governments served Queen Victoria – first the Conservatives and then the Liberals – and used the diplomatic power and moral influence of Great Britain to work for the end of papal temporal power as then constituted.

2   Peter Partner, *The lands of St. Peter: The Papal State in the Middle Ages and early Renaissance* (London: Eyre Methuen, 1972), ch. 1; Jeffrey Richards, *The popes and the papacy in the early Middle Ages, 476–752* (London: Routledge and Kegan Paul, 1979); and Walter Ullmann, *The Growth of papal government in The Middle Ages: A study in the ideological relation of clerical to lay power*, 3rd ed. (London: Methuen, 1970), ch. 2.

3   According to government sources, the population of the Papal State (1853) was 3,124,668, approximately the same as Piedmont-Sardinia (1861), 3.3 million; and Lombardy (1861), 3.1 million. Two Sicilies was much larger (1861), 9 million. The population of Rome (1859) was about 182,000, making it the fifth largest city (1861) after Naples, 484,000; Milan, 267,000; Genoa, 242,000; and Palermo, 199,000; followed by Turin, 173,000; Venice, 164,000; Florence, 150,000; and Bologna, 116,000. The population of the whole Italian peninsula (1861) was about 25 million. See, for the Papal States: *Statistica della popolazione dello Stato pontificio dell'anno 1853* (Rome: 1857); and *Stato dell'anime per l'alma città di Roma per l'anno 1859* (Rome: 1860); for all Italy: *Popolazione residente e presente dei communi al censimenti dal 1861 al 1961* (Rome: Istituto centrale di statistica, 1967). The figure 200 million was the estimate used by the Irish hierarchy in their Pastoral 5 Aug. 1859.

Introduction

To be sure, in the practice of their diplomacy the two British governments differed dramatically. The Tories, who held office from February 1858 until June 1859, with Lord Derby as prime minister and the Third Earl of Malmesbury as foreign secretary, were comparatively conciliatory toward the papacy. They hoped to induce the papal government to adopt reforms and to contribute thereby to stabilizing the troubled situation in Italy and maintaining the peace in Europe. The Liberals, by contrast, who served from June 1859 onward, with Lord Palmerston as prime minister and Lord John Russell as foreign secretary, were vigorously hostile to papal interests and sought more deliberately to assist the overthrow of the temporal power. The differences in approaches of the two governments were as much due to the change in the historical situation – the revolution occurred in the Romagna just as Palmerston and Russell took office – as they were to any relative differences in outlook or ideology.

The Conservative and the Liberal governments fundamentally agreed on a number of basic points, indicative of a shared view of history and a relatively common socio-cultural vision. First, they regarded England as the best society in Europe, the model of civil and religious liberty and material prosperity. Second, they considered the papal government in the States of the Church as undeniably the worst, the epitome of political and religious tyranny and economic backwardness. Third, they believed that Piedmont-Sardinia, with Victor Emmanuel as king and Count Cavour as prime minister, offered the best means of establishing in Italy a stable social order led by a constitutional monarch, liberal aristocrats, and men of property, committed to material prosperity, and 'equally opposed to the excesses of democratic license and to the thraldom of ecclesiastical and political domination'.[4]

Both governments, with the support of the vast majority of the British population, understood their policy and activity toward the pope and Italy as a means of promoting what they regarded as 'the moral and material progress of mankind'. This purpose deserves to be listed as a basic aim of British foreign policy at the time, along with maintaining British security, and creating and preserving British trade opportunities.[5] In Italy the promotion of moral and material progress gave the British governments functions to undertake diplomatically in a situation where little threatened British security and trade, or as Russell phrased it once, where 'Great Britain has no wish, and no interest which would lead her to interfere in the internal concerns of Northern and Central Italy.'[6] A crucial difference of method distinguished the British in Italy from the

---

[4] Lord John Russell to James Hudson, 31 March 1860, no. 66, *Le relazioni diplomatiche fra la Gran Bretagna e il Regno di Sardegna*, ed. Giuseppe Giarrizzo (Rome: Istituto storico italiano per l'età moderna e contemporanea, 1962), vol. VIII, 62–3.

[5] Compare with D.C.M. Platt, *Finance, trade, and politics: British foreign policy, 1815–1914* (Oxford: Oxford University Press, 1968), 363.

[6] Russell to Hudson, 31 March 1860, no. 66, *Gran Bretagna e Sardegna*, vol. VIII, 62–3.

Introduction

British in India where, in part, the aim was the same: in India, where Queen Victoria became queen in 1858, the English exercised direct political rule and possessed a direct and comprehensive power to implement their desires for moral and material progress, whereas in Italy their only instruments were diplomacy, moral influence, hints of armed force, and indirect action in support of others.[7]

The English complaint against the papacy was a radical one. The problem with the States of the Church was not merely that the pope and his government misgoverned, but that the States of the Church was an ecclesiastical state ruled by priests and prelates. Such a state, subservient to churchly and papal needs, was an affront to English *laissez-faire* and Erastian convictions and ways. During the 1850s, and finally through the events of 1858 to 1861, the British governments only slowly came to believe that the solution to what contemporaries sometimes called the Papal Question lay not in reforming the government but in abolishing the Papal States.

Pius IX knew well that the nature of papal temporal power was under attack, but he had difficulty understanding why the English found papal government so objectionable. Repeatedly through the crisis, he emphasized in his encyclicals, in his allocutions to the Sacred College of Cardinals, and in his audiences with the high and the low, that the States of the Church was a patrimony held in trust for St Peter and given by Providence through the course of the ages. Its function was to render the popes subject to no earthly ruler and to provide the temporal freedom necessary for the exercise of the popes' spiritual calling as head of the church of Christ universal. In the very nature of the case, public government and the instruments of public justice in the land were meant to serve ecclesiastical purpose. As Pius IX saw it, the States of the Church was not 'his' to relinquish; his duty was to preserve the patrimony and convey it to the next Vicar of Christ.[8]

In the Italian context, the people and the governments divided into three main tendencies which contemporaries, including the English and the papacy, recognized offered three different types of politics for the settlement of the Papal Question. They, indeed, provided alternative views of history and alternative visions for the make-up of the totality of socio-cultural life. The pope's

7   In 1861, the British government published the *Statement exhibiting the moral and material progress and condition of India during the year 1859–60* (Great Britain, Parliament, *Parliamentary Papers* (Commons), *1861*, vol. 47 (*Accounts and Papers*)). The *Act for the Better Government of India*, passed in 1858 (21 and 22 Vict. c. 106) removed India from the jurisdiction of the East India Company, placed it directly under The Crown, and required that detailed reports on 'the moral and material progress' of India be made. Such a statement was published annually thereafter until 1937.

8   The standard treatment of Pius IX in the Risorgimento during these years, based on Vatican sources, is still Pietro Pirri, *Pio IX e Vittorio Emanuele II dal loro carteggio privato*, vol. II; 'La questione romana, 1856–1864' (Rome: Pontificia Università Gregoriana, 1951). Roger Aubert's, *Le pontificat de Pie IX, 1846–1878* (Paris: Bloud et Gay, 1952) is still the best volume on his period as pope. See Giacomo Martina, *Pio IX, 1846–1850* (Rome: Università Gregoriana Editrice, 1974).

Introduction

supporters in Italy were the first tendency, known as the *papalini*, or the blacks. They included the vast network of the hierarchy of the church, from cardinal to parish priest, as well as the usually anonymous and inert masses of 'the faithful', both in the Papal States and throughout the peninsula. They relied especially upon Austrian influence for support. In Rome itself the pope enjoyed support from most of the Roman nobles, the great majority of the tradition-oriented population of Rome, and, of course, the clergy and the Curia. Cardinal Antonelli was the pope's loyal, if less than perfect, secretary of state who ran the government. The pope and the *papalini* wanted to maintain a Christian society loyal to the pope, in continuity with the Apostles of Christ, and implementive of the spiritual and moral precepts of the Catholic Church, which they regarded as the focal point of God's Providence. The British consciously opposed not only the papal government but also the *papalini* who influenced so much of the social life throughout the peninsula.[9]

The other two tendencies opposed the temporal power. The democrats, also known as the reds, the republicans, or the Mazzinians, challenged not only priestly government, but aristocratic and bourgeois government as well. They advocated the regeneration of Italy through the achievement of a secular society of the people, perhaps even a religion of the people, and led by a government whose authority derived not from God, the church, property, or aristocratic privilege, but from popular sovereignty. The pope experienced the Mazzinians first hand when they overthrew him in 1849 and erected the Roman Republic. The English generally opposed these democracies as revolutionaries, even though Mazzini himself frequently resided in London, and he and his followers exercised very little political power except through the imagination of the established authorities.[10]

The liberals were the third tendency, and were known as the whites or the national party. These liberal nationalists, mostly aristocrats and urban professionals and middle classes – 'the respectable classes' – placed their hope in the Piedmont-Sardinia government and looked to Cavour and Victor Emmanuel as their leaders. Many were organized into the Italian National Society. The liberals, with the Piedmont government, were the pope's worst enemies. They truly believed that rule by priests was wrong, an impediment to personal freedom and advancement. Their aim was to build a strong secular and constitutional monarchy in which priests and things ecclesiastical were legally

9   See Fiorella Bartoccini, *La 'Roma dei romani'* (Rome: Istituto per la storia del Risorgimento italiano, 1971), 60, 76–9. Much work remains before we will know who the *papalini* are and what the ordinary faithful in Italy, including Rome, were like. Anna Maria Isastia, *Roma nel 1859* (Rome: Istituto per la storia del Risorgimento, 1978), virtually neglects them, even though she notes that they no doubt composed the great majority of the Roman population. See Guido Verucci, *Il movimento cattolico italiano: dalla Restaurazione al primo dopo guerra* (Messina and Florence: D'Anna, 1978).

10 Emilia Morelli, *1849–1859: I dieci anni che fecero l'Italia* (Florence: le Monnier, 1977), 10–21. There is a large literature on Mazzini.

Introduction

subordinant to the state and public law. They believed in the progress of 'mankind', and wished to build a society shaped by capitalist material development. The English counted on Piedmont and the liberals to usher in the moral and material progress of Italy. Garibaldi, that astonishing guerrilla warrior and charismatic figure, combined two tendencies in one, loyalty to Victor Emmanuel with the democratic vision, and won wholehearted English support.[11]

On the international plane, a number of governments and peoples were involved in the Papal Question. All European governments opposed the democrats, but they divided over their support for or opposition to the papal temporal power and Piedmont-Sardinia. Most important and most complicated were the French. The pope depended upon Napoleon III as his protector, especially as expressed through the garrison of 5000 to 7000 French troops who, since 1849, kept public order and maintained French influence in Rome and the surrounding region. But the pope also dreaded Napoleon who simultaneously acted as Cavour's co-conspirator and colleague-in-arms against the pope. The French Catholic clergy and the mass of the French faithful compelled Napoleon to stay on the pope's side as much as he did. The English, meanwhile, continually endorsed actions of the French government detrimental to the pope and supportive of Piedmont, while guarding against the aggrandizement of French power and influence in Italy, and even fearing the possibility of a French invasion of England.

The Austrians were the pope's most consistent friends, the defenders of the Vienna settlement of 1815 in Italy. Since 1849, they had garrisoned 6000 to 8000 troops on the Adriatic side of the Papal States at Bologna and Ancona to keep public order and insure Austrian influence there. But the Austrian government behaved erratically and eventually hurt the pope irremediably by evacuating their troops without warning in June 1859. The English government lamented the Austrian presence in Lombardy and Venetia, as well as the Papal States, but needed the Austrians to remain a great power to offset Prussia and Russia, as well as France.

Russia and Prussia usually remained on the periphery, except when congresses of the powers were planned, at which times the pope imagined them as schismatics and Protestants grouped against him.

Of the lesser powers, the pope and his government sought help from Spain in the form of troops or diplomacy. Queen Isabella II and the Spanish Catholic faithful were, on the whole, devoted followers of the pope, sufficiently so to keep the English alert against a repetition of the Spanish armed intervention in Rome in 1849.

---

11 See Raymond Grew, *A sterner plan for Italian unity: the Italian National Society in the Risorgimento* (Princeton: Princeton University Press, 1963); and Denis Mack Smith, *Cavour and Garibaldi, 1860* (Cambridge: Cambridge University Press, 1954).

Introduction

Some of the pope's most effective support, which the English found most difficult to handle, came from the Catholics of Great Britain and Ireland. Under Queen Victoria's rule in the 1850s, there were perhaps 750,000 Catholics in England, including 100,000 in London itself, with a Roman Catholic hierarchy under Cardinal Wiseman, plus perhaps four-and-a-half million Catholics in Ireland with their hierarchy under Archbishop Cullen. These English and Irish Catholics worked almost as one in defence of the pope and Catholic interests. In 1859, thirty-six Catholics sat in the British parliament, all but one from Irish constituencies.[12] The Conservative and the Liberal governments constantly paid attention to this sizeable number of Catholics under British rule, and the pope appealed to them repeatedly for assistance.

In both the Italian and the international context, then, English opposition to papal temporal power stood out and made a decisive difference in the outcome of the course of events in 1858 to 1861. For the liberal opponents of the pope in Italy, England provided the model and the inspiration for the creation of the new Italy, liberated from 'foreigners and priests'. The English government, through all the twists and turns of the events, was the one great power who acted as a consistent critic and opponent of the papal government. The English served as the major facilitator of the attack on the temporal power. They were always present, using their diplomacy and moral influence, and occasionally hinting or threatening armed intervention, working to enable the pope's Italian opponents to succeed, and to ensure that he and his friends failed. The English followed, not a pre-conceived plan, but a direction which at every conjunction led them to pursue the way that went against the papacy.

This English opposition was formidable partly because of the sheer economic, naval and political power it entailed. In financial, industrial and commercial terms, England in the 1850s and 1860s was undisputedly the dominant power in the world. It was an economic power which included even the Papal States within its network of trade and trade treaties. From a naval viewpoint, the English regarded the Mediterranean as virtually an English sea, and the powerful English Mediterranean fleet, based in Malta, encircled the Italian peninsula and included the papal ports of Civita Vecchia and Ancona in its sphere of influence. Politically, the English parliament in the 1850s was working as well as it ever had, and by using the method of gradual reform, the English appeared to succeed in avoiding, as did no other European power, the extremes

---

12 For the English Catholic figures, see John Bossey, *The English Catholic community, 1570–1850* (London: Darton, Longman and Todd, 1975), 298 and 313. The total Irish population (1861) was about 5.7 million, of which easily 80 per cent were Catholic. The population of the whole of the United Kingdom (1861) was about 29 million, with about 20 million in England and Wales; Scotland had about 3 million. The population (1861) of London was 2.8 million, while Liverpool, Glasgow, Dublin, Manchester and Birmingham ranged from 472,000 down to 351,000; and Leeds, Edinburgh and Sheffield had around 200,000 each. For the names of the Catholic M.P.s, see *The Catholic Directory of the Whole World* (Dublin, 1860), 21.

Introduction

of authoritarian rule and revolution. From this position the English could hit the papacy with unremitting criticism and opposition.

But the English opposition to the papacy was powerful, too, because it arose out of an essential feature of English identity. Since the sixteenth century, through the struggles of the English reformation, to be truly English meant to be against the pope. Those who remained loyal to the pope, the Catholics, in a most profound sense ceased to be regarded as fully English, and were looked upon as agents of a foreign power. The anti-papal element originated almost two centuries earlier in the controversies out of which came the statutes of *provisors* and *praemunire* of the fourteenth century.[13] Through the experiences of the Henrican Reformation, the Elizabethan settlement, the Puritan revolution, and the 'glorious Revolution' of 1688–9, anti-papalism broadened into an anti-Catholicism which sought to cleanse England from 'papists' and 'popery' in all its forms. To be English meant to be Protestant; to enjoy English liberties meant, in part, to be free from the pope.[14]

The place of Catholics in English society was far from settled in the 1850s. It would seem a better reflection of the situation in the 1850s and 1860s to regard anti-Catholicism, not as gradually dying out and visible only through occasional dying spasms, and not as merely a peculiar belief of some intolerant Evangelicals,[15] but as a continuing element in a common English experience and identity which came to active political and social expression from time to time. One of these times came during 1859 and 1860, when virtually all English people, excepting Catholics and Puseyites, were excited to hope for the political downfall of the pope. Seen in this way, England's approach to the loss of papal temporal power in 1858 to 1861 may be understood as an expression in foreign policy and diplomatic action of an anti-Catholic and particularly anti-papal element in the English way of life. Anti-Catholicism figured as an important factor in British diplomacy toward Italy. Denis Mack Smith makes the point: 'One of the reasons why so many people in England were enthusiastic supporters of either Cavour, Garibaldi, or Mazzini was that those three had in common a

13   The earliest statutes of *provisors* came under Edward III: in 1350 (25 E3. st. 5. c.22) and (25 E3. st. 6); in 1352 (27 E3. st. 1); and in 1363–4 (28 E3. st. 2). The first statute of *praemunire* came in 1392–3 under Richard II (16 R2. c. 5).
14   On anti-Catholicism, see esp.: E.R. Norman, *Anti-Catholicism in Victorian England* (London: George Allen and Unwin, 1968). Then see Richard Bauckham, *Tudor apocalypse* (Abingdon, Oxon.: Sutton Courtenay, 1978); John Miller, *Popery and politics in England, 1660–88* (Cambridge: Cambridge University Press, 1973); J.R. Jones, *The Revolution of 1688 in England* (New York: W.W. Norton, 1972); G.I.T. Machin, *The Catholic question in English politics, 1820 to 1830* (Oxford: Clarendon, 1964); Sheridan Gilley, 'Evangelical and Roman Catholic missions to the Irish in London, 1830–1870' (Ph.D. thesis, Cambridge University, 1970); and G.F.A. Best, 'Popular Protestantism in Victorian England', in Robert Robson, ed., *Ideas and institutions of Victorian Britain: essays in honour of George Kitson Clark* (London: G. Bell, 1967), 115–42.
15   See Sheridan Gilley, 'Protestant London, no-popery, and the Irish poor, 1830–1860', *Recusant history* 10 (1969–70), 210–30, and 11 (1971–72), 21–46; and G.I.T. Machin, *Politics and the Churches in Great Britain, 1832 to 1868* (Oxford: Clarendon, 1977), *passim*.

Introduction

strong anti-clericalism, and to this extent Italian nationalism coincided not only with British political interests against France, but also with Protestant anti-Catholicism.'[16] Anti-Catholicism was, in relation to the pope, the negative side of the English hope for the moral and material progress of Italy.

The aim of this study is to examine the intriguing relations between England and the papacy in the Italian and European contexts during 1858 to 1861, and to explain the process by which two English governments, in changing circumstances and with increasing intentionality, used their influence to contribute to the overthrow of the papal temporal power in the Romagna, the Marches and Umbria. The study begins with the movement toward war at the end of 1858, continues with a detailed analysis of the complex and irregular course of events, and concludes with the official incorporation of the papal territory into the kingdom of Italy in 1861. The years 1859 and 1860 were the decisive years both for the end of the temporal power and for the culmination of the Risorgimento, that general cultural movement which yielded the Italian kingdom. They were years of intense and concentrated activity, during which, like 1789–91 for the French, 1775–7 for the Americans, 1688–9 for the English, or 1919–22 for the Irish, things ended and things began in the political realm which affected the life of the whole society.

England and the papacy had no direct diplomatic relations with each other in these years, but they found a way for each to make their desires known to the other. The British government maintained an unofficial diplomatic envoy in Rome, Odo Russell, nephew of Lord John Russell, who established an unusual *rapport* with both Pius IX and Cardinal Antonelli. He provided a unique and direct channel between the two states which both sides used for diplomatic communication.[17]

These were the years of what may be called the Papal Question, when the political status of the papacy in Italy became a central historical issue, and when the essential element of a future settlement of the Papal Question was determined by depriving the pope of his extensive political rule. What historians have called the 'Roman Question' should perhaps be said to begin in November 1860, after the papal loss of the Romagna, the Marches and Umbria, when all those involved turned their attention to the question of depriving the pope of Rome and to forming relations between the pope and the new Italy. Only recently have historians shown considerable interest in the Papal States and Rome in the few years *before* 1861.[18]

16   Mack Smith, *Victor Emanuel, Cavour*, 157.
17   Noel Blakiston renewed interest in English relations with the papacy by publishing many of Odo Russell's letters, or extracts from his letters: *The Roman Question: extracts from the despatches of Odo Russell from Rome, 1858–1870* (London: Chapman and Hall, 1962; reprint, Wilmington, Delaware: Michael Glazier, 1980).
18   These works fill many holes in our knowledge of the Papal States before 1861. Noteworthy are three volumes published by the Istituto per la storia del Risorgimento italiano whose

9

Introduction

This study treats the end of the temporal power both as an important subject in its own right, and as a significant dimension of the making of Italy. Similarly, English policy and diplomatic action on the Papal Question, and the papal response to the English are regarded as special topics of their own, as well as dimensions of Italian affairs. By pointing out how actively the English were involved in the Papal Question, the study wishes to help shift attention in our historiography of the pope and the Risorgimento away from an over-emphasis on France, Sardinia and Austria;[19] and by indicating how central the Papal Question was to the English in their assessment of Italy and their approach to the Italian Question, to help correct an over-emphasis on English consideration of the balance of power, concern over France's position in Europe, and sympathy for Italian nationalism.[20]

In the most specific sense, this is a study of the diplomatic and political relations between two states, and the intercourse among many of the great and small powers of Europe. And this is appropriate, given that the Papal Question, like the question of Italian unification, was approached by the governments and people involved at the time as, in large part, a matter for war and diplomacy to decide. Diplomats and political rulers made decisions and performed actions which, to a large degree, determined the course of things. These men were a relatively small handful of wealthy and privileged aristocrats who knew each other well and observed common social rules. However, small in number though they were, we should not forget that they acted not as individuals, but as officials of governments who possessed the power to make large decisions affecting war

offices are in the top of the Victor Emmanuel monument in Rome: Fiorella Bartoccini, *La 'Roma dei romani'* (1971); Romano Ugolini, *Cavour e Napoleone III nell'Italia centrale: il sacrificio di Perugia* (1973); and Anna Maria Isastia, *Roma nel 1859* (1978). Three volumes published by Giuffré of Milan are: two by Mario Tedeschi, *Francia e Inghilterra di fronte alla questione romana, 1859–1860* (1978); and *Cavour e la questione romana, 1860–1861* (1978); plus Salvatore Bordonali, *Riflessi diplomatici e politici nella crisi del potere temporale negli anni formativi dell'Unità italiana, 1859–61* (1979).

19 The mainline of the historiography of the pope and the Risorgimento has concentrated on France, Sardinia and Austria. For example, I think of: Lynn M. Case, *Franco-Italian relations, 1860–1865: the Roman question and the convention of September* (Philadelphia: University of Pennsylvania Press, 1932); Pirri, *Pio IX e Vittorio Emanuele II*; and Franco Valsecchi, *L'Italia del Risorgimento e l'Europa delle nazionalità: l'unificazione italiana nella politica europea* (Milan: Giuffré, 1978). Ivan Scott, *The Roman question and the powers, 1848–1865* (The Hague: Martinus Nijhoff, 1969), devotes little attention to England, partly because his focus is mainly upon French–papal relations, but also because he believes incorrectly that 'England, as an insular and Protestant power, would stand outside this confused religious and political quarrel' (96).

20 For example, Harry W. Rudman, *Italian nationalism and English letters* (London: Allen and Unwin, 1940) is about English sympathies for Italian liberty; Mack Smith, *Victor Emanuel, Cavour*, acknowledges that anti-Catholicism is a factor, but concentrates on the other factors; Derek Beales, *England and Italy, 1859–1860* (London: Thomas Nelson, 1961), is usually quite good at noticing the anti-Catholic factor in the making of English foreign policy toward Italy, but in his conclusion he overstates the importance of the French factor: 'In reality England was not pursuing an Italian policy so much as a French policy' (169).

Introduction

and peace as well as justice, law and order, which touched the lives of nearly everyone. Nevertheless, when the topic involves the pope and England, other factors are unavoidably operative, as the diplomats and political rulers themselves recognized. The study, thus, includes social, economic and naval factors, newspapers, public opinion and domestic politics, ecclesiastical affairs, theology and religious movements both Catholic and Protestant, in so far as these are necessary to understand and explain the course of English–papal relations concerning the end of the temporal power of the pope.

The events and processes which this study examines hover around issues of church and state, and religion and politics. The pope inherited a political structure which conflated church and state to the advantage of the church. As Catholics and Nonconformists were quick to point out, the British possessed their own structures which conflated church and state to the advantage of the state and the established Church of England. Bourgeois and aristocratic liberals in the Papal States saw themselves as suffering under priestly government which they claimed inhibited the development of commerce and industry and a lay political leadership. They looked to the British as their model, and they appealed to them for help. The pope scarcely understood the liberals' discontent. On the other side, the British faced the complaints of the Catholics in England and Ireland. The English Catholics pressed for the end of all anti-Catholic legislation, while the Irish objected to their status as the only country in Europe where the religion of a minority was state-established, and the religion of a majority systematically disadvantaged. The British, however, could see no analogy between the papal situation and British rule over Catholic Ireland or Hindu and Muslim India.[21] The majority of the British parliament and both the Conservative and Liberal governments continued to maintain British supremacy in Ireland and they carefully safeguarded the Protestant church established in Great Britain and Ireland as well as the Protestant succession to the Crown.

Pius IX confronted all the hostility of the new secular forces associated with secular state power, capitalist and bourgeois industrialization, liberal and democratic politics, and the new ideologies. He perceived the conflict as a spiritual struggle, and so responded to diplomatic action, political revolution, and war with religious and ecclesiastical means: excommunication, calls for prayer and pious devotion, the enhancement of papal authority. He sought to consolidate the Catholic Church with its centre in Rome as a bulwark against the secular spirits of the age. The English government only partly understood what the pope was doing. The conflict between England and the papacy, inter-related

---

21   Cardinal Cullen to Sir Culling Eardly, Dublin, 9 Dec. 1859, in Peader MacSuibhne, ed., *Paul Cullen and his contemporaries, with their letters 1820–1902* (3 vols., Naas, Ireland: Leinster Leader, 1961–5, vol. II, 322–3; J.R. McCulloch, *A descriptive and statistical account of the British Empire* (London: Longman, Brown, Green and Longman, 1854), vol. II, 305–11.

Introduction

with all the other parties to the Papal Question, involved weighty matters pertinent to the secularization of modern society.²²

Through all the complicated events and conjunctures from 1858 to 1861, both England and the papacy knew that something deeply significant was happening. When the crisis reached a resolution of sorts with the Piedmontese annexation of the Marches and Umbria at the end of 1860, Palmerston commented to Russell about what they had just helped to accomplish:

> This great change in the condition of the existence of the Papacy is a great and important event and the more important because what is now doing in regard to the Temporal Power of the Pope will never be undone.²³

22 On secularization, see David Martin, *A general theory of secularization* (Oxford: Basil Blackwell, 1978); Owen Chadwick, *The secularization of the European mind in the nineteenth century* (Cambridge: Cambridge University Press, 1975); Martin E. Marty, *The modern schism: three paths to the secular* (New York: Harper and Row, 1969); and Herman Dooyeweerd, *Roots of Western culture: pagan, secular, and Christian options* (Toronto: Wedge, 1979).
23 Palmerston to Russell, 6 Oct. 1860, Russell papers, PRO, 30/22/21.

1 'English Liberties' and 'The Government of Priests'

The coming crisis

War and revolution in Italy which could extend to all of Europe were, by January 1859, considered frightfully distinct possibilities by all governments of Europe, including the English. The Italians who would most welcome war, those who looked to Cavour, Mazzini or Garibaldi, whatever the differences among them, were agreed that it would be a war of independence – from Austria and from the pope.

Austria was the obvious foreigner, and Italian liberals and democrats found its presence in Italy offensive. The Treaty of Vienna of 1815, which all governments regarded as the stabilizing constitution of Europe,[1] allowed Austria to hold a position of predominance in Italy by assigning it possession of the choice states of Lombardy and Venetia, along with some papal territory on the left bank of the Po. The Austrian government negotiated special treaties with the duke of Tuscany and, after 1847, with the dukes of Parma and Modena. In 1849 Austria added to its hegemony direct influence over the eastern half of the Papal States by successfully using its troops to help restore the rule of Pius IX. The troops remained to occupy the provinces known as the Romagna and the Marches, with major garrisons in Bologna and Ancona.[2] In addition, Austria exercised considerable influence over the southern Italian Kingdom of Naples.

According to Italian liberals and democrats, the pope was equally a threat to the independence of Italy. They considered the papacy offensive on two grounds: pope and priests exercised great influence over many people in all the states of Italy, including Piedmont, and thereby rivalled governmental power; and 'a government of priests' in the States of the Church politically controlled the whole middle of Italy, including the historically pre-eminent city of Rome.

Of the many Italian refugees from the papal rule who came to England and served as political 'missionaries', none was more effective than Felice Orsini. In

---

[1] Count Rechberg to Count Apponyi, 25 March 1860, *Gran Bretagna e Sardegna*, vol. VIII, 59.
[2] Richard Lyons to Lord Normanby, 27 Dec. 1856 and 15 May 1857, *Despatches from Mr. Lyons respecting the condition and administration of the Papal States*, in *Parliamentary Papers* (Commons), *1860*, vol. 68, 39–40, 47.

'English Liberties' and 'The Government of Priests'

a series of very popular public lectures given in many parts of England in 1856 and 1857, he sought to reinforce the English belief that the pope was indeed a foreigner to Italian liberty: 'That Popery has ever been the principal cause of Italian servitude is undeniable. This truth has always been recognized by our greatest statesman and philosophers, from Machiavelli downwards; and until the Italians cast off the incubus of Papacy, considered as a temporal power, they can never hope to behold the triumph of true liberty and independence.'[3] Orsini, a native of the Papal States, believed that England provided Italians with their model of liberty, and that Napoleon III possessed the practical power to determine whether the pope and Austria would continue to enslave Italians.[4] Orsini took the matter in his own hands, and in January 1858 very nearly succeeded in assassinating Napoleon III. In the public trial which followed, the French were enraged when they learned that the bombs, and the plot, were made in England. The affair led to the resignation of Palmerston's government and to the election of the Conservatives under Lord Derby and Lord Malmesbury.[5] Orsini's deed, the fourth assassination attempt by an Italian in two-and-a-half years, seemed to push Napoleon into action over Italy. When Napoleon published in *Le Moniteur* Orsini's letter pleading that the Emperor 'deliver my country, and the blessings of 25 million people will go with you for ever',[6] politically attuned people could detect a rise in the potential for war and revolution in Italy.

Napoleon met privately with Cavour at Plombières, in France, in July 1858, and the unease intensified, although no one at the time, least of all the English and papal governments, knew that what happened there was historically definitive for the future of Italy and the papacy. The English tended to undervalue the meeting,[7] and both Derby and Malmesbury persisted in believing until as late as January 1859 that Napoleon certainly had no intention of making war against Austria over Italy.[8]

3   Felice Orsini, *Memoires and adventures ... containing unpublished state papers of the Roman Court*, trans. George Carbonel (Edinburgh: Thomas Constable; London: Hamilton, Adams, 1857), 58. See Bernard Porter, *The refugee question in mid-Victorian politics* (London: Cambridge University Press, 1979).
4   Orsini, *Memoires, passim*, and 193–4, 217.
5   Michael St John Packe, *The bombs of Orsini* (London: Secker and Warburg, 1957), 235ff. The plot was assisted by Dr Simon Francis Bernard, George Holyoake and Thomas Allsop, who were Secularists, as well as by some Italian exiles.
6   Porter, *Refugee question*, 61; Orsini to Napoleon III, 11 February 1858, in Mack Smith, *The making of Italy, 1796–1870*, 230–1.
7   See James Hudson to Malmesbury, 19 July 1858, private, *Gran Bretagna e Sardegna*, vol. VI, 286.
8   Derby to Malmesbury, 30 Dec. 1858, copy, Derby papers, 186/2: 'Still I do not think we shall have an Italian war ...' Also see Malmesbury to Queen Victoria, 18 Jan. 1859, *The letters of Queen Victoria*, ed. A.C. Benson and Viscount Esher (1st ser.; London: Longmans, 1907), vol. III, 399. Malmesbury wrote to Queen Victoria, 10 Dec. 1858, 'Lord Malmesbury thinks he can assure your Majesty that none [war] is at present contemplated by the Emperor Napoleon (who has just contradicted the report officially) ...', *Letters of Queen Victoria*, vol. III, 390–1.

In fact, as we now know, the Plombières meeting was a deliberate war plot which had as its objective the political reorganization of Italy, including the Sardinian takeover of most of the pope's territory. Cavour had been talking of a war at least since 1856, even hoping that England might help him fight against Austria. But he soon realized that only Napoleon might be interested in such a thing. Now Cavour went to Plombières to plan with Napoleon how to start a war, and what strategy and objective to pursue. He returned with a war pact.[9] Throughout the complex vicissitudes preceding the start of the Austro–Sardinian war in April 1859, the events were often beyond the control of Cavour and Napoleon and their comrades, but surprisingly the war came off much as the Plombières pact envisioned.

Some points of the pact directly concerned the Papal States.[10] First, both in principle and in concrete detail, Napoleon agreed to allow – that was all that was necessary – the planned overthrow of papal temporal power in at least the Romagna and perhaps in the Marches down to Ancona. The Romagna, the plan said, would be incorporated in a new Kingdom of Upper Italy, which would include the territory north of the natural line of the Apennines, and be placed under the House of Savoy, i.e., under Victor Emmanuel and Cavour.

Second, and crucial to the whole scheme, Napoleon agreed to back Cavour and the Piedmontese party in Italy and to work consciously against the Mazzinian democrats. Napoleon could not accept democratic revolution in the *social* structure prevailing in Italy, but he could permit the overthrow of priestly rule in most of the Papal States which he might regard as merely a *political* rearrangement in Italy. That was the meaning of the term 'nonrevolutionary' to Napoleon.

Third, Napoleon would stand firm on Rome. French troops had helped restore the pope after the Roman revolution of 1849, and they remained to occupy Rome and the Lazio, parallel to the Austrian occupation on the Adriatic side. Napoleon would continue to protect Rome, not because of any profound solidarity with the pope, but 'so as not to stir up French Catholics against me'. For the same opportunist reason the pope would be given the presidency of a proposed Italian Confederation, 'to console him for losing the best part of his estates'. The French Catholic faithful, out of devotion to the pope, made it necessary for the not-very-devout Napoleon to play the part of the defender of the head of the church, or else risk losing his place as emperor.[11] The Plombières

9   Mack Smith, *Victor Emanuel, Cavour*, 26–7. *Tutti gli scritti di Camillo Cavour*, ed. Carlo Pischedda and Giuseppe Talamo (4 vols., Turin: Centro Studi Piemontesi, 1978), vol. IV, 1976–81.
10   The account of the Plombières meeting is Cavour's. Cavour to King Victor Emmanuel, 24 July 1858, Baden Baden, in *Il carteggio Cavour–Nigra dal 1858 al 1861* (4 vols., Bologna: Zanichelli, 1926–9), vol. I, 103–10; translated in Mack Smith, *Making of Italy*, 238–47.
11   Two standard books on the Napoleon–papacy–French Catholics triangle are: Lynn M. Case, *French opinion on war and diplomacy during the Second Empire* (Philadelphia: University of Pennsylvania Press, 1954); and Jean Maurain, *La politique ecclésiastique du Second Empire de 1852 à 1869* (Paris: Felix Alcan, 1930).

plan initiated a programme of calculated dissimulation: Napoleon would appear to defend the pope while actually trying to undermine him.

Napoleon and Cavour agreed that England had to be kept neutral. Cavour was 'to make every effort to influence opinion in that country to compel the government (which is a slave to public opinion) not to side with Austria'. Cavour would need to play delicately on England's developing sympathy for constitutional liberty in Sardinia, and antipathy to priestly government in the Papal States.

On Christmas eve 1858, Napoleon laid out his war strategy in a memorandum to Count Walewski, the French foreign secretary. In January, Napoleon and Sardinia concluded a formal war alliance in the Treaty of Turin which was kept secret and backdated to 12 December.[12]

For the Plombières plot to get rolling, there needed to be an insurrection somewhere. Napoleon was hesitant about having one started in papal Romagna. He would not, however, mind Cavour manufacturing one in the Austrophile duchies in central Italy, nor would he object to its spread from there into the Papal States.

It was probably in the autumn of 1858 that Cavour took up contact with the Italian National Society about just such an insurrection. He took Giuseppe La Farina, the secretary of the National Society's central committee in Turin, into his confidence and informed him of the Plombières agreement.[13] That organization had already formulated a clear objective and method: to form a united Italian nation, independent of Austria and the pope, by means of war and revolution.[14] The National Society was organized throughout the duchies and the Papal States. In the Romagna, where as one historian remarked, 'clandestine political activity was almost a way of life', it achieved its greatest success organizationally. The strongest committee was in Bologna, and it had committees in most of the other larger cities of the province. It had little organization of its own in the Marches, but it did establish ties with existing committees, some of which were Masonic. In Rome the Comitato Nazionale Romano remained in constitution and in its programme relatively independent of the National Society.[15] The National Society regarded its subversive work as a 'holy cause', and wanted to help Victor Emmanuel earn a 'holier and more splendid crown, that of redeemer of the most glorious of nations'.[16] It was

12 Napoleon III to Walewski, 24 Dec. 1858, in Franco Valsecchi, *L'unificazione italiano e la politica europea dalla guerra di Crimea alla guerra di Lombardia, 1854–1859* (Milan: Istituto per gli studi di politica internazionale, 1955), 336–41. Pirri, vol. II, part 1, 16–25. *Cavour-Nigra*, vol. I, 312–14. The important part of the text is translated in Mack Smith, *Making of Italy*, 259–60.
13 Grew, 122.
14 Grew, 139–61, 153. 'Our way is clear. War and insurrection as means; national independence as goal; all Italian forces under the dictatorial power of King Victor Emmanuel... Without blood there is no redemption' (La Farina to Eugenio Canevazzi of Bologna, 12 May 1859, Giuseppe La Farina, *Epistolario*, ed. Ausonio Franchi (Milan: E. Treves, 1869), vol. II, 172).
15 Grew, 97–9. Isastia, 60–1.
16 Grew, 154–5.

devoted to Piedmont and Cavour's *realpolitik*, and was vigorously anti-clerical, anti-Papal States, and anti-Jesuit.

In October 1858, La Farina formulated with Cavour a detailed plan for revolution which the National Society pledged itself to implement. Cavour proposed the plan to Napoleon.[17] The insurrection would begin on the following 1 May in Massa and Carrara, then move across the Apennines to Parma, down the old Roman Emilian road directly to Modena, and on to Bologna. Garibaldi would be chosen to lead the volunteer forces along this route. If Venetia and Lombardy revolted as well, he was to carry on from Bologna into the Marches. The Piedmont regular army would be used only limitedly and only after the Garibaldi forces had succeeded. The plan itemized the guns and other equipment the volunteers would need, presumably supplied, at least partially, by Cavour's government. The idea was that this insurrection would probably force Austria to declare war on Piedmont, and Napoleon and Cavour would then have their war. La Farina carried on an extensive correspondence with his committees throughout the duchies and the Romagna to plan the revolution and the war for the spring.[18]

Cavour was heady about the whole design. He came to regard Sardinian possession of the pope's territory, particularly the Romagna and the Marches, as essential to Piedmont's well-being. 'Sardinia', he wrote, 'can never be made safe unless it has its head supported upon the Alps and its feet at Ancona.'[19] Cavour boasted to Odo Russell, who stopped in Turin *en route* to Rome in December 1858, that 'I shall force her [Austria] to declare war on us.' Unbelieving, Odo wondered when Cavour would perform this feat. Cavour candidly responded, 'about the first fortnight in May'.[20]

England: reform and rearrange the Papal States

Lord Malmesbury, the Conservative foreign secretary, was slow to believe the rumours of a coming war, even when Lord Cowley, the British ambassador in Paris, informed him in early December that it seemed Napoleon believed that a war against Austria '*for the freedom of Italy*' might help him with English public opinion. The suggestions greatly alarmed Queen Victoria, who urged action. Benjamin Disraeli, Chancellor of the Exchequer, came close to falling out with Malmesbury in the weeks that followed because he felt the foreign secretary needed to take decisive action against war.[21]

17   Plan dated 19 Oct. 1858 and enclosed with La Farina to Felice Bolognini, 20 Oct. 1858, La Farina, vol. II, 80–5. *Tutti gli scritti di Camillo Cavour*, vol. IV, 1982–5.
18   La Farina, vol. II, *passim*.
19   Cavour to Count Villamarina, 25 Nov. 1858, *Cavour–Nigra*, vol. I, 213–15.
20   Odo Russell interview with Cavour, 14 Dec. 1858, quoted in A.J. Whyte, *The political life and letters of Cavour, 1848–1861* (Oxford: Oxford University Press, 1930, 1962), 269.
21   Cowley to Malmesbury, Paris, 6 Dec. 1858, copy, RA J14/1 (underlining Cowley's); Queen Victoria to Malmesbury, 9 Dec. 1858 draft, RA J14/2; Malmesbury to Queen Victoria, 10 Dec. 1858, RA J14/4; Derby to Disraeli, 6 Jan. 1859, draft, Derby papers, 187/1.

Malmesbury's approach was cautious at first. On 7 December he wrote a lengthy private letter to Cowley assessing the crisis, and Cowley discreetly conveyed Malmesbury's view to Napoleon.[22] But Cowley's further reports from Paris and Napoleon's remarks on New Year's Day to the Austrian ambassador in Paris, Count Hübner, made the danger of war seem so likely that it could hardly be doubted any longer.[23] On 10 January, Malmesbury finally sent Cowley a major official policy statement on the Italian crisis, and on 12 January sent comparable statements to Sir James Hudson, ambassador in Turin, and Lord Augustus Loftus, ambassador in Vienna. He drafted a despatch to Lord John Bloomfield, ambassador in Berlin, designed to persuade the Prussian government as another Protestant power to act together with England, but Queen Victoria stopped the letter. She thought it too unmercifully castigated the pope. The queen managed to tone down Malmesbury's language against the papal government in the various despatches that were sent, but she did not alter his analysis of the Italian problem. On 13 January the queen pressed for an immediate increase in the navy, which the cabinet approved on the 18th. These January policy papers, backed by the strengthening of the British navy, mark the beginning of English involvement in the Italian crisis and show how central to the whole affair the English government considered the papacy to be. England acted alone, without the Prussians, and upon the basis of Malmesbury's assessment of the nature of the Italian crisis.[24]

In these documents, Malmesbury denied the feasibility of Italian nationalist aspirations. He thought Italy was too deeply and anciently divided by provincial and municipal loyalties for a true nation to be made of it. Even independence from Austria he did not consider a worthy aspiration. In his opinion, 'it is *sound policy*, as well as sound honesty, to leave Austria in quiet possession of her Italian Dominions'. The Austrian archduke viceroy, he thought, actually governed Lombardy and Venetia well. Moreover, the Austrian presence in Italy was guaranteed by the Treaties of Vienna in 1815, which were essential to uphold as the constitution of Europe; they had insured 'the longest peace on record' and still served to maintain the balance of power.[25]

22   Malmesbury to Cowley, 7 Dec. 1858, private, Cowley papers, PRO, FO, 519/196.
23   According to Hübner, Napoleon remarked to him at the New Year's reception at the Tuileries: 'I regret that our relations are not as good as I would desire that they be, but I beg you to write to Vienna that my personal feelings for the Emperor are always the same' (Count Joseph Hübner, *Neuf ans de souvenirs d'un ambassadeur d'Autriche à Paris sous le Second Empire* (Paris: Plon-Nourrit, 1904), vol. II, 244–5, 1 Jan. 1859). The episode occasioned a European-wide war scare.
24   Malmesbury to Cowley, 10 Jan. 1859, no. 47; Malmesbury to Hudson, 12 Jan. 1859, no. 6; Malmesbury to Loftus, 12 Jan. 1859, no. 22, *Gran Bretagna e Sardegna*, vol. VI, 321–8. What follows is drawn from these letters and Malmesbury's 7 Dec. 1858 letter to Cowley. See also Malmesbury to Bloomfield, 7 Jan. 1859, draft, with the queen's extensive comments in the margin, RA J14/19.
25   Queen Victoria to Derby, 13 Jan. 1859; and Malmesbury to Queen Victoria, 18 Jan. 1859, *Letters to Queen Victoria*, vol. III, 395 and 399.

England: reform and rearrange the Papal States

In Malmesbury's view, what were justified were the Italian complaints against despotic government in central Italy, by which he meant the Papal States. The Papal States, he told the queen in December, was 'the worst governed country [of Italy]'.[26] In his draft to Bloomfield he asserted 'that the dominions of the Pope are the most grievous sore of Italy, and that from that central point arises the principal heap of misery and just discontent'. On top of this, in the statement to Cowley in January, he charged that Piedmont inflamed the discontents and sought to foment war between France and Austria in order to 'increase its territory and fortify their personal position'. Malmesbury wanted to warn everyone that such agitation could lead to 'a war of opinions', in which 'all the worst passions of conflicting theorists, exiled pretenders, and adverse races, would be mingled in a deadly struggle', and from which the only real winner would be the republicans who accomplish their ends 'in anarchy alone'.

Malmesbury believed that the entire crisis could be eased if Sardinia would stop manoeuvering toward war, and, more fundamentally, if 'an amelioration and gradual improvement of the condition of the Italians' were achieved by introducing reforms in the papal government. In his draft to Bloomfield he claimed, 'In the opinion of Her Majesty's Government, if that portion of Italy were well-governed and happy, we should hear far less of the general oppression of the Italian people, and of that long and vain dream of Italian unity.' He urged France and Austria, instead of working themselves up into war, to co-operate in pressing the pope to reform the States of the Church. It was inappropriate, or so he said, for England as a Protestant state to 'take too prominent a part, lest she should excite a suspicion that she was swayed by motives of a sectarian character'. He would nonetheless employ English diplomacy to persuade France and Austria to put pressure on the pope.

Malmesbury was prepared to go farther than papal reform, however. He was willing to use English influence and perhaps naval power to effect a partitioning of the pope's ancient states. In the private letter to Cowley in December he stated the idea most explicitly: '[England] could give her moral, and if necessary her material assistance to establish another distribution by Catholic Powers of the Pope's Territory, or a forced improvement of the Pope's Government.' To Derby on 4 January he spoke of 'a remodeling of the territorial arrangements of the Papal Dominions'.[27] In the Bloomfield draft he proposed 'a redistribution of Central Italy'. When the queen objected that the proposal undermined the Vienna treaties as well as the exercise of the pope's spiritual power, he phrased the proposal more guardedly to Cowley and Loftus, referring to 'modification of the existing territorial arrangements in Central Italy' provided that it be 'sanctioned by all the powers and accomplished without enfeebling the spiritual power of the Pope'. He no longer explicitly referred to using English force or

---

26   Malmesbury to Queen Victoria, 10 Dec. 1858, *Letters of Queen Victoria*, vol. III, 390–1.
27   Malmesbury to Derby, 4 Jan. 1859, Derby papers, 144/2.

material assistance. However much Malmesbury muted his proposal, Napoleon and the Austrians would have no difficulty hearing his message – the English conservative government, contrary to the Vienna treaties, was prepared to promote the rearrangement of at least some of the Papal States, precisely what Napoleon at Plombières planned with Cavour to do. Malmesbury himself was quite aware of the significance of what he proposed.[28]

It should be noted here that Lord John Russell, the future Whig–Liberal foreign secretary, stated in December 1858 that he too was ready to give up papal territory. He was less cautious than Malmesbury: 'I'm not afraid about Rome and Naples. Rome with fifteen miles around should be guaranteed to the Pope, with a Spanish garrison paid by the Catholic Powers, who should also give the guarantee.'[29] Russell would have his day beginning in June 1859 when he could work to achieve this vision of papal rule.

At least two observations can be made about Malmesbury's policy toward Italy and the papacy. In the first place, his view that the papal government was the root of the trouble in Italy and that reform of papal government constituted the way toward Italian and European peace in the matter continued the traditional approach of English governments, both Whig and Tory, to the problems of Italy. On two major occasions since 1815, England was involved with other powers in urging the popes to introduce certain governmental changes. The first was the conference of ambassadors of France, Austria, Prussia and Russia, with England represented unofficially by Sir Brook Taylor, which met in Rome throughout the spring of 1831, following the February–March revolution in Romagna. The powers agreed on a memorandum addressed to Pope Gregory XVI on 21 May 1831, proposing a re-organization of the papal government.[30] The second occasion came in May 1856, after the Congress of Paris. Richard Lyons, then unofficial English envoy at Rome, presented a message from Lord Clarendon, then English foreign minister, to Cardinal Antonelli, which proposed changes in the papal government.[31] The English pressed the matter into 1857 when the French and Austrians exchanged correspondence about papal reforms. The French produced a proposal for papal reform and the Austrians responded with a revised proposal, but the effort collapsed for want of agreement, and was dropped.[32] Both the memorandum of

---

28   The papal territorial question was the first thing Count Buol, the Austrian prime minister, responded to when Loftus presented Malmesbury's message to him: Loftus to Malmesbury, Vienna, 20 Jan. 1859, copy, RA J14/77. Malmesbury to Cowley, 7 Jan. 1859, private, Cowley papers, PRO, FO, 519/196.

29   Russell to Lord Clarendon, 26 Dec. 1858, *The later correspondence of Lord John Russell, 1840–1878*, ed. G.P. Gooch (London: Longmans, Green, 1925). vol. II, 229.

30   G.F.-H. Berkeley, *Italy in the making*, vol. I (Cambridge: Cambridge University Press, 1932, 1968), especially ch. 7 and 8. The complete text is published in R. del Piano, *Roma e la rivoluzione del 1831, con documenti inediti* (Imola: n.p., 1931), 343.

31   Lyons to Normanby, 8 May 1856, *Lyons' despatches*, 4–6.

32   The French plan for papal reforms, June 1857, together with the Austrian modifications, are published in full in Pirri, vol. II, part 2, 104–8.

England: reform and rearrange the Papal States

1831 and the French plan of 1857 served as important texts for the ongoing discussion of papal reform throughout 1859 and 1860.

There is a second point to observe about Malmesbury's emerging policy. In another respect, Malmesbury broke sharply with the traditional English policy toward the Papal States. For the first time since 1815, an English government was prepared to allow, indeed even to promote, the end of papal temporal power in at least some, perhaps most, of the historic Papal States. From 1814 through 1849, all of the powers, including England, assumed that the States of the Church, in spite of difficulties, were a lasting feature of the European international scene. At the Congress of Vienna in 1815, Lord Castlereagh, then English foreign secretary, as a matter of course supported the restoration of the Papal States under Pius VII, commenting that 'in this all England has Catholic sentiments'.[33] When the pope was overthrown in the Romagna during the revolution of 1831, England again joined the other powers to support papal restoration, this time, as already noted, with some urging that the pope effect certain reforms. It was taken for granted that Austrian troops would put down the revolution in the Romagna and restore papal rule. At the time of the revolution of 1848–9, the story was only slightly different. The English government, with Lord Palmerston then as foreign secretary, assumed that the pope would be restored, although he favoured arranging it by diplomatic intervention which would include papal reforms, and not by the use of armed force. When the French, then under Napoleon as president of the French Republic, sent troops to restore the pope by force, Palmerston called it 'a most unfortunate proceeding' in which the English did not participate, but he did not object. Neither did he object when the Austrians followed with their troops on the Adriatic side.[34]

By the end of 1858, however, the whole matter was changed. Both the English Conservative government and the Whig–Liberal opposition were ready to give up the pope to those who wished his political overthrow in perhaps the greater portion of the States of the Church. This point constitutes one of the crucial historical changes which shaped the events of 1859 and 1860: this time no one moved to restore the ancient Papal States to the pope, and England played its part in effecting papal overthrow and in not effecting papal restoration. The grounds for this change in English relations with the papacy are to be found in the 1850s and must be explored after we have looked at the papal response to the coming crisis.

---

[33] Quoted by Mgr Testaferrata, 13 April 1814, after his talk with Lord Castlereagh, in John Tracy Ellis, *Cardinal Consalvi and Anglo-papal relations, 1814–1824* (Washington: Catholic University Press, 1942), 20. Gary Mooney, 'British diplomatic relations with the Holy See, 1793–1830', *Recusant history* 14 (1978), 198–201.

[34] Hansard's, CV, col. 1368–70, 11 June 1849; CVI, col. 734–40, 22 June 1849.

'English Liberties' and 'The Government of Priests'

The papacy: maintain the temporal power

Pope Pius IX, in contrast to Malmesbury, was very quick to see that a crisis was coming in Italy and that it involved him and his states. For him, the matter at issue was quite clear: the nature and the existence of the temporal power of the popes. Pius' policy from the start was to defend and seek to maintain the temporal power and to appeal to the Catholic faithful to support it vigorously.

Early in January 1859, Monsignor Sacconi, papal nuncio in Paris, alerted Antonelli to the possibility of war over Italy.[35] In his view the main source of the trouble was the activity of Napoleon and Cavour in pursuit of 'the so-called Italian cause'; they were stirring up the revolutionary party of Italy and preparing to destroy the tranquillity of the peninsula, especially in the Papal States and the Austrian states. England contributed to this, he thought, by resurrecting the question of papal reforms at the end of 1858. Sacconi's comment may have reflected some knowledge of Malmesbury's private overture to Napoleon via Cowley on 7 December. The English, Sacconi believed, were especially unable to understand and appreciate Catholic and papal concerns. Cardinal Antonelli, the papal secretary of state, noted that there were those, including presumably the English, who tried to blame the present troubles of Italy on the political conditions of the papal government. In Antonelli's judgment, however, such people were searching for a pretext to deprive the head of the church of his temporal dominions.[36]

The pope communicated his views of the crisis to the English government directly in a private audience with Odo Russell at the Vatican on 14 January.[37] The occasion was especially amicable, in spite of the gravity of the subject discussed, because it was the pope's first meeting with the newly arrived unofficial English envoy. Pius was eager for Odo to understand what the main issue was: the nature and continued existence of the States of the Church, the temporal power of the popes. He believed the source of the troubles was clear. 'Evil spirits are at work even in my dominions', Pius told Odo, 'and the late speech of the King of Sardinia is calculated to inflame the minds of all the revolutionary men of Italy.'[38] Pius added that there were those outside Italy who

35 Sacconi to Antonelli, Paris, 7 Jan. 1859, ASV,ASdS, 1859, 165/1/33–8, and *Il carteggio Antonelli–Sacconi, 1858–1860*, ed. Mariano Gabriele (2 vols., Rome: Istituto per la storia del Risorgimento italiano, 1962), vol. 1, 10–12.
36 Antonelli to Sacconi, Rome, 11 Jan. 1859, ASV, ANParigi, 1859, SdS, AD/P and *Antonelli*, vol. 1, 13.
37 Odo Russell to Corbett, Rome, 14 Jan. 1859, no. 1, most confidential, PRO, FO, 43/70, and *Odo Russell*, 1–3. The letter was passed on to Queen Victoria.
38 On January 10, Victor Emmanuel opened the new session of the Piedmontese parliament with the Royal Address, in which he acknowledged 'the cry of sorrow [*grido di dolore*] that reaches us from so many parts of Italy'. The wording was carefully chosen by Cavour and explicitly approved by Napoleon before delivery (Arnold Blumberg, 'The diplomacy of the Austro-Sardinian War of 1859' (Ph.D. dissertation, University of Pennsylvania, 1952), 102–6).

pressured the pope to make reforms, and by so doing agitated the revolutionaries. The way to peace in Italy would be for the agitators in Sardinia-Piedmont and their agents in the Papal States to cease their disruptive action and for the powers of Europe to stop pressing for changes in the papal government. They did not understand, Pius contended, that to make the kind of reforms they insisted on would require that the very nature of papal government be transformed, something the pope could never allow. According to Odo's account of the audience, Pius expressed the point succinctly:

> We are advised [the pope said] to make reforms and it is not understood that those very reforms which would consist in giving this country a government of laymen would make it cease to exist. It is called 'States of the Church' (États de l'Église) and that is what it must remain. It is true, I have lately appointed a layman to a post formerly held by an ecclesiastic, and I may do so again occasionally, but, however small we may be, we cannot yield to outer pressure and this country must be administered by men of the Church.

In other words, both revolutionaries and reformers, each in their own way, Pius thought, were bent on the end of papal temporal power as it now stood, whether they were self-consciously aware of that or not. In Pius' view, when he had introduced reforms in 1846 and 1847, some of the very changes the powers had urged in 1831, it had led not to peace but to revolution and his temporary exile. Pius was determined that this time there would be no reforms. At the same time he identified the source of his strength:

> For my part I shall fulfill my duties according to my conscience and should governments and events turn against me they cannot make me yield. I shall go with the faithful to the Catacombs as did the Christians of the early Centuries and there await the will of the Supreme Being, for I dread no human power upon earth and fear nothing but God.

Pius meant what he said, and therein he laid bare the profoundly Catholic Christian character of his motives, which provides the key to interpreting his perspective, policy, activity and formative power throughout the long years of crisis surrounding the end of the temporal power.[39] It gave him a personal strength which allowed him to withstand the most vehement threats of war and revolution. He was able to convey the honesty and depth of his spiritual conviction to the faithful everywhere. In the process a very concrete political power accrued to him which even his least agreeable foe *could* understand: Catholics in France would oppose any French efforts to unsettle the pope, and, if Napoleon wished to retain their political backing, he had better beware of it; and even though smaller in number, Irish Catholics and English Catholics felt the same, and both the Conservative and Whig–Liberal governments had to take

---

39 It is common for historians not to pay attention when Pius IX says such things, especially when discussing political and diplomatic history as we are here. The passages must be read and taken seriously, however, if we are to get to the core of Pius' work.

account of it. Pius probably gave little thought to his political influence, but Antonelli was more calculating. Antonelli told Odo Russell:

> The Pope does not belong to himself, he belongs to the Catholicks of England, Ireland, France, Germany, Austria, Spain, Portugal, to the Catholicks of all the world and to God whose Vicar he is on Earth... The Catholicks of the whole world will speak out when he is in distress and will not forsake him, but far be it from us to wish the subjects of foreign Sovereigns to assume a hostile attitude towards their governments, when their Holy Father is threatened with injustice.[40]

That Pius IX enjoyed such spiritual *rapport* with the faithful in France, Ireland, England and elsewhere, was due to the revival of Catholic religion which produced among the clergy and faithful renewed Catholic devotion in their everyday lives, and a distinct orientation toward the pope and Rome. Pius was both the beneficiary and the spiritual leader of the revival, the movement opponents usually referred to as Ultramontanism. The pope himself encouraged personal veneration of the Holy Father, and he supported it during the 1850s by instituting some very practical measures which helped to centralize the church around Rome. In church government, he battled French Gallicanism with an encyclical in 1852. He encouraged judicial appeals to Rome from all countries, he increased the number of papal appointments to bishoprics, and he helped found new national seminaries in Rome, including the Irish College. In liturgy and vestments, he ordered (1850) the Roman clergy to wear the cassock instead of breeches and frock coat, and he encouraged the use of the Roman missal to standardize the mass everywhere. In devotion, he defined the Immaculate Conception of Mary (1854) and set the example of prayer to the Virgin Mary and devotion before the crucifix.[41]

In Ireland the Catholic revival was especially associated with Pius' appointment of Cardinal Cullen as Archbishop of Armagh (1850), later Dublin (1852). During thirty years Cullen led a reorganization of the Irish church which Romanized the church and consolidated a devotional transformation in which the great mass of Irish people became practising Catholics.[42]

In England the Catholics experienced a similar revival under Cardinal Wiseman who was appointed by Pius as Archbishop of Westminster when he established the English Catholic hierarchy in 1850. The act completed the transformation of the English Catholics from a mission into a denomination.[43] Wiseman's coming coincided with the immigration of masses of Irish into England in flight from the famine of the 1840s. The new Irish gave the Catholic

---

40 Odo Russell to Russell, Rome, 4 Jan. 1860, no. 4, PRO, FO, 43/76, and *Odo Russell*, 75.
41 Aubert, *passim*; J. Derek Holmes, *The triumph of the Holy See: a short history of the papacy in the nineteenth century* (London: Burns and Oates, 1978), 134–59.
42 Emmet Larkin, 'The devotional revolution in Ireland, 1850–1875', *American Historical Review* 77 (1972), 625; Desmond Bowen, *The Protestant crusade in Ireland, 1800–1870: a study of Protestant–Catholic relations between the Act of Union and Disestablishment* (Montreal: McGill–Queen's University Press, 1978).
43 Bossey, 362.

church real numerical presence in England, added to a Catholic population already increasing through natural growth and frequent conversions from the Church of England.[44] In the 1850s, the number of churches and chapels in Great Britain increased from 680 to 950, and the number of priests from just over 800 to nearly 1240. By 1860 there were many more convents and religious houses, Catholic booksellers, schools and agencies. Priests now walked the streets of London in distinctive dress, churches followed Roman liturgy and styles, and the faithful expressed devotion to the Virgin and before the crucifix. Church government was centralized and integrated with Rome. Above all, the faithful felt near to their Holy Father and closely followed his lead.[45]

By the end of the 1850s, in other words, in Ireland and England as well as France and elsewhere, Catholic revival was well underway. It provided the foundation of English and Irish Catholic loyalty to the pope and of their support of the temporal power. It meant that the pope's policy to stand firm and uncompromisingly defend the temporal power could have both spiritual and political consequences.

It was crucial to the pope's policy to define the meaning and importance of the temporal power. This he did by means of encyclicals and allocutions, and through his letters and audiences with every sort of person. The Jesuit journal in Rome, *Civiltà Cattolica*, often elaborated on what the pope said.[46]

Pius IX issued his earliest, and perhaps most authoritative, formal definition of the temporal power in June 1859 in an encyclical and an allocution to the Sacred College of Cardinals in response to the revolution in the Romagna. In the encyclical he gave the temporal power the highest status he could without making it a formal dogma of the Church: 'We openly declare that the Civil Power is necessary to this Holy See in order that it may be able, without any impediment, to exercise its sacred duties for the benefit of religion.' To make his intent clear he formally excommunicated all those who perpetrated what he called a sacrilege against the States of the Church. In the allocution, he elaborated on his declaration:

44 Bossey, 362, 306–7. Perhaps 80 per cent of the 750,000 Catholics in England were Irish.
45 *Catholic Directory* (London) for 1850, and for 1860. See Wiseman's statistics in his address to the Catholic international congress at Malines, Belgium (1863), in Wilfred Philip Ward, *The life and times of Cardinal Wiseman* (2 vols., London: Longmans, Green, 1897), vol. II, 459. Still helpful is Paul Thureau-Dangin, *The English Catholic revival in the nineteenth century*, trans. Wilfred Wilberforce (2 vols, London: Simpkin, Marshall, Hamilton and Kent, 1914); but see Jean Alain Lesourd, *Les catholiques dans la société anglaise, 1765–1865* (Paris: Honoré Champion, 1978).
46 The most comprehensive collection of documents by Pius IX is *Pii IX, pontificis maximi Acta* (part 1, 7 vols.; part 2, 2 vols., Graz: Akademische Druck, 1971 reprint of the original edition, n.d.). However I have used the Italian version of the principal encyclicals and allocutions of 1859–61 as they were forwarded by Odo Russell to the Foreign Office, sometimes with his own English translation (in PRO, FO, 43). The main Jesuit articles are those in the series, 'Il principato civile del Papa tutela della dignita personale', *Civiltà Cattolica*, 1st ser., II (1850), 637–54; III (1850), 89–102, 201–19, plus a large number published in the journal during 1859 and 1860.

'English Liberties' and 'The Government of Priests'

> [B]y the singular Counsel of Divine Providence, it happened that, in so great a multitude and variety of secular Princes, the Roman Church also should have a Temporal dominion, subject to no other Power, to the end that the Roman Pontiff, the Chief Pastor of the whole Church, without being placed under (or subject to) any Prince whatsoever, might, with the fullest liberty, exercise over the entire Orb, (sphere or world) the supreme Power, and the supreme Authority given to him by God, to feed and to uphold (or rule over) the whole Flock of the Lord, and at the same time, more easily to propagate His Divine Religion from day to day, to provide for the various wants of the faithful, to give aid to suppliants, and to procure all the other kinds of good, which according to times and circumstances, should, by him be known to confer most advantage to entire Christendom.

The temporal power, thus given by Providence, was, through history,

> confirmed to her [the Church] by continued possession for so many ages and recognized and defended by the common consent of the People, and the Princes of many nations, (and even of many who are not Roman Catholic), as the Sacred and inviolable patrimony of the Prince of the Apostles.[47]

English and Irish bishops, clergy and popular writers interpreted the temporal power to the Catholic faithful by means of pastoral letters, sermons, lectures, pamphlets, books and public mass meetings. The English Catholic press, especially the *Tablet* and, beginning in 1860, the *Universe* for working class Catholics, kept the pope's tribulation and ideas constantly before the people. In these years a major public discussion of the temporal power developed, which spread to Parliament, the general press, upper class drawing rooms, working class neighbourhoods, and the general pamphlet circuit.[48] It appears that, during 1859 and 1860, the pope and his definition of the temporal power were supported by all English and Irish Catholics. This included even Sir John Acton, John Henry Newman and the liberal Catholics whose misgivings on the temporal power did not develop until after most of the temporal power was

---

[47] The translation of both the encyclical (18 June 1859) and the allocution (23 June 1859) were provided by Odo Russell, and enclosed in Odo Russell to Russell, 1 July 1859, no. 79, PRO, FO, 43/71.

[48] Four especially significant English Catholic writers on the subject were: John Maguire, *Rome: its ruler and its institutions* (London: Brown, Green, Longmans and Roberts, 1857); Henry Edward Manning, *The Temporal Power of the Vicar of Jesus Christ* (London: Burns and Lambert, 1862); M.J. Rhodes, *His Holiness Pope Pius IX and the temporal rights of the Holy See as involving the religious, social, and political interests of the whole world* (London: Thomas Richardson, 1859); and Nicholas Wiseman, *Recollections of the last four popes and of Rome in their times* (London: Hurst and Blackett, 1858; new rev. ed., 1859). Pius IX considered Maguire's book to be an able 'vindication' of him and Roman institutions (Pius IX to J.F. Maguire, 15 Sept. 1859, in *Tablet*, 8 Oct. 1859). Manning's volume presents his public lectures on the theme and is clearly the most complete piece of political theology on the subject published anywhere in Europe, including Rome. Wiseman's is an endearing anecdotal autobiographical memoir showing how devout and fatherly the popes were. See Philip Hughes' observation: in the English Catholic press, the temporal power was 'the most insistent topic, continuously, for all this quarter of a century ... To the English Catholic of the time this was not, and could not be, any academic problem of continental politics merely' (in 'The coming century', G.A. Beck (ed.), *The English Catholics, 1850–1950* (London: Burns, Oates, 1950), 15).

lost in 1860, when it became necessary to discover some way out of the *impasse* over Rome.[49]

The very structure of the States of the Church revealed in concrete political, social, and economic idiom what the temporal power meant.[50] As Pius IX emphasized to Odo Russell, it was a state belonging to the church, administered for the church by men of the church. The men of the church were of four kinds: priests who were the actual clergy; deacons who were like clergy and eligible to be cardinals, but without the authority to administer the sacraments; prelates who were persons devoted to service of the church or the government of the Papal States, and called by the title 'monsignore'; and monks and nuns who were members of convents and religious orders. In Rome (1859) there were nearly 7000 persons in these four categories, one for every six families in the city. In the Papal States there were perhaps 35,000 of them.

The pope was bishop of Rome, head of the universal church, and monarch of the Papal States. He was elected by the Sacred College of Cardinals, all men appointment by the pope. The Consistery of the College of Cardinals, other than electing the pope and receiving papal allocutions, possessed little power. Political power was held by Cardinal Antonelli, the pope's secretary of state since 1846, and a deacon, who was also president of the Council of Ministers. The Council of Ministers included the ministers of the Interior, of Grace and Justice, of Finance, of War, and of Commerce, Agriculture and the Fine Arts. All had to be at least prelates, and were appointed by the pope. The papal diplomatic

49   Edward Norman (*The Catholic Church and Ireland in the age of rebellion, 1859 to 1873* (Ithaca: Cornell University Press, 1965), 47), is misleading when he says that Newman and the *Rambler* were against the temporal power. Newman was convinced that the pope could not rightly be a subject of anyone. What he opposed was some versions of the defence of the temporal power (Newman to Acton, 7 June 1861, in *The letters and diaries of John Henry Newman*, vol. XIX, ed. Charles Stephen Dessain (London: Nelson, 1969), 507–19). However he kept silent publicly until 1866 when he gave his notable sermon in support of the temporal power, *The pope and the revolution* (London: Longman, Green, Reader and Dyer, 1866). See his own account of his views written long after the events (Newman's *Memorandum*, 22 May 1882, *Letters of Newman*, vol. XIX, 561). Acton, who, with Richard Simpson, published the *Rambler*, supported the temporal power. In 1861 he argued against Simpson's criticism of Manning's lectures on the temporal power: 'There is no other way of securing him [the pope]. You are quite right against Manning's theory, but in point of fact we cannot devise an alternative for sovereignty . . . The temporal sovereignty is the only plan we can devise to secure liberty for the pope . . . The extent, therefore, is not essential' (Acton to Simpson, Munich, 8 Oct. 1861, Joseph Altholz and Damian McElrath, ed., *The correspondence of Lord Acton and Richard Simpson* (Cambridge: Cambridge University Press, 1971), vol. I, 182–3.

50   The main sources upon which this brief comment on the structure of the Papal States is based are: *Annuario pontificio*, 1858–61; *Statistica della popolazione dello Stato pontificio dell'anno 1853* (Rome: 1857); *Stato dell'anime per l'alma città di Roma per l'anno 1859* (Rome: 1860); the *Almanach de Gotha*, 1859, 1860, 1861; the *Lyons' despatches*, especially Lyons to Normanby, 26 and 28 May 1856; 'La questione italiana nel 1859', appendix, *Civiltà Cattolica*, 4th ser., vol. I (1859), 643–56, translated by John Maguire as 'Internal administration of the Papal States', in Maguire, 2nd ed., appendix xxxiii–xlvi; Robert Graham, *Vatican diplomacy: a study of church and state on the international plane* (Princeton: Princeton University Press, 1959), 133–43; and Paolo dalle Torre, *L'opera riformatrice ed amministrative di Pio IX fra il 1850 e il 1870* (Rome: n.p., 1945).

representatives were the nuncios, who could be priests, deacons, or prelates, and were responsible to the Cardinal Secretary of State, and were papal appointments.

The rest of the state structure manifested thorough-going papal centralism. The fundamental law, the *Motu proprio*, issued at Portici on 12 September 1849, was created exclusively on the authority of the pope himself. Other specific laws were papal proclamations channelled through Antonelli. At the central, provincial and municipal levels, including the courts, police and prisons, all chief officials were appointed, or selected from lists, by the pope and subject to the pope via Antonelli. All the significant offices at the central and provincial levels were occupied by clerics or prelates. Although the fundamental law provided for it, there were as yet no councils or bodies of electors in the municipalities, as *Civiltà Cattolica* explained, due to 'the excitement of political passions ... [T]he government, by means of its officers supplies the want of this assembly, whilst it gives effect to the other provisions of the law.' In any case, Bologna and Ancona were under Austrian martial law from 1849 to 1857. Only people of irreproachable political and ecclesiastical conduct possessed civil rights. There was no 'opposition' within the state structure; the pope's opponents were forced to operate outside the established political institutions. Ecclesiastical excommunication meant loss of civil rights, and improper political activity could mean excommunication.

The political–administrative organization explicitly troubled the British. However, to understand the extent of papal–ecclesiastical centralism in the Papal States, reference must be made to how other nonpolitical sectors related to the church's central structure. The tempo of life in Rome and the rest of the Papal States was set by the church calendar and liturgical year. The church was the single largest landowner and landlord in the state. Almost 80 per cent of the population, being rural and oriented to the land, was integrated by means of the traditional church-sanctioned social hierarchy of clergy, aristocracy, and peasant. The economy of the largest city, Rome, was primarily based on the church and its administration, the pilgrimages of the faithful, and the manufacture and sale of ecclesiastical goods, such as statuary, religious souvenirs, gold and silver objects. Institutions of charity and welfare, such as hospitals and poor houses, were run by religious orders, or in some cases by papal government authorities. Probably a majority of the population of Rome lived on papal and church welfare.[51] Schools were run and staffed by religious orders, the bishops, or the communes, in which case they were supervised by the church. Professors at the universities were appointed by the pope. On top of all this, the departments of the Curia for ecclesiastical matters administered the affairs of the entire Catholic Church throughout the Papal States – and, for that matter, throughout the entire Catholic world. Hence the hierarchy of the church in the

---

51   Isastia, 184.

England turns against the papal temporal power

Papal States, including the archbishops, bishops and parish clergy, spread minutely into every city, town and village.

In short, the temporal power of the popes meant an ecclesiastically dominated and integrated state and society, with Rome as an ecclesiastically dominated and integrated city, which quite explicitly implemented the papal cultural vision and view of history. This was the papal temporal power Pius IX could not give up or secularize, but which he determined to defend and maintain in the name of God and the church.

England turns against the papal temporal power

The difference on a fundamental level between the English and papal responses to the coming crisis in Italy could not be more radical. Both governments agreed on the immediate need to keep Sardinia-Piedmont from agitating for war between France and Austria, but they were divided into opposite sides over the question of the nature and the continued existence of the papal temporal power.

The pope was correct in his claim that the powers of Europe, including non-Catholic powers, had until now sanctioned the existence of the papal monarchy. The English Conservative government under Derby and Malmesbury was the first power to break with that tradition and to begin to turn against the papal temporal power. This change in English policy was a response to the course of events in Italy and England from the restoration of Pius IX in 1849 onward. It entailed an extension into foreign policy of the English motif of anti-Catholicism, especially anti-papalism.

As already noted, the English government did assume that the pope would be restored in 1849, and it did not object to the use of French troops to put down the Roman Republic under Mazzini. But the English had misgivings about it. For one thing, Russell and Palmerston, who were then prime minister and foreign minister, along with many English people, were not completely unattracted to the Mazzinian republic. John Freeborn, the English consular agent in Rome, wrote appreciative reports of the conduct of the republican government and the population. Many English considered Garibaldi's defence of Rome against the French no less than heroic.[52] By contrast, the English were profoundly disappointed with Pius IX's reaction to the revolution, and with his acts and outlook after the French troops regained Rome. They interpreted him as undoing the reforms which, to their satisfaction, he had instituted during the first three years of his pontificate, and which had earned him the reputation of being a liberal pope.[53] People in England talked of the pope reverting to the old

---

52 Freeborn to Palmerston, Rome, 23 March 1849, *Correspondence respecting the affairs of Rome, 1849*, in *Parliamentary papers, 1851*, vol. 57, 6. G.M. Trevelyan, *Garibaldi's defence of the Roman Republic* (London: Longmans, 1907).

53 Before the revolution, Lord John Russell stated in the House of Commons: 'I have seen with very great pleasure, the course which the present pope has pursued; and I think it will tend

superstitious, despotic and backward ways of the papacy. Richard Lyons, the English unofficial envoy in Rome during the 1850s, agreed with the outlook of those Romans who looked favourably on Pius' first three years: 'They do not compare Pius IX with Gregory XVI, but with his former self. The contrast they draw is..., to use their own expression, between the reign of "Pio Nono Primo" and the reign of "Pio Nono Secondo".'[54]

Disappointment and misgivings turned into outright opposition to the pope when he officially established the hierarchy of the Roman Catholic Church in England in 1850. It made no difference that Rome and Wiseman had planned and decided long before the revolution to create a proper hierarchy in England, or that Rome had informed Lord Minto during his special governmental mission to Italy in 1847 of its intention to proceed to that end. Nicholas Wiseman, whom the pope appointed cardinal and first Archbishop of Westminster, and who was full of hopes for the conversion of England to Catholicism, announced the new hierarchy in an exuberant pastoral sent from Rome, dated 7 October 1850. When it was published in England the holocaust broke. It was the most severe anti-Catholic tumult of the century. It emerged from all levels of society, from the working classes to the prime minister, and from nearly all Protestants, broad church to Evangelical, Anglican to Nonconformist, educated Protestantism to popular Protestantism. Lord John Russell himself led the anti-Catholic outrage. He wrote a letter to the Bishop of Durham which was published in *The Times*:

> There is an assumption of power in all the documents which have come from Rome; a pretension of supremacy over the realm of England, and a claim to sole and undivided sway, which is inconsistent with the Queen's supremacy, with the rights of our bishops and clergy, and with the spiritual independence of the nation, as asserted even in Roman Catholic times.[55]

The 'no-popery' panic was most intense in October, November and December 1850 and continued throughout 1851. It brought to near universal expression an underlying anti-papal conviction common to nearly all non-Catholic English. Lord Clarendon, later to become foreign secretary, confessed that he did not

much to increase the happiness of the people of Italy' (Hansard's, XCII, col. 854–5, 14 May 1847). Queen Victoria wrote Pius IX a letter applauding his 'many proofs of being animated by a sincere desire to improve the condition of the People'. (Queen Victoria to Pope Pius IX, Windsor Castle, 8 Jan. 1849, ASV, Archivio Pio Nono, Inghilterra, Sovrani.)

[54] Lyons to Normanby, Rome, 6 June 1856, *Lyons' despatches*, 21. Berkeley, *Italy in the Making*, vol. II, 37–52; E.E.Y. Hales, *Pio Nono: A study in European politics and religion in the nineteenth century* (London: Eyre and Spottiswoode, 1954), *passim*; Livia de Ruggiero, *Inghilterra e stato pontificio nel primo triennio del pontificio di Pio IX* (Rome: Società romana di storia patria, 1953), ch. 1 and 2. The contrast is real on the level of political policy and acts in a changed setting (before and after a revolution), but Berkeley, Hales and other historians overlook the point that on a more foundational level Pius IX was always a deeply Catholic Ultramontanist, and never a liberal.

[55] Russell to Dr Maltby, Bishop of Durham, Downing Street, 4 Nov. 1850, in *The Times*, 7 Nov. 1850, reprinted in E.R. Norman, *Anti-Catholicism in Victorian England* (London: George Allen and Unwin, 1968), 159–61. See also Norman's ch. 3, 'Papal aggression', 52–79; and, Hales, *Pio Nono*, 144–9.

regret 'the anti-Pope feeling', since it was 'high time to resist the encroachments of Rome and to let His Holiness know that we are still Protestants'. Song-sellers in the streets peddled a piece whose chorus went like this:

> Monks and Nuns and fools afloat,
>   We'll have no bulls shoved down our throat,
> Cheer up and shout "down with the Pope,
>   And his bishop cardinal Wiseman".[56]

The objection to the pope's act centred on its political and not its spiritual or ecclesiastical implications. The Russell government believed it demonstrated how the pope, a foreign monarch, intended to interfere with the temporal affairs of the United Kingdom. Sir Alexander Cockburn, the solicitor general, noted that the pope's act presumed to create dioceses in England, which both Catholics and the Church of England regarded as territorial divisions of the country, and to appoint bishops with territorial titles, thereby elevating towns to cities and granting bishops many temporal prerogatives. These were all acts that, in England, only the Crown had the authority to perform. A foreign political ruler had no right to invade the realm of the queen of England in this manner.

To oppose what they regarded as a political encroachment, the Russell government, in February 1851, introduced a bill regulating ecclesiastical titles and proposed to place civil penalties against the use of episcopal titles related to cities or areas in England unless approved by the Crown. In March the measure passed the Commons by an overwhelming majority, and became law in August.[57]

After what the English regarded as the pope's illiberal restoration and his unilateral act in establishing the Catholic hierarchy in England, the question of the pope being a political ruler stood out. A number of persons and events contributed to keep the Papal Question and Italy before the public during the 1850s.[58] As a result, a national consensus with two distinct foci gradually formed and developed: on one hand, the judgment that the papal monarchy was an intolerable tyranny, and, on the other, the conviction that the cause of Italian liberties, especially as represented in Piedmont-Sardinia, was a marvellous glory.

With the Catholic revival and the mass influx of Irish, fears of Catholic

---

56 Lord Clarendon to Sir George Lewis, 29 Oct. 1850, in Sir Herbert Maxwell, *The life and letters of George William Frederick, fourth Earl of Clarendon* (London: Edward Arnold, 1913), vol. I, 313–15. This song and others were collected by Henry Mayhew, *London labour and the London poor*, enlarged edition (4 vols., London: Griffin, Bohn, 1861–2), vol. I, 227.

57 14 et 15 Vict., c. 60. Russell's and Cockburn's speeches: Hansard's, CXIV, col. 187–211, 7 Feb. 1851; and CXV, col. 87–101, 17 March 1851. The vote was 438–95; a third of the negative votes were cast by Catholics.

58 The decade was a time of exceptional public interest in foreign affairs, and the Papal Question, no doubt, was responsible for creating a sizeable share of it, Beales, *England and Italy*, 19ff. See also Noel Blakiston, 'L'opinione pubblica inglese e la Questione italiana del 1859 al 1866', in *Inglesi e italiani nel Risorgimento* (Catania: Bonanno, 1973), 125–6.

progress in England were easily generated, and any information against Catholics and the pope's temporal power was eagerly believed. The hundreds of Italian refugees escaping the restoration in Italy, who offered first-hand evidence of papal superstition and political tyranny in 'priest-ridden' Italy, were especially welcomed. Giuseppe Mazzini and Aurelio Saffi, two of the three Triumvirs of the Roman Republic, came to London, as did Felice Orsini, and Antonio Gallenga, who became a journalist with *The Times*.[59] Many refugees made links with the social élite, some through the Society of the Friends of Italy. Several priests and monks who converted to Protestantism wrote and lectured on popery with a knowledge and style that attracted large readership and audiences – especially Camillo Mapei, Salvatore Ferretti, Luigi DeSanctis, Alessandro Gavazzi and Giacinto Achilli.[60] Antonio Panizzi, who arrived much earlier, had become keeper of the British Museum, and during the 1850s acted as a channel of information between Italian liberals and many English aristocrats. Panizzi and Giacomo Lacaita frequently communicated with William Gladstone concerning liberty and despotism in Italy.[61]

Numerous English people who did the *giro d'Italia* returned with first hand stories of despotisms in the Papal States and Naples. None was more influential in shaping the public opposition to papal temporal power than Gladstone. During one visit to Rome and Naples in 1849, shortly after French troops overthrew the Roman Republic, and during another to Naples over the winter of 1850–1, he read and heard reports of despotism which alarmed him. He was so captivated by a new book on the injustices of the papal government by Luigi Carlo Farini, a Romagnol exiled in Turin, that he began to translate its four large volumes for the English public almost as soon as he read it in Naples. Farini convinced him that 'Rome unites the evils of the worst government and the most entire anarchy.'[62] When the volumes appeared in the early 1850s they provided the English reading public with the detailed information it needed to show that the 'government of priests' was so despotic that, as Farini asserted, 'there is not a breath of liberty, not a hope of tranquil life'.[63] While still in Naples, Gladstone personally witnessed the sentencing of Baron Carlo Poerio to twenty-four years imprisonment for political offences. His talk with Poerio in prison afterwards

59 Porter, *The refugee question*, 22–3, 32–3, 39–40.
60 Valdo Vinay, *Evangelici italiani esuli a Londra durante il Risorgimento* (Turin: Claudiana, 1961), *passim*; Giorgio Spini, *Risorgimento e protestanti* (Naples: Edizione scientifiche italiane, 1956), 274–314; Basil Hall, 'Alessandro Gavazzi: a Barnabite friar and the Risorgimento', *Studies in church history* 12 (1975), 303–56.
61 William Gladstone, *The Gladstone diaries* (6 vols., Oxford: Clarendon, 1968–78), vols. IV and V *passim*; Charles Lacaita, *An Italian Englishman: Sir James Lacaita* (London: Grant Richards, 1933).
62 Gladstone to Marquis Dragonetti, 1854, quoted in John Morley, *The life of William Ewart Gladstone* (London: Macmillan, 1903), vol. II, 12. Luigi Carlo Farini, *The Roman state from 1815 to 1850*, trans. W.E. Gladstone (4 vols., London: John Murray, 1851, 1852, 1854). See *The Gladstone diaries*, 27 Nov. 1850 and 19 Dec. 1850.
63 See Farini to Gladstone, 20 Dec. 1852, in Farini, vol. IV, 328.

convinced him that the government of the Kingdom of Two Sicilies committed tyranny against the best sectors of 'that upper part of the middle class'. Outraged, he wrote two public letters to the Earl of Aberdeen which dramatically brought Italian despotism to British attention. These experiences occasioned Gladstone's permanent conversion to the Risorgimento.[64]

Among the English, Evangelicals served as the *avant-garde* of 'no-popery' during the 1850s. They focussed public consciousness on the gains of Catholic revival in England, and provided an almost polar opposition to what they called 'the progress of priestcraft'. Most Protestants held anti-Catholic and anti-papal convictions, but Evangelicals expressed them with greater intensity and fewer qualifications than the rest, and emphasized the explicitly theological and moral meaning of popery in addition to the political. They still believed the sixteenth-century doctrine of eschatology that the pope was the Anti-Christ prophesied in Revelation, the Scarlet Woman whose name was written on her forehead:

MYSTERY, BABYLON THE GREAT,
THE MOTHER OF HARLOTS
AND ABOMINATIONS OF THE EARTH.[65]

Evangelical organizations were many, and very active in the cause of anti-Catholicism during the 1850s. Especially influential were the Evangelical Alliance, the Protestant Reformation Society and the National Protestant Society. There were countless public meetings, lectures, and sermons on popery, including no-popery topics in the long-running series of lectures at Exeter Hall in London. Many newspapers, such as the *Record*, an evangelical paper in the Church of England, carried news on popery. The number of published books, pamphlets, tracts and sermons on popery was immense.[66] Evangelical action, besides disseminating news and theological interpretations against popery, concentrated on evangelism of Catholics and circulation of Bibles. Three of the organizations for the evangelism of papists were the Society for the

---

64 Gladstone, *Two letters to the Earl of Aberdeen, on the state prosecution of the Neapolitan government* (London: John Murray, 1851). The letters went through eleven editions in 1851 and fourteen by 1859. *The Gladstone diaries*, vol. IV, 4 Jan. 1851 and 13 Feb. 1851). D.M. Schreuder, 'Gladstone and Italian unification, 1848–70: the making of a liberal?' *English historical review* 85 (1970), 478.

65 Revelation 17: 3–6. The key biblical passages in which Evangelicals saw the papacy foretold were Daniel 7 and 8, and Revelation 10–18. See the commentary and illustrations in the popular *Cassell's illustrated family Bible* (London and New York: Cassell, Petter and Calpin, 1860).

66 See G.I.T. Machin, *Politics and the Churches in Great Britain, 1832 to 1868*, passim. The *Times* and the *Record* gave notices and reports of lectures. Notable publications were: R.P. Blakeney, *Popery in its social aspect, being a complete exposure of the immorality and intolerance of Romanism* (London: Protestant Reformation Society, 1854); William Bennett, *Popery, as set forth in Scripture: its guilt and its doom* (London, 1850); J.A. Wylie, *Rome and the workings of Romanism in the Papal States* (London: Hamilton and Adams, 1854); Antonio Gavazzi, *My recollections of the last four popes, and of Rome in their times* (London, 1858); Luigi DeSanctis, *Popery and Jesuitism at Rome* (London, 1852); M. Hobart Seymour, *Evenings with Romanists* (London: Seeley's, 1854).

'English Liberties' and 'The Government of Priests'

Evangelization of Foreigners in London, the Society for the Religious Care and Instruction of Foreigners, and the London City Mission.[67] The Society for the Promotion of Christian Knowledge (SPCK) published (1853) an Italian translation of the Bible known as the Giucciardini Bible, and the British and Foreign Bible Society had an Italian version of its own. Bible salesmen, known as colporters, spread these Bibles in Italy.[68] Cardinal Cullen, while objecting to the anti-Catholicism of all sectors of Protestants, singled out the Evangelicals as the Catholics' most awful opponents, charging that they gave money and assistance to a committee which provided guns for attacks on the Papal States. Pius IX himself opposed the excursions of the colporters into the Papal States.[69]

Meanwhile, the long love affair that educated and socially advantaged English people had enjoyed with Italy and things Italian continued, and perhaps, because of the political agonies of the peninsula, even intensified. They loved Italy because it was the land of classical Rome, of the Renaissance, and, paradoxically, of the pope. It was to them a land of grandeur, and the arts, and Rome was the eternal city. Italy was the source of modern civilization. Generations of the sons and daughters of nobles and gentry, and now of the middle classes, journeyed to Italy. English poets in the line of Byron and Keats, and artists in the tradition of Turner went to Rome for inspiration.[70] In the 1850s, more English than ever before went to Italy with Murray's guidebook in their hands to gaze on the forum, to view the statues in the Vatican galleries, and to experience the pomp of St Peter's.[71] At home they studied Italian with refugees, viewed the greats of Italian art in the increasingly popular National

---

67 *The Times* carried notices of these societies. See Gilley, 'Evangelical and Roman Catholic missions', *passim*.
68 Vinay, 139–40; Spini, 351.
69 See Cardinal Cullen's address, 3 Sept. 1859, and Cullen's exchange in 1859 with Sir Culling Eardley, president of the Evangelical Alliance, in *Paul Cullen*, vol. II, 293–4, 312–23. Pius IX to Leopold II, Rome, 20 Jan. 1859, in *Pio IX e Leopoldo II*, ed. Giacomo Martina (Rome: Pontificia Università Gregoriana, 1967), 499. In the Papal States it was illegal to circulate Bibles without approval. After French troops restored papal temporal power in 1849, Roman police seized 3000 copies of the New Testament from a Roman printer who had been commissioned to publish them by Captain Pakenham; they were burned in 1850 (Spini, 276).
70 See *Italy: classical, historical, and picturesque, illustrated in a series of views by the leading landscape painters of Great Britain with descriptions of the scenes*, 2nd ed. (Glasgow, Edinburgh, and London: Blackie and Son, 1859), containing an introductory essay by Camillo Mapei; the third edition, completed in 1862, appeared in 1864 with a new title: *Italy illustrated and described, with a review of its past condition and future prospects*. See also James Fergusson, *The illustrated handbook of architecture* (2 vols., London: John Murray, 1855), vol. II, 473. G.M. Trevelyan, 'Englishmen and Italians', in *Clio, a muse and other essays*, 2nd ed. (London: Longmans, Green, (1930), 1949), 104–23; J.P.T. Bury, 'England and the unification of Italy', *Il Risorgimento e l'Europa* (Rome: Accademia Nazionale dei Lincei, 1964), 163–78; and Rudman, *passim*.
71 Octavian Blewitt, *Handbook for travellers in Central Italy*, part 1; 'Southern Tuscany and Papal States', 4th ed. (London: John Murray, 1857); part 2: 'Rome and its environs', 4th ed. (London: John Murray, 1856). The fifth edition of part 2 appeared in 1858, and of part 1 in 1861; the first edition on central Italy appeared as one volume in 1843. See R.S. Pine-Coffin, *Bibliography of British and American travel in Italy to 1860* (Florence: Olschki, 1974).

Gallery in London, and attended Italian opera at the Royal Italian Opera in Drury Lane, and, after 1858, in the new Royal Italian Opera at Covent Garden.[72] Italy satisfied both the classically-minded and the romantic.

As they experienced the glories of the Italian past, they could not help but long for what they regarded as the revival of Italian liberties to wipe away the degradation and despotism into which they believed Italy had fallen. Events in Piedmont-Sardinia during the 1850s soon gave many English people reason to hope for the moral and material progress of Italy. The government, headed by Massimo d'Azeglio, which came to power under King Victor Emmanuel in 1849 instituted numerous political, social and ecclesiastical changes of which the British greatly approved. Notable were the restoration of the constitution known as the *statuto*, and the passage of the Siccardi laws against Catholic church power. Count Cavour, in 1850, became minister of agriculture and commerce, and later of finance, and undertook a series of economic changes based on capitalist and *laissez-faire* principles he learned in England. These he continued as prime minister from 1852 onward. Among other things, he built railway track, extended gas lighting, increased Piedmont's exports, and lowered the tariff, permitting English manufacturers and traders to profit from a sizeable 50 per cent increase in their exports to Piedmont from 1850 to 1853.[73] Piedmont thus manifested all the tangible evidences of progress before the discovery of the G.N.P. As long as the English did not look too closely at how Cavour's government, his economic policy and the Piedmont parliament actually functioned during the 1850s, they could allow their hopes for Italian liberties and progress to be translated into enthusiasm for Piedmont.[74]

The two tendencies in the rising English consensus – against the papacy, and for Piedmont – conjoined in the Congress of Paris of 1856 when the powers of Europe met to settle the Crimean War. Cavour got next to Lord Clarendon, who was now British foreign secretary, and gave him a memo on Italy and against the Papal States written by the Marchese Gualterio in Rome. He played on Clarendon's attraction for Italy and dislike of the papal monarchy. In a forceful speech, Clarendon went beyond simple reforms, called the papal government the most appalling on the peninsula and publicly proposed Cavour's suggestion of separate treatment for the Romagna.[75] Palmerston brought the matter im-

[72] *The Times* regularly published notices and reviews on the opera and the gallery.
[73] Rosario Romeo, *Cavour e il suo tempo* (2 vols., Rome and Bari: Laterza, 1969–77), esp. vol. II, ch. 6 and 7. For the British trade statistics see: *Parliamentary papers, 1856*, vol. 56, *Trade and navigation: annual statement*. The exports from the United Kingdom to Sardinia, in pounds sterling were: 1850: £774,512; 1851: £706,108; 1852: £924,225; 1853: £1,112,447; it stayed around the 1853 level during the rest of the 1850s.
[74] See the ambivalent reports on Piedmont's economy by E.M. Erskine, Turin, 1 Jan. 1858, *Parliamentary papers, 1857–1858*, vol. 50, 88–96; and L.S. Sackville West, Turin, 1 July 1860, *Parliamentary papers, 1861*, vol. 63, 152–6. Mack Smith, *Victor Emanuel, Cavour*, ch. 2 and 3.
[75] Valsecchi, *L'unificazione italiana e la politica europea dalla guerra di Crimea alla guerra di Lombardia, 1854–1859*, 204–210; Harry Hearder, 'Clarendon e l'Italia', *Il Risorgimento e l'Europa* (Catania: Bonanna, 1969), 173–86; Mack Smith, *Victor Emanuel, Cavour*, ch. 4.

mediately to the attention of the English Parliament by claiming that 'the Holy City had not of late years been better governed than it was during the temporary absence of the Pope'. Both Palmerston and Clarendon were willing to consider armed coercion against the government of Naples and maybe even Rome to secure reforms. What they did was immediately to promote reforms by diplomacy through Richard Lyons in Rome, with the French joining in a year later. Both England and France anchored their naval fleets in the bay of Naples to scare King Ferdinand II, known as King Bomba, and then broke diplomatic relations with his government.[76] Cavour tried to cement a bond with England by arranging the marriage of Victor Emmanuel with Princess Mary of Cambridge, a cousin of Queen Victoria, but failed when the princess declined to marry a Catholic. The English were actually a little wary of Cavour in the coming years, but the events in Paris put England squarely on Cavour's side, willing to accept Piedmont's dominance in Italy, and some kind of assault on the Papal States as the sore spot of Italy. For his war strategy, Cavour had to turn hereafter to Napoleon.[77]

In England during 1857 and 1858, many English people from various parties feared that Catholicism was in new ways infiltrating even the Church of England. It was bad enough that Cardinal Wiseman had introduced Roman liturgical style into the English Catholic church, but now high churchmen in the Tractarian tradition appeared to be Romanizing the established church itself. More churches began using candles, crucifixes and elaborate vestments, held frequent eucharists, installed organs and organized choirs. It was the use of private confession, however, that aroused the greatest furor. In the summer of 1858 women from St Barnabas, Pimlico and Boyn Hill, Maidenhead, claimed that their priests asked them improper questions in the confessional. All the worst suspicions of Catholic priestly power and immorality now seemed applicable to the 'Puseyites', as they were called. Archibald Tait, Bishop of London, withdrew the licence of the curate at St Barnabas, but Samuel Wilberforce, Bishop of Oxford, acquitted the curate at Boyn Hill, stating that private confession to priests was good and appropriate for Anglicans. The episodes seemed to confirm that the progress of priestcraft was reaching inside even the home sanctuary.[78]

Late in 1858, the case of Edgar Mortara, a Jewish child in the Papal States, brought papal temporal power to public attention in a very existential manner. People learned the news that church officials in the Papal States had taken a Jewish boy in Bologna from his parents and placed him under church care in a

---

76 Hansard's, CXLII, col. 131, 6 May 1856. See the report of Palmerston's speech in *Giornale di Roma*, 14 May 1856. Maxwell, *Clarendon*, vol. II, 123–4.
77 Maxwell, *Clarendon*, vol. II, 124–5. Mack Smith, *Victor Emanuel, Cavour*, 26, 92.
78 Owen Chadwick, *The Victorian church* (2 vols., London: Adam and Charles Black, 1966–70), vol. I, 501–20. *Punch* mocked the Puseyites repeatedly during 1857 and 1858; see especially the cartoons of the week for 26 Sept. 1857, 9 Oct. 1858, 16 Oct. 1858, and 27 Nov. 1858; Norman, *Anti-Catholicism in Victorian England*, ch. 5.

religious order. The Mortara family had employed a Christian servant girl who had secretly baptized the boy as a baby when his life was endangered by an illness. The law of the Papal States, in conformity with canon law, required that, since by the act of baptism the child was regenerated and made a member of the Christian church, he must be removed from his parents and raised as a Christian. To English Protestants this was an outrageous abduction of an innocent child which could only be performed because of the existence of papal temporal power with the legal authority of a state. Protests went up across England and a Mortara committee of leading figures in church and state was organized to publicize the Mortara case. They put pressure on the papal government, raised the question of the papal government's treatment of Jews, and wanted the English government to take action against the pope.[79]

By the end of 1858, a definite consensus against the 'government of priests' and for Italian liberties as represented in Piedmont-Sardinia was well developed. It was a political consensus concerning vital questions of foreign policy towards the Italian peninsula. It arose from a still more fundamental consensus which bound together virtually all non-Catholics in England, excepting perhaps the Puseyites, and which underlay differences in party, church and social position. Protestant English people at this time tended to share a view of the world and history and the place of England which centred on three commitments, symbolized by three common and frequently used terms, or their synonyms: material prosperity, civil liberty and religious liberty. These added up to a commitment to 'the moral and material progress of mankind'. These commitments can be distilled from the writings and actions to which this study refers.

Material prosperity, in the still freshly exciting world of bourgeois capitalist industrialization and commerce, meant very tangibly producing, selling and acquiring more and better material goods. The Great Exhibition of 1851 at The Crystal Palace in London had displayed it: steam engines, railways, telegraphs, gas lighting, industrial machinery, consumer goods for the home. In the 1850s England led the world in factories, trade and finance. The English had achieved this prosperity, they believed, by enlightened hard work and ingenuity, free trade, the movement of history, and the blessings of God. By contrast, the pope's domains were regarded as the least prosperous – they were predominately rural and peasant, with almost no railways, and few gas lights, or steam engines. The priest-ridden people were lazy, backward, and clearly lacking in the blessings of God.

Civil liberty meant the English constitution, the carefully ordered relationships among all parts of the temporal body so that every sector, under God, knew its place and its duties to the others. Civil liberty culminated in the English Parliament wherein met all the Lords, temporal and spiritual, plus the representatives of the common people. Parliament, the courts and the laws

79 Rhodes, 25–6; Cullen to Sir Culling Eardley, Dublin, 9 Dec. 1859, in *Paul Cullen*, vol. II, 320–2. *The Times*, 8 Nov. 1859, and 9 Nov. 1859. Norman, *Catholic church and Ireland*, 40–3.

safeguarded and maintained English liberties and the rights of English people. When differences arose they could be settled by the method of gradual reform under the leadership of the government of the Crown. The Crown benevolently superintended the whole. By these standards, the papal government easily appeared perverse – there was no parliament, the lords temporal and the common people were excluded from government, the priests ruled all, and the pope resisted all reforms which the English and others proposed during the 1850s.

Religious liberty meant the Protestant religion, whether Anglican or Nonconformist. Three times, in effect, the English had broken from the papacy: under Henry VIII against Rome, with Elizabeth against 'bloody' Mary, and with William and Mary against James II. The Church of England was established by law as the Protestant state church, and the law guaranteed the Protestant succession to the Crown; the United Kingdom of Great Britain and Ireland was a Protestant state under a Protestant Crown. Many Nonconformists in the 1850s opposed the legal establishment of the Church of England, but they shared with Anglicans the belief that the Christian religion in its Protestant form was the only true religion, and to it could be attributed all the blessings of civil liberty and material prosperity that the English enjoyed. On the face of it, to these Protestants, the pope and the priests of the Catholic church and the Papal States were the antipode to religious liberty – they followed false doctrine, practised superstition and idolatry, and bound the conscience and faith of the people.

These three convictions, given the course of events of the 1850s, were readily translated into support for Piedmont-Sardinia which people believed most closely followed the English model in Italy. Malmesbury appealed to all three convictions in a comment about England and Sardinia in his January policy statement to James Hudson in Turin: 'England has always viewed in Sardinia the model for Europe of a young Constitutional State daily increasing in prosperity, as the fruit of her liberty... Sardinia until now has vindicated those principles of civil and religious liberty which both England and Sardinia represent.'[80] These three convictions were just as easily applied against the temporal power of the pope. It made sense to Lord Derby for him to write to the queen in December 1858 that the Papal States was 'the worst governed country', and to Malmesbury for him to claim in January 1859 that 'the dominions of the Pope are the most grievous sore of Italy'. It also made sense to Derby and Malmesbury to take a new course against the papacy and to suggest the redistribution of the papal temporal power.

In the events that lay ahead, the English pressed their convictions and acted on their political consensus. They construed English–papal relations as a contrast between 'English liberties' and the 'government of priests', and made the existence of the papal temporal power increasingly the centre of attention.

80 Malmesbury to Hudson, 13 Jan. 1859, no. 10, *Gran Bretagna e Sardegna*, vol. VI, 331.

England turns against the papal temporal power

The pope, on his side, felt English pressure and the force of their convictions. He came to view the English as undoubtedly the source of the trouble behind the scenes. This he expressed to Odo Russell: 'I do not doubt the good intentions of England, but unfortunately you do not understand this country and your example is dangerous to the Italian minds. Your speeches in Parliament excite them, and you fancy because Constitutional liberties and institutions suit you that they must suit all the world.'[81]

81 Odo Russell to Russell, Rome, 14 July 1859, no. 88, PRO, FO, 43/71, and *Odo Russell*, 37.

2 Odo Russell and the network of English–papal relations

The English government's headlong entrance into Italian affairs and the Papal Question was, in the nature of the case, primarily a matter of diplomatic activity and international politics. In this way, Malmesbury began a new period of English involvement with the papal temporal power. The person on whom the English relied for their diplomatic relations with the pope was Odo Russell, a talented young envoy who arrived in Rome to take up his new appointment in December 1858, just as the international crisis was beginning. He ended up remaining in Rome until 1870 when the Italians took the city of Rome away from the pope. Odo Russell's position and activity in Rome during the political and diplomatic crisis of 1858 to 1861 were the centre of a complex configuration of relations – social, ecclesiastical, consular, diplomatic, naval and commercial – between the English and the papal temporal power.

English society in Rome

In Rome during these years there was a sizeable visiting population of English people residing annually in the city for 'the season'. John Freeborn, the English consul in Rome at the start of 1859, reported that about 1500 British subjects visited Rome each year during the 1850s. They joined probably thousands of others who came from France, Austria, the German areas, and Scandinavia. In spite of the prospect of war, the 1859 season attracted the highest incursion of visitors of the decade, but as the papal crisis worsened, the numbers apparently dropped off considerably in 1860.[1] These English visitors were the source of much fervent pro-Italian and anti-papal propaganda.

The season began in January and, following the Roman liturgical calendar, ran through the festival of Carnival, then Lent and Easter. Some people arrived before Christmas, but for most December was too cold, and the real interest came later, when it was also warmer – 10° Fahrenheit warmer than London. The

---

[1] John Freeborn, Memorandum, Rome, 9 Jan. 1857, in 'Report from the Select Committee on Consular Service and Appointments', *Parliamentary papers, 1857–1858*, vol. 8, 644–5. *The Times*, 15 March 1859. 'English chapel at Rome', Jan. 1860, PRO, FO, 43/81. Isastia, 248.

special attractions began with the weeks of festivities and extravagance of Carnival, culminating in three days of costume balls, masked parades and carriage drives by the social élite along the Corso, Rome's central avenue. Then, after four contrastingly drab weeks of Lent, came the drama and pageantry of Good Friday and Easter at St Peter's Basilica.

Murray's *Handbook for travellers in Central Italy*, bound in red, was the mandatory guide which provided everything for the traveller – the rationale for the journey, an educational introduction to the history and current society and politics of Rome and the Papal States, and all the practical information necessary for a well-rounded sojourn in the eternal city. It was careful to avoid any anti-Catholic references so both Protestants and Catholics could use it as Englishmen. The English were seen carrying it everywhere, and one writer complained that they did things because Murray's *Handbook* told them to. Odo Russell boasted to his mother, as he travelled through Italy and approached Rome: 'I made up my mind as to what I thought good, bad, or indifferent and was vastly pleased on reading over Murray's Handbook that I had been well guided by instinct and had been able to feel correctly.'[2]

The great majority of the visiting English population were wealthy people, whether of the nobility, gentry, or middle classes. They had time and money to spend, and were either among the last to do the Grand Tour, or the first to be tourists; some, especially the older ones, came for their health to a warmer climate in stimulating social surroundings. In 1859, Lord Granville and Lord and Lady Stratford de Redcliffe were there, and above all, the young Prince of Wales, whose presence for the season helped to account for the larger number of English than usual. All the English enjoyed the presence of visiting royalty, who were numerous in 1859 – the King and Queen of Prussia, the Dowager Queen Christina of Spain, the Russian Grand Duchess, the Prince and Princess of Hesse, the Austrian Archdukes William and Regnier.[3]

There was a smaller number of Catholic English who came as pilgrims, like many before them for centuries, to express their devotion in the Holy City. The troubles Pius IX experienced drew many of the devout who wanted to be near their Holy Father, and if possible secure an audience with him. There were also visits from the Catholic clergy and lay leaders who came for ecclesiastical purposes. During 1859 and 1860 Cardinal Wiseman, Dr Henry Edward Manning, Cardinal Cullen, Bishop Ullathorne, Bishop Errington and Sir

2   Murray's *Handbook*, 4th ed., part 1, xvii. *The Times*, 12 March, and 14 April 1859. Odo Russell to Lady William Russell, Dec. 1858, quoted by Noel Blakiston, 'Introduction', *Odo Russell*, x.
3   Pine-Coffin, 49–52. 'Guidebooks and tourism: the British in Italy' (London: British Museum, 1980). Odo Russell to Russell, Rome, 17 July 1859, no. 89, PRO, FO, 43/71, and *Odo Russell*, 38. *The Times*, 15 March 1859. Colonel Bruce to Prince Albert, Rome, 17 Feb. 1859, RA Z444/54. RA *Diary of Albert Edward, Prince of Wales, 1859*, passim. *Giornale di Roma*, passim.

George Bowyer all spent time in Rome, and saw the pope or the officials at Propaganda Fide.[4]

A rather distinct English society existed in Rome, comparable to the French and Germans, with its own institutions and practices, and dependent on a small permanent English population. Socially, the English tended to visit each other, giving teas and champagne suppers; very few except for the highest social élite enjoyed social contact with Italians. They tended to group in the most northern section of the city around the Piazza del Popolo, the Piazza di Spagna and the Via Condotti. The wealthiest took rooms at the Locanda del'Isole Brittaniche, where the Prince of Wales resided, or the Locanda del'Europa, run by an English woman, Mrs Melga, or else took apartments in the *palazzi* of the great Roman nobility. The rest could find rooms or suites in the Locanda di Londra, the Locanda d'Inghilterra, or in private houses. Piale's Reading Room on the Piazza di Spagna carried English and American newspapers, and the English Club had premises first in Palazzo Lepri on Via Condotti, later in Palazzo del Gallo on Via della Croce. Dr Diomede Pantaleoni, an Italian who had lived in England and had the manners and language of an Englishman, was the most sought after physician; he became Odo Russell's physician in these years. There was a full line of English businesses – Lowe's on the Piazza di Spagna, Mrs Muller's English bakery, an English tailor, an English saddlemaker, Mr Shea's house agency on the Piazza di Spagna, MacPherson's for photography – and banks – Macbean and Co., and Plowden, Cholmley and Co. on the Corso, Freeborn and Co. on Via Condotti, and Packenham and Hooker on the Piazza di Spagna. Odo Russell's banker was Macbean. Some English artists had studios in Rome, the foremost being John Gibson, R.A., but also Penry Williams, Shakespeare Wood, R. MacPherson, and others. English artists joined with Americans to organize the British and American Artists Club on Via della Croce. Murray's *Handbook* encouraged the English to patronize English bankers as well as shops: 'As a general rule in Rome, as throughout Italy, we would advise our countrymen to employ English tradespeople when possible; they are more to be relied upon for punctuality, good attitudes, and honesty, than the native shopkeepers.' The English spent a large part of their time viewing the classical sights of the city, visiting the Vatican galleries and the studios of artists, socializing together, strolling on the Pincio, and enjoying the events of Carnival and Holy Week. The Vatican arranged special seating and issued special tickets for Protestants inside St Peter's for the important church occasions. English ladies, in 1859, had a reputation for whispering and eating biscuits during the ceremonies, and the Vatican issued a notice instructing ladies to have proper decorum during Holy Week.[5]

4   *Odo Russell, passim*; *The Times, passim*; Edward Sheridan Purcell, *The life of Cardinal Manning* (2 vols., London: Macmillan, 1895), vol. II, 75–112.
5   Murray's *Handbook* 5th ed., part 2, xxi, and *passim*. *The Times*, 14 April and 22 April 1859. Odo Russell to Lady William Russell, Rome, 6 Nov. 1860, Ampthill papers, PRO, FO,

English society in Rome

The English chapel in Rome, which observed the form of the Church of England, was located in a large apartment just outside the northern walls of Rome near the Porta del Popolo. It was included within the Anglican Diocese of Gibraltar embracing the Mediterranean region. In the season, attendance was high, reaching perhaps 800 in February 1859. The sermons by the chaplain, Rev. F.B. Woodward, were popular, especially with the young Prince of Wales. On 27 February 1859, Woodward preached against Protestants hearing sermons by the Catholic Henry Edward Manning, and the young Prince of Wales thought it excellent. Nonconformists could attend services according to Presbyterian form in the legation of the United States of America in Palazzo Braschi. William Davis, of Thames Street, Windsor, at least requested the English government to appoint a 'missionary extraordinary' to the Court of Rome to convert the pope and proclaim a modern-day Reformation for the church.[6] Catholics had English language services at the English College on Via Monserrato where Wiseman stayed in Rome, or at the new Irish College where Cullen stayed. These colleges prepared men for the priesthood according to Roman style and liturgy, and were centres of English and Irish Catholic presence in Rome. A fair number of clergy circulated to and from England and Ireland through these colleges, and in 1860 and 1861 the colleges served as conduits of money from Great Britain and Ireland to the pope. English and Irish Catholics, in church matters, could call upon the assistance of a number of English prelates in Rome, above all Mgr George Talbot, a private chamberlain of Pius IX, who was apparently one of the pope's closest confidants. Many English bishops communicated with the pope through Talbot, and when in Rome Catholic laity and clergy might arrange an audience with the pope through him as well. Talbot arranged for the Prince of Wales to have two audiences with the pope, but other English Protestants usually had to pass their requests for a papal audience through the Hanoverian or Prussian envoys. It was Talbot who supplied John Maguire with the inside information he needed for his book *Rome: its ruler and institutions*, and who befriended Lady William Russell, Odo Russell's mother, during her times in Rome.[7]

Several English newspapers, including the *Tablet*, the leading Catholic paper,

---

918/85/265–7. Odo Russell to William Corbett, Rome, 4 Oct. 1859, PRO, FO, 170/89. For a contemporary map of Rome I have used 'Pianta della città di Roma publicata nel'anno MDCCCLX' designed by Dom Feltrini, drawn and engraved by Augusto Fornari, Rome; it names all the major buildings and classical monuments.

6   'English Chapel at Rome', Jan. 1860, PRO, FO, 43/81.RA *Diary of Albert Edward, Prince of Wales, 1859*, esp. 6 Feb., 13 Feb., 27 Feb., 10 April, 24 April 1858. Also compare with RA *Prince of Wales' Journal, Rome 1859* for the same dates. Vinay, 13. William Davis to Russell, 14 April 60, PRO, FO, 43/81.

7   ASV, ASdS, 1860, 165, and 1861, 165 *passim*. In George Talbot's papers there are letters from Wiseman, Manning, Cullen, Bishop Vaughan, Bishop Clifford, Archbishop MacHale, and many others. John Maguire to Talbot, 15 Jan. 1857, Talbot papers, letter 470, English College Archives, Rome. See Aubert, 284. Odo Russell to Lady William Russell, Rome, 4 Dec. 1860, copy, Ampthill papers, PRO, FO, 918/85/276.

and *The Times*, the most influential English paper of the day, kept a staff journalist in Rome, or secured news correspondence from persons resident in the city. *The Times* transferred its correspondent Henry Wreford from Naples to Rome in March 1859, with the specific assignment to investigate the reports of papal oppression and popular discontent: 'Is this all true? Let us bring the Pope and his cardinals to trial, make a specific charge against them and prove it. That should be your task. It is in the hope that you will execute it, that *The Times* has sent you to Rome.' Wreford was already known for his political opposition to the régime of King Bomba at Naples. In Rome, both he and his sister sent reports which did little to improve on the impartiality of the freelance correspondent *The Times* had been using, as this piece written before Wreford's arrival illustrates: 'The Papal Government is a loaded tester; it descends, gently if you like, upon the public mind, but it effectually destroys its vitality, prevents all power of motion, and then takes merit to itself, as it has recently done, for the tranquillity and contentment which generally prevail.'[8] Later, as the papal crisis continued, *The Times* sent Antonio Gallenga, the Italian exile and naturalized British subject, to Italy, particularly Rome, to move around and gather information, not from the governments, but from the liberal nationalists. The papal government at first allowed him to settle in Rome, but when they feared he might also be a subversive agent, they expelled him from the Papal States. John Delane himself, the editor of *The Times*, visited Italy, including Rome, in the autumn of 1859 to meet his correspondents and find ways to improve *The Times*' coverage. He concluded that what the discontented population in the Papal States detested was 'the priests and their government'.[9]

In practical and official matters, the life of the English society in Rome depended upon the British consul on Via Condotti. There were three successive consuls in Rome during 1858 to 1861. John Freeborn served as consular agent, as he was entitled, from 1831 until his death in 1859. He doubled as a banker with his own firm, Freeborn and Co. on Via Condotti. Antonelli always regretted that Freeborn had given so much support to the Roman Republic, and considered the relations between him and the papal government to be strained.[10] Freeborn's successor from June 1859 to January 1861 was Charles Newton, an archaeologist

8   Morris (manager of *The Times*), to Henry Wreford, 28 March 1859, in *The history of 'The Times'*, vol. II: *The established tradition, 1841–1884* (London: The Times, 1939), 282–4. *The Times*, 26 March 1859, dated from Rome, 19 March 1859. The Wreford reports appear to begin in April; notable are *The Times*, 15 April and 22 April, 1859.
9   *The history of 'The Times'*, vol. II, 284–8. Charles Newton to Russell, Rome, 30 Jan. 1860, no. 13, PRO, FO, 43/79B; Newton to Antonelli, 24 Jan. 1860, ASV, ASdS, 1860, 297. Russell to Newton, 10 March 1860, no. 5, PRO, FO, 43/79A. Gaetano Tortone to Antonelli, Turin, 12 Jan. 1860, and 20 Jan. 1860, ASV, ASdS, 1860, 165/10. John Delane to G.W. Dasent, 1 Nov. 1859, in A.I. Dasent, *John Thadeus Delane, editor of 'The Times': his life and correspondence* (2 vols., New York: Scribner, 1908), vol. I, 322–3.
10 Odo Russell to Malmesbury, Rome, 22 May 1859, no. 62, PRO, FO, 43/71, and *Odo Russell*, 21. John Freeborn, memorandum, Rome, 9 Jan. 1857, in *Parliamentary papers, 1857–1858*, vol. 8, 644–5.

and later keeper of Greek and Roman Antiquities at the British Museum, who combined his duties with his research in classical Roman remains. He was named full consul without papal agreement, but after discussion the papal government gave its approval, and then, astonishingly, asked whether the English government would object to the appointment of a papal consul in England, possibly at Liverpool. On the advice of the Duke of Newcastle, the colonial secretary, and Sir George Lewis, the home secretary, the British cabinet agreed to it, although no such appointment was ever made. Newton was excited by the political significance of events in Rome and prepared long despatches on political affairs, neglecting some consular duties, to Odo Russell's dismay. He was followed by Joseph Severn, an artist, who sought time in Rome to paint. He remained in Rome from 1861 until 1872. A. Ercole, an English-speaking Italian, served as a consular assistant for nearly thirty years under Freeborn and Newton.[11]

There were other consular positions in the Papal States. Consular relations between England and the Papal States began in 1816, and at various times vice-consuls were located at Ferrara, Porto d'Anzio, Porto Sant'Elpidio, and the two major ports of Civita Vecchia and Ancona. There was also a consul at Ancona, George Moore, who held the post since 1836. Gustavus Gaggiotti was vice-consul at Ancona since 1851, and John Thomas Lowe was vice-consul at Civita Vecchia since 1845.[12]

Consuls and vice-consuls were the only official representatives of the English government in the Papal States. Their duty was to oversee and assist the affairs of British subjects while they were in papal territory. Consular officials provided documents such as passports, facilitated commerce, assisted economic and business dealings with the papal government, handled grievances against the papal government, processed admissions to public institutions and art galleries, solemnized marriages, executed wills, arranged burials, managed the property of deceased, and much more. Beginning in 1859, however, they were prohibited from engaging in banking or commerce for personal profit. Newton, not Odo Russell, negotiated with the papal government concerning the expulsion of Antonio Gallenga, and Lowe, Newton and Gaggiotti handled the Irish who enlisted in the papal army in 1860. Gaggiotti, partly because of his interest, and partly because Ancona was so far from Rome, provided extensive political

11 On papal consuls, Odo Russell to Russell, Rome, 9 Jan. 1860, no. 9, PRO, FO, 43/76; Merivale to Edmund Hammond, 21 Feb. 1860, and Sir George Lewis to Edmund Hammond, 10 Feb. 1860, in PRO, FO, 43/81: Russell to Odo Russell, 28 Feb. 1860, no. 8, draft, PRO, FO, 43/75; and Odo Russell to Antonelli, 20 March 1860, ASV, ASdS, 1860, 297. Odo Russell to Lady William Russell, Rome, 17 March 1860, Ampthill papers, PRO, FO, 918/85/259–60. On Newton and Severn, see Noel Blakiston, 'Introduction', *Odo Russell*, xxvii–xxxiii. Newton to Mgr Giuseppi Berardi, 1 Feb. 1860, ASV, ASdS, 1860, 297.
12 'Report from the Select Committee on Consular Services and Appointments', in *Parliamentary papers, 1857–1858*, vol. 8, 623. Louis Hertslet, *Memorandum respecting the relations of Great Britain with the Holy See*, 16 July 1848, PRO, FO, 45/661. *The Foreign Office list, forming a complete diplomatic and consular handbook* (London: Harrison, 1856–62).

reports on events in the Marches upon which the British government relied for information. After the papal government broke diplomatic relations with Sardinia in 1859, it was Newton who provided official protection for Sardinian subjects in the Papal States, and served as the only official link between the two enemy countries. Gaggiotti prepared extensive annual summaries of papal trade, manufacturing, and agriculture from 1858 onward.[13]

Odo Russell, the Whig: a two-way diplomatic medium

When Odo Russell arrived in Rome just before Christmas 1858, he fitted easily into both the English society and the diplomatic world in the city. Because of his family connections, his talent and his personality, he very soon became both a social attraction for the English in Rome and the essential political link between England and the papacy.

By family heritage Odo Russell was a Whig. He was highly class conscious, and observant of the rules of 'the class I live in and belong to'. He was a member of the renowned Russell family and close to three successive dukes of Bedford whose seat was Woburn Abbey in Bedfordshire.[14] Lord John Russell was his uncle. This family connection gave Odo a special standing in Rome that everyone recognized and which compensated for his relative lack of experience and age – he was only twenty-nine when he arrived in Rome. Cardinal Antonelli and Pius IX were always conscious that he was the nephew of Lord John Russell. Pius once complained to Odo, '[O]ur bitterest enemy in England, and I will say so even before you, is Lord John Russell. His dislike to the Papacy and to the Catholic religion is so violent that he seems to tremble all over with hatred ... when he speaks against us.'[15]

13 See John Freeborn, Memorandum, Rome, 9 Jan. 1857, in *Parliamentary papers, 1857–1858,* vol. 8, 644–5. On Gallenga, Odo Russell to Russell, Rome, 26 Jan. 1860, no. 15, PRO, FO, 43/76. Gaggiotti's political reports were addressed to the British minister in Florence, see PRO, FO, 79. On Newton and Sardinia, Russell to Newton, 20 Oct. 1860, no. 18, PRO, FO, 43/74A. Gaggiotti's commercial reports for the years 1858, 1859, 1860 and 1861 are in *Parliamentary papers, 1859* (sess. 2), vol. 30, 550–1; *Parliamentary papers, 1862,* vol. 58, 490; and *Parliamentary papers, 1862,* vol. 59, p. 96.

14 For biographical details I have relied mainly on Noel Blakiston, 'Introduction', *Odo Russell,* ix–xxxviii, and *The Foreign Office list, forming a complete diplomatic and consular handbook,* (1862), 139. Blakiston's wife, Georgiana Russell Blakiston, is a granddaughter of Arthur Russell, Odo's brother. Cosmo Russell, Odo's grandson, kindly shared passages on Odo Russell from *Contacts*, a private memoir by Odo's son, who was Cosmo Russell's father, also named Odo Russell. Odo Russell's personal papers were discovered a hundred years after the events of 1859 to 1861 in a trunk hidden away in Woburn Abbey. For additional treatment of Odo Russell, see Blakiston, 'Rome in 1860', *History today* 10 (1960), 488–5, but see E.E.Y. Hales' response in the same volume, 572; see Alec Randall, 'A British agent at the Vatican: the mission of Odo Russell', *Dublin review* 479 (1959), 37–60. Note: C.T. McIntire, 'Mid-Victorian anti-Catholicism, English diplomacy, and Odo Russell in Rome', *Fides et historia* 13 (1980), 13–23.

15 Antonelli to Sacconi, Rome, 17 Dec. 1859, very private, ASV, ANParigi, 1859, SdS, AD/P. Odo Russell to Russell, Rome, 17 July 1859, no. 89, secret, PRO, FO, 43/71, and 31 Jan. 1860, no. 19, secret, PRO, FO, 43/76, and *Odo Russell,* 37, 85.

Odo Russell, the Whig: a two-way diplomatic medium

Officially Odo was appointed as a low-level paid *attaché* to the British diplomatic mission at Florence, with instructions to reside in Rome in order to observe and report on events in the papal city. His despatches were to be addressed to the *chargé d'affaires* at Florence, Edwin Corbett, who would forward them to the Foreign Office in London. He remained attached to Florence until the annexation of Tuscany to Piedmont in March 1860, when the English terminated the mission there. He was then attached to the British mission in Naples until the autumn of 1860, when Naples too was absorbed by Piedmont. Thereafter he was attached directly to the Foreign Office in 'Special Service under the immediate orders of the Secretary of State for Foreign Affairs'.[16] The arrangement, in itself a product of the English tradition of anti-Catholicism, continued a long-standing diplomatic charade. Odo was the fourth diplomatic agent since 1832 to reside in Rome while attached to Florence. Thomas Aubin, the first, had accompanied the English minister at Florence, Hamilton Seymour, on a special mission to Rome after the February revolution of 1832, and ended up remaining there until 1844. William Petre, a Catholic, held the appointment from 1844 to 1853, and was succeeded by Richard Lyons from 1853 to 1858, with whom Antonelli and the pope enjoyed especially good *rapport*.

This roundabout relationship was necessitated by a long series of statutes, but especially one Elizabethan law which was interpreted as forbidding official communication with the pope on the grounds that it would attribute 'jurisdiction, authority, or pre-eminence to the See of Rome'. In 1848 Parliament actually passed a law permitting the government to establish diplomatic relations with Rome, but since it referred to the pope merely as 'the Sovereign of the Roman States', and prohibited receiving as envoy anyone who was a priest or a member of a religious order, the pope found it offensive, and nothing came of it.[17]

In practice, Odo began to act, and to be accepted, as the English ambassador in Rome. Early in January 1859, he began exchanging telegrams directly with Malmesbury, by-passing Corbett. In February, as the importance of the papacy in the Italian crisis became clearer, Malmesbury instructed Odo to address official

---

16   Russell to Odo Russell, 17 Nov. 1869, no. 38, draft, PRO, FO, 43/75. Russell had intended to attach Odo to the Turin mission under Hudson, but Odo objected, at Antonelli's request, on grounds that it would be too provocative to the papacy. Russell to Odo Russell, 29 Oct. 1860, private, copy, Russell papers, PRO, 30/22/111, and Odo Russell to Russell, Rome, 6 Nov. 1860, private, Russell papers, PRO, 30/22/75, and excerpted in *Odo Russell*, 135–7. Also, Hammond to Odo Russell, 25 March 1860, draft, PRO, FO, 43/75.

17   5 Eliz. I, c. 1.s.2. Hertslet, *Memorandum*, 16 July 1848, PRO, FO, 45/661. 11 et 12 Vict., c. 108. See Hansard's, CI, col. 201–35, 17 Aug. 1848; col. 487–525, 24 and 25 Aug. 1848; and col. 625–9, 29 Aug. 1848. See Norbert Miko, 'Die diplomatischen Beziehungen zwischen England und dem Heiligen Stuhl im 19 Jahrhundert', *Zeitschrift für Katholische theologie* 78 (1956), 206–25; Alec Randall, 'British diplomacy and the Holy See, 1555–1925', *Dublin review* 482 (1959–60), 291–303; and Gary Mooney, 'British diplomatic relations with the Holy See, 1793–1830', 193–210.

despatches directly to him at the Foreign Office instead of to the mission in Florence.[18] The new arrangement disturbed the Duc de Gramont, the French ambassador in Rome, who was sure the English were up to something.[19] Both Malmesbury and Russell addressed despatches and policy statements directly to Odo and instructed him specifically to obtain information and views from the papal government. One occasion will illustrate the point. In mid-February 1859 Malmesbury told Odo, 'You should now begin to speak to Antonelli about politics and shew him how *impossible* it is ... to leave everything in Italy in *statu quo*.' And then, 'What does Antonelli wish as regards them [French and Austrian troops]. Would he do without them with Swiss regiments? Would he do with a small garrison only at Civita and Ancona of French and Germans? Send me a telegram when you have seen him.'[20] Cardinal Antonelli received Odo as if he were the English envoy and responded freely to his policy inquiries. Antonelli and Odo could only speak unofficially to each other, but that they did well and often. Odo was not permitted to attend the two annual papal audiences with the diplomatic corps, but he was invited instead to private audiences with the pope, which were longer and more meaningful than the larger and more ceremonial official ones. The diplomatic corps also accepted him as if he were the English envoy. The Austrian ambassadors – Count Colloredo until mid-1859, and Baron von Bach thereafter – regarded him with the highest respect, although they had only a moderate amount of social and diplomatic interaction with him.[21] Gramont, the French ambassador, socialized and talked regularly with Odo and both gathered information from each other for their governments.[22] Moreover, the English society in Rome admired Odo's social position with other diplomats, the Roman princes, and visiting royalty and nobility. 'I am always treated as the British minister and placed according to this imaginery rank at table above my elders and betters', he told his mother.[23]

There is an even more remarkable point about Odo's position in Rome. The

18 Copies of Odo's earliest telegrams are in PRO, FO, 170/89; Malmesbury to Odo Russell, 9 Feb. 1859, s.n., PRO, FO, 43/69; Hammond to Scarlett, 9 Feb. 1859, PRO, FO, 79/202.
19 Gramont to Walewski, Rome, 29 Jan. 1859, no. 7, and 9 April 1859, no. 28, AMAE, CP, Rome, 1009/199 and 332–3. The 29 January letter is misdated 1858.
20 Malmesbury to Odo Russell, 12 Feb. 1859, private, Ampthill papers, PRO, FO, 918/6.
21 For example, see Bach to Rechberg, Rome, 3 Feb. 1860, no. 5B, 16 March 1860, no. 11B, 13 July 1860, no. 28A–H, and no. 28F, and 29 Sept. 1860, no. 41E, HHSA, PA, XI, 201. Also Bach to Rechberg, Rome, 6 July 1860, HHSA, PA, XI, 202.
22 For example, see Gramont to Walewski, 22 Feb. 1859, no. 14, and 9 April 1859, no. 28, AMAE, CP, Rome 1009/246–9, and 332–42, 20 Dec. 1859, no. 127, AMAE, CP, Rome 1012/281–2, and Gramont to Thouvenel, 22 Jan. 1861, no. 9, AMAE, CP, Rome 1016/256–65. Gramont especially asked Walewski not to let Lord Cowley know that Odo Russell allowed news of English activity to pass to Gramont 'because that would cause embarrassment to Mr. Russell, and take away facilities of information here which could be useful at a given moment' (Gramont to Walewski, Rome, 23 April 1859, private, Papiers Walewski, 17).
23 Odo Russell to Lady William Russell, Rome, 13 March 1860, copy, Ampthill papers, PRO, FO, 918/85/257–8. Odo's way with the Prince of Wales was much admired, for example; see Colonel Bruce to Prince Albert, 5 March and 7 March 1859, RA Z444/65, 66.

extraordinary nature of English–papal relations meant not only that the English used Odo as if he were the English envoy in Rome, but also that the papal government, which had no comparable way of placing an 'unofficial nuncio' in London, used him as its principal and only direct means of communication with the English government. Antonelli gladly received from Odo information about English policy, and in fact expected him to give it.[24] At the same time, significantly, Antonelli and the pope used Odo as *their* means of communicating *their* information and *their* policy to the English government. Important papal documents, such as encyclicals or allocutions which Antonelli communicated to papal nuncios to present to European governments the cardinal gave to Odo to submit to the English government.[25] More importantly, Antonelli and Pius IX used their frequent interviews with Odo as their prime means of presenting or explaining papal policy and views to the English government. An example will illustrate. During the Austro-Sardinian war of 1859, papal territory was threatened in spite of the pope's declaration of neutrality. Antonelli talked at length about this with Odo. Afterward Odo telegraphed Malmesbury: 'Sardinia will not acknowledge the Pope's neutrality. The Cardinal alarmed, wishes me to inform Your Lordship.'[26] In the despatch describing this talk, Odo reported to Malmesbury, 'I had never seen him so much alarmed before, and he thanked me with great warmth when I promised to report faithfully, all he had told me, to Your Lordship.'[27] The medium could not, of course, be fully satisfying to the papal government, but it was all there was.

There were other means than Odo by which the papal government learned information about England and the English government, but none was very systematic. The Paris nuncio, Monsignor Sacconi, regularly passed on news of English activities which he learned about through means such as talks with Lord Cowley.[28] Monsignor DeLuca, the nuncio in Vienna, and Monsignor Franchi, the nuncio in Florence until the Tuscan revolution in 1859, similarly reported on English diplomacy in those capitals.[29] Sometimes the Austrian and French ambassadors in Rome informed Antonelli of English diplomatic activity relevant to the papacy. The Vatican received English newspapers, and the *Giornale di Roma*, the official papal newspaper, regularly carried English news, sometimes

24	See Odo Russell to Russell, Rome, 1 May 1860, private, Russell papers, PRO, 30/22/75, and *Odo Russell*, 101.
25	For example, Antonelli to Odo Russell, 18 June 1859, PRO, FO, 43/71. Usually Antonelli gave Odo the documents directly without a covering letter.
26	Odo Russell to Malmesbury, Rome, 26 May 1859, no. 66, PRO, FO, 43/71.
27	Odo Russell to Malmesbury, Rome, 25 May 1859, no. 65, secret, PRO, FO, 43/71, and *Odo Russell*, 23.
28	For example, see Sacconi to Antonelli, Paris, 1 Feb. 1859, no. 1190, ASV, ASdS, 1859, 165/1/64–5.
29	For example, see DeLuca to Antonelli, Vienna, 21 April 1859, no. 642, and 22 April 1859, no. 644, ASV, ASdS, 1859, 165/2/83–4, and 79–80. See Franchi to Antonelli, Florence, 31 March 1859, no. 318, ASV, ASdS, 1859, 165/11/33–5, and Colloredo to Buol, Rome, 3 April 1859, HHSA, PA, XI, 200.

extracted whole from the English continental press.[30] For their general understanding of England, the pope and Antonelli relied especially on the English Catholic primate, Cardinal Wiseman, and Dr Henry Edward Manning, Wiseman's confidant and successor, when they came to Rome.[31] George Bowyer, the leader of the Catholics in Parliament, was helpful to the papal government when he came to Rome, and his speeches in the House of Commons were a faithful reflection of the papal perspective. He seemed to regard himself as the chief political spokesman for the pope in England, and was recognized as such by Lord John Russell.[32] And Mgr George Talbot, Pius IX's private chamberlain, channelled information to the pope which he gathered from his many sources.[33] While all these means of gaining information and impressions about England were helpful in filling the gap created by the lack of a papal nuncio in London, none was a means of direct communication with the British government.

Odo Russell filled the need and became, in practice, a two-way diplomatic medium between Rome and London. Both the papal and English governments used Odo as their primary means of gaining knowledge of each other's policy and of conveying their policy to each other.

When Odo first arrived in Rome, he was uncertain about what views to hold concerning the Papal Question, or even what were the viable alternatives for Italy and the papacy. During his journey from London to Rome he had heard strongly conflicting emphases and opinions along the way – from Lord Cowley in Paris, from Sir James Hudson, Cavour and Giuseppe Massari, Cavour's confidant, in Turin, from Lord Normanby in Florence.[34] After his session with Normanby, Odo summarized his confusion so far:

> Lord Normanby and Sir J. Hudson take diametrically opposite views of everything relating to Italy. They both make such strong cases in favour of their own views that it becomes most perplexing and I could not for the life of me judge who was

30   *Giornale di Roma* took reports from *The Times*, *Morning Star*, *Daily News*, *Morning Herald* and other papers. For example, see the reports from *The Times* in *Giornale di Roma*, 18, 20 and 21 Jan. 1859.

31   'The Pope considers Cardinal Wiseman as the best authority on English politics . . .' (Odo Russell to Russell, Rome, 26 June 1860, no. 90, secret, PRO, FO, 43/77, and *Odo Russell*, 112).

32   'Mr. Bowyer, M.P. (who has been very active at the Vatican and constantly with the Pope and Antonelli) leaves tomorrow for London. His judgement is highly thought of at the Vatican . . .' (Odo Russell to Russell, Rome, 7 Jan. 1860, private, Russell papers, PRO, 30/22/75, and *Odo Russell*, 80–1). Hansard's, CLVI, col. 1968, 28 Feb. 1860; Russell to Odo Russell, 6 March 1860, private, Ampthill papers, PRO, FO, 918/7.

33   Talbot apparently exercised great influence on the pope, particularly with respect to English Catholic affairs; see Dom Cuthbert Butler, *The life and times of Bishop Ullathorne, 1806–1889* (London: Burns, Oates, and Washbourne, 1926), vol. I, 227; and Ward, *Wiseman*, vol. II, 58.

34   See Cowley to Malmesbury, Paris, 17 Jan. 1859, private, Cowley papers, PRO, FO, 519/224/273, and Cowley to Hudson, Paris, 13 Feb. 1859, private, Cowley papers, PRO, FO, 519/225/54–5. Hudson to Odo Russell, Turin, 14 Dec. 1858, Ampthill papers, PRO, FO, 918/42. Giuseppe Massari, *Diario dalle cento voci, 1858–1860*, ed. Emilia Morelli (Bologna: Cappelli, 1959), 87–9. Whyte, *Cavour*, 269.

right and who was wrong. I shall have to make up my mind one way or the other in Rome, but not for a long time, I hope, as these questions are truly difficult and require thought and experience.[35]

In spite of his Whig heritage, he did not automatically adopt Whig convictions at the start of his tenure in Rome.

His first impressions of papal Rome ran in two directions – the city seemed dirty and dark, and the people unlikable, while the papal regalia and ecclesiastical grandeur seemed impressive if not believable. He confided to his mother:

> I observe that everybody is so *exceedingly* fond of Rome that I suppose I must *end* by feeling like them? – at present I am still at a loss to make out what it is that fascinates people to such an extraordinary extent in a stinking, dirty, comfortless place inhabited by a race of chimpanzees cheating a legion of Englishmen from morning till night.

Then, on Christmas day:

> I went to St. Peter's and saw the Pope carried round the church – altogether the finest sight of its kind.[36]

His first meetings with Cardinal Antonelli and Pius IX established immediately one characteristic of his relations with them: Antonelli showed Odo 'the utmost kindness and cordiality of manner', and Pius IX was especially 'benevolent' to him, as Odo aptly put it. In his first private audience with the pope, Pius presented his version of the affairs of Italy and the condition of the Papal States, suggested a criticism of the English, and pleaded with Odo not to be too rash in judging the papacy. During the audience, as he reports it, Odo made no retort, and offered no argument in defence of England or in criticism of the papal government. His own comments were simple inquiries to help him learn.[37]

Odo's view of the papal government slowly took shape during the coming months. It was at the end of January that Odo raised his first hesitant objection to something Antonelli said in an interview. In mid-March, according to his account, he engaged in cautious argumentation with Antonelli on the occasion of presenting a new policy statement by Malmesbury. It is evident from the same account that Odo was already gaining a good knowledge of the nationalist party and tending to accept its perspective.[38] A month later, without adequate means

---

35   Odo Russell to Lady William Russell, Florence, 18 Dec. 1858, copy, Ampthill papers, PRO, FO, 918/85/185.

36   Odo Russell to Lady William Russell, Rome, 25 and 30 Dec. 1858, copies, Ampthill papers, PRO, FO, 918/85/189 and 190. Underlining is Odo's.

37   Antonelli to Lyons, Rome, 27 Dec. 1858, draft, ASV, ASdS, 1858, 284/2. Odo Russell to Corbett, Rome, 23 Dec. 1858, PRO, FO, 43/68, and *Odo Russell*, 1. Odo Russell to Corbett, Rome, 14 Jan. 1859, no. 1, most confidential, PRO, FO, 43/70, and *Odo Russell*, 1–3.

38   Odo Russell to Corbett, Rome, 28 Jan. 1859, no. 8, confidential, and 15 March 1859, no. 31, confidential, PRO, FO, 43/70, and *Odo Russell*, 5, 10–13.

to corroborate it, he confirmed to Malmesbury the plausibility of a rumour of extreme violence in the Romagna involving even 'the assassination of priests in their churches'. Odo added, with approval, 'Certain it is that the Piedmontese or national party is now admirably organized throughout Italy.'[39] Odo reported a demonstration in Rome against the papal government at Easter, and included the unconfirmed information that Antonelli had ordered the arrest of the leaders who, Odo emphasized, were 'all respectable men of the middle classes'.[40] At the end of May, in response to a special request by Malmesbury, to describe the condition of things in Rome, Odo reported as fact that the pope was in effect a prisoner of the French, papal supporters were few, and 'the power of Count Cavour over the minds and hearts of the Roman subjects is beyond all belief'.[41]

The one major restraint on the free development, or at least the free expression, of his ideas in a Whig direction was his need to work for the Tory government which had appointed him. He sought to serve the Tories conscientiously, even to the point of explicitly urging Antonelli, at Malmesbury's request, to follow 'conservative principles'.[42] He believed a diplomat has 'no right to party feeling', but is 'appointed and paid to serve the government and not to serve the opposition'.[43]

Two events occurred in June which settled the outcome of the formation of Odo's views of Italian affairs. First, because of the war which eventually broke out with Piedmont, Austrian troops withdrew from the Marches and Romagna. Immediately some persons related to the Italian National Society in Romagna revolted and established a provisional government pledged to King Victor Emmanuel. Similar uprisings occurred elsewhere. Papal troops acted to re-establish papal authority in various towns, including Perugia, where after a bloody battle they succeeded. The events at Perugia were interpreted in England as a 'papal massacre' and aroused renewed anti-papal revulsion. Perugia shook Odo personally.[44]

Second, and simultaneously, Lord Palmerston and Lord John Russell quite unexpectedly came to office with their very definite convictions in favour of Piedmont and against the papacy. The change meant that Odo now corresponded with his Whiggish uncle at the Foreign Office. Lord John, in his first private letter to his nephew, nonchalantly expressed a derogatory comment

39 Malmesbury to Odo Russell, 9 April 1859, private, and Odo Russell to Malmesbury, Rome, 16 April 1859, private, Malmesbury papers, 1859/7.
40 Odo Russell to Malmesbury, Rome, 26 April 1859, no. 46, PRO, FO, 43/70, and *Odo Russell*, 17–18.
41 Malmesbury to Odo Russell, 20 May 1859, no. 43, PRO, FO, 43/69. Odo Russell to Malmesbury, Rome, 28 May 1859, no. 69, PRO, FO, 43/71, and excerpted in *Odo Russell*, 23–5.
42 Malmesbury to Odo Russell, 10 March 1859, private, Ampthill papers, PRO, FO, 918/6. Odo Russell to Malmesbury, Rome, 15 March 1860, no. 31, confidential, and 9 April 1860, no. 38, confidential, PRO, FO, 43/70, and *Odo Russell*, 11, 15.
43 Odo Russell to Malmesbury, Rome, 26 March 1859, private, Malmesbury papers, 1859/7.
44 Odo Russell to Russell, Rome, 1 July 1859, no. 80, PRO, FO, 43/71, and *Odo Russell*, 29.

against the pope: 'I am sorry to see by the telegram received this morning that the Pope has been setting his Swiss wolves upon his poor sheep at Perugia.'[45] Malmesbury had never used such language. Lord John's candour helped remove all of Odo's restraint. In reply Odo drafted his first private letter to his uncle, which revealed that he had finished sorting out the perplexity he experienced five months earlier:

> Nothing can be more rotten or despicable than the Papal Government and for my part I cannot conceive any settlement of Italian affairs complete and satisfactory that does not deprive the Pope of his temporal power.[46]

Three weeks later he had gained confidence in expressing anti-papal opinions to Lord John:

> Pharoah's heart is hardened! Pio Nono regrets the concessions he made to the wonders performed by the Emperor in the land of Lombardy and if he can succeed in promising and *procrastinating* at present, he will do nothing in the future for the three millions of individuals doomed to be his slaves. As in the case of Napoleon I the Pope will prove an insurmountable difficulty to the policy of Napoleon III and I am more than ever convinced that no satisfactory settlement of Italian affairs is possible so long as the temporal power of the Pope is tolerated in the Peninsula. However, there it is, and there it will remain, until someday or other it will die a victim to its own internal corruption.[47]

The basis of Odo's opposition to the temporal power was religious. In mid-September 1859, soon after his return to Rome after the summer holidays, he prepared for Lord John a new assessment of the condition of the Papal States. There was, he thought, 'an awful absence of true religious feeling ..., the want of some pure religion'. The situation was analogous to the dearth of true religion in the days of heathen Rome. Early Christianity had redemptively filled that void, but now – the implication was unmistakable – papal religion could not satisfy a similar need. Odo continued briefly to develop his line of thought, but he stopped, and scratched out the whole section before sending it. There is no reason not to believe, however, that the portion omitted from the final draft expressed his convictions on the matter. In the deleted section Odo penetrated to the heart of the issue as he saw it. The papacy and the Roman church were an idolatry desperately in need of a shake-up at least as radical as the Protestant Reformation:

> [The] curse which now seems to rest on the Papacy and its surroundings must once more burst forth like the thunderstorm after the Reformation. The more I see with my own eyes what this Papacy really is, the more grateful do I feel to those men who freed England from her unwholesome influence . . . The progressive

45 Russell to Odo Russell, 23 June 1859, private, Ampthill papers, PRO, FO, 918/7, and *Odo Russell*, 27.
46 Odo Russell to Russell, Rome, 6 July 1859, private, draft, Ampthill papers, PRO, FO, 918/10.
47 Underlining is Odo's. Odo Russell to Russell, Rome, 30 July 1859, private, Russell papers, PRO, 30/22/75, and excerpted in *Odo Russell*, 43–4.

degeneration and corruption of the Roman Church becomes apparent to the naked eye at Rome. So much corruption and folly cannot last forever. It has developed into a species of idolatry. The religion of the Greeks and Romans did not last forever. Why should the *forms* of this Church of Rome?[48]

Odo could not understand the Catholic devotion and spirituality he saw around him as anything other than 'so much imbecility and corruption': 'At present the Pope resorts to every kind of procession and Church Festival. Miraculous crosses, virgins, relics, saints and idols are paraded about the streets, and carried from one Church to the other. Indulgences are offered at every altar and the poor man is said to be deeply convinced that a miracle will be performed in his favour.'[49] Papal Catholicism was awry at the foundations: '[I]f there is a thing these Papists, Prelates, Priests and Princes of the Roman Catholic Church abhor more than anything else it is – Truth.'[50] At the end of the tumultuous events which overthrew most of the temporal power, in December 1860, he exclaimed to Lord Cowley: 'There is not a day passed here in Rome where I don't feel the blessings of the Reformation and I thank God with all my heart that we at home have broken for ever with this infernal Papacy.'[51] However he put it, it meant the same thing – Odo came to hold intensely anti-papal and anti-Catholic convictions.

There was one very important consideration which appears to have had some modifying influence on his views. His mother, Lady William Russell – the person with whom he was most intimate – converted to the Roman Catholic Church in 1860. It was to his mother at Christmas 1860 and at Easter 1861, after she began attending mass, that Odo expressed a more tempered hope that the Roman Catholic Church itself might be revived if only the pope would care more for the spiritual tasks of the church and relinquish the temporal power. Perhaps a renewal of Catholicism, rather than its overthrow as in the English Reformation, would suffice: 'The Roman Catholic Church, once freed from the millstone of Temporal Power around her neck and able to turn all her attention once more and exclusively to her spiritual interests, would be regenerated to an extent no one can foresee at present.'[52]

Odo came to describe his own beliefs as the principles of Whiggism, which he

48 Underlining is Odo's. Odo Russell to Russell, Rome, 16 Sept. 1859, private, Russell papers, PRO, 30/22/75, and excerpted in *Odo Russell*, 47–9.
49 Odo Russell to Russell, Rome, 12 June 1860, private, Russell papers, PRO, 30/22/75.
50 Odo Russell to Hammond, Rome, 7 Dec. 1859, draft, Ampthill papers, PRO, FO, 918/37.
51 Odo Russell to Cowley, Rome, 5 Dec. 1860, Cowley papers, PRO, FO, 519/205, and excerpted in *Odo Russell*, 144.
52 Odo wrote his mother, 'Monsignor Talbot enquires very tenderly after you and hints that he knows you go to Mass. He is most anxious for your arrival in Rome' (Odo Russell to Lady William Russell, Rome, 4 Dec. 1860, copy, Ampthill papers, PRO, FO, 918/85/276). Georgina Blakiston, Lady William's great-granddaughter, writes, 'She was received into the Roman Catholic Church in 1860' (*Lord William Russell and his wife, 1815–1846* (London: John Murray, 1972), 544). See Odo Russell to Lady William Russell, Rome, St Sylvester Day, 1859, and 6 March 1860, copies, Ampthill papers, PRO, FO, 918/85/240, 256; for Odo's modified views, see Odo Russell to Lady William Russell, Rome, 25 Dec. 1860, 13 April, and 20 April 1861, copies, Ampthill papers, PRO, FO, 918/85/279, 292–4.

interpreted in an Erastian and broad church Protestant way.[53] The events in Italy and the need to take a stand on the papacy had helped him to match his Whig background and family connections with his own personal convictions. Anti-Catholic and anti-papal beliefs were an important element of his credo.

Odo learned to present a Whig interpretation of events in Rome, but without revealing in the official world the anti-papal and anti-Catholic aspects of his Whiggish views and language.[54] This he was free to express privately to his mother and his uncle, but it would have been regarded as improper for public expression. In the official world of his despatches, liable as they were to being published in the Parliamentary Blue Books, he was careful to present himself as tolerant, non-dogmatic and liberal-minded.

Beginning with the Perugia affair, partly following the example of Lord John, Odo became much more aggressive in his interviews with Antonelli and the pope. Before hearing from Lord John, Odo confronted Antonelli with 'the ferocious behaviour' of the papal-Swiss soldiers at Perugia and charged that they had 'murdered, pillaged, burnt houses and committed other outrages'.[55] The following week, at Lord John's request and using his uncle's language, he accused the papal soldiers of committing 'atrocities' and 'butcheries'.[56]

In his first audience with Pius IX after Perugia and after the beginning of Lord John's term of office he debated with the pope as well. He disputed the pope's criticisms of Lord Minto, Lord Palmerston and a whole list of Englishmen – Granville, Gladstone, Cobden, Stratford de Redcliffe, Disraeli. He challenged, politely, the pope's view of the temporal power by claiming that it existed only because it was imposed on three million people by French and Austrian bayonets. Then, to Pius' face, he accused papal troops of pillage and murder. Odo was aware that he took a more aggressive approach in the audience and described it as a time of speaking freely and openly.[57] At his next audience with the pope six months later, in January 1860, Odo was ready for even more straightforward promotion of his political convictions. As he described it,

> In answering His Holiness's enquiries respecting the nature of our [English] administration I dwelt with warmth on the blessings of free institutions and self-government which were productive of confidence between the people and their authorities and animated all with loyalty to the Sovereign, but the Pope merely observed that we English were unlike other people and that what suited us would not suit anyone else.[58]

---

53 Odo Russell to Russell, Rome, 19 Nov. 1859, private, Russell papers, PRO, 30/22/75, and *Odo Russell*, 60.
54 See Herbert Butterfield, *The Whig interpretation of history* (London: Bell, 1931).
55 Odo Russell to Russell, Rome, 1 July 1859, no. 81, secret, PRO, FO, 43/71, and excerpted in *Odo Russell*, 30–1.
56 Russell to Odo Russell, 1 July 1859, no. 2, draft, PRO, FO, 43/69. Odo Russell to Russell, Rome, 7 July 1859, no. 82, PRO, FO, 43/71, and excerpted in *Odo Russell*, 32–3.
57 Odo Russell to Russell, Rome, 17 July 1859, no. 89, secret, PRO, FO, 43/71, and *Odo Russell*, 36–9.
58 Odo Russell to Russell, Rome, 31 Jan. 1860, no. 19, secret, PRO, FO, 43/76, and *Odo Russell*, 84–7.

Odo Russell and the network of English–papal relations

Odo's audience in January 1861 was extremely vigorous as he earnestly tried to persuade Pius to accept the overthrow of the temporal power and to give his blessing to the new Kingdom of Italy.[59] Odo, in his enthusiasm, apparently exceeded the proprieties of a papal audience, for the French complained of the excesses of his language, and the pope, it turned out, did not grant him an audience again for a year-and-a-half.[60]

Odo used his frequent interviews with Antonelli and his papal audiences to promote the English case for material prosperity and civil and religious liberty. He did so with increasing missionary-like zeal as he followed a distinct personal policy: 'I avoid giving offence by volunteering opinions or advice, but when asked I frankly uphold constitutional principles.'[61]

Odo was convinced that he presented in his despatches only the most accurate reports from the most authentic sources.[62] There is no doubt, as he testified later, that he sought conscientiously to be fair, just and truthful and to avoid exaggeration and uncalled for abuse of the papal government. At the same time, however, everything he wrote in his despatches and letters was filtered through a perspective which, as he said, did 'not approve of this rotten administration and admit the necessity of imposing it by force on a suffering, bleeding, prostrate nation'.[63] He saw Roman affairs through frankly partisan eyes, and that fact must be taken into account in order to appreciate his reports adequately. Odo's despatches did not, like Hudson's from Turin, explicitly argue in favour of Cavourian policy, but they nonetheless aided the nationalist cause through the selection and interpretation of what he reported.

Odo tended to neglect giving reports about the views and activities of those who opposed or were uninvolved with the Risorgimento – the clerical party and the *papalini* in Rome as well as the great mass of the Roman and peasant population. These were the people to whom Pius IX referred when he claimed that his children were loyal to him and loved him. Odo was not able to comprehend the pope's spiritual power and purpose, or his relation with the faithful. Concomitantly, Odo tended to over-stress the nationalist party in Rome, at least in proportion to their numbers and their influence. He came to know some of their leaders well, especially Dr Pantaleoni, the physician preferred by the English in Rome, and he adopted their, and the Sardinians', view of the struggle. These were the people to whom he referred when he wrote reports like this: 'The Romans look on, laugh, curse the Priests and the "*Neri*"

59   Odo Russell to Russell, Rome, 16 Jan. 1861, no. 5, secret, PRO, FO, 43/83A, and *Odo Russell*, 152–9.
60   Odo Russell to Russell, Rome, 17 Feb. 1863, private, Russell papers, PRO, 30/22/76, and *Odo Russell*, 264–5.
61   Odo Russell to Hammond, Rome, 7 Dec. 1859, private, draft, Ampthill papers, PRO, FO, 918/37.
62   Odo Russell to Russell, Rome, 20 March 1860, no. 41, PRO, FO, 43/76, and *Odo Russell*, 95.
63   Odo Russell to Russell, Rome, 19 May 1863, private, Russell papers, PRO, 30/22/75, and *Odo Russell*, 274.

and pray for their own Idols, Victor Emmanuel, Cavour, and Garibaldi.'⁶⁴

The overall historical framework within which Odo depicted the events in Rome and the Papal States during 1859 to 1861 was a straightforward mid-Victorian Whig interpretation of history. He interpreted the events of 1859 to 1861 as a great movement of the people of Italy irresistibly pressing forward toward the achievement of free institutions based on liberal principles according to the English model. He saw the papacy, especially the temporal power, as the great obstacle which one day, again irresistibly, would succumb to the movement toward the liberty of Italy. This interpretative overview helped him to place day-to-day details in a context.

Nevertheless, making allowances for his Whig perspective, Odo's despatches from Rome provided a generally competent representation to the English government of papal policy and responses to English policy, and recorded well how he as English envoy implemented English policy toward the papacy.⁶⁵ Moreover, his despatches were delightfully witty and literate. As Lord John observed, 'They give a lively picture of the decline and fall of the Temporal Power.'⁶⁶

The Mediterranean fleet and the papal trade

Rome was the centre of English attention regarding the papal temporal power, but the English always maintained a peripheral vision which allowed them to locate the pope in the wider context of what they called 'British interests'. Through all the events of war, revolution and diplomacy, the two British governments did not forget for a moment two ways in which British interests encompassed the Papal States and the Italian peninsula – the British navy in the Mediterranean, and British trade. These two interests worked together.

When Queen Victoria insisted on 13 January that the Cabinet increase the naval allotment, her concern was to keep up British superiority at sea, especially over France. She enunciated the conviction shared, no doubt, by virtually every member of Parliament: 'there will be no safety to the honour, power and peace of this country except in Naval and Military strengths'.⁶⁷ The Derby government increased the naval force, as did the Palmerston government again later. The concern close to home was France, and a genuine fear that the French would invade Great Britain rolled over the population during 1859 and 1860. Farther away, the concern was the Mediterranean. The British possessed naval bases in the Mediterranean at Gibraltar, Malta and the Ionian Islands. They made plans to increase the Gibraltar and Malta garrisons in the spring of 1859 by 21 per cent,

---

64 Odo Russell to Russell, Rome, 22 Feb. 1860, no. 31, PRO, FO, 43/76, and *Odo Russell*, 90, and 12 June 1860, private, Russell papers, PRO, 30/22/75.
65 Hammond to Odo Russell, 26 Dec. 1859, Ampthill papers, PRO, FO, 918/37.
66 Russell to Odo Russell, 29 Oct. 1860, private, copy, Russell papers, PRO, 30/22/111.
67 Queen Victoria to Derby (for communication to Cabinet), 13 Jan. 1859, Derby papers, 136/6.

to 5400 and 6500 men, plus commissioned officers and crews. This included both new recruits and a shift to Malta of men from the base at Jersey in the Channel Islands. They would increase the Ionian base by 36 per cent to 4100 men. The Malta harbour was enlarged in 1860. During the summer of 1859, Parliament provided for the creation of a reserve volunteer force of 30,000 seamen. By the end of 1860, 150,000 Englishmen had enrolled in the Volunteer Rifle Corps designed to defend the homeland, especially if the regular British armed forces were needed to defend Malta and Gibraltar.[68]

The bases at Malta and the Ionian Islands gave the British a commanding position in both the Tyrrhenian and the Adriatic Seas. From these two bases, the British fleet literally surrounded the Italian peninsula by patrolling the coasts and regularly calling in ports where there were British consuls or vice-consuls, especially Palermo, Naples, Civita Vecchia, Livorno (Leghorn), and Genoa on the Tyrrhenian coast, and Ancona and Venice on the Adriatic. The British had the most advanced steam-powered fleet there was, with a variety of screw steam ships, paddle wheel steam frigates, steam sloops, and steam gun-vessels. With the outbreak of war, the government sent ships to several ports around the peninsula. On 21 May 1859, H.M. Steam Sloop *Argus*, under Commander H.W. Ingram, despatched from Malta, arrived in Ancona harbour, where, under orders from the Foreign Office, it remained for the duration of the Austro-Sardinian war. In June and July, a squadron of six large screw steam ships, also from Malta, sailed in powerful display up the Tyrrhenian coast and then up the Adriatic, calling in the major ports. The squadron was commanded by Vice-Admiral Fanshawe in the lead ship, the *Duke of Marlborough*, and among the ships behind him, as if to indicate where British sympathies lay, was the *Victor Emmanuel*. Three steam ships from Malta – the *Conqueror*, the *Terrible* and the *Centurion* – and one from the Ionians – the *Vigilant* – kept individual schedules up and down the coasts during the crisis of 1859 and 1860.[69]

The duties which the two English governments assigned to the Mediterranean fleet were well summarized by the instructions given to Commander Ingram, the effect of which, in this case, kept the *Argus* anchored in Ancona harbour for almost two-and-a-half months in 1859: 'affording protection to British Subjects and Interests *alone*'.[70] Protecting British subjects was straightforward enough. If the war and revolution swept into the Papal States,

68 'Memorandum of the present and proposed garrisons in the Mediterranean Islands, and the Channel Islands', 15 April 1859, RA J 17/114. 'Navy estimates for the year 1860–1861', *Parliamentary papers, 1860*, vol. 42. Queen Victoria to Derby, 1 June 1859, Derby papers, 136/6. *British almanac and directory* (1860), 42–52. 22 et 23 Vict. c. 40, and 22 et 23 Vict. c. 42. *The Times*, 31 Dec. 1860.
69 See the vice-consular reports to the Florence ministry, in PRO, FO, 170/89. Derby to Malmesbury, 26 April 1859, Derby papers, 188/1. Two engraved drawings of Fanshawe's majestic squadron were published in *The Illustrated London News*, 9 July 1859, 37.
70 Commander H.W. Ingram to Peter Campbell Scarlett, Ancona, 21 May 1859, PRO, FO, 170/89. Underlining is Ingram's.

The Mediterranean fleet and the papal trade

many British might need to be evacuated. It had happened in May 1849 when Commander A. Cooper Key and the *Bulldog* had assisted the British leaving Rome. In May 1859, the Prince of Wales was taken away from the Papal States at short notice by the H.M.S. *Scourge*, which had anchored at Civita Vecchia as the crisis worsened.[71] While they were at it, the ship commanders might serve in lieu of a diplomatic or even consular agent, and make contact with government authorities and prepare political reports on the state of affairs in the area. This Commander Key did in Rome and Civita Vecchia in 1849, as did Ingram in Ancona in 1859.[72]

Protecting 'British interests' was a more flexible matter, however, and it tended to enlarge according to need. One obvious interest was British trade, which at both Civita Vecchia and Ancona was not inconsiderable; more will be said about this shortly. Keeping the ports and the seaways open for British merchants selling their wares had long been an aim of British foreign policy. The *Argus* and the other ships in 1859 and 1860 repeated the work of the *Frolic* at Ancona, and the *Bulldog* at Civita Vecchia ten years earlier.[73] A second obvious interest was the self-perpetuating act of maintaining British presence in the Mediterranean. The fleet had the duty of defending the British possessions of Gibraltar, Malta and the Ionian Islands which were the mainstays of their superiority at sea, their influence in the Italian peninsula and their access to the Middle East, Central Asia and above all, British India.[74]

There were other interests, such as giving assistance to refugees, an act whereby the English believed they could demonstrate the excellence of their material prosperity and institutions of civil and religious liberty. The British in these years of crisis reiterated that they were proud for their ships to receive refugees equally from 'the arbitrary acts of Monarchial Government' or 'the lawless violence of a Revolutionary Committee'.[75] In August 1859, the Foreign Office decided as a matter of policy to make available to the pope, should he request it, a ship from the Malta fleet to take him to any destination he desired. Talk of the pope leaving Rome first arose in April 1859 and frequently recurred during the 1860s. The English could imagine the evacuation of the pope from Rome as the quick solution to the Papal Question, for there would be no

---

71 Commander A. Cooper Key to Vice-Admiral Sir W. Parker, Civita Vecchia, 10 and 12 May 1849, *Correspondence respecting the affairs of Rome in 1849*, in *Parliamentary papers, 1851*, vol. 57, 29–30. Prince Albert to Col. Bruce, 23 April 1859, copy, and Col. Bruce to Prince Albert, 7 May 1859, RA Z444/93. Odo Russell to Malmesbury, Rome, 3 May 1859, private, Malmesbury papers, 1859/7.
72 Ingram's reports to Peter Campbell Scarlett in Florence are in PRO, FO, 170/89.
73 Platt, 85. See Vice-Admiral Sir W. Parker to W.A.B. Hamilton (Secretary of the Admiralty), Malta, 1 May 1849, in *Correspondence respecting the affairs of Rome in 1849*, in *Parliamentary papers, 1851*, vol. 57, 18.
74 Russell to Queen Victoria, 3 Nov. 1860, RA J31/43. See Edward Ingram, *The beginning of the Great Game in Asia, 1828–1834* (Oxford: Clarendon, 1979).
75 Porter, *The refugee question, passim*. Addington (of the Foreign office) to C. Paget (Secretary of the Admiralty), 4 Aug. 1860, *Parliamentary papers, 1860*, vol. 68, 378.

possibility of another papal restoration. Spain and Bavaria were the destinations most often mentioned, but in January 1860 Antonelli asked Odo Russell confidentially whether the pope might be taken away safely by a British ship and given asylum in England. In July 1862 Pius himself inquired about protection by a British ship and asylum in England. The British government responded formally by offering the pope asylum in Malta where he would be safely surrounded by the British fleet.[76]

The fleet directly served British diplomatic interests in the Papal States and throughout the peninsula by providing the underlying and ever present threat of armed coercion in support of British policy. The fleet was essential to the much emphasized doctrine of non-intervention. Both English governments were constantly aware of this mode of power, and were ready to have recourse to it if necessary. It was a little like peeling off the layers of an onion. To achieve desired ends, the English might be content to serve as a model against the pope and for the liberals in Italy, or they might actively employ varying degrees of moral suasion, or they might use a graded range of commercial or diplomatic instruments. Underneath these lay a further option, what they called 'material force' or 'material assistance'. By such euphemisms they referred to a variety of hints and threats and armed measures, the last resort being war. They meant using the Mediterranean fleet. In April 1859, Lord Derby seriously considered adopting the policy of armed neutrality, which utilized the Mediterranean fleet, and discussed what it would take for England to be engaged in actual war. Malmesbury suggested to the queen that the crucial matter determining whether England entered the war would be the neutrality of the Adriatic and the Baltic. Palmerston, in June 1859, was willing to use a squadron from Malta to blockade both Genoa and Venice in order to keep a prospective kingdom of North Italy, which would include papal Romagna, amenable to British interests. Several times in the course of events, both English governments considered using 'material force' to achieve desired results relevant to the Papal Question. The first, already seen, was Malmesbury's suggestion in December 1858 that England 'could give her moral, and if necessary her material assistance' to redistribute papal territory or force reforms upon the pope. One Englishman in Ancona claimed that the presence of the British ship *Argus* in Ancona harbour kept papal troops from using extreme measures against the populace. There would be more occasions to refer to 'material force'.[77]

76 Hammond to the Admiralty, 20 Aug. 1859, draft, PRO, FO, 43/73; Bruce to Prince Albert, Rome, 28 April 1859, RA Z444/87; Odo Russell to Russell, Rome, 21 Jan. 1860, private and secret, PRO, 30/22/75, and *Odo Russell*, 82; Odo Russell to Russell, Rome, 26 July 1862, PRO, FO, 43/86B, and *Odo Russell*, 234–6; Russell to Odo Russell, 25 Oct. 1862, no. 46, PRO, FO, 43/85.
77 Derby to Queen Victoria, 9 April 1859, copy, Derby papers, 187/2. Malmesbury to Queen Victoria, 2 May 1859, RA J19/14. Palmerston, Cabinet Memorandum, 28 June 1859, in Blakiston, 'L'opinione pubblica inglese', 142. 'An Englishman' to *The Times*, Ancona, 30 July 1859, in *The Times*, 15 Aug. 1859. The Evangelical politician Sir R.H. Inglis (M.P.,

The Mediterranean fleet and the papal trade

The politicians, the diplomats, including Odo Russell, the English society in Rome, and the merchants could all assume the surrounding presence of the English fleet and carry on with their activities.

The British encompassed the Papal States in another way – British trade. In 1859 and 1860, England was the top of the world in economic terms, enjoying superiority not only at sea, but also in industry, commerce and finance. During the 1850s, as Gladstone noted in his 1860 budget speech, England had profited by a great increase in the wealth of the nation. The 'career of commercial improvement', he stated, had promoted the prosperity of the country and the security of its institutions. The Tories agreed, and both parties would support Malmesbury's conviction, which underlay Tory commercial diplomacy, that the surest guarantee of international peace and amity was 'the maintenance and extension of commercial and social intercourse between nations'.[78]

This was the period in which English governments were the most missionary-like about advancing 'Free Trade' throughout Europe and around the world. They included even the Papal States within a tight global network of commercial treaties. In 1848, Palmerston argued that the advancement of English commercial interests in the Papal States required diplomatic relations with the pope. But even without diplomatic relations, the English won their commercial treaty. On 17 November 1853, Scarlett for England and Antonelli for the Roman States signed a reciprocity treaty declaring that each government would impose on each other's produce, manufacturing, or vessels only such duties or taxes as were the same for any other country. With this English–papal commercial treaty, England completed its first round coverage of the whole Italian peninsula. The papal treaty was due to last for seven years, until 1860.[79] English example and pressure toward freer trade following the conclusion of the treaty was part of what induced the papal government to lower customs tariffs by considerable amounts twice, once in June 1855 and again in May 1857. The British succeeded at least once in obtaining a special exemption from export duties on a contract for oak timber going to England.[80]

British–papal trade was relatively small, but, as Palmerston phrased it,

---

Oxford University) reviewed the various options the Russell government could consider in resisting 'papal aggression' in 1850, and concluded that a visit by a British squadron to Civita Vecchia or Ancona was one: Hansard's, CXIV, col. 1368–9, 14 March 1851.

78 Gladstone, 'Financial statement of 1860', 10 Feb. 1860, in *The financial statements of 1853, 1860–1863* (London: John Murray, 1863), 111, 115, 122. Malmesbury, Foreign Office circular, 8 March 1858, in Platt, xv.

79 Hansard's XCVII, col. 203–4, 17 Aug. 1848. 'Declaration exchanged between the governments of Great Britain and of the Roman States for securing national treatment to the vessels and commerce of the one country in the ports of the other', in *Parliamentary papers, 1854*, vol. 72, 781–6. 'Treaties of Commerce', F.O. 15 March 1860, *Parliamentary papers, 1860*, vol. 68, 637–41: Austria, including Lombardy and Venetia (1838), Two Sicilies (1845), Tuscany (1847), Sardinia (1851), Roman States (1853).

80 Lyons to Normanby, Rome, 6 June 1856, and Rome, 22 Jan. 1857, in *Lyons' despatches*, 404 and 424. H.L. Bulwer to George Moore, 4 Jan. 1855, PRO, FO, 170/70.

'nevertheless it is of growing and annually increasing importance'.[81] Merchant ship traffic passed between the English ports of Liverpool, Newcastle and London, primarily, and the papal ports of Civita Vecchia and Ancona, with perhaps 60–70 per cent going to Ancona. According to English statistics, the number of ships clearing English ports to papal ports, and entering English ports from papal ports were:

Papal States	1856	1857	1858	1859	1860
Clearing to:	62	71	194	61	62
Entering from:	48	22	31	26	13

The ships to the Papal States increased in number until the crisis years, while ships from the Papal States decreased. In pounds sterling, the value of English exports carried by these ships to the Papal States was:

1850–5 (avg.)	1856	1857	1858	1859	1860
£196,965	£311,114	£318,797	£409,543	£260,077	£294,175

This indicated a steady increase in British exports to the Papal States after the English–papal trade treaty until the crisis years. The papal trade represented a generally steady 6–7 per cent of the total British exports to the Italian states until 1860 when it declined to about 5 per cent. Meanwhile during the same 1850 to 1860 period British imports from the Papal States fluctuated around a £75,000 average, except for the high year of 1856, representing 2–3 per cent of British imports from the Italian states. The imports consisted mainly of wheat, wood, lamb skins and cream of tartar. Papal oaks went to build Thames dock yards while papal cream of tartar supplied about 10 per cent of British needs for their baking powder and hard sweets.

While the figures for English exports to the Papal States are not large relative to the total British trade with the Italian peninsula, or relative to total British world exports, the results in the Papal States were very significant. English merchants sold to the Papal States the products of the English 'career of commercial improvement'. The main articles were textile manufactures – both yarn and cloth, in cotton, wool and linen – hardwares and cutlery, wrought and unwrought iron, and coal. British merchants supplied nearly all the coal, most of the cotton cloth and cotton yarn, and most of the wrought iron used in the Papal

---

81 Hansard's, XCVII, col. 203–4, 17 Aug. 1848. The data on English–papal trade which follow are collated from *The Trade and Navigation: annual statement*, in *Parliamentary papers*, every year from 1850 to 1880, which for some categories give data back to 1840. The first export figures by Italian states are for 1846, and import figures start for 1854. The data on merchant ships is given in 'Vessels, sailing and steam, by country', in *Parliamentary papers, 1861*, vol. 60, 45–8.

States.[82] The papal government during the 1850s awarded contracts to English firms for several major projects. The new gas lighting system in Rome was built, financed and operated by the Anglo-Roman Gas Illumination Company, managed by James Shepherd in Rome. Shepherd trained papal subjects to follow English discipline and factory methods in order to manufacture the gas lamps locally out of English wrought iron. Another English company built an iron drawbridge extension onto the famous Ponte Rotto across the Tiber in Rome. The Thames Iron Works and Ship Building Company designed and manufactured a handsome screw steam ship for Pope Pius IX, which was christened *The Immaculate Conception* and launched on the Thames in 1859. The mainline railway between Rome and Civita Vecchia, which opened in April 1859, was built by a Spanish company, but with help from English entrepreneurs. By such means the English profited from the advancement of material progress even in the Papal States.[83]

During the 1850s, by comparison, British exports to Sardinia-Piedmont, according to English statistics, moved in a general, but fluctuating trend upward from £0.7 million (1850) to £1.8 million (1860), accounting for a generally steady 30 per cent of the total British exports to the Italian States. British exports to the Two Sicilies from 1850 to 1860, except for two low years in 1853 and 1854, fluctuated around a £1 million to £1.2 million average, and moved from a share of the total British exports to the Italian states that was greater than Sardinia's to one that was less. Total British exports to the Italian states moved generally upward from £3.4 million (1850) to £5.5 million (1860). Then after unification, from 1861 until 1870, total British exports to Italy stopped increasing and instead fluctuated up and down around a £5.5 million average. And after unification, 1861 to 1870, British exports to southern Italian ports tended to be greater than those to northern Italian ports, a reversal of the pre-1861 trends. Meanwhile, total British world exports increased in a gradually steady line upward from £71 million (1850) to £135 million (1860) and £238 million in 1870, with the greatest increases going to the United States, the German states, Holland and British India.

In other words, before 1861 British exports to all the Italian states, including the Papal States, tended to rise, along with British world exports, and there was a general shift from south to north, namely to Sardinia. After unification, British exports to the new Italy levelled off, with a general shift from north to south, while British world trade continued to rise, bypassing Italy. British exports to Italy did not significantly increase until the late 1870s and the 1880s when the

82   Gaggiotti, 'Report . . . on the trade and navigation in [Ancona] for the year 1858', in *Parliamentary papers, 1859* (Sess. 2), vol. 30, 550–1.
83   *Giornale di Roma*, 7 March and 18 April 1859; Maguire, ch. 33. *Tablet*, 7 May 1859, and *Illustrated London News*, 20 Aug. 1859, 179; also ASV, ANParigi, Sacconi, Ministri pontifici, 1854–8 ott. 1860, Finanze. See L.H. Jenks, *The migration of British capital to 1875* (New York: Knopf, 1927).

Italian economy began its period of rapid and intense industrialization.[84] During the period 1850 to 1870, it was France, and not Britain, which controlled the largest share of imports by the Italian states as well as the new Italy, although the British dominated in textiles, industrial products and coal.

The important thing to observe about these economic trends and events is that there was no obvious motive of economic profit which tended to tilt England toward Sardinia and against the pope. From the standpoint of direct economic gain for British merchants, the merchants stood to win whichever way the political events in Italy went. The British had no direct economic need to act against the pope. They already dominated the papal economy in the essential products of industrialization and had every expectation of continuing to increase their sales and investments, and there were no exceptional treaty or tariff reasons to impede the development of that dominance. If anything, there were reasons to fear actual economic loss which worked against English support for Sardinia-Piedmont. The officials at the British legation in Turin regularly reported that Sardinian finances and commerce were chaotic and not progressing according to expectations, although they excused the government on the grounds that it necessarily devoted its attention to political and military objectives. The Piedmontese tariff was, in fact, higher on some items of importance to English merchants than the Tuscan or papal tariffs, so that the extension of Piedmont's tariff to these territories would harm British merchants unless things were changed.[85]

If immediate economic profit was not a factor bending English interest toward Piedmont and against the pope, there was an economic concern that did. It was the English conviction that Piedmont offered the best prospects in Italy of achieving the material prosperity which the English model glorified. Sackville West from Turin and Gaggiotti from Ancona both expressed this socio-economic conviction when they stressed in their commercial reports that, in spite of all signs to the contrary, the Piedmontese, and not anything priestly, could be expected to prosper as soon as the political crisis passed. The practice of free trade and the free course of 'speculative enterprise', especially by the British, could not help but issue forth with incessant progress. Soon after taking office, Palmerston was quick to assert that, whatever happened, the English had no economic reason to fear the enlargement of Sardinia; such a state would be sure to devote itself to commerce and would certainly be compatible with British

---

84   Valerio Castronovo, 'The Italian take-off: a critical re-examination of the problem', *Journal of Italian history* 1 (1978), 492–510.

85   E.M. Erskine, Report, Turin, 1 Jan. 1858, in *Parliamentary papers, 1857–1858*, vol. 50, 93–4; L.S. Sackville West, Report, Turin, 1 July 1860, in *Parliamentary papers, 1861*, vol. 63, 152–3; Sackville West, Report, Turin, 1 Jan. 1861, and Report, Turin, 30 Jan. 1861, in *Parliamentary papers, 1861*, vol. 63, 316–19, and 432–7; Sackville West, Report, Turin, 1 Jan. 1863, in *Parliamentary papers, 1863*, vol. 70, 684. Blakiston, 'L'Inghilterra e la tariffa piemontese, 1859–1860', in *Inglesi e italiani nel Risorgimento*, ch. 3. See Palmerston to Queen Victoria, 8 Aug. 1859, RA J22/70.

interests as long as British trade and the British fleet maintained their superiority.⁸⁶

With this understanding of British commerce and the British navy, both English governments were free to pursue diplomatic activity in which economic, political and religious concerns readily fitted together. Theirs was the mission to help deliver Italians from the backwardness, the despotism, and the superstition of the papacy, and to set Italy properly on the way of moral and material progress. The complicated network of English–papal relations, with Odo Russell at the centre, directly contributed to this mission.

86   See reports from Sackville West and Gaggiotti already cited. Palmerston, Cabinet Memorandum, 28 June 1859, in Blakiston, 'L'opinione pubblica inglese', 142.

3 Tories, the pope, and peace

Tory–papal *rapprochement*

The Tory government's policy, as formulated in Malmesbury's statements to his ambassadors early in January 1859, could not easily be construed as friendly to the papacy. Of all the states of Italy he had singled out the States of the Church as the root of the trouble and had proposed to France and Austria that the solution of Italy's ills lay in making changes in the papal government and perhaps partially redistributing the Papal States.

Malmesbury decided not to reveal this proposal directly to the papal government, but instead prepared a special version to guide Odo Russell in his relations with Cardinal Antonelli and Pius IX.[1] This version was meant to appeal to the pope to consider the effect of the current international crisis on the temporal power. It talked of the just discontent of the peoples of Italy, warned of a revolution which would overthrow the entire Italian social system, and described his formula that France and Austria together press for changes in the papal government. But, remarkably, the statement sent to Odo stopped there. Unlike the letters to Cowley, Hudson and Loftus, it contained no reference to the papal government as the core of the problem, and implied that all the Italian states needed reform and not merely the Papal States. It also relativized England's role in Italian affairs by claiming that England had no 'material interests' involved, cared only for the maintenance of the general peace of Europe, and, as a Protestant state, would remain a 'spectator' of papal affairs, offering only occasional advice. The statement contained no hint of Malmesbury's idea of remodelling papal territory.

Odo was instructed not to discuss the statement with Antonelli or Pius IX, but merely to convey to them that only the most amicable intentions lay behind the English government's diplomatic initiatives. Since Malmesbury did not give

---

1   Malmesbury to Odo Russell, 13 Jan. 1859, no. 5, confidential, draft, PRO, FO, 43/69. Derek Beales notes that Malmesbury adapted each version of his policy statement to the recipient, giving each government, including France and Austria, an especially fitted impression of what the implications of his policy would be in the event of war (*England and Italy*, 39–40). On Malmesbury generally, Harry Hearder, 'The foreign policy of Lord Malmesbury, 1858–1859' (Ph.D. thesis, University of London, 1954).

Odo the statements sent to the other capitals, Odo did not know what else Malmesbury had proposed to do. Malmesbury's strategy was to pursue an understated, even conciliatory, approach to the papacy directly in the hope that Antonelli and the pope would be persuaded to carry out reforms, and thereby help secure the peace of Europe.

What impelled Malmesbury to try to conciliate the papal government was the awful foreboding of war and revolution. He had finally come to believe that the French, the Sardinians and the Italian nationalists might indeed be contemplating war. He also feared that 'undoubtedly any moment may bring forth a revolution in the Papal States'.[2]

When Gramont, the French ambassador in Rome, learned what Malmesbury wished Odo to do, he interpreted this English action toward the papacy, correctly, as 'the first indications of an attempt at diplomatic rapprochement'. But, Gramont observed, 'I cannot believe that the Court of Rome is the least disposed to lend itself to it for the present, and for my part, I see nothing to be desired in this consequence either for it [the papal government] or for us.'[3]

Malmesbury was worried about Cavour's ambition for territorial aggrandizement, even though he continued to respect Sardinia for what he took to be its liberal institutions on the English model. The danger in Cavour's policy, he thought, was that it would impede true reform in the Papal States, and benefit only the revolutionaries. Lord Shaftesbury, an Evangelical aristocrat who was close to the Piedmontese ambassador in London, Emanuel d'Azeglio, warned Cavour that he was on the verge of losing English support because of his agitation against Austria and encouragement of revolutionaries. Emanuel d'Azeglio suggested to Cavour that he would more easily get what he wanted with England if he directed attention not against Austria but against Rome and the Papal States.[4]

When Cavour learned of Malmesbury's policy from Hudson, the English envoy in Turin, he replied with an argument Hudson had already made for him – that Piedmont, far from inciting revolt in the Romagna and Lombardy, actually calmed it by giving them reason to be patient. The surest way to peace, Cavour argued, would be for England and the other powers to support the aspirations of the Italians who looked to Piedmont's leadership. For his part Cavour claimed he was ready to support any English plans to achieve reform in the Papal States, but he warned there was small chance of success unless the pope's temporal power were separated from his spiritual power. So important did Cavour consider the matter that he himself dictated the parts of Hudson's dispatch to Malmesbury which reported Cavour's views on the Papal Question.[5]

2   Malmesbury to Derby, 27 Jan. 1859, Derby papers, 144/2.
3   Gramont to Walewski, Rome, 27 Jan. 1859, no. 7, AMAE, CP, Rome, 1009/199–200.
4   Shaftesbury to Emanuel d'Azeglio, 15 Jan. 1859, and Emanuel d'Azeglio to Cavour, London, 20 Jan. 1859, *Cavour e l'Inghilterra*, vol. II, part 1, 248–9, and 250.
5   Hudson to Malmesbury, Turin, 19 Jan. 1859, no. 28, *Gran Bretagna e Sardegna*, vol. VI, 337–9. Massari, *Diario*, 20 and 21 Jan. 1859, 122–3.

Cardinal Antonelli first learned from the newspapers something about English policy as sent to the other capitals. Then Count Colloredo, the Austrian ambassador in Rome, told the cardinal of private talks between Malmesbury and Count Apponyi, the Austrian ambassador in London, held during the first week of January at Heron Court, Malmesbury's country house. Malmesbury had there unmistakably indicated that English sympathies were against the pope and Austria in the coming crisis. Colloredo described Antonelli's reaction: 'The vast projects of which Lord Malmesbury had spoken with Count Apponyi were not very appealing to the cardinal, who recognized that they originated in the Anglicanism and the Protestantism from which English politicians knew very rarely how to free themselves.'[6] Antonelli, thus, had clear reason not to be receptive to any overtures from the English.

Not long after Odo Russell received the policy statement from the foreign office he got an opportunity to approach Antonelli in the manner Malmesbury desired. Malmesbury heard, via Vienna, that Antonelli had protested at an increase of the Austrian garrison at Ancona. He considered such a step by Austria to be a deliberately negative response to the English idea of Austrian and French co-operation to effect improvements in the Papal States.[7] The cardinal's protest delighted him, for it was the first time under the new circumstances of crisis that the papal government acted in a direction the English government wanted. Malmesbury instructed Odo by telegraph on 25 January to encourage Antonelli in that course.[8] Odo went to see Antonelli, and the cardinal informed him that he had indeed made such a protest, and that as a result the Austrians had decided not to increase but only to replace their troops in the Papal States. Antonelli expressed his gratitude for England's support. Since the subject of the troops was raised, the cardinal took the chance to reply to an argument often put forward in the past by the English and the Cavourians – that the need for foreign troops was convincing evidence of the incompetence and corruption of papal civil government. The troops, Antonelli argued, had been necessary originally to restore order after the revolution of 1849, and their continuation was needed to restrain the subversive activities of small numbers of devoted revolutionaries. But he was happy to report that this need was disappearing. The Papal States was now tranquil and the pope could govern his own people in security. The cardinal confidently told the English envoy, 'I can again return to the accomplishment of my favourite scheme, namely, the withdrawal of the French garrison to Civita Vecchia. For their presence here is in my opinion quite unnecessary and I have plenty of Papal troops at my disposal to maintain order at Rome.' Antonelli had last requested the withdrawal of the troops in October

6   Apponyi to Buol, London, 1 Jan. 1859, no. 1D, private, HHSA, PA, VIII, 47; and Colloredo to Buol, Rome, 15 Jan. 1859, no. 2A, HHSA, PA, XI, 200.
7   Malmesbury to Queen Victoria, London, 25 Jan. 1859, *Letters of Queen Victoria*, vol. III, 399–400.
8   Malmesbury to Odo Russell, 25 Jan. 1859, telegram, no. 10, draft, PRO, FO, 43/69.

1858.⁹ Antonelli's policy on the troops offered common ground on which the English and papal governments could meet.

The receptions of Malmesbury's statements in Vienna and Paris were not generally so hopeful, even though there were a few positive signs in Paris. Surprisingly, the best response came from the papal nuncio in Paris. Count Buol, the Austrian foreign minister, considered the suggestion of redistributing papal territory to be subversive of the treaties upon which the peace of Europe rested and thought it would create war instead of discouraging it. He regarded the idea of Austrian–French co-operation on papal reforms to be unworkable. They had tried it in 1857, but France, he claimed, had allowed the negotiations to drop. England ought to see France about that. In any case, he could no longer see any basis of agreement in proposing reforms to the pope, their Catholicism notwithstanding.¹⁰

In Paris, Cowley found Walewski equally aware of the differences between the Austrian and French governments. The 1857 negotiations had stopped, Walewski maintained, not because of French negligence but because of their failure to agree on the basis of reforms to recommend to the pope. Nonetheless, Walewski was willing at least to try to open negotiations once again. He suggested that England might serve as 'the medium of communication between the two Imperial Governments'.

The question of the redistribution of papal territory was another matter. Someone in the French Ministry of Foreign Affairs, possibly Walewski himself, had written in the margin of Malmesbury's policy statement 'utopia', and 'proposal to dismember the Roman States by common agreement'. Cowley thought the topic so controversial that he declined to raise it with Napoleon or Walewski. He thought Napoleon took seriously his role as guardian of the full integrity of the temporal power and so under present circumstances would not 'consent to any forced diminution of the Pope's temporal authority, still less to any encroachment on his dominions'. Cowley did not understand the duplicity of Napoleon's policy. He told Malmesbury his own opinion 'that nothing short of the overthrow of the Pope's temporal authority can afford a chance of better government; and even then, the elements for it must be looked for elsewhere than in the Papal dominions'.¹¹

Cowley's work in Paris left an unexpectedly good impression on the papal nuncio, Mgr Sacconi. He wrote to Antonelli saying that Cowley had spoken quite firmly to the emperor and urged him not to engage in war. Sacconi was sure

9   Odo Russell to Corbett, Rome, 28 Jan. 1859, no. 8, confidential, PRO, FO, 43/70, and *Odo Russell*, 4–6. Antonelli to Sacconi, Rome, 9 Oct. 1858, Pirri, vol. II, part 2, 43–4.
10   Loftus to Malmesbury, Vienna, 20 Jan. 1859, no. 52, and 27 Jan. 1859, no. 68, PRO, FO, 425/51/33–5, 49–50.
11   See copy of Malmesbury to Cowley, 10 Jan. 1859, no. 47, in AMAE, CP, Angleterre, 712/43–9. Cowley to Malmesbury, Paris, 14 Jan. 1859, no. 71, 19 Jan. 1859, no. 97, and esp. 19 Jan. 1859, no. 105, PRO, FO, 425/51/14–15, 29–31.

Tories, the pope, and peace

Cowley had given Napoleon the understanding that in the event of war England would at first remain neutral, but upon the first prospect of French victory would have to join with Austria in order to prevent French domination in Italy, an eventuality alien to English interests. This strong language, Sacconi happily reported, had caused the French government, including the emperor himself, to stop talking as if war were a likely possibility and to begin saying that only the violation of treaties would induce France to go to war. This Sacconi interpreted as a positive development.[12] Sacconi's report was not an accurate account of what Cowley explicitly *said* – for Malmesbury's policy statement, intended for Napoleon's ears, nowhere explicitly talked about English neutrality or English belligerence on the Austrian side – but it did more or less reflect the *impression* Malmesbury wanted Cowley to give.[13]

By the end of January, England was the only power to resist the movement toward war in Europe. The English government had assessed the crisis in such a way that it came to regard the question of the temporal power as central to the whole affair. Without mitigating its policy critical of the papacy, England had attempted to make the papacy amenable to its diplomacy. Remarkably, Malmesbury had found a point of contact with the papal government and had caused it to take an active interest in English efforts to prevent war. The papal government was beginning to realize that its own welfare depended, at least partly, on England's success in preventing a French–Sardinian war with Austria. Ironically, as the English government understood it, success in preventing war was related to its ability to convince Europe to put pressure on the pope to make reforms, the very reforms which the papal government believed could only endanger the welfare of the Holy See. It was, for the papacy, a complex state of affairs.

Naples, the papacy and England

While the English government pursued its diplomacy against war in the European theatre, two other sets of events unfolded which supported *rapprochement* between England and the papacy. They developed independently of the wider questions, but both had an important bearing on papal reactions to English policy. The first was the papal attempt to persuade England and France to renew diplomatic relations with the Kingdom of Naples. The second was the visit to Rome of the Prince of Wales, son of Queen Victoria and heir to the Protestant throne of England.

In October 1856, when Palmerston was prime minister, England had joined with France to break diplomatic relations with the Kingdom of Naples. The act was a protest against illiberal government in Naples, and, more precisely, against

12   Sacconi to Antonelli, Paris, 17 Jan. 1859, no. 1179, ASV, ASdS, 1859, 165/1/44–51, and Antonelli, vol. I, 16–17.
13   Beales, *England and Italy*, 40.

the refusal by the king of Naples, Ferdinand II, to adopt reforms proposed jointly by the English and French. As Cowley described it, they 'stigmatized the Neapolitan Government as perpetuating atrocities disgraceful in a civilized nation'.[14] In the autumn of 1858, the king of Naples hoped to re-establish those relations. The English and French did too. The times had changed, and so had the English government. Malmesbury did not consider the faults of King Bomba to be as great as Palmerston had. Moreover, as the international crisis developed and began to cause the English government grave concern, Malmesbury added two other reasons why he wanted renewed relations with Naples: it would help calm the troubles of Italy by reducing the range of animosities, and, quite practically, it would permit England to place a diplomatic minister at a crucial spot on the peninsula.

The English government allowed negotiations to begin in Berlin via the Neapolitan *chargé d'affaires* at the Prussian court. The English strategy was to find a formula requiring some reforms which, although genuine, were not too demanding. Malmesbury proposed that King Ferdinand release his political prisoners, including the well-known Luigi Settembrini and Carlo Poerio – whose trial in 1850 was so influential in turning Gladstone into an activist against the temporal power – and exile them to America.[15] Malmesbury's eagerness to restore relations with King Bomba, and the relative mildness of this formula, underscored, by contrast, how much more heinous he reckoned the papal government to be than the Neapolitan. In the meantime King Ferdinand asked Pius IX to act as a mediator in the negotiations with France.[16] The mediation never formally occurred, but since Pius cared about what happened to the king of Naples, who had so amply aided him in 1849, and since the pope considered Ferdinand's welfare to be tied to his own, he promised to do anything he could to help normalize the king's relations with the two great powers.

Early in January, on the occasion of the marriage of his son, the king proclaimed the amnesty Malmesbury had suggested, and sixty-six political prisoners were released and duly exiled.[17] Immediately afterward, on 14 January, Odo Russell received his first audience with the pope. Pius IX talked to Odo about the amnesty and commended it as an exceptional act of mercy. 'I hope this event may have the effect of making your Government and that of France renew diplomatic relations with Naples', he urged. Pius was anxious for Odo to convey this message to Malmesbury.[18]

Before anything else could happen, however, King Bomba proclaimed martial

14 Cowley to Malmesbury, Paris, 8 Oct. 1858, private, copy, Cowley papers, PRO, FO, 519/224/156–8.
15 Malmesbury to Cowley, 14 Oct. 1858, private, Cowley papers, PRO, FO, 519/196.
16 Cowley to Malmesbury, Paris, 17 Oct. 1858, private, copy, Cowley papers, PRO, FO, 519/224/164–5.
17 See Odo Russell to Malmesbury, Rome, 13 Jan. 1859, telegram, PRO, FO, 43/74.
18 Odo Russell to Corbett, Rome, 14 Jan. 1859, most confidential, PRO, FO, 43/70, and *Odo Russell*, 2–3.

law at Naples. Under such circumstances, Malmesbury decided on 18 January that in spite of the amnesty, he could not proceed to re-establish relations with Naples.[19]

The papal government did not know of Malmesbury's decision and continued its efforts to persuade the English and the French to restore relations with Naples. Antonelli instructed Sacconi, partly at Gramont's request, to approach Walewski about the subject.[20] On 21 January, Antonelli talked with Odo Russell about it, and Odo described the discussion to Malmesbury:

> His Eminence expressed to me in the strongest terms his anxious hope that the Governments of England and France would soon be induced to renew diplomatic relations with the King of Naples. 'Such a measure,' he said, 'would go a long way in calming the disturbed spirits of Italy, and would, more particularly at this moment, have a most beneficial effect throughout the country'.[21]

On 23 January Sacconi met with Lord Cowley in Paris to discuss the same issue. Then he spoke to Walewski.[22] On 5 February Antonelli wrote to Sacconi saying that he hoped the nuncio could find further opportunity to pursue the matter with Cowley.[23]

As things turned out both the papal and English governments simply dropped the subject. The sixty-six exiles persuaded the ship taking them to America to let them off in Ireland instead. They made their way to London, where a committee of Panizzi, Lacaita, Gladstone, Shaftesbury and the Duke of Argyle, publicized their case and offered them financial assistance appropriate to their class.[24] English–Neopolitan relations were not restored until June 1859, after the death of Ferdinand II and upon the accession of his son, Francis II.[25]

This papal–English interaction concerning Naples indicated that the concerns of the two governments for peace and social tranquillity in Italy coincided, although they arose from different grounds. Moreover, for a time, the papal government was trying to persuade the English of something, just as the English were hoping to persuade the pope of reform. The whole affair contributed to a mutual spirit of conciliation between the two governments.

19 Cowley to Malmesbury, Paris, 17 Jan. 1859, private copy, Cowley papers, PRO, FO, 519/224/272–3; and Malmesbury to Cowley, 18 Jan. 1859, private, Cowley papers, PRO, FO, 519/196.
20 Antonelli to Sacconi, Rome, 17 Jan. 1859, s.n., ASV, ANParigi, 1859, SdS, AD/P.
21 Odo Russell to Corbett, Rome, 21 Jan. 1859, no. 7, PRO, FO, 43/70, and *Odo Russell*, 4.
22 Sacconi to Antonelli, Paris, 23 Jan. 1859, no. 1185, and Paris, 1 Feb. 1859, no. 1190, ASV, ASdS, 1859, 165/1/55–7 and 64–5.
23 Antonelli to Sacconi, Rome, 5 Feb. 1859, no. 1595, ASV, ANParigi, 1859, SdS, AD/P.
24 *Gladstone diaries*, 8 March 1859 and *passim*; *The Times*, 15 April 1859.
25 See Sacconi to Antonelli, Paris, 3 June 1859, no. 1285, draft and Antonelli to Sacconi, Rome, 8 June 1859, no. 3907, ASV, ANParigi, 1859, SdS, AD/P. Also Pietro Giannelli to Antonelli, 28 May and 4 June 1859, ASV, ASdS, 1859, 165/9.

Queen Victoria's heir in Rome

Preparations for the visit of the Prince of Wales to Rome also drew the English government and the papacy together, although the occasion aroused new 'nopopery' discussion in England. No heir to the Protestant throne of England had gone to Rome since the Reformation, so when it was rumoured in November 1858 and finally publicly announced early in January 1859 that Albert Edward, the Prince of Wales, would reside in Rome for several months, considerable public concern was expressed.[26] There were fears expressed that the prince would be subjected to attempts to convert him or that he might become too friendly or too indifferent to popery, or perhaps be made susceptible to the temptations of Puseyism.[27] English and Irish Catholics, on the other hand, were absolutely delighted with the interest shown in Rome by the royal visit. They thought it could help improve the position of Catholics in England, the relations between the Irish and England, as well as the relations between England and the papacy. And there were Catholic hopes for his conversion.[28]

Queen Victoria and Prince Albert arranged the trip as part of their son's education upon his coming to the age of 17. The plan called for the young man to take the Grand Tour culminating in Rome, where he would study religion, history, art, Italian and music. After Rome would come sojourns in Edinburgh, Oxford and Cambridge, followed by some travel to North America.[29] The queen was particularly distressed about 'Bertie' and his seeming lack of interest in learning. She hoped that his new governor, Colonel Bruce, would do him good, as would the stay in Rome. There would be, she thought, 'opportunities of seeing and coming across much that is interesting'.[30] The visit was to be non-

26 Official court circular, in *Record*, 7 Jan. 1859. See *Record*, 17 Nov. 1858, for the early rumours of the visit. The *Record* was a general newspaper of low-church and evangelical Anglican perspective.
27 For example see: *Record*, 17 Nov. 1858, 5 Jan. 1859, and a letter from Mr J. Smith of Cambridge in the 16 Feb. 1859 issue. Also *The Times*, 28 March 1859, and *Tablet*, 15 Jan. 1859. Captain E.A.J. Harris/Malmesbury, Berne, Switzerland, 28 Feb. 1859, Malmesbury papers, 1859/2: 'I am not afraid of his becoming a Roman Catholic, but Puseyism is rampant there amongst our countrymen and women there, and I am afraid of his getting from them *unenglish* ideas' (underlining by Harris).
28 For example see: *Tablet*, 6 and 15 Jan. 1859, etc. Also Patrick F. Moran (a member of the Irish College, Rome) to Hugh Cullen, Rome, 27 Jan. 1859, *Paul Cullen*, vol. II, 225. The *Record*, 25 Feb. 1859, reproduces a leaflet picked up in a shop in Exeter: 'Novena for the Conversion of Albert Edward, Prince of Wales. Patron St. Peter. The Angelus at twelve o'clock – One Pater. Memorara.'
29 Prince Albert to Prince of Wales, 9 Nov. 1858, RA Z141/36; 'List of studies for Rome', n.d., RA Z444/30. Philip Magnus, *King Edward the Seventh* (London: John Murray, 1964), 28.
30 RA Queen Victoria's *Journal*, 6 Jan, 1859. Queen Victoria to Princess Victoria, Windsor Castle, 17 Nov. 1858, Roger Fulford (ed.), *Dearest child: letters between Queen Victoria and the Princess Royal 1858–1861* (London: Evans, 1964), 144. Prince Albert to Baron Stockmar, 15 Jan. 1859, Theodore Martin, *The life of the Prince Consort* (London: Smith, Elder, 1875–80), vol. IV, 353.

political and strictly educational, and no doubt, from the standpoint of the welfare of Albert Edward, it was. Victoria and Albert stipulated that he should travel officially as Baron Renfrew rather than as the Prince of Wales, so that all official ceremony and status due royalty could be waived in favour of the educational objectives of the Roman residence.

There were, however, inescapable political ramifications of the visit, not the least of which was its meaning to the papal government. In December 1858, at the queen's request, Odo Russell officially informed Pius IX and Cardinal Antonelli of the royal visit which would commence in February. They were overjoyed at the prospects of the son and heir of Queen Victoria residing for 'the season' in Rome and the States of the Church, especially at such a time of pending crisis. Pius, who had read the discussion about the visit in the press, said he considered it a great honour to Rome and himself, and he would be happy to receive the prince at the Vatican at any time. Antonelli took the greatest personal interest in the visit and promised to make it as congenial as possible.[31] It was the pope's desire that the future king of England would, as he told Odo, 'preserve a pleasant recollection of Rome in the future', and help transform English understanding of the condition and character of the papal government.[32]

For the queen and Prince Albert the royal visit required certain decisions which implied a will on their part to foster good relations with the papacy. First, even though the threat of war increased in January, they chose not to cancel the prince's journey, so valuable would the time in Rome be. They simply added the precaution of stationing a British warship at Civita Vecchia in case of sudden need to take the prince away.[33] The Rome correspondent of the *Tablet* reflected Catholic opinion in Rome on the importance of the visit not being cancelled: 'Should he [the prince] proceed on his journey in the face of proclaimed danger, and even seek this especially proscribed den of assassins, priestly and political, the world will regard the step as the best evidence of England's estimate of the state of affairs here.'[34] Secondly, Victoria requested that her son be granted an audience with the pope in spite of advice to the contrary and vocal anti-Catholic sentiments against it at home. She did so cautiously, of course, by stipulating as a safeguard the condition that her son be accompanied during the audience by Colonel Bruce. She explained afterward, 'It would never have done to have let Bertie go alone as they might hereafter have pretended God knows what

[31] Malmesbury to Odo Russell, 10 Dec. 1858, private, and Odo Russell to Malmesbury, Rome, 23 Dec. 1858, private, draft, Ampthill papers, PRO, FO, 918/6.
[32] Odo Russell to Corbett, Rome, 14 Jan. 1859, no. 1, most confidential, PRO, FO, 43/70, and *Odo Russell*, 1–3.
[33] Prince Albert to Baron Stockmar, 15 Jan. 1859, Martin, vol. IV, 353. Malmesbury to Queen Victoria, 11 Jan. 1859, RA J14/25. Malmesbury to Odo Russell, 13 Jan. 1859, no. 4, confidential, draft, PRO, FO, 43/69, approved by Lord Derby and the queen.
[34] *Tablet*, 22 Jan. 1859.

Bertie had said.'³⁵ The pope willingly agreed to the condition although it went against long-standing papal protocol for royal audiences.³⁶

Thirdly, with Malmesbury's approval, Victoria risked snubbing Victor Emmanuel and Cavour by the visit. In November 1858 when the Sardinian ambassador, Emanuel d'Azeglio, reported from London the rumour of the Prince of Wales' journey to Rome, he told Cavour that if the itinerary did not include Turin, it would be clear evidence of ill-will toward Sardinia.³⁷ Cavour agreed, and contended that it would slight the honour and credit of Victor Emmanuel and 'could not fail to affect the Political Condition of Italy'.³⁸ Cavour realized he had to avoid being affronted by the English if he could, and so asked Emanuel d'Azeglio to tell Malmesbury that he and Victor Emmanuel really liked the Tories and that the Whigs were a hundred times worse, and that the heir to the British throne really would be well-received if he were routed via Turin.³⁹ At Hudson's suggestion, Cavour wrote a flowery letter for the queen to see about the wonders of Sardinia's and England's liberal institutions, about Sardinia's special friendship toward England, and about how honoured the king would be to provide a brilliant reception for the young prince if he would travel by way of Turin. Simultaneously he wrote to d'Azeglio telling him to use all his eloquence 'to persuade Malmesbury of the necessity of doing something serious on behalf of Italy'.⁴⁰

The Prince of Wales, in fact, did not pass through Turin. Prince Albert gave as the official reason that the young prince needed to hurry to Rome for educational purposes; the real reason was Victoria and Albert's low opinion of Victor Emmanuel's personal character.⁴¹ Instead of taking the normal English route via Paris and Turin, he journeyed to Italy via Brussels, Augsburg and the Brenner Pass in Austrian Italy. He continued to Rome via Bologna, Ancona and the length of the Papal States.⁴² And instead of being fêted *en route* by Victor

35   Malmesbury to Queen Victoria, 10 Dec. 1859, RA J14/4. Clarendon to Prince Albert, 4 Jan. 1859, RA Z444/25. Queen Victoria to King Leopold, 15 Feb. 1859, *Paul Cullen*, vol. II, 285.
36   Odo Russell to Malmesbury, Rome, 12 Jan. 1859, private, Malmesbury papers 1859/7. Catholics thought the queen insisted on the prince being accompanied during the interview in order to prevent the pope from influencing him toward Catholicism. See for example: Cullen to Dr Leahy, Rome, 9 Feb. 1859, *Paul Cullen*, vol. II, 284.
37   Massari, *Diario*, 23 Nov. 1858, 70.
38   Hudson to Malmesbury, Turin, 12 Dec. 1858, copy, RA Z444/15. Massari, *Diario*, 27 Nov. 1858, 75.
39   Cavour to Emanuel d'Azeglio, Turin, 1 Dec. 1858, no. 69, *Cavour e l'Inghilterra*, vol. II, part 1, 240–3. Massari, *Diario*, 12 Dec. 1858, 85.
40   Massari, *Diario*, 3 Jan. 1859, 105. Cavour to Hudson, 5 Jan. 1859, *Gran Bretagna e Sardegna*, vol. VI, 313–14. Cavour to Emanuel d'Azeglio, Turin, s.d. (6 Jan. 1869), no. 70, *Cavour e l'Inghilterra*, vol. II, part 1, 244–5.
41   Prince Albert to Malmesbury, copy, 26 Dec. 1858, RA Z444/23; Hudson to Malmesbury, Turin, 12 Dec. 1858, copy, RA Z444/15.
42   Bruce to Odo Russell, Augsburg, 17 Jan. 1859, Ampthill papers, PRO, FO, 918/16. The prince received his visa to enter the Papal States at the Brussels nunciature. Mgr Matteo Eustachio Gonella (Brussells Nuncio) to Antonelli, Brussels, 13 Jan. 1859, no. 1107, ASV,

Emmanuel at Turin, he was guest of the papal apostolic delegate at Bologna and occupied the papal box at the opera.[43] The papal government followed the prince's journey at every stage, and the papal legates throughout the States of the Church received the English royal heir in the very best manner.[44] The journey from London to Rome occurred between 10 January and 3 February, during the period when the English government began to pursue its conciliatory policy toward the papacy and its resistance to the Sardinian manoeuvres toward war. Antonelli could be happy with the statement attributed to Colonel Bruce at Bologna: 'It is a matter of great importance that a hereditary prince of England visits Rome after so many centuries. I am pleased that this ice is broken.'[45]

The prince arrived in Rome without fanfare on 3 February and took up residence at the Locanda del 'Isole Britanniche on the Piazza del Popolo. He met Cardinal Antonelli at the Vatican the next morning and the cardinal returned the visit at the prince's hotel suite in the evening. 'We are in the midst of shoals and quicksand', Colonel Bruce reported to Prince Albert.[46] On 7 February the prince was received in audience by Pius IX, accompanied by Colonel Bruce as the queen had stipulated. The audience, which lasted ten minutes, was most congenial. After exchanging cordialities, the pope commented approvingly on Queen Victoria's emphasis on peace in her recent speech from the throne. He then lamented that the restoration of the Catholic hierarchy had caused such misunderstanding in England. Thinking the subject too delicate, Colonel Bruce decided to terminate the audience.[47] Although done politely, his action caused

ASdS, 1859, 227/79. The prince followed this itinerary through the Papal States: Bologna, Rimini, Ancona, Loreto, Foligno, Terni, Narni, Civita Castellana, Rome the same route, in reverse order, that Pius IX took on his triumphal tour of his states in 1857. A. Ercole (chancellor of the British consulate in Rome) to Cardinal Berardi (undersecretary of state), 24 Jan. 1859, ASV, ASdS, 1859, 227/83.

43 Cardinal Milesi (Papal apostolic delegate at Bologna) to Antonelli, Bologna, 27 Jan. 1859, ASV, ASdS, 1859, 227/85-6.

44 Antonelli to the apostolic delegates, Rome, 24 Jan. 1859, circular, draft, ASV, ASdS, 1859, 227/82. Odo Russell to Malmesbury, Rome, 15 Jan. 1859, telegram, PRO, FO, 43/74. See *Giornale di Roma*, 14 Jan. 1859.

45 Spoken to Count Diamoncini and reported by Cardinal Milesi to Antonelli, Bologna, 27 Jan. 1859, ASV, ASdS, 1859, 227/85.

46 Bruce to Prince Albert, Rome, 4 Feb. 1859, RA, Z444/46. Odo Russell to Malmesbury, Rome, 4 Feb. 1859, no. 10, PRO, FO, 43/70. The Rome correspondent of the *Tablet* commented on the fact that there was a heavy rain as the prince arrived in Rome: 'Had Shaftesbury and Co. engaged implurial Jove for an exhibition of his entire water works on the occasion, in order to throw cold water on his first impressions, the effect could not have been more complete' (*Tablet*, 11 Feb. 1859).

47 *Giornale di Roma*, 7 Feb. 1859. There are four accounts of the papal audience, one by Bruce (Bruce to Prince Albert, Rome, 7 Feb. 1859, RA Z444/48); and three by Prince Albert Edward: 1) RA *Diary of Albert Edward, Prince of Wales, 1859* for his personal use, in which he wrote one telegraphic sentence; 2) RA *Prince of Wales' Journal, Rome 1859* which he kept for practice in composition, to be corrected by his father, in which he wrote one plain paragraph – his father was so disappointed by it that he asked Edward to compose another entry about what was said and its historic significance; and 3) 'Visit to the Pope', a long and very interesting account of the papal audience, written to fulfil Prince Albert's request (included in the *Journal*).

some dissatisfaction, since protocol demanded that only the pope properly could end an audience. In spite of this *faux pas*, however, Antonelli and the pope expressed their pleasure with the occasion. Queen Victoria was pleased too.[48]

The Prince of Wales remained in Rome until 2 May when, because of the outbreak of the Austro-Sardinian war, he left for Gibraltar on the British warship stationed at Civita Vecchia. He never did visit Turin. While in Rome he followed a rigorous schedule of study under the tutelage of C.F. Tarver, went sight-seeing, and visited the Vatican museum and galleries, including a special night viewing as Antonelli's guest. He enjoyed some of the aristocratic social life of Rome, especially at Carnival time. He visited St Peter's often, once to see the tombs of the never-crowned Catholic Stuart kings of England. On St Patrick's day, he visited the Irish College where he was received by the rector and Archbishop Cullen; on Easter Eve he visited the English College. Both the English and Irish Catholics were pleased by his kindness toward them. He was not at all attracted to Catholicism, which he thought was filled with 'absurdities', and encumbered by 'monotonous', if impressive, rituals. In all, he thoroughly enjoyed his stay in Rome.[49]

In a second hour-long papal audience on 1 May, just before leaving Rome, he found Pius IX eager to talk. The pope told the prince that he thought the war would lead to troubles like those of 1848 and 1849, but that his trust was in God. He terminated the audience this time, urging the English royal heir 'to protect the Catholics, and ... be kind to them'.[50]

The Times and the *Tablet* both reported that the prince had won all hearts in Rome.[51] Mgr George Talbot, the pope's private chamberlain, thought the prince did badly, however – not only had Colonel Bruce terminated the first papal audience himself, but the prince's entourage in Rome had acted in 'the most shabby manner'.[52]

One event of special political consequence occurred in connection with his stay. Victoria and Albert had avoided Cavour on Bertie's journey to Rome, but Cavour had kept looking for a way to make some use of the visit. He needed to soften English opposition to him as his war plans unfolded. Two weeks after the prince's arrival in Rome he got the idea of having Victor Emmanuel award the

48   Bruce to Prince Albert, Rome, 17 Feb. 1859, RA Z444/54. Queen Victoria to King Leopold, 15 Feb. 1859, *Paul Cullen*, vol. II, 285.
49   *Diary of Albert Edward, Prince of Wales, 1859, passim*; Prince of Wales to Prince Albert, Rome, 20 Feb. and 25 March 1859, RA Z461/89 and 95. As a personal favour from Antonelli, the Prince requested permission to have photographs made of a number of paintings. Bruce to Antonelli, 11 Feb. 1859, Archivio Antonelli, Carteggio personale del Cardinal Giacomo Antonelli, Busta 1.
50   *Prince of Wales' Journal, Rome 1859*, 1 May 1859. Odo Russell to Malmesbury, Rome, 3 May 1859, private, Malmesbury papers, 1859/7. Bruce to Odo Russell, Rome, 25 April 1859, Ampthill papers, PRO, FO, 918/16.
51   See especially: *Giornale di Roma*, 8 March, 27 April 1859; *The Times*, 12, 26 and 28 March 1859; *Tablet*, 18 Feb., 16 and 30 April, 7 and 21 May 1859; *Record*, 18 Feb. 1859.
52   Talbot to Patterson, Vatican, 7 March 1859, Wiseman papers, Pre-1865/137/5.

prince the Order of Annunciation, the king's highest honour, as an expression of gratitude that 'the Prince of Wales has honoured Italy with a visit'.[53] To make sure the queen would approve the act, he asked Massimo d'Azeglio, who had a reputation with the queen as a conservative gentleman, artist and statesman, to agree to go on a special mission to Rome to present the award.[54] Victoria then agreed to it as well. The Prince of Wales duly attended a special ceremony in his honour in Rome on 5 March, apparently unaware of Cavour's ulterior motives.[55]

But there was a further purpose to Cavour's design than mere flattery to soften Queen Victoria. Cavour used the Prince of Wales as a cover to allow Massimo d'Azeglio to get into Rome to help maintain Cavourian influence over the nationalist party there. Odo Russell was aware of Cavour's use of the Prince of Wales in this way, and he mentioned it to Malmesbury after the award ceremony.[56] Massimo d'Azeglio's message to the Roman nationalists was twofold: they must bind their hopes to Piedmont's so that all nationalists can act with unity, and they must be tranquil and patient so that Cavour has time for his policy to unfold and Europe to act. So long as revolution did not break out in Rome, they could organize peaceful demonstrations and encourage soldiers to desert from the papal army and volunteer for the coming revolution in the Romagna.[57] The point was to do nothing which would create difficulties for Napoleon by disturbing the pope, or that would antagonize the English government by obvious conspiracy with Cavour. To the dismay of the papal government, which was well aware of what he was up to, Massimo d'Azeglio remained in Rome throughout March, in constant communication with members of the nationalist party.[58]

The visit of the Prince of Wales to Rome, clearly Queen Victoria's and Prince Albert's act, supported the Conservative government's strategy for *rapprochement* with Rome. It served the papal government's interest in good feelings with England, and, by a curious twist, even benefited Cavour, if only a little. Queen Victoria and Pius IX exchanged cordial letters of gratitude for the other's kindness.[59] Colonel Bruce summarized the balance he believed was achieved:

53   Victor Emmanuel to Prince of Wales, Turin, 20 Feb. 1859, copy, RA, Z444/67. Hudson to Malmesbury, Turin, 18 Feb. 1859, no. 56, *Gran Bretagna e Sardegna*, vol. VI, 362–3.
54   Hudson to Odo Russell, Turin, 20 Feb. 1859, Ampthill papers, PRO, FO, 918/43. Massari, *Diario*, 19 Feb. 1859, 142–3. The event marked the end of a political estrangement between Cavour and Massimo d'Azeglio.
55   Bruce to Prince Albert, Rome, 5 March and 7 March 1859, RA Z444/65 and 66.
56   Odo Russell to Malmesbury, Rome, 5 March 1859, private, Malmesbury papers, 1859/7. Isastia, 64–7, 70–4.
57   Cavour to Massimo d'Azeglio, Turin, 27 Feb. 1859, Chiala, *Cavour*, vol. III, 377–9. Massimo d'Azeglio to Eugene Rendu, 30 March 1859, and 10 April 1859, Eugene Rendu (ed.), *L'Italie de 1847 à 1865, correspondance de Massimo d'Azeglio* (Paris: Didier, 1867), 94–9. Alberto Maria Ghisalberti, *Massimo d'Azeglio: un moderator realizzatore* (Rome: Edizioni dell'Ateneo, 1953), 199–223. Ronald Marshall, *Massimo d'Azeglio: an artist in politics, 1798–1866* (London: Oxford University Press, 1966), 261–2.
58   Pirri, vol. II, part 1, 26–7. See Gramont to Walewski, Rome, 26 Feb. 1859, no. 15, AMAE, CP, Rome 1009/255.
59   Queen Victoria to Pius IX, Buckingham Palace, 20 May 1859, ASV, Archivio Pio Nono, Inghilterra, Sovrani. Pius IX presented gifts of gratitude to Queen Victoria and the prince,

Parliament and the question of the foreign troops

'[L]iberality and tolerance ... were shown by His Royal Highness contrasting in so marked a manner with the tone which too often pervades the press and society at home. Nevertheless I think that there were no undue concessions to papacy or the papists.'[60]

Parliament and the question of the foreign troops

By remarkable coincidence, the day the Prince of Wales arrived in Rome, 3 February, the English Parliament began a new session and devoted a major portion of its opening debate to the papacy. The French, Austrian and Piedmontese governments, as well as the papacy, had awaited the new Parliament with great interest. In analysing French conduct, Mgr Sacconi, the nuncio in Paris, conjectured that whether the emperor made war depended in part on the attitude taken by England in the new Parliament.[61] Sacconi thought that if there were a change in governments from Tory to Whig, bringing with it a stronger anti-papal and pro-Italian policy, Napoleon would feel freer to pursue war against Austria and thereby risk danger to the temporal power. Sacconi felt that the pope would be safer with the Tories.[62] It was not to be quite so simple.

When the new English Parliament convened on 3 February, both Tories and Whigs, in the Lords and the Commons, used the occasion to castigate the papal government. To everyone's surprise the principal focus of debate quickly became the question of the foreign troops in the Papal States. Up to this time the Conservatives had not raised questions about the Austrian and French occupation of the Papal States. Their policy depended on the analysis that reform of bad government was more fundamental than withdrawal of the troops or even termination of revolutionary initiatives. The Foreign Office survey of foreign affairs at the end of 1858 had even described the continued French occupations of Rome as 'not without advantage in some respects, as serving in some measure to control the proceedings of Austria in the north of Italy'.[63] Lord Derby had observed privately on 6 January that the evacuation of foreign troops

---

which he described as 'the work of Roman Artists, and thus a part of the industry of this country', no doubt a gentle reply to English criticisms of papal economic backwardness (Pius IX to Queen Victoria, Vatican, 3 June 1859, RA Z444/102). The gifts were: for the queen, a black and gold marble tripod table inlaid with scenes of papal and classical Rome, now at Osborne House, Isle of Wight, Queen Victoria's favourite residence; and for the prince, a mosaic picture of St George and the dragon, kept for a time at Marlborough House, London.

60 Colonel Bruce to Odo Russell, Holyrood Palace, Edinburgh, 13 Aug. 1859, Ampthill papers, PRO, FO, 918/16. Prince Albert Edward visited Rome again at the end of 1862, and Pius IX inquired about him several times during the 1860s. After he became king in 1901, he again visited the pope, the first reigning English sovereign since the Reformation to do so. He had a reputation of being friendlier to Catholics than Queen Victoria (see Owen Chadwick, *The Victorian church*, vol. II, 407). The 1859 visit perhaps had some enduring influence on the young prince.

61 Sacconi to Antonelli, Paris, 24 Jan. 1859, no. 1189, ASV, ASdS, 1859, 165/160-2, and *Antonelli*, vol. I, 20–1.

62 Sacconi to Antonelli, Paris, 31 Jan. 1859, no. 1195, ASV, ASdS, 1859, 165/1/70–3, and *Antonelli*, vol. I, 22.

63 'Confidential memorandum on the state of foreign relations at the close of the year 1858', 1 Jan. 1859, Derby papers, 144/2.

might even be sufficiently harmful to the state of affairs in the Papal States 'to induce England to pause before she takes the initiative in urging on either or both parties such a course of action'.[64] Only at the end of January – when Antonelli repeated to Odo Russell his desire for French troops to withdraw from Rome to Civita Vecchia – did the Conservative government take an interest in the topic.

It was the Whigs in Parliament who made it the vital issue. Lord Palmerston, responding to the queen's speech from the throne, singled out the expansion of French influence in Italy as a particular worry, and asserted that the presence of French troops in the Papal States was the facet of French influence which he found most objectionable. That Austria had troops there too only made it worse. This was, he urged, an exceptional state of things that was 'founded on a principle which we in this country do not approve', and it must be brought to an end. He largely agreed with Malmesbury's line of argument about reform and revolution, except that he regarded the use of foreign troops as the distortion most needing immediate attention.[65]

Benjamin Disraeli, responding for the Tories, had to agree with Palmerston's criticism of the troop occupations. He accepted the strategy of calling them the cause, at least externally, of the unsettled relations between France and Austria. He then explained the government's policy of trying to influence the papacy to make reforms.[66]

When it became Lord John Russell's turn to speak, he too attacked the presence of French and Austrian troops in the Papal States, but he made it part of a general attack on the whole papal government. He based his criticism on Gladstone's translation of Luigi Carlo Farini's history of the Roman States. The situation was so serious, he said, that it called for a far-reaching solution. It was good for England to encourage papal reform, but, he argued, 'There is one plan better than any of these, and that is that the people should be allowed to settle the law for themselves.' This was Russell's first public statement of the principle he would enunciate and follow when he came to power in June. If France and Austria would withdraw their troops now, without delay, the people of the Papal States would solve the problem themselves. He proclaimed, 'Let the people of Bologna, let the people of Romagna, form laws for themselves, and I believe the difficulty of Italy would be almost entirely solved. I believe there would be no need of this bloody war.' Russell envisioned the sort of plan for the separate treatment of the Romagna that Cavour had promoted at Paris in 1856, and suggested that the Romagnol electors would adopt a plan leaving them under the nominal suzerainty of the pope.[67]

The debate in the House of Lords followed a somewhat similar course. Lord Granville, leader of the Whigs in the Lords, also focussed his remarks on the

64 Derby to Disraeli, 6 Jan. 1859, draft, Derby papers, 187/1.
65 Hansard's, CLII, col. 74–5, 3 Feb. 1859.
66 Hansard's, CLII, col. 85–8, 3 Feb. 1859.
67 Hansard's, CLII, col. 94–100, 3 Feb. 1859.

Parliament and the question of the foreign troops

Papal States and especially the foreign troops which he claimed were the most urgent problem. He had just returned from a stay in Rome where he experienced papal rule for himself.[68] This brought Lord Derby to his feet to articulate the government's policy. He put the case against the Papal States with great force, just as the Conservatives had stated it in Malmesbury's January statement. In doing so, he emphasized that both the opposition and the government shared a common view on the subject. And like Disraeli in the Commons, he too now joined in the condemnation of the French and Austrian military occupations of the Papal States. This constituted an important revision of his own views. The principal cause of the current anxieties in Europe was, he proclaimed, 'that unhappy portion of Central Italy which is subject to the temporal jurisdiction of the spiritual head of the Roman Catholic Church'. He called it 'the real plague spot of Italy'. He agreed that the subjects of the pope would rise in revolution were it not for the presence of two foreign armies whose purpose was to maintain, not the liberties of Italy, but an incompetent and unjust government. Derby then explained in detail the government's strategy, through France and Austria, to urge reforms upon the pope. Nowhere in the debates in either House did the Conservatives mention their notion about the redistribution of the Papal States.[69]

The texts of the speeches in Parliament were published as usual in the newspapers, and for the first time the papal government heard from the English themselves an unmistakable account of what they were up to with their diplomacy. Pius IX himself read the speeches.[70] To make matters worse for the pope, the English debate in Parliament was followed on 4 February by the publication of a new French pamphlet sanctioned by Napoleon, *L'Empereur Napoleon III et l'Italie*, and by Napoleon's address at the opening of the French legislature on 7 February, both of which criticized the continuation of the foreign military occupations of the Papal States. Sacconi believed that Napoleon spoke as he did in order to echo the English Parliament, hoping thereby to impress the English with his pacific intent and his willingness to accommodate himself to their policy. At the same time he would make Italian nationalists happy.[71]

The seemingly unanimous attacks on the papal government in the English Parliament deeply troubled Cardinal Antonelli, especially since they occurred at the very time 'when the Pope heaped kindness and politeness upon the hereditary prince of the crown of England'. There was a real danger that the

---

68   Hansard's, CLII, col. 28–9, 3 Feb. 1859.
69   Hansard's, CLII, col. 42–6, 3 Feb. 1859.
70   Odo Russell to Russell, Rome, 17 July 1859, no. 89, secret, PRO, FO, 43/71, and *Odo Russell*, 38.
71   Sacconi to Antonelli, Paris, 12 Feb. 1859, no. 1203, ASV, ASdS, 1859, 165/1/85–90, and *Antonelli*, vol. I, 26. Napoleon's words in his address were: 'The state of Italy and the abnormal situation where order is maintained only by foreign troops has justly disturbed diplomacy' (quoted in Scott, 110).

Tories' conciliatory display toward the papal government would be taken as a ploy. The point that disturbed him most was the accusation that the pope could only maintain his political throne by means of two foreign armies. This was the charge which a new article in *Civiltà Cattolica*, the Jesuit journal, sought to answer.

Antonelli made a decision, and on 12 February he met with Gramont, and hinted that he thought the time had come for the pope to dispense with the help of foreign troops altogether, even without small garrisons at Civita Vecchia and Ancona.[72] Antonelli conveyed the same impression to Colloredo on the same day. The cardinal was anxious to talk about what the English were doing, about the Parliamentary debates and their diplomatic initiatives among the powers. Colloredo had kept Antonelli informed about English diplomacy in Vienna. Antonelli was pleased that Austria refused to co-operate with the English plan about papal reform which 'in the present time of excitement' could only embarrass and harm the papal government. The extraordinary idea of redistributing some of the Papal States appalled him. He praised Austria's view that the idea was subversive of the treaties upon which the good order of Europe rested. The question of troop withdrawal was different, however. Antonelli began describing to Colloredo the tranquillity of the Papal States and the strength and loyalty of the papal army, now numbering, he claimed, 17,000 men, and suggested that the papal government might be ready for the complete evacuation of the Papal States as early as the beginning of the new year.[73]

The following week Antonelli continued to be pre-occupied with the question of troop withdrawal. The criticisms from the English Parliament in particular still bothered him. Meanwhile Odo Russell began talks with Gramont on the kinds of reforms to urge on the papal government.

On 19 February Antonelli spoke to Gramont and Colloredo again. He affirmed his belief that the occupation of the Papal States was not responsible for creating unrest. Nevertheless, he indicated that since the foreign troops were an object of so much international concern the papal government was considering preparations to do without them. It was important, he said, that the papacy take the initiative in the matter and not act under outside pressure. Gramont raised the issue of reforms which, he suggested, would help remove the need for the occupation armies. Antonelli replied with a lengthy defence of the papal government as it stood, and emphasized that if he asked the French and Austrians to remove their troops, it would be because he regarded the situation in the papal territories to be stable as it was.[74]

72 Gramont to Walewski, Rome, 12 Feb. 1859, no. 11, AMAE, CP, Rome, 1009/214. 'La questione italiana nel 1859', *Civiltà Cattolica*, 4th Ser., vol. I (1859), 608–42, esp. sections 4, 5 and 6.
73 Colloredo to Buol, Rome, 12 Feb. 1859, no. 4A–B, HHSA, PA, XI, 200/45–8.
74 Colloredo to Buol, Rome, 19 Feb. 1859, telegram, HHSA, PA, XI, 200/51. Gramont to Walewski, Rome, 19 Feb. 1859, no. 12, AMAE, CP, Rome, 1009/223–33.

Parliament and the question of the foreign troops

Following the debates in Parliament, Palmerston and Russell felt that they, as opposition leaders, needed to act. Russell wrote to Palmerston:

> [I]t seems to me we shall be wanting in our duty if we allow the affairs of Italy to drift to war without urging upon our government the necessity of endeavouring to prevent such a calamity while it is yet time. This can only be done by the withdrawal of Austrian and French troops from the Pope's dominions. You are the best person to move in this matter, but if you do not like to interfere, I would do so. The question how is another matter.[75]

Before the Whig leaders could do anything, however, Malmesbury responded on his own to the parliamentary debates and their emphasis on the question of the foreign troops. He sent Odo Russell new instructions and told him to begin talking 'politics' with Antonelli. Two weeks earlier Malmesbury had sent Odo copies of the policy despatches to Cowley, Hudson and Loftus, so that he finally knew first-hand the full English policy.[76] He wrote to Odo on 12 February: '[S]hew him [Antonelli] how impossible it is after the cloud that has nearly burst over us and that still hovers to leave everything in Italy in statu quo. Her Majesty's Government want to prevent revolution and to thwart Cavour's ambitions and fatal policy.' Malmesbury was offering to the pope the opportunity for English–papal *rapprochement* in a common cause against common enemies – revolution and the ambitions of Cavour. For this to work, the pope had to make some changes in his government. The immediate problem, Malmesbury now made clear, was the presence of French and Austrian troops in the Papal States: 'What does Antonelli wish as regards them? Would he do without them with Swiss regiments? Would he do with a small garrison only at Civita Vecchia and Ancona of French and Germans? Send me a telegram when you have seen them.'[77]

Odo saw Antonelli on 21 February and presented Malmesbury's questions very cautiously, he said, in order not to overstep the limits of his unofficial status. But Antonelli, to Odo's amazement, responded precisely and conclusively.[78] With the Cardinal's authorization, Odo summarized Antonelli's reply in a telegram to London:

> The Cardinal desires me to inform Your Lordship confidentially that the condition of the Papal States is so satisfactory that he has demanded, in the name of the Pope, the early and complete withdrawal of the French and Austrian troops from the Papal States, and that their complete evacuation and the fulfillment of this request now rests with the governments of France and Austria.[79]

Antonelli thus took the step he had been moving toward for two weeks. Odo was

---

75 Russell to Palmerston, 13 Feb. 1859, Palmerston papers, 1859, GC/RU/496.
76 Malmesbury to Odo Russell, 28 Jan. 1859, no. 11, PRO, FO, 43/69.
77 Malmesbury to Odo Russell, 12 Feb. 1859, private, Ampthill papers, PRO, FO, 918/6.
78 Gramont to Walewski, Rome, 22 Feb. 1859, no. 14, AMAE, CP, Rome, 1009/246–9.
79 Odo Russell to Malmesbury, Rome, 22 Feb. 1859, telegram, PRO, FO, 43/74, and *Odo Russell*, 6.

the first to be informed of it; Gramont learned of it from Odo, since a request was not made to Gramont and Colloredo until the next day.[80] Pius IX himself had decided that the request should be made. He looked upon it as a reply to the criticisms raised by the English and French at the Congress of Paris in 1856 and by the French and Austrians in 1857.[81]

Malmesbury was elated with the outcome of his inquiry, especially since it allowed him to outrun Palmerston and Russell. He telegraphed Odo:

> Express the great satisfaction of Her Majesty's Government at the Cardinal's request for the withdrawal of troops. It would be of great use to us for the maintenance of peace and for the Cardinal's object if he would allow me to state in Parliament that he has done so or meant to do so, as Lord Palmerston is on Friday going to attack the Cardinal's policy and that of Her Majesty's Government in Italy. Reply immediately.[82]

Thus Malmesbury again sought to make common cause with the papal government. If he could break Antonelli's news in Parliament, it would help a lot of things – the cause of peace, Antonelli's aims, and, not the least, the Tory position against the Whig challenge. Malmesbury implied that Antonelli would be wise to work with the Tories in this way, since Tories would be better for the pope than the Whigs. Odo telegraphed Antonelli's response:

> Your Lordship is at liberty, to state in Parliament the facts reported by me, but the Cardinal begs you will not say they come direct from him and will remember that we have no official relations with Rome. The request for the withdrawal of the troops is official, earnest and sincere. France and Austria, he assures me, can confirm it to Your Lordship.[83]

As expected, Lord Palmerston delivered a vigorous speech in the Commons on 25 February. He asked the government to give an account of its policy and its efforts to calm the international crisis. As in the 3 February debates, he directed his chief criticism against the foreign military occupation of the Papal States and the distorted condition of the papal government which made it necessary.[84]

Disraeli seized the moment. He regretted he must decline to discuss the government's activity on the grounds that public debate could endanger the success of delicate undertakings then in progress. Nevertheless, he said he did have something to disclose: Her Majesty's Government had reason to believe that, at the pope's request, the troops of France and Austria would soon be evacuated from the Roman States. Lord Malmesbury revealed similar news to the House of Lords.[85]

80   Gramont to Walewski, Rome, 22 Feb. 1859, no. 13, and Rome, 22 Feb. 1859, no. 14, AMAE, CP, Rome, 1009/244–5, 246–9.
81   Pius IX to Antonelli, 22 Feb. 1859, Pirri, vol. II, part 2, 55–6.
82   Malmesbury to Odo Russell, 23 Feb. 1859, telegram, no. 22, PRO, FO, 43/70, and excerpted in *Odo Russell*, 7.
83   Odo Russell to Malmesbury, Rome, 24 Feb. 1859, telegram, PRO, FO, 43/74, and *Odo Russell*, 7.
84   Hansard's, CLII, col. 869–78, 25 Feb. 1859.
85   Hansard's, CLII, col. 878–81, and 855, 25 Feb. 1859.

Parliament and the question of the foreign troops

It was a coup for the Tories. The impact of these announcements was immense both in Parliament and among the politically-aware public. In the Commons there was loud and prolonged cheering as soon as Disraeli broke the news. Lord John Russell immediately commended the government for achieving such early success in its diplomacy in support of European peace, especially in relation to the Roman states.[86]

In Rome, Gramont and Colloredo assured Antonelli that their governments would certainly agree to the request of the papal government. Both ambassadors gave Odo the same assurance, although Odo felt they were somewhat displeased with the manner in which Antonelli made the request. Colloredo observed that complete evacuation would no doubt end the unhappy pressures placed on the papacy by English diplomacy, the debates in Parliament, and the French Emperor. Sacconi thought the same thing. General Goyon, the commander-in-chief of the French forces in Rome, openly talked about preparations for leaving. According to Odo, the news of the withdrawal of the troops was welcomed by virtually all parties of the Roman population, except for the staunchest ultramontanes, and 'the pleasure seeking members of the Roman aristocracy'.[87]

Cavour was terribly upset by the prospect of evacuation. He thought it could ruin his plans for the Papal States. He told Hudson that Disraeli's announcement complicated the Italian crisis. Cavour meant that the removal of the troops could lead to a premature revolution in Rome which would force Napoleon, under French Catholic pressure, to resume the occupation of the city with even greater stringency, upsetting thereby Cavour's time schedule for war and antagonizing England.[88] Suddenly Massimo d'Azeglio's mission to Rome, under the guise of giving honour to the Prince of Wales, seemed even more important to Cavour. 'What great fortune that Massimo will now be in Rome', he said. Cavour told Tito Lopez and Raffele Caraffa, two delegates from the *Comitato Romano* who had come to Turin for advice, to keep Roman liberals patient and obedient to Piedmont's strategy.[89] Cavour was forced to revise the memorandum he was preparing in answer to a request from Malmesbury that he specify his complaints against the papal government and Austria. The whole situation was embarrassing for him. He had to argue for measures he did not believe in: for the necessity of substantial reforms before evacuation and even for what he now considered to be the half-way measure of a separate administration for the Romagna and the Marches. What he really wanted was war and the absorption of the Romagna by Piedmont. Hudson, not knowing all of Cavour's

---

86   See the account in the *Tablet*, 4 March 1859. Hansard's, CLII, col. 881, 25 Feb. 1859.
87   Odo Russell to Malmesbury, Rome, 26 Feb. 1859, private, draft, Ampthill papers, PRO, FO, 918/6, Odo Russell to Malmesbury, Rome, 8 March 1859, no. 28, confidential, PRO, FO, 43/70, and *Odo Russell*, 7–10. Colloredo to Buol, Rome, 26 Feb. 1859, no. 5C, HHSA, PA, XI, 200/61–2,. Sacconi to Antonelli, Paris, 6 March 1859, no. 1215, ASV, ASdS, 1859, 165/1/119–24.
88   Hudson to Malmesbury, Turin, 26 Feb. 1859, telegram, no. 74; 26 Feb. 1859, no. 64; 27 Feb. 1859, no. 75, confidential; 28 Feb. 1859, private, *Gran Bretagna e Sardegna*, vol. VI, 369–76.
89   Massari, *Diario*, 28 Feb. 1859, and 11 March 1859, 153, 167. Isastia, 61–2.

intentions, took up Cavour's cause and warned Malmesbury that the evacuation project was probably a device of Napoleon and that it would harm the interests of Italy.[90]

The papal government formally requested the complete withdrawal of the troops on 11 March in identical letters to the French and Austrian ambassadors. The request carefully stated that the condition of the Papal States was healthy and that the papal government was now capable of maintaining order on its own, so that there was no longer any need for the foreign troops which the Catholic powers, sanctioned by all others, had so freely offered.[91]

There were risks in requesting evacuation, of course. Revolution could occur. Speculation abounded that Spanish troops might come to the pope's defence as replacements for the French and Austrians, an idea which, apparently, the Spanish government did not take lightly.[92] Pius IX revealed to Gramont that, in spite of the risks, he took this step with confidence, but he admitted that he experienced 'hesitations which tormented his soul'. Then, as Gramont described it, the pope explained why he went ahead anyway: '[T]he circumstances were urgent, and after *the unqualified insults* which had been heaped on him in the British Parliament, he could no longer hesitate. This decision placed on him obligations which he had weighed in advance and which he had resolved to accomplish.'[93]

It is clear that the English diplomatic campaign and the parliamentary debate of 3 February were a vital influence in leading Pius IX and Cardinal Antonelli to request the end of the military occupation of the States of the Church. It was the English, rather than the French, who had made the Papal Question paramount in Europe. Malmesbury was getting nowhere with his idea about new projects for papal reform and the redistribution of papal territory, but by drawing attention to these comprehensive concerns, and stimulated by the Whig opposition in Parliament, he contributed to Antonelli's and the pope's belief that troop evacuation was, by comparison, a simple step, and perhaps even a plausible one. The pope and Antonelli thought that requesting the removal of the troops would be the way for them to demonstrate that the Papal States was tranquil and that there was no need for papal reform or the partitioning of papal territory. They hoped in this way to stop the diplomatic pressures on the papal government. The

---

90   Mack Smith, *The making of Italy*, 266. Malmesbury to Hudson, 12 Feb. 1859, no. 33; Cavour to Hudson, Turin, 2 March 1859, *Gran Bretagna e Sardegna*, vol. VI, 355–8, and 377–8. Sardinian memorandum, 1 March 1859, PRO, FO, 425/51/114–18.

91   Antonelli to Colloredo, Rome, 11 March 1859, no. 1400, HHSA, PA, XI, 200/83–6. Antonelli to Gramont, Rome, 11 March 1859, copy, *Antonelli*, vol. I, 44–5. Odo Russell to Malmesbury, Rome, 13 March, 1859, telegram, PRO, FO, 43/74.

92   Barrot (French ambassador in Madrid) to Walewski, Madrid, 9 March 1859, no. 44, *La guerra del 1859 nei rapporti tra la Francia e l'Europa*, ed. Armando Saitta (Roma: Instituto storico italiano per l'età moderna e contemporanea, 1961), vol. IV, 1475–6.

93   Gramont to Walewski, Rome, 17 March 1859, no. 22, AMAE, CP, Rome, 1009/302–3. Underlining is Gramont's: '*les insultes inqualifiables*'.

Parliament and the question of the foreign troops

English government's essentially anti-papal appraisal of the States of the Church continued to underlie its policy toward the papacy, but in the interests of thwarting the ambition of Cavour and preventing the possible involvement of France in a war with Austria, Malmesbury believed it necessary, not only to conciliate the papacy, but to find common cause with the papacy directly. The outcome, to this point in time, of the question of the foreign troops in the Papal States seemed to him to validate his approach.

English–papal relations at the end of February now became absorbed in a second development which Disraeli disclosed in Parliament on 25 February.

4 Tories, the pope, and war

The Cowley mission and the pope

When Benjamin Disraeli announced on 25 February that the pope would soon request the withdrawal of the French and Austrian troops from the States of the Church, he made a second announcement which equally gratified Parliament. The English government, he said, had decided to send Lord Cowley to Vienna on a special mission of peace, and at that moment, in fact, the English ambassador was *en route* to the Austrian capital.[1] Cowley arrived on 27 February and remained until 10 March, during which time he held extensive talks with Emperor Francis Joseph, Count Buol, and many other persons. The papacy figured as a major issue in the discussions.

The mission could not have been more timely from the standpoint of the Papal Question, although neither the papacy nor the English government knew just how timely it was. While Cowley was in Vienna, the pope and Antonelli were preparing the official request for the complete evacuation of the two armies; the document was finally issued on 11 March.[2] At the same time, unknown to the papal government, the Italian National Society intensified its conspiracy to overthrow papal temporal power in the Romagna, the very thing the troop occupations had been designed to protect the pope against. On 1 March the National Society sent secret instructions, signed by La Farina as secretary and Garibaldi as vice-president, to all its agents in central Italy. It was a fifteen point scheme outlining how to start a revolutionary uprising as soon as Cavour succeeded in precipitating war against Austria, and how to form a provisional government to take over when the established authorities were overthrown. The Bologna committee immediately began extensive preparations for the coming revolution.

---

[1] Hansard's, CLII, col. 878–81, 25 Feb. 1859. See also Lord John Russell's pleased response, col. 881–2, 25 Feb. 1859. Two articles which usefully discuss the Cowley mission more generally are: Franco Valsecchi, 'L'Inghilterra e la questione italiana nel 1859, la missione Cowley (27 febbraio–10 marzo 1859)', *Archivo storico italiano*, CXXVI (1968), 479–94; and Magda Jaszay, 'La questione italiana nei rapporti anglo-austriaci duranti la crisi del 1859', *Rassegna storica del Risorgimento* 52 (1965), 557–78.

[2] Malmesbury to Queen Victoria, 22 Feb. 1859, and Derby to Queen Victoria, 23 Feb. 1859, RA J15/84 and 86.

The Cowley mission and the pope

Simultaneously, on still another front, Mazzini issued a declaration in London intended to coalesce the revolutionary democrats in Italy. None of these conspirators could be pleased with the Cowley mission.[3]

Lord Malmesbury and Lord Derby came to the idea of sending Cowley to Vienna in response to Walewski's suggestion that England might serve as 'the medium of communication' between France and Austria. Malmesbury picked up some remarks by Walewski, and turned them into concrete topics to serve as the focus of Cowley's mission.[4] Cowley sounded out the French government, and was told on 16 February that Napoleon accepted the English proposal. This meant the special mission would indeed take place, even though the English did not know that Napoleon's support actually was worth very little. As the emperor told Cavour's agent in Paris, he was quite sure nothing would come of the mission, but it was important 'to have the appearance of believing in the possibility of a diplomatic solution'.[5] Cowley went to London where, on 22 February, Malmesbury gave him a summary of four points which the English government believed and hoped were obtainable. These objectives of the English mediation were, according to Malmesbury's formulation:

(1) Evacuation of the Roman States by Austrian and French troops;
(2) Reforms of administration in the same States, either on the plan put forward by the Great Powers in 1832, or by France and Austria in 1856–7;
(3) A security for the better relations between the governments of Austria and Sardinia;
(4) The abrogation or modification of the Austro-Italian Treaties of 1847, which are peculiarly obnoxious to the feelings of this country, inasmuch as the 111th Article of that between Austria, Modena, and Parma, lay the former under an obligation to interfere with and suppress any popular expressions of opinions in the latter States.[6].

A few observations about these points can be made. It is noteworthy that three of the four points were directly relevant to the papacy. In fact, Malmesbury contemplated designing the mission 'to refer entirely to the position of the Papal States as recommended in my despatches to Paris and Vienna of last month'.[7] Two of them – evacuation and reform – exclusively pertained to the papacy. Point four would involve the papacy since talk about abrogating the Austrian

---

3   La Farina, vol. II, 137. Grew, 181–90. Mazzini's declaration was dated 28 Feb. 1859 (Mack Smith, *Making of Italy*, 263–65).
4   Cowley to Malmesbury, Paris, 10, 11 and 14 Feb. 1859, private, copies, Cowley papers, PRO, FO, 519/225/47, 50 and 55–7; Malmesbury to Cowley, 13 Feb. 1859, separate, PRO, FO, 425/51/76–7.
5   Nigra to Cavour, Paris, 28 Feb. 1859, *Cavour–Nigra*, vol. II, 42.
6   Malmesbury to Cowley, 22 Feb. 1859, separate, PRO, FO, 425/51/92. The four points were finally formulated during Cowley's conversations with Derby and Malmesbury at the Foreign Office. Disraeli, who had an acute sense of the crisis character of Italian affairs, offered his own four points which were partially reflected in the final version (Disraeli to Derby, 20 Feb. 1859, Derby papers, 145/6).
7   Malmesbury to Prince Albert, 17 Feb. 1859, RA J15/56.

anti-revolutionary treaties naturally raised the question of what should take their place. Any new device would have to embrace all the central Italian areas, including the Romagna. The emphasis given to troop evacuation meant that England accepted the task of getting Antonelli actually to make the official request, and then of obtaining Austrian and French compliance with it. Malmesbury persisted in his standing analysis that, ultimately, only reform of the worst state in Italy could avert war and revolution, yet out of prudence he dropped all reference to possible redistribution of the States of the Church. All this meant that, contrary to Antonelli's hopes, the papal request for troop evacuation did not silence talk against the papacy or stop English diplomatic pressure in favour of papal reform. Instead, with the Cowley mission, England increased its pressure on the papacy all the more.

Odo Russell informed Cardinal Antonelli of the mission on 26 February.[8] Antonelli chose to regard the mission favourably while awaiting word of its outcome. But there were some misgivings in papal circles. During Cowley's time in Vienna, Antonelli was preoccupied with the mission and very anxious to get news about it, especially when the nuncio in Vienna failed to send him any reports immediately.[9] The nuncio in Paris was pleased that England, along with Prussia, was acting so 'moderately' during the crisis and that Cowley's mission was devoted to preventing war, but he had hesitations about it. The way he analysed things, the Cowley mission could force Austria to take one of two routes. Either Austria could accept the Cowley points, and begin to withdraw from predominance in central Italy as well as to promote reforms in the Papal States, actions the pope could not support, or it could reject them, and move irresistibly toward a war which would certainly not benefit the Papal States. Thus Sacconi believed the papacy would lose either way. He urged Antonelli to determine what policy to follow should either route be taken. DeLuca, the nuncio in Vienna, admitted that he too was deeply troubled, especially by the prospect of a premature evacuation of troops from the Papal States, and by England's and Cowley's urgent insistence on the evacuation. He acknowledged that this anxiety had led to his silence on the Cowley mission. He had not known what to do.[10]

8 Malmesbury to Odo Russell, 25 Feb. 1859, no. 21, telegram, PRO, FO, 43/69. Odo Russell to Antonelli, Rome, 26 Feb. 1859, private, draft, Ampthill papers, PRO, FO, 918/11. Sacconi to Antonelli, Paris, 24 Feb. 1859, no. 1209, ASV, ASdS, 1859, 165/1/110–17, and *Antonelli*, vol. 1, 36–7.
9 Antonelli to Mgr Alessandro Franchi, Rome, 14 March 1859, no. 1410, draft, ASV, ASdS, 1859, 165/11/19. Odo Russell to Malmesbury, Rome, 5 March 1859, private, Malmesbury papers, 1859/7. Gramont to Walewski, Rome, 5 March 1859, no. 18, AMAE, CP, Rome, 1009/272. Antonelli to DeLuca, Rome, 12 March 1859, s.n., draft, ASV, ASdS, 1859, 165/1/137.
10 Sacconi to Antonelli, Paris, 24 Feb. 1859, no. 1209, ASV, ASdS, 1859, 165/1/110–17, and *Antonelli*, vol. 1, 36–7. DeLuca to Antonelli, Vienna, 18 March 1859, private, ASV, ASdS, 1859, 165/1/137–8. Antonelli to DeLuca, Rome, 25 March 1859, no. 1780, draft, ASV, ASdS, 1859, 165/1/139–40.

The Cowley mission and the pope

Lord Cowley found Emperor Francis Joseph and Count Buol very amenable to discussion, and the talks, punctuated by balls and ceremony, went easily. At the end, Cowley surveyed what he thought had happened. He believed that the two points which directly concerned the papacy – evacuation and reform – had created little difficulty. Austria was ready to comply with the request for troop withdrawal, perhaps considering with France an intermediate withdrawal to Civita Vecchia and Ancona. On reforms, according to Cowley, Buol was willing to press again for papal reforms, preferably along the lines of the 1832 recommendations, although the 1856–7 negotiations between France and Austria could be resumed if France would take the next step. According to the papal nuncio in Vienna, however, Buol gave him a different impression, that Austria would never co-operate in imposing reforms on the papacy or any other Italian state.[11] On point four, Cowley reported that the Austrians were not adverse to the abrogation of the Austro-Italian treaties of 1847, provided that some effective replacement for them could be found. He said that Buol would prefer the alternative of neutralizing Piedmont, but that he would consider the formation of a league among the smaller Italian states for their mutual security against civil disorder; the league might include the Papal States. Buol's appearance of co-operation with the English was not entirely sincere, but he did win Malmesbury's favour by it and gained some points in the diplomatic game against France and Sardinia.[12]

Malmesbury considered the Cowley mission successful and requested Odo Russell to discuss these results with Antonelli. Malmesbury reported to Odo that Austria had agreed 'to advise and support Reforms in the Papal States on the basis she proposed in 1856 and 1857', but he instructed Odo not to tell this to Antonelli. Instead he should give the cardinal this report:

> As to Reforms say that I have told Austria, France, and Sardinia that we are persuaded that Reforms would tend both to the benefit of the Roman people and to the security of the Papal Authority but that as a Protestant country we do not desire to take the initiative or to appear in the front line. Still for the sake of Peace and conservative principles we hope he will himself stop Cavour by putting public opinion on his side.[13]

On 15 March, Odo had a lengthy interview with Antonelli in which he spoke just as Malmesbury instructed him. The cardinal said he took for granted that Austria would withdraw its troops as requested, and he thought the duchies

---

[11] Cowley to Malmesbury, Vienna, 9 March 1859, separate, PRO, FO, 425/51/141–3. See also: Cowley to Malmesbury, Vienna, 3, 4 and 6 March 1859, private, copies, Cowley papers, PRO, FO, 519/225/68–9, 72 and 75. Banneville to Walewski, Vienna, 22 Feb. 1859, no. 22, *La guerra del 1859*, vol. I, 132–4. Buol to Colloredo, Vienna, 12 March 1859, circular, draft, HHSA, PA, XI, 199/71–2. DeLuca to Antonelli, Vienna, 16 March 1859, no. 609, and 18 March 1859, private, ASV, ASdS, 1859, 165/1/135–6, 137–8.
[12] Cowley to Malmesbury, Vienna, 9 March 1859, separate, PRO, FO, 425/51/141–3. A.J.P. Taylor, *The struggle for mastery in Europe, 1848–1918* (Oxford: Clarendon, 1954), 109.
[13] Malmesbury to Odo Russell, 10 March 1859, private, Ampthill papers, PRO, FO, 918/6.

surely had the right to make treaties for their own safety without European interference. As Malmesbury expected, however, Antonelli was not at all ready to discuss the subject of papal reform. He said, strangely, he could not recall any reform plans proposed in 1856 and 1857. He spoke only a few words in justification of the papal government and then would say no more. In general Antonelli insisted that England was putting its diplomatic pressure on the wrong spot. In his judgment it was the Sardinian government and its agents throughout the peninsula who were responsible for bringing the crisis upon Italy and Europe, not the papal government. Nevertheless, he told Odo, he was 'convinced of the good intentions of Her Majesty's Government'.[14]

The English perhaps had some reason to be pleased with the ambivalent response by the papal government. It is likely that the Cowley mission was an influence in leading Antonelli to go ahead with the official evacuation request, dated 11 March; as Odo Russell observed, the request was by no means automatic, and the papal government did hesitate and delay in preparing and issuing it.[15] Antonelli could have taken a position of outright rejection of the results, and closed off any further communication with England on the subject. It seems evident that Malmesbury was aware of this possibility, and for that reason worded the report to Odo about the results of the talks on reforms the way he did. He still hoped to persuade the pope and Antonelli to adopt reforms. With this goal in mind, he did not want them to feel that England had achieved a *fait accompli* with Austria, or that the English were even pressing for reforms, although they certainly were. Instead he wanted the papal government to feel itself on England's side, bound by common Tory and papal abhorrence of Cavour and commitment to 'conservative principles'. Taking all this into account, Malmesbury could be glad that at least Antonelli believed the Tory government was not hostile to the papacy but had only good intentions, an admission the cardinal continued to make to France and Austria during the next two weeks. Nonetheless the papacy moved no closer to considering reforms as the English desired. At the same time Antonelli seems to have felt an underlying hurt because of English diplomatic activity. When Sacconi complained that the English, along with the pope's enemies in France, put too much pressure on the papacy and spread too many false tales about the papal government, and that the pope needed to put a stop to it by publicizing the truth about the Papal States, Antonelli simply replied that they already knew the truth, but they preferred to dwell on falsehoods.[16]

14 Odo Russell to Malmesbury, Rome, 15 March 1859, no. 31, confidential, PRO, FO, 43/70, and *Odo Russell*, 10–13.
15 Odo Russell to Malmesbury, Rome, 8 March 1859, no. 28, confidential, PRO, FO, 43/70, and *Odo Russell*, 7–10.
16 Sacconi to Antonelli, Paris, 19 March 1859, no. 1229, ASV, ASdS, 1859, 165/1/141–4, and *Antonelli*, vol. I, 52–4; Antonelli to Sacconi, Rome, 26 March 1859, no. 1802, ASV, ANParigi, 1859, SdS, AD/P, and *Antonelli*, vol. I, 57–8. Colloredo to Buol, Rome, 26 March 1859, no. 9A–C, HHSA, PA, XI, 200/104–5.

The proposed congress

On other fronts, the English government had reason to feel the Cowley mission had been less than successful. The Austrians, though remaining amicable, spread the word that since Cowley's mission was informal in status and carried no direct propositions to Vienna, the Austrian government could accept no propositions nor offer any alternative ones. The nuncio in Vienna claimed that when everything had settled down after Cowley's departure 'the condition of things remains unchanged'.[17] When Cowley returned to the French court and saw Walewski on 17 March, the foreign minister expressed disappointment with the results of the mission to Vienna, and then told Cowley some astonishing news: France had agreed with Russia to support the proposal of a congress of the five powers on the Italian question. Napoleon had gone ahead with his own separate project without waiting to discuss with Cowley his findings at Vienna. The French Emperor had not given the Cowley mission a chance to succeed; he did not even allow it to reach completion.[18]

The proposed congress

It seems that the idea of a congress originated with Napoleon himself as a device to undercut the Cowley mission and English mediation while appearing nonetheless to support a diplomatic effort to prevent war.[19] By diverting attention to a congress, which in any case might never convene, Napoleon could perhaps evade English diplomatic pressure.

Malmesbury decided to take the initiative and, although not favouring a congress, he set out to predetermine its agenda. On 19 March, before the Russians officially proposed a congress, the English Cabinet agreed to support it on the condition that the powers adopt as the basis of their discussion the four points which Cowley took with him to Vienna.[20] The version of the four points now presented by Malmesbury modified the one used by Cowley earlier. The two points which pertained directly to the Papal States – evacuation and reform – remained the same except that the one on reform was enlarged to include the duchies of Parma, Modena and Tuscany. The point about securing better relations between Austria and Sardinia was unchanged. The principal change was a modification of point four about the Austrian treaties with the duchies. As a result of the Cowley mission this one was reworded to emphasize what should replace the treaties. The text read: 'The substitution for the Treaties between

---

17 DeLuca to Antonelli, Vienna, 20 March 1859, no. 613, ASV, ASdS, 165/1/146–7.
18 Cowley to Malmesbury, Paris, 18 March 1859, separate, and 25 March 1859, no. 330, confidential, PRO, FO, 425/51/168–70, and 193.
19 This is a point debated by historians, but see Prince Napoleon to Cavour, 30 March 1859, *Cavour–Nigra*, vol. II, 146. Also see Valsecchi, 'La missione Cowley', 493–4. Especially helpful on the congress in general is Hearder, 'Foreign policy of Lord Malmesbury', ch. 8.
20 Malmesbury to Malakoff, 19 March 1859, *La guerra del 1859*, vol. III, 221. Cowley to Malmesbury, Paris, 18 March 1859, separate, PRO, FO, 425/51/168–70. Hearder, 'Foreign policy of Lord Malmesbury', 318–28.

Austria and the Duchies of a confederation of the minor States of Italy among themselves for their mutual internal and external protection.' The new confederation was intended to include the Papal States. Thus three of the four points in this new version proposed by England as the basis of the congress explicitly involved the papal government. The English government added a further condition, sometimes treated as a fifth point, that a congress should not consider anything which interfered with the present territorial arrangements in Italy, or in any other way meddled with the treaties of 1815. What this meant for the papal territory remained to be seen.[21]

Malmesbury vigorously sought to persuade the powers to accept England's condition about the four points. Parallel to this he led a complex negotiation to determine the composition of the congress, a question which involved whether or not Sardinia and the pope would be included.

The French, partly to pacify the English, quickly agreed to adopt the four points for the congress. Besides diverting English pressure away from France directly, Napoleon could actually promote one of his long-standing special interests, which the new fourth point included – an Italian confederation involving the pope. He had even incorporated a confederation point in the Plombières agreement with Cavour in July 1858. Moreover, by accepting the authority of the congress to decide on evacuation, Napoleon could escape personal blame for any bad consequences resulting from the withdrawal of his troops from the Papal States.[22]

Prussia and Russia readily agreed to adopt the four points for the congress. If a congress occurred, Protestant and Orthodox powers – England, Prussia and Russia – would have a hand in determining the pope's affairs.

Getting Austria to accept the four points as the basis of the congress was a different story. Count Buol's first response was firmly opposed to submitting either the question of papal reforms or the evacuation of the Papal States to a European congress. Such matters concerned the internal affairs of the States of the Church, he argued, and lay beyond the competence of a congress. Similarly, Buol considered the subject of the Austrian treaties to be primarily a topic of discussion between Austria and the Italian states, and not the concern of a congress either. The only things the Austrian government believed a congress would be competent to take up were support of the rights of treaties and opposition to the disruptive activities of Sardinia on the Italian peninsula.[23]

21 Malmesbury to Malakoff, 22 March 1859, *La guerra del 1859*, vol. III, 226–9. Malmesbury to Cowley, 21 March 1859, no. 298, PRO, FO, 425/51/166. The version Loftus gave to Buol combined the two points on evacuation and reform into one and treated as the fourth point the condition that no territorial arrangements be discussed nor the 1815 treaties be touched. Malmesbury later corrected Loftus on this. Loftus to Buol, Vienna, 28 March 1859, and Malmesbury to Loftus, 6 April 1859, *Parliamentary papers, 1859* (Sess. 2), vol. 32, 173, 198.

22 Walewski to Malakoff, Paris, 24 March 1859, no. 43, and Walewski to Banneville, Paris, 17 March 1859, telegram, and 22 March 1859, no. 36, *La guerra del 1859*, vol. III, 1056–8, and vol. I, 153 and 157–8.

23 Loftus to Malmesbury, Vienna, 21 March 1859, no. 193, PRO, FO, 425/51/204; Banneville to Walewski, Vienna, 24 March 1859, no. 36, *La guerra del 1859*, vol. I, 161–3.

The proposed congress

Malmesbury combated these arguments both in talks with the Austrian ambassador in London and by means of a flurry of telegrams between London and Vienna during the last ten days of March. He disclaimed any desire for England or a congress 'to impose any such reforms upon any independent state', but he did believe the European powers possessed the competence to propose 'a kind of Reform Bill for their administrations', as he described it to Count Apponyi, and urged that the advice be accepted. Concerning evacuation, Malmesbury argued emphatically that the European powers not only were competent to handle the issue, but they had a duty to help end 'a permanent occupation never contemplated by any school of statesmen or any category of Treaties'. Malmesbury would not accept the separation of the two primarily papal issues from the four points.[24]

Malmesbury reassured Austria that territorial questions in general would be excluded from the congress, but in the process he revived the issue of the redistribution of the pope's territory which he had left dormant since early in January. He told Apponyi that while the congress must not discuss territorial issues, England thought it could properly consider territorial changes in the States of the Church provided Austria and France could reach prior accord on what changes ought to be made. Malmesbury wished to keep the way open to consider the radical solution of the Papal Question: taking away at least some of the pope's territory.[25]

Malmesbury's and Loftus' work in Vienna brought results. By the end of March the Austrian government gradually came to accept the four points as the basis of the congress, although it insisted on a distinctive interpretation of them. Buol agreed to let the congress discuss the evacuation of the Papal States, but only to determine that they be evacuated and when it should occur. He agreed, too, that the congress could debate the question of papal reforms, and that the results of its debate could be presented to the papal government and other Italian states, but only as advice; the powers should use no coercion to enforce their will. He also agreed that the congress could consider the alternatives to the Austro-duchies treaties, including the proposal of a league formed by the states of central Italy. He added that the validity of the treaties could not be discussed and that all the other powers must allow their treaties with Italian states to be raised for discussion as well.[26]

By 1 April Malmesbury essentially had what he wanted on the matter: it appeared that the powers were taking diplomatic steps to forestall war, and the troublesome Papal Question remained at the centre of European diplomacy. But as soon as he gained his way, Austria and Sardinia were, on their own, rushing

---

24 Malmesbury summarized his arguments of the ten-day period in Malmesbury to Loftus, 30 March 1859, no. 174, PRO, FO, 425/51/221–3. See also: Apponyi to Buol, London, 21 March 1859, no. 25B, and 22 March 1859, no. 26, HHSA, PA, VIII, 48/521 and 544–6.
25 Apponyi to Buol, London, 21 March 1859, no. 25 A–B, HHSA, PA, VII, 48/517/518.
26 Loftus to Malmesbury, Vienna, 29 March 1859, and Buol to Loftus, Vienna, 31 March 1859, *Parliamentary papers, 1859* (Sess. 2), vol. 32, 174, and 188–9.

toward war, and the powers became fully absorbed with the problem of the mutual disarmament of Sardinian and Austrian troops.[27] By then the disarmament question became entangled with the other topic of vital significance to the papacy, the composition of the congress.

The problem of the membership of the congress emerged as soon as the project was proposed. The question of whether to include the papacy in the congress was always important to the negotiations. Malmesbury initially wanted to exclude the Papal States as well as the other Italian states, and restrict the congress to the five major powers. His grounds were partly the Tory principle that only the five powers had the authority to settle issues of European consequence, partly his disdain of conducting European affairs with Sardinia, and partly his desire to avoid the 'Babel' of the Italian states fighting among themselves. He envisioned that if the major powers met alone they would check off the four points by a neat process:

> The Five Powers to meet at Aix and begin by the question of the Reform for the Papal States (query Duchies also?). Having framed our scheme send it for submission to Rome and the Three Duchies for observations and approval. *By this we save time* and while they consider our Reforms the Conference to proceed with the question of finding a substitute for the *Austro-Italian Treaties* and the best mode of *Evacuation*.[28]

Both France and Austria, for different reasons, objected to excluding the Italian states. Napoleon took the position that all the Italian states ought to be represented on equal terms with the five major powers, although he eventually accepted a modified solution thought up by England. Count Buol at first also argued that all the Italian states should be present, especially the pope, since the congress would deal so much with papal affairs.[29]

Faced with this opposition Malmesbury suggested a compromise on 23 March – the Italian states could be admitted to the congress 'on a consultative basis', although not as full deliberating members. He pictured the representatives of the Papal States and the duchies being allowed to submit points via a major power, and then receiving the results of the deliberations. As precedent for this structure he cited the conference in London of 1831 which decided the status of Belgium.[30] Meanwhile Buol shifted his ground and began to *oppose* the inclusion of the papacy and the duchies in any status, especially as he moved toward his qualified acceptance of England's four points by the end of March. He now perceived the overwhelming disadvantage to Austria of giving Sardinia

27   Malmesbury was a leader in seeking agreement on this point as well, consistent with his policy to try any angle to keep war from erupting.
28   Underlining is Malmesbury's. Malmesbury to Cowley, 19, 20 and 25 March 1859, private, Cowley papers, PRO, FO, 519/196.
29   Cowley to Malmesbury, Paris, 24 March 1859, private, Cowley papers, PRO, FO, 519/225/102–3. Malmesbury to Loftus, 19 March 1859, no. 150, PRO, FO, 425/51/156.
30   Malmesbury to Loftus, 23 March 1859, no. 165, PRO, FO, 425/51/176.

The proposed congress

– probably represented by Cavour in person – the platform of a congress to promote its plans for Italy. Furthermore, he now considered it gross effrontery to invite the pope to send a representative to a congress that had presumed to decide papal affairs.[31] Then, during the first week of April, Malmesbury modified his position once more, this time to satisfy the French and the smaller Italian states and possibly to catch the Austrians. He advocated as a new model the congress of Laibach of 1821, where the smaller states were admitted during the final sessions to full membership on equal terms with the major powers. He was willing to go further.[32] On 18 April, as the momentum toward war increased, Malmesbury made his final move and tied the question of the composition of the congress to the question of mutual demobilization of Austria and Sardinia. Austria finally rejected Laibach as a valid precedent for the present crisis, sent Sardinia the ultimatum, and went ahead to invade Sardinia on April 26.[33]

Throughout the long negotiations, Malmesbury tried everything he knew to secure the pope's acceptance of the congress on the basis of the four points and with the status for the pope's representative the English government proposed. On 19 March he sent Odo Russell the news that the English cabinet had just agreed to participate in a congress provided it was restricted to the four points. Once again Malmesbury employed the method of selective disclosure he had used on previous occasions with Antonelli and the pope. He instructed Odo to withhold some information which would be disconcerting to them and to emphasize other details which they would like to hear. Regarding the content of the four points he told Odo: 'Keep this strictly to yourself and if you see Antonelli alarmed, tell him no territorial change will be discussed and that our object is to preserve peace in Italy which can only be done by a Conference on these points.' Neither Odo nor Antonelli knew that Malmesbury had already revived the proposition to divide up the States of the Church.[34]

When Odo went to see Antonelli on 25 March, the cardinal was already quite alarmed about the effect of a congress on the Papal States. He told Odo that the papal government considered any kind of congress to be a direct interference in the internal affairs of Italy and an unwarranted stimulation of the revolutionary hopes of the Cavourian party. Odo tried to calm the cardinal with Malmesbury's assurance that no territorial changes would be discussed and that England desired only to use the congress to preserve the peace in Italy. Odo did not

31 Banneville to Walewski, Vienna, 24 March 1859, no. 36, *La guerra del 1859*, vol. 1, 161–3.
32 Malmesbury's memorandum on the Congress of Laibach, 4 April 1859, PRO, FO, 425/52/105. Malmesbury to Loftus, 6 April 1859, s.n., *Parliamentary papers, 1859* (Sess. 2), vol. 32, 197.
33 Malmesbury to Malakoff, 18 April 1859, PRO, FO, 425/52/2. Malmesbury to Cowley, 25 April 1859, no. 514, PRO, FO, 425/52/98.
34 Malmesbury to Odo Russell, 19 March 1859, confidential, Ampthill papers, PRO, FO, 918/6.

mention the four points. Antonelli was only partly pacified by these remarks. He expressed gratitude for Malmesbury's good will and his effort in 'the cause of order and peace', but reiterated his view that Malmesbury excited people against their established governments by promoting discussion of things which were of no direct concern to England.[35]

Malmesbury on 26 March asked Odo to persuade the papal government to accept the proposal that the Papal States be represented at the congress 'on a consultative basis'. The Italian states, he explained, would sit *at* the congress but not *in* it; they would be heard and give their opinions, but the five powers would retain the prerogative of 'laying down the law'.[36] Malmesbury appeared insensitive to the fact that such a notion could scarcely appeal to the pope. Nevertheless he did realize that he had to say something to soften his proposal. He chose Parliament as a suitable platform to do so on 28 March in reply to a question by Lord Clarendon: 'Our object will naturally be, not to impose – either on the question of Reform or on any other point – any conditions upon the Italian States and people, but to recommend to them what we consider for their own benefit and for the safety of Europe.'[37] He sent Odo the text of this speech and asked Odo to read it to Antonelli 'to reassure him'. He instructed Odo to play down any idea that Malmesbury intended 'to pass a reform Bill for his States though I cannot pass one here'.[38]

By the time Odo could get to Antonelli with Malmesbury's reassurance, it was already too late to win the pope's and Antonelli's acceptance of a congress on the terms England promoted. By the first week of April, Antonelli had gathered enough information about the project to know quite clearly that he could not have anything to do with it. During the last ten days of March the Austrian and French ambassadors in Rome had discussed the congress with him. The nuncio in Paris summarized the crux of the papal complaint against a congress:

> I cannot understand why the strong have such little regard for the rights and the independence of the small states, and why a congress composed of one schismatic power, two Protestant powers systematically hostile to the Holy See, and only two Catholic powers now fighting between themselves, has to concern itself with, and propose solutions for the dominions of the pope.[39]

DeLuca, the nuncio in Vienna, who kept Antonelli better informed of the congress diplomacy than he had about the Cowley mission, impressed the cardinal with the vigour of Malmesbury's and Loftus' activity to persuade

---

35 Odo Russell to Malmesbury, Rome, 26 March 1859, private, Malmesbury papers, 1859/7.
36 Malmesbury to Odo Russell, 26 March 1859, private, Ampthill papers, PRO, FO, 918/6.
37 Hansard's, CLIII, col. 918, 28 March 1859.
38 Malmesbury to Odo Russell, 30 March 1859, private, Ampthill papers, PRO, FO, 918/6.
39 The schismatic power was Russia, whose established Orthodox Church derived from the Great Schism of 1054, and the Protestants were England and Prussia. Only France and Austria were Catholic. Sacconi to Antonelli, Paris, 22 March 1859, no. 1232, ASV, ASdS, 1859, 165/1/151–2, and *Antonelli*, vol. I, 55.

Austria to accept the four points, and made it clear to him that the congress had become in reality England's special project.⁴⁰

Antonelli was particularly incensed by the idea of being offered merely a consultative voice in the proceedings. He issued a brief policy statement on 31 March to both Sacconi and DeLuca which opposed the idea of the congress and especially objected to the idea of consultative status. Such a congress, he declared, was totally unacceptable to the pope: '[T]he Supreme Head of the Catholic Church, ... in his two-fold capacity, can in no way tolerate other governments, and especially non-Catholic ones, calling him as if before a tribunal to subject him to a trial, and demanding he give a defence of his system of government.'⁴¹ Antonelli presented his objection to Odo Russell on 1 April. According to Odo's report, Antonelli remarked wryly, 'The Governments of Italy had not asked for advice and therefore he "was at a loss" to know what would be discussed by the five powers in Congress.' The cardinal made it very clear that he would not under any circumstances accept the congress as the English promoted it. Indeed, Antonelli said, he would no longer take any notice of it.⁴²

Malmesbury was surprised and unsettled by Antonelli's strong words to Odo. He had formulated his policy on the congress fully assuming that the papal government would accept it. Now that Antonelli had expressed his opposition to it, he was faced with the more difficult task of having to change Antonelli's mind. This he tried to do. His method was to depict an alternative which he thought the cardinal might regard as a prospect worse than the congress, and so induce him to choose for the congress. He telegraphed Odo on 3 May: 'If the Cardinal wishes to avert a war of opinion and of national hatreds in Europe, he will assist in promoting this Congress as we propose.' Malmesbury evoked the image of a revolutionary war which would overthrow the established social and political order of Italy. Malmesbury told Odo to press Antonelli on the point.⁴³ A few days later Malmesbury sent Odo an inflated account of bloodletting in the Romagna which he had received from an 'excellent though villainous authority'. It was a report of 'the most extreme violence, including even the assassination of priests in the churches'. Malmesbury held it up as an example of what would happen on a wide scale if Antonelli did not go along with the English proposal for a congress.⁴⁴

40 DeLuca to Antonelli, Vienna, 21 March 1859, no. 614; 23 March 1859, no. 615; 24 March 1895, no. 615 (*sic*), ASV, ASdS, 1859, 165/1/149–50, 153, 155. DeLuca to Antonelli, Vienna, 31 March 1859, no. 619, ASV, ASdS, 1859, 165/1/180–1.
41 Antonelli to DeLuca and Sacconi, Rome, 31 March 1859, no. 1964, ASV, ANVienna, 376/77–8, and ASV, ASdS, 1859, 165/2/5, and *Antonelli*, vol. 1, 66.
42 Odo Russell to Malmesbury, Rome, 2 April 1859, no. 34, PRO, FO, 43/70, and *Odo Russell*, 14.
43 Malmesbury to Odo Russell, 3 April 1859, telegram, and 4 April 1859, no. 28, PRO, FO, 43/69.
44 Malmesbury to Odo Russell, 9 April 1859, private, Ampthill papers, PRO, FO, 918/6.

Odo met with Antonelli on 9 April and vigorously pressed the argument about the 'war of opinion'. Antonelli was not moved at all. Once again Antonelli acknowledged the good intentions of the Tory government, and then he countered with his own arguments. The congress would be seriously misled, he claimed, if it kept the four points as the basis of its deliberations. If the powers wanted to prevent war and not cause damage to Italy, they would be wise to devote their energy, not to the affairs of the Papal States and the duchies which were troublesome to no one, but to the real problem – Piedmont's intrigues and war-mongering throughout the peninsula. Antonelli went further:

> The Papal Government has shewn that it requires no assistance from without, by demanding the withdrawal of foreign troops. That being done, the Powers of Europe have no right to interfere with us. The Pope has never asked for the advice of any foreign Government, does not require it, and will never accept it, and therefore His Holiness will not send a Representative to appear at the bar of a self constituted tribunal such as the proposed Congress is.

The discussion ended when Antonelli gave an answer which showed how little the threats of war and revolution ultimately worried him: 'Our destinies are in the hands of God, in Him let us confide, beyond that I can say no more.' The papal government quite simply wanted to be left alone to handle its own affairs.[45]

Antonelli told both the Austrian and the French ambassadors of this interview with Odo Russell. Gramont considered it an important event. He described to Walewski Odo's activities in Rome during the last ten days. 'Some very categorical questions coming from the British Cabinet have led the Papal Government to make formal declarations which do not leave any more doubt', Gramont observed. 'I am tempted to believe', he concluded, 'that for the affairs of his states, he [Antonelli] has found the war less disquieting than the Congress.'[46]

The official invitation to the congress was presented to Antonelli by Gramont in Rome on 15 April, which Antonelli now formally rejected.[47] Yet, Malmesbury tried one more time to change Antonelli's mind. He telegraphed Odo: 'Let me know if the Pope would send a Representative to Congress on equal footing with Five Powers.' Odo replied on 17 April without even going to ask Antonelli. He knew the answer: 'No, he would not – under no conditions whatever, I believe'.[48] It was too late even for an offer of equality with the major

45 Odo Russell to Malmesbury, Rome, 9 April 1859, no. 38, confidential, PRO, FO, 43/70, and *Odo Russell*, 15–16.
46 Gramont to Walewski, Rome, 9 April 1859, no. 28, AMAE, CP, Rome 1009/332–42. Colloredo to Buol, Rome, 9 April 1859, no. 13B, HHSA, PA, XI, 200/134–5.
47 Odo Russell to Malmesbury, Rome, 16 April 1859, no. 40, PRO, FO, 43/70, and *Odo Russell*, 17. Walewski to Gramont, Paris, 10 April 1859, no. 20, and Gramont to Walewski, Rome, 16 April 1859, no. 29, AMAE, CP, Rome, 1009/345–50 and 353–60.
48 Malmesbury to Odo Russell, Rome, 16 April 1859, telegram, and Odo Russell to Malmesbury, Rome, 17 April 1859, telegram, cited in Odo Russell to Malmesbury, Rome, 17 April 1859, no. 41, PRO, FO, 43/70.

powers in the congress. Perhaps if Malmesbury had begun his efforts with this proposal a month earlier, the papal government might have looked more favourably on the whole project.

At this point in the negotiations for the congress the only thing the papal government would entertain at all was an offer from Austria to speak in the interests of the pope if a congress were held. He accepted Austria's aid and commissioned the nuncio in Vienna to begin talks designed to prepare the Austrian defence of the papacy.[49]

On 18 April Malmesbury addressed the House of Lords and gave his first and only public account of the Conservative government's diplomacy regarding the congress. And Lord Clarendon, speaking for the opposition, once again severely lambasted the Papal States and echoed a similar analysis presented by Disraeli. On the pope, there was no essential difference between Tories and Whigs.[50]

By then, however, even though negotiations continued with Austria for another week over demobilization and the composition of the congress, a meeting of the powers was no longer a possibility. Even if a congress met, it could not hope to succeed on the terms demanded by the English. The papal government's categorical boycott of everything about the congress insured that it could only fail. Beginning in December 1858, when the threat of war first dawned on the English, Malmesbury and the Conservative government had analysed the troubles of Italy, devised a solution, formulated a policy, and entered into complex diplomacy, all of which directly pertained to the States of the Church, but none of which had taken seriously the perspective and needs of the papacy. When Antonelli rejected the congress, Gramont commented to Walewski, 'It appears that at London they had not expected this response, although it was easy to foresee, if one knew the habits and traditions of the Court of Rome.'[51]

The war: English and papal neutrality

The Austrian ultimatum to Sardinia to demobilize or be invaded was delivered on 23 April, Easter weekend, and took every government by surprise. Not the least surprised was Cavour himself. During the last few weeks, England's diplomatic pressure against war had virtually foiled Cavour's 'project of calculated aggressions'. His plans to produce a revolt in the Romagna as a pretext for war had failed miserably during March and April.[52] Massari found Cavour on 19 April in agitated despair: 'The only thing left for me now is to blow out my brains', Cavour exclaimed. 'English policy has won. All is lost. N. III has abandoned us.' Cavour was ready to resign.[53] The ultimatum and the Austrian

49 Colloredo to Buol, Rome, 17 April 1859, no. 14A, HHSA, PA, XI, 200/145–7.
50 Hansard's, CLIII, col. 1830–55, and 1863–81, 18 April 1859.
51 Gramont to Walewski, Rome, 9 April 1859, no. 28, AMAE, CP, Rome, 1009/233.
52 Mack Smith, *Victor Emanuel, Cavour*, 94, 130.
53 Massari, *Diario*, 19 April 1859, 212, translated in Mack Smith, *Making of Italy*, 274–5.

invasion of Sardinia on 26 April saved him, and, among other things, saved his plans for the Papal States.

Cavour had succeeded in provoking the Austrians to the breaking point. The war that all European governments had talked about for months and that Malmesbury had worked so long to prevent began in northern Italy. It lasted into July. Austria's invasion gave Napoleon the technicality he needed to join the war against Austria. The war has commonly been called the Austro-Sardinian war of 1859, but because French troops actually carried most of the work of the war and Sardinian troops usually mishandled their operations, the war was in effect a Franco-Austrian war which Napoleon conducted in support of his ward, Cavour.[54] As it turned out the war started as a factor in Austro-Sardinian relations very much as the original Plombières scheme had envisaged, but with the major exception that Sardinia's irritation of Austria had little to do with the outbreak of revolt or with the Papal States. The only one of the four points which might have helped to prevent the war as it actually unfolded was the point about Austro-Sardinian friction, and not the other three points about the Papal States and the duchies. In the short term, Malmesbury would have done better to follow Antonelli's advice and work to stop Cavour's provocations.

When the war began, Malmesbury and the English government moved immediately to implement a wartime policy, and they did not stop to reflect on the efficacy of their pre-war diplomacy. Indeed, just before the war began, Malmesbury offered still once more to mediate between France and Austria on the basis of the four points via a renewal of the personal diplomacy of the Cowley mission. Even after the invasion, he reaffirmed to Lord Derby his confidence in the four points.[55]

The outbreak of war changed many things, of course. One immediate concern was whether the war would spread southward. Under such a circumstance, the English and papal governments expressed parallel second thoughts about the evacuation of the French and Austrian troops. The English government was glad when Antonelli declared immediately that the papal government would maintain strict neutrality, and demanded that the belligerent powers respect the neutrality of the papal territory.[56]

The papal government's obvious fear was that the French and Austrians would, by means of their occupation troops, engulf the Papal States in the fighting. Antonelli was alarmed when he learned that the Austrians added 2000 soldiers to their forces at Ancona.[57] But then, when news arrived of the revolution in Tuscany on 27 April and the flight of the grand duke, Antonelli had

54   Mack Smith, *Victor Emanuel, Cavour*, ch. 5.
55   Malmesbury to Loftus, 23 April 1859, no. 291, PRO, FO, 425/52/58–9. Malmesbury to Derby, 27 April 1859, Derby papers, 144/2.
56   See Derby's addition to Malmesbury's despatch to Odo Russell, 14 April 1859, no. 32, confidential, draft, PRO, FO, 43/69.
57   Antonelli to Gramont and Colloredo, Rome, 26 April 1859, *Antonelli*, vol. I, 92–3. The declaration of papal neutrality was sent to the diplomatic corps in Rome, dated 3 May, and

The war: English and papal neutrality

a competing fear that the Austrians and French might reduce their troops too much or even leave papal territory too soon. Antonelli was told that the increase of Austrian troops at Ancona was to be achieved by transferring troops from Bologna, a manoeuvre which he regarded as doubly uninviting. Antonelli was forced to turn about in his policy. He wrote to both Sacconi and DeLuca that the war made evacuation inopportune, and instructed them to express the papal government's desire that no evacuation occur before papal troops were adequate to cope with the needs of the defence of the papal territory. At the same time he issued a protest against the enlargement of the Ancona garrison as an act which violated papal neutrality. What Antonelli wanted was the *status quo ante bellum* indefinitely perpetuated.[58]

The English government likewise wanted to prevent the foreign troops from serving as an occasion, or an excuse, to extend the war into central Italy. Malmesbury's policy was to localize the war. He also wanted to end the war as soon as possible. Antonelli publicly approved England's policy on the war in his declaration of papal neutrality on 26 April. The Tory government declared its own policy of strict neutrality, and Malmesbury indicated to the queen his willingness to make it *armed* neutrality if necessary.[59] This is when England decided to move a squadron from Malta to parade around the peninsula and to station the *Argus* in Ancona harbour to be ready for any contingency. England could stay out of the war if the Adriatic coast remained neutral. By a curious twist, the papal government welcomed the presence of the British fleet, and the papal newspaper, *Giornale di Roma*, reported the fleet's movements regularly.[60] The English government also announced that it was anxious to serve as mediator in the war if by that means 'the cause of peace and reconciliation', and the cause of the 'general improvement of the administrations throughout the peninsula of Italy' could be served. Malmesbury's wartime policy continued his pre-war hopes for the reform of the Papal States and the duchies.[61]

In papal circles hope was expressed that England's neutrality would be weighted in favour of Austria.[62] Queen Victoria and Prince Albert no doubt

---

unofficially communicated to Odo Russell on 28 May (see Antonelli to Odo Russell, 28 May 1859, PRO, FO, 43/71). However, Odo had reported the news of papal neutrality when it was first declared to the French and Austrian ambassadors (Odo Russell to Malmesbury, Rome, 27 April 1859, no. 47, PRO, FO, 43/70, and *Odo Russell*, 18).

58 Mack Smith, *Victor Emanuel, Cavour*, ch. 7. Antonelli to DeLuca, Rome, 30 April 1859, s.n., draft, and Antonelli to Sacconi, Rome, 30 April 1859, no. 2810, draft, ASV, ASdS, 165/2/80–1, and 68–9, and *Antonelli*, vol. I, 98–9.

59 Hearder, 'Foreign policy of Lord Malmesbury', 356, 379. Derby to Queen Victoria, 9 April 1859, copy, Derby papers, 187/2. Apponyi to Buol, London, 2 June 1859, 53A–K, HHSA, PA, VIII, 49/405.

60 *Giornale di Roma*, 5 May, 6 May, 10 May, 23 May, 10 June 1859, *inter alia*. F.A. Simpson, 'England and the Italian war of 1859', *Historical Journal* 5 (1962), 111–12.

61 Malmesbury to Cowley, 4 May 1859, no. 678, *Gran Bretagna e Sardegna*, vol. VII, 78.

62 Sacconi to Antonelli, Paris, 29 April 1859, no. 1262, ASV, ASdS, 1859, 165/2/99–104, and *Antonelli*, vol. I, 95. DeLuca to Antonelli, Vienna, 25 April 1859, no. 645 NP, and Vienna, 10 May 1859, no. 662, ASV, ASdS, 1859, 165/2/90 and 139–40. *Tablet*, 30 April and 7 May 1859.

thought the government ought to give priority to achieving understanding with Austria, but Malmesbury's activities, in fact, were scrupulously neutral, and if anything, tended to be partial to France, even though remaining on guard against French expansion in Italy.[63] In any case, Malmesbury, with the queen's and Lord Derby's approval, wanted to assure the papal government that England would remain strictly neutral.[64]

France and Austria both announced their intentions to respect the pope's neutrality.[65] The papal government, however, had trouble with the Piedmontese. Sardinia was trying to push the new king of Naples, Francis II, to join the war on the Franco-Sardinian side. Antonelli expressed to Odo his fear that Neapolitan troops might use papal territory as a corridor to the war.[66] Then, the Sardinian envoy, Count della Minerva, informed Antonelli that Cavour's government would not respect papal neutrality unconditionally. Cavour, it seems, wanted to keep open the possibility of attacking the Austrian garrisons on the Adriatic side of the Papal States. These negative prospects forced Antonelli to turn to England for help. Odo telegraphed the gist of the cardinal's message to Malmesbury: 'Sardinia will not acknowledge the Pope's neutrality. The Cardinal alarmed, wishes me to inform your Lordship.'[67] Antonelli asked if England could influence the young king to stay clear of Cavour. On this Malmesbury instructed Odo both at Rome and on a special mission to Naples to speak against any violation of papal neutrality.[68] He asked Hudson in Turin to determine what Cavour intended. Hudson's reply was candid. As a matter of fact, he reported, Cavour was quite ready to extend the war into central Italy:

> I have the honour to report to your lordship that the Sardinian Government, having refused to accept an unconditional neutrality on the part of Rome, is organizing a force, with which it is intended to occupy a part of the Papal States, the moment that matters are sufficiently advanced in this quarter to allow them to attack the Austrians at Ancona and Bologna.
>
> Her Majesty's Government must therefore be prepared to see the Legations, and the Duchies follow in the wake of Tuscany, as soon as a victory over Austria shall allow Sardinia and France to follow out their plans with regard to Central Italy.

Cavour continued to encourage Sardinian agents to entice papal soldiers to defect and to join volunteer units in Piedmont's army. Visions of a Piedmontese northern and central Italy enticed him – Piedmont, as he once told

63 See Hearder, 'Foreign policy of Lord Malmesbury', 363–9.
64 Malmesbury to Odo Russell, 20 May 1859, no. 43, draft, PRO, FO, 43/69.
65 Buol to Apponyi, Vienna, 10 May 1859, PRO, FO, 425/53/79. Antonelli to DeLuca, Rome, 10 May 1859, no. 3103, ASV, ASdS, 1859, 165/2/152.
66 Odo Russell to Malmesbury, Rome, 19 May 1859, telegram, no. 56, PRO, FO, 43/71.
67 Odo Russell to Malmesbury, Rome, 25 May 1859, no. 65, secret, PRO, FO, 43/71, and *Odo Russell*, 21–3. Odo Russell to Malmesbury, Rome, 26 May 1859, telegram, no. 66, PRO, FO, 43/71.
68 Malmesbury to Odo Russell, 20 May 1859, telegram, no. 41, PRO, FO, 43/69. Malmesbury to Odo Russell, London, 20 May 1859, private, Ampthill papers, PRO, FO, 918/6.

The war: English and papal neutrality

Odo, with 'its head supported upon the Alps and its feet at Ancona'.[69] Cowley, in the meantime, learned that, in effect, France had fully backed Cavour's position on papal neutrality which, Cowley observed, 'leaves ample scope for excuse to attack the Austrians in the Legations, whenever it may suit the convenience of France to do so'.[70] For the time being, however, Cavour was content merely to make threats.

The time had come for the Derby government to conduct a thorough appraisal of the complex state of affairs developing in central Italy. Malmesbury asked Odo Russell to prepare 'an exact report of what has lately taken place in the Papal dominions, and a statement of your opinion as to the probable course of events in the Capital'. Odo's analysis was ready on 28 May. According to him, sympathy for France and Sardinia in the Papal States was spreading while support for Austria was decreasing. Among the nationalist party, he claimed, respect for England was weakening because the Tory government's policy was considered too Austrophile and too kindly to the papacy. Odo fully expected that the French, supported by Cavour's policy of tranquillity in Rome itself, would be able to keep the capital quiet. Antonelli and the pope, Odo believed, were virtual prisoners of the French. He said it was different across the Apennines. He predicted the outbreak of a revolution in the Romagna as soon as Cavour wanted it. Odo's report, which so one-sidedly emphasized the position and views of the nationalist party, may have been partially designed to influence Malmesbury and the Conservative government to be more sympathetic to Piedmont. His account of the Romagna, of which he had no direct knowledge, contrasted markedly with the story told by Charles Lever, the English vice-consul at La Spezia, who had just visited the Romagna. He observed that things were remarkably quiet there, that the mass of ordinary people supported the pope, and that partisans of Piedmont were only a minority, albeit a vocal one. Odo's analysis, nevertheless, had its impact on Malmesbury. The foreign minister wrote these words on the margin of Odo's despatch: 'Important. Assuming this description of Italy to be correct what chance is there of arresting the war?'[71]

The papal government and the English found themselves together about the first of June in resisting the spread of war and revolution from northern Italy into the States of the Church, and down into Naples – in short, enveloping the whole of the Italian peninsula. Austria only belatedly and half-heartedly decided to reduce its troops at Ancona and Bologna to something like the pre-war level.[72] Volunteers continued to defect from the Romagna to the Piedmont side. Naples

69   Malmesbury to Hudson, 30 May 1859, no. 130, and Hudson to Malmesbury, Turin, 1 June, no. 228, and 4 June 1859, no. 234, *Gran Bretagna e Sardegna*, vol. VII, 107, 110 and 111. Cowley to Malmesbury, Paris, 7 June 1859, no. 834, PRO, FO, 425/53/307.
70   Cowley to Malmesbury, Paris, 3 June 1859, no. 796, PRO, FO, 425/53/281.
71   'Arresting the war' means preventing the extension of the war. Odo Russell to Malmesbury, Rome, 28 May 1859, no. 69, PRO, FO, 43/71, and excerpted in *Odo Russell*, 23–5. Charles Lever to Hudson, 20 May 1859, *Gran Bretagna e Sardegna*, vol. VII, 102.
72   DeLuca to Antonelli, Vienna, 12 May 1859, no. 664, ASV, ASdS, 1859, 165/2/153–4.

received additional pressure from Piedmont to join the war. The new Tuscan provisional government declared for King Victor Emmanuel and let Tuscany serve as the base for provocative forays by nationalist agents into the Papal States. Cavour awaited the moment to attack Austria in papal territory. On 4 June the French army defeated the Austrians in the bloody battle of Magenta and on 8 June Napoleon, joined by Victor Emmanuel, entered Milan to take the city from Austria. With this, Austria, the pope's defender, lost the province of Lombardy which soon would be added to Piedmont's holdings. The prospects of preventing war and revolution in the States of the Church appeared increasingly poor.

The parliamentary election: Tories and papal influence

Malmesbury and Derby ran out of time in which to try to stop the fiery developments in central Italy. On 11 June, after losing a vote of 'no confidence' in Parliament, the Derby government resigned. The outcome was not entirely expected since in the springtime elections the Conservatives had actually increased their numbers in the House of Commons, partly because of Catholic votes in Ireland. The relationship between the Conservatives, the papal government, and English and Irish Catholics was one important factor in those elections.

Ever since Lord John Russell's protest against the establishment of the Catholic hierarchy in 1850 and the Ecclesiastical Titles Act of 1851, Catholics in England and Ireland began to question the support they had generally given to the Liberals, especially to Lord John. By the time of the second Derby ministry of 1858–9 some Catholic M.P.s had begun to support the Conservatives in spite of the long-standing Tory position as the party of Protestant domination of the Catholic majority in Ireland. In mid-1858 a tenuous collaboration between some Irish Catholics and the Conservatives emerged, which, however, began to break up early in 1859.[73]

In March 1859 the Derby government foresaw that the forthcoming vote on its reform bill would become a test of its policy and power to govern. Some Catholic M.P.s, led by J.F. Maguire and Sir John Bowyer, decided that the most important thing about the vote was whether or not to continue the Derby ministry, which they were coming to look upon in both foreign policy and domestic policy as less hostile to Catholic interests than what they could expect from the Liberals.[74]

Derby and Malmesbury contemplated their possible defeat while Lord Cowley was in Vienna. Malmesbury knew that Antonelli tended to look favourably on the Cowley mission and that the cardinal responded well to his

---

[73] J.H. Whyte, *The independent Irish party, 1850–1859* (Oxford: Oxford University Press, 1958), 147, 151–4; Altholz, 'The political behavior of English Catholics, 1850–1867', *The journal of British studies* 4 (1964), 96–8.

[74] *Tablet*, 12 March 1859.

The parliamentary election: Tories and papal influence

attempts at *rapprochement*. Not wanting to overlook any means of strengthening the Tories' political position, Malmesbury thought of adding a postscript to an otherwise innocuous note to Odo Russell on 12 March. What he wrote was full of implications: '*Tell Antonelli* that if we are beaten on the Reform Bill the end of this month we shall dissolve – and that we expect greatly to improve our Parliament.'[75] The thrust of the postscript, understood in the context of the surrounding events, was to interest the papal government in the political welfare of the English Conservatives. Malmesbury had already endeavoured several times to convince Antonelli that the diplomatic interests of the two governments converged on their desires to maintain 'Conservative principles' and to prevent war and revolution in Italy. This note of 12 March now proposed that the two governments ought to share an interest in continuing Tory rule in Great Britain and Ireland.

Malmesbury now chose an extraordinary line of action which he pursued in tandem with his diplomacy to persuade the papal government to accept the congress and consider reforms. He decided to request the help of the papal government in securing Catholic votes for the Tories in Ireland in the elections which surely were coming. His desire for papal political influence in Ireland may well have affected his diplomacy toward the pope. He asked Odo Russell, the nephew of the most controversial Liberal, to serve as the intermediary in making this unusual request. At the end of his letter to Odo on 19 March he added: 'Are you sufficiently *honest* to tell Antonelli to help *us* in the Conservative Elections in Ireland. We shall have a dissolution in a month.'[76] As if he needed to make the point clearer, he wrote Odo a week later: 'Antonelli is quite right. If your relative comes in it will be "go it Cavour".'[77] In pursuing this strategy, he actually relied on a long tradition of courting papal influence to perpetuate British rule over Catholic Ireland. By a curious irony, the British desire for political and economic domination over Ireland, with all its anti-Catholic implications, coincided with the papal desire for Roman domination over the Irish Catholic church. The strategy had been tried under the previous governments of Robert Peel, Russell, and Derby, and now Malmesbury was ready to try again.[78]

Odo Russell fulfilled his extraordinary mandate by 26 March, well aware of its delicate character. In a lengthy conversation with Antonelli, Odo raised the subject so that the cardinal would himself get the idea of helping the Conservatives in Ireland without Odo actually suggesting it. This is the complete text of Odo's account of the interview:

75 Malmesbury to Odo Russell, 12 March 1859, private, Ampthill papers, PRO, FO, 918/6. Underlining is Malmesbury's.
76 Malmesbury to Odo Russell, 19 March 1859, private, confidential, Ampthill papers, PRO, FO, 918/6. Underlining is Malmesbury's.
77 Malmesbury to Odo Russell, 26 March 1859, private, Ampthill papers, PRO, FO, 918/6.
78 Machin, *Politics and the churches*, 167–8, 177–8, 211–14, 246.

> I asked him whether a change of Government in England would seriously affect the interests in Italy. He said the name[s] of Lord Palmerston and Lord John were too well know[n] in Italy not to be dangerous to the cause of peace, that a change of Ministry which would bring them into Power would be a great misfortune and he asked me with much concern whether I thought it likely to occur.
>
> 'I told Your Emminence the other day', I replied, '[the present] Government of Lord Derby if beaten intend to dissolve and then their future tenure of office will depend on the result of the elections.'
>
> 'And what are the chances and probabilities', he said, with considerable anxiety reflected in his bilious countenance.
>
> 'Well', I said, 'I understand that Government will obtain a favourable parliament, certainly in England, but the stumbling block will be Ireland, of course.'
>
> 'How do you mean?' said His Eminence.
>
> 'It is all your own fault', I replied laughing. 'Your Irish Clergy is ignorant, their tendencies are far from being conservative and they naturally exercise all this influence on the Roman Catholic electors.'
>
> 'Rome has never interfered in such matters', said the Cardinal who seemed much interested.
>
> 'No doubt', I answered, 'but it is strange enough to think that your own priests will in the end and indirectly be acting against the interests of Rome, thro' ignorance and hostility to the Conservative cause.'
>
> I paused to see what effect this had made on him. He rubbed his forehead thoughtfully for some time and then said, 'We have plenty of the Irish clergy here, many of whom are going home. One might say a word to them and tell them to assist in keeping the present Government in Power.'
>
> 'Well', I said, 'that is your look out', and I wished him good-bye. As I left the room I saw him take up a bit of paper from his table and make some rapid notes.[79]

Antonelli had got the point.

On the day of the vote on the reform bill, 31 March, Odo drafted a letter to Antonelli which described the urgency of the matter:

> They have written me from London that Lord Palmerston and Lord J. Russell have a good chance of coming to power. Tonight the Parliament at London will vote on Reform. The Irishman MacHale has addressed publicly a circular to the Irish Catholic Members to tell them to vote against the government of L. Derby and L. Malmesbury and this circular has been approved, they say, by Cardinal Wiseman. There will be therefore a majority against the present Government, made by the Irish Catholic Members. The vote will have taken place tonight. This complication is serious.[80]

The day before the vote, Malmesbury reminded Odo, 'Do not lose the point relating to home affairs at the proper time.'[81]

79   The copy of this letter that I have seen is the original draft in which the punctuation marks and quotation marks are incomplete. For clarity, I have supplied them where it is obvious they are missing in the draft. Odo Russell to Malmesbury, Rome, 26 March 1859, private, confidential, draft, Ampthill papers, PRO, FO, 918/6.
80   Odo Russell to Antonelli, n.d. (31 March 1859), draft, Ampthill papers, PRO, FO, 918/11. It is not certain that Odo sent the letter. He was mistaken about Wiseman who consistently advocated Catholic support of the Tories.
81   Malmesbury to Odo Russell, 30 March 1859, private, Ampthill papers, PRO, FO, 918/6.

The parliamentary election: Tories and papal influence

As expected, the Conservative reform bill did lose, and Parliament was dissolved, and new elections were called. Odo continued his special assignment during the elections, and even gave it a turn the other way around. In order to win Antonelli's support for Conservative diplomacy he suggested on 9 April that the papal government would do well to go along with Tory policy while they still had Tories to deal with. Antonelli was unmoved: 'We sincerely acknowledge the good intentions of Her Majesty's Government and hope they may continue long to govern England, but, as I have said before, the proposed Congress is uncalled for, and not desired by the Governments of Italy.' Odo tried the same argument one week later, but with no better results.[82]

Odo met Antonelli on 14 April in the home of the Austrian ambassador, Count Colloredo, and reminded him of his promise to help in the Irish elections. Odo reported Antonelli's reply: 'He [Antonelli] assured me again that it had been constantly on his mind, that he had already done all in his power, and that he felt sure the effects would be such as Your Lordship wished.'[83]

No direct evidence has yet been found to indicate precisely with whom Antonelli spoke or corresponded about this delicate matter. However, Antonelli did identify to Odo the channel he expected to use – the clergy in Rome. There were many Irish and English clergy residing in Rome in the Irish College, the English College, or in one of several Irish and English religious establishments. As devout Catholics living near the papacy they would be able to articulate in their letters or during visits to Ireland how much the political crisis in Italy endangered the pope's temporal power. Clergy in Ireland commonly influenced how Catholics voted,[84] so it was important that some clergy publically spoke in favour of the Conservatives, partly because of the question of the temporal power. Noteworthy were the fifty-one clergy of the diocese of Meath who published a statement in April which asked: 'Is it now that we should entrust to Russell or Palmerston the whole power of the British Empire to be employed in snatching from the Holy Father his temporal dominions and independence?'[85] There were many other meetings of clergy to support specific candidates. Cardinal Wiseman, himself Irish, son of a Waterford family, made public a letter he wrote stating that he supported the Conservatives. His pastoral letter for Lent had earlier awakened Catholics to the potential effect of the Italian crisis on the papacy and summoned them to pray and work for the well-being of the Holy See.[86] The Vatican itself publicly revealed its wishes for the English elections

---

82   Odo Russell to Antonelli, Rome, 9 April 1859, no. 38, confidential, PRO, FO, 43/70, and *Odo Russell*, 15–16. Odo Russell to Malmesbury, Rome, 16 April 1859, private, Malmesbury papers, 1859/7.
83   Odo Russell to Malmesbury, Rome, 16 April 1859, private, Malmesbury papers, 1859/7.
84   See Wiseman to Talbot, 11 July 1856, and Cullen to Talbot, 29 June 1859, in Talbot papers, 1028 and 182.
82   *Tablet*, 7 May 1859.
86   Wiseman to T.F. Strange (of Waterford), 13 April 1859, reproduced in *Tablet*, 7 May 1859. Wiseman told Mr Strange, who was a member of Mr John A. Blake's election committee at Waterford, to make public use of this letter. The text of Wiseman's Lenten pastoral letter appeared in the *Tablet*, 12 March 1859.

by conspicuously reproducing on 19 April in *Giornale di Roma* an editorial from the French Catholic newspaper *Univers* which categorically supported the Derby government over a potential Palmerston or Russell government. The editorial stated:

> We are far from approving every act of this [Derby] ministry. We know that Catholics have just complaints to make against it, and that Ireland is still a long way from receiving the justice which is owed to it..., but in judging him [Lord Derby] by his foreign policy, we believe that the peace of Europe is in less danger with him than with Lord Russell or Lord Palmerston, who find themselves somewhat compromised with revolution: in a word Derby seems more conservative than his opponents.[87]

Such an editorial probably would not have been published without Antonelli's approval. In these ways, the Papal Question became an issue for the first time in Irish politics.

The election results in May showed a gain for the Conservatives of eight seats in Ireland, and gave them a clear majority in Ireland, fifty-five to fifty, for the first time since the Reform Bill of 1832. In England the Conservatives gained eighteen seats but did not win a majority. Conservatives remained a minority in the Commons by about fifty votes. In England the Tories benefited from 'the completely conservative spirit of the country', and their foreign policy apparently did not figure very strongly in the election.[88] Even so, the *Tablet* claimed that a majority of English Catholic voters supported the Derby government, partly because of foreign policy, and that Catholic votes helped elect two liberal-conservatives in South Lancashire, an area of Catholic concentration, which normally went against Tories and where Catholics usually voted for Liberals.[89] In Ireland, Catholics remained divided, but large numbers of Catholics voted for Tories for the first time, and the issue of foreign policy toward Italy and the papacy was relatively significant.[90] An Irish Catholic seemed to turn away from traditional Liberal or independent positions when he came to believe that defending the papacy by voting in effect against a Russell or Palmerston government outweighed all other considerations. Such a switch of loyalties was not easy, however. Archbishop Cullen and Bishop MacHale, for instance, both expressed great concern for the rights of the papacy, but both considered the overriding matters still to be government policy on such things as Irish tenants' rights, the religious rights of Catholics in workhouses and prisons, equality for Catholic education, and legal recognition of a Catholic university in Ireland, and so they supported Liberals and independents respectively.[91]

87   *Giornale di Roma*, 19 April 1859.
88   *The Times*, 21 May 1859; Norman, *Catholic Church and Ireland*, 37; Beales, *England and Italy*, 72–3; C.C.F. Greville, *The Greville memoirs, 1814 to 1860*, ed. Lytton Strachey and Roger Fulford (London: Macmillan, 1938), vol. VII, 417, 27 (17) May 1859.
89   *Tablet*, 14 May 1859. *The Times*, 9 May 1859.
90   Beales, *England and Italy*, 74–5. See Derby to Queen Victoria, 11 May 1859, Derby papers, 188/1.
91   Norman, *Catholic Church and Ireland*, 33–40, 45. See *Tablet*, 12 March 1859.

The parliamentary election: Tories and papal influence

The shift of so many Catholic votes to the Conservatives angered some opponents, who charged that Lord Derby had 'a compact with the pope', or that Catholics acted 'under orders from Rome'. Wiseman denied the charge by *The Times* that he made an alliance with Derby to influence Catholics to vote for the Conservatives. Disraeli felt compelled when the new Parliament convened to deny what he called the most serious charge, that Lord Derby 'entered into any compact or contract, or understanding with any hierarchy in this country, or with any agent of any foreign Prince, to influence the elections of our own country'.[92] The charge was surely overstated; no evidence of any such formal agreement or compact has come to light. Catholic votes for Tories quite likely came freely due to new assessments of what was best for Catholic interests. Nevertheless, decisions to influence Catholics in favour of Tories were made by some clergy, including Wiseman, and the leading English Catholic lay politician, Sir George Bowyer, actively called for votes for Tories.[93] Disraeli acknowledged this support privately in this farewell letter to Bowyer:

> I do not wish to retire from office without offering you my thanks for the valuable and truly independent support which during the trying period of our existence, as ministers, we unvariably received at your hands.
>
> I should feel gratified also, if, thro' your medium, I might convey to Cardinal Wiseman my sense of the generous and courageous manner, in which His Eminence accorded us his assistance.
>
> It was given ungrudgingly, without solicitation and without condition, and with that true feeling, which can only be prompted by a high sentiment of duty.[94]

We do not know whether more lies behind this letter, whether, for example, Disraeli or any other Tory leaders approached Catholic leaders for assistance in the elections. Nor do we know what Disraeli would have answered if anyone had confronted him with Malmesbury's secret request for Vatican intervention in the Irish elections on behalf of Tories. Antonelli appears to have been quite discreet, and his and Malmesbury's actions did not become public knowledge, no doubt to Malmesbury's relief.

On 7 June, the motion of 'no confidence' was proposed in Parliament as the best strategy to achieve agreement among disparate Whigs, Liberals and Radicals against the Derby ministry.[95] Even though Malmesbury's despatches had not yet been published in the parliamentary Blue Books, the opposition speakers in the debate hurled great missiles against Tory foreign policy on Italy

---

92 *Greville memoirs*, vol. VII, 418, 27 (17) May 1859. *The Times*, 21 May 1859. *Tablet*, 4 June 1859. Hansard's, CLIV, col. 125–8, 7 June 1859. The Protestant Alliance warned Protestants to vote against Tories because the Tories had compromised with Catholics (*Record*, 15 April 1859).

93 On Catholic voting generally, see John Vincent, *The formation of the British Liberal party, 1857–1864* (Harmondsworth: Penguin, 1971), appendix one, 'The Catholic vote', 293–4. George Bowyer to the editor of the *Tablet*, 19 May 1859, in *Tablet*, 21 May 1859.

94 Disraeli to Bowyer, Grosvenor Gate, London, 25 June 1859, copy, Wiseman papers, Pre-1865, 137/2. Bowyer apparently gave this copy to Wiseman.

95 Beales, *England and Italy*, 79–80. Vincent, *passim*.

and the papacy. They charged Malmesbury with being too Austrophile, too inactive in seeking to impede the outbreak of war, and too uncritical toward the papacy. All three charges were largely unwarranted; their purpose, however, was not clarity, but the upset of the Conservative ministry.[96] The Derby ministry lost the 'no confidence' vote by 323 to 310, a margin of only 13 votes. Irish members, of whom 36 were Catholics, voted 63 to 38 in favour of the Derby ministry. The *Tablet* was displeased with the result and remarked that if only seven of those Irish Catholics who voted against Derby would have voted otherwise, they would have reversed the result. Catholics, the *Tablet* observed, should be judged responsible for turning out the Conservatives.[97] Seen another way, however, it could be said that Catholics nearly kept the Conservatives in office.

Many months later when Malmesbury's despatches were published in the parliamentary Blue Books,[98] Catholics debated Conservative policy among themselves. Cardinal Cullen, who in the spring elections had not supported the Tories, pointed out somewhat angrily that Malmesbury's diplomacy all along had been, in fact, very hostile toward the papal government, and that there was a discrepancy between his approaches to the powers of Europe and to the papacy directly. The *Tablet* agreed that the mainline of Tory diplomacy was anti-papal, but emphasized that it was still *less* hostile to papal interests than what the Liberals had to offer under Palmerston and Russell.[99]

Even if Malmesbury had been given more time, the configuration of people and parties pushing toward war possessed greater force than Tory policy and method could cope with. Malmesbury's solutions – papal reform, perhaps rearrange papal territory, evacuate the troops, confederation – although appropriate to his analysis, required long stretches of peace in order to implement them. His conciliatory approach directly with the papacy appeared to influence Pius and Antonelli only once – their request for troop withdrawal. The rest of the time they welcomed Tory policy when it coincided with theirs, and ignored it when it did not. In practice, Malmesbury's papal policy was one dimension of his peace policy. In the short term, if he had concentrated more on Cavour, and Austria, and less on the pope, he may have done more to prevent the outbreak of war, but his anti-papal assessment of the troubles in Italy did not point him that way.

The defeat of the Derby government early in the morning of 11 June[100] was followed that evening by the Austrian government suddenly withdrawing its

---

96   Hansard's, CLIV, col. 165, 179–81, 211–13, 341–3, 408, 7 June 1859.
97   *Tablet*, 18 June 1859.
98   *Correspondence respecting the affairs of Italy, January to May 1859*, in *Parliamentary papers*, 1859 (Sess. 2), vol. 32.
99   *Tablet*, 28 Jan. 1860.
100 See, Third Earl of Malmesbury, *Memoirs of an ex-minister*, 3rd ed. (2 vols., London: Longmans, Green, 1884), 9 and 11 June 1859.

troops from Bologna and Ancona. The next day members of the Italian National Society overthrew papal temporal power in the Romagna and quickly established a provisional government loyal to Cavour. A few days later Queen Victoria was obliged to offer Lord Palmerston the office of prime minister, and Lord John Russell became foreign minister. These two series of events transformed the entire situation and suddenly confronted Pius IX and Antonelli with a new state of affairs. For the papacy, the worst had come, in the Romagna as well as in England.

5 Liberals and the revolution in the Romagna

'Let the Italians govern their own affairs'

The advent to power of the reunited Liberal party in England decisively affected the pope's prospects in Italy and Europe. Queen Victoria tried her best to avoid having Lord Palmerston and Lord John Russell, leaders of the old Whigs, at the head of the new government. Among other things, she abhorred their unmitigated Whig favouritism for Piedmont and the Italian nationalists. She would have felt safer with Lord Granville as prime minister and Lord Clarendon as foreign minister.[1] When Gladstone joined Palmerston and Russell as the chancellor of the exchequer, the pope faced a formidable triumvirate. The Duke of Argyll, as Lord Privy Seal, and Milner Gibson, as president of the Board of Trade, gave them full support in the Cabinet.[2]

Leaders on all sides of the Italian and papal crisis expected the new government to transform England's role in the course of events. Count Persigny, the French ambassador in London, felt sure that Napoleon could count on Russell being 'perfectly disposed to follow us on this terrain'. The Austrian ambassador in London, Count Apponyi, foresaw that the new government would undermine Austrian interests in Italy and pressure Austria to accept the revolutionary *fait accompli* in Italy. He anticipated a *rapprochement* between England and France due to Italian affairs.[3]

Cavour and the Romagnol nationalists were elated with the new government. Cavour once confessed, 'Despite his outbursts of ill temper, Lord John is one hundred times more preferable than Malmesbury by whom I felt threatened.' Marco Minghetti, a Romagnol leader who figured prominently in Cavour's plans for the Papal States, summarized the convictions of the pope's adversaries in the Romagna: 'England can put in the balance a great weight in our favour. And I must thank God that the Malmesbury Government has fallen. Palmerston and

---

1   RA Queen Victoria's *Journal*, 11, 12 and 13 June 1859.
2   *The Gladstone diaries*, 13 June 1859, and notably his memorandum on the views of Cabinet members, 30 May 1860. Gladstone, who had voted with the Tories in the 'no confidence' motion, joined the Liberal Cabinet to help Palmerston and Russell on the Italian Question.
3   Persigny to Walewski, London, 17 June 1859, no. 67, *La guerra del 1859*, vol. III, 1129–31; Apponyi to Rechberg, London, 14 June 1859, no. 59B, HHSA, PA, VIII, 49/511.

'Let the Italians govern their own affairs'

Lord John seem to me to have understood perfectly the condition of things in Italy.'[4]

Pius IX quickly understood what Palmerston and Russell would mean for his states: 'They have always sympathized with the turbulent spirits of Italy and their accession to power will greatly increase the hopes of the Piedmontese party. Indeed I know what the English Government want; they want to see the Pope deprived of his temporal power.'[5] The *Giornale di Roma*, the papal newspaper, carried a brief political and social biography of each cabinet member.[6]

The revolution in the Romagna began on 12 June in Bologna and extended to other cities and towns in the Romagna, the Marches and Umbria during the next two weeks. Similar revolutions occurred in the duchies of Parma and Modena on 9 and 11 June. Pro-Piedmontest activists had been at work in the Romagna causing desertions from the papal army, and both Piedmontese and Tuscan regular army troops had already crossed the papal border and appeared at the outskirts of Bologna. The Tuscan provisional government let rebel Romagnol fighters use Tuscany as a base for infiltration against the papal government.[7]

The locus of the conspiracy in the Romagna was the Bologna chapter of the Italian National Society, one of the best organized and most powerful chapters of the whole peninsula. When the Austrian troops suddenly withdrew from Bologna, the officers of the National Society proclaimed themselves to be a provisional government. In many places throughout the Romagna in the next two weeks, similar actions occurred.[8] In Bologna itself, the provisional government, backed by the Piedmontese and Tuscan army troops nearby, repressed all political opposition from both *papalini* and republicans, secured a police force and municipal bureaucracy loyal to the new régime, and published an official paper to control the flow of news. To the surprise of Cavour and the liberal nationalist leaders, however, only a minority of the total population rallied to the new provincial government.[9] Cavour's big argument, echoed by Hudson and Odo Russell, had been that the people needed only the removal of

4   Cavour to Emanuel d'Azeglio, 28 March 1861, *Cavour e l'Inghilterra*, vol. II, 202. See also Marliani to Cavour, London, 4 Feb. 1860, *Cavour e l'Inghilterra*, vol. II, 15–17: 'The present government is for us the ideal of good will – our cause is its cause, our future its future ...' Minghetti to Emanuel d'Azeglio, Turin, 7 and 18 July 1859, Adolfo Colombo (ed.), *Carteggi e documenti diplomatici inediti di Emanuele d'Azeglio* (Turin: Istituto per la storia del Risorgimento, n.d.), vol. II, 204, 208.
5   Odo Russell to Russell, Rome, 17 July 1859, no. 89, secret, PRO, FO, 43/71, and *Odo Russell*, 37.
6   *Giornale di Roma*, 27 June 1859.
7   Antonelli to Sacconi, Rome, 9 June 1859, no. 3935, ASV, ANParigi, 1859, SdS, AD/P, and *Antonelli*, vol. I, 129–31. See Hudson to Russell, Turin, 1 July 1859, no. 11, *Gran Bretagna e Sardegna*, vol. VII, 124, which acknowledges, and defends, the presence of Piedmontese troops inside the boundary of the Romagna.
8   Grew, 212.
9   Mack Smith, *Victor Emanuel, Cavour*, 100–1. Grew, 213. Victor Emmanuel complained to George Cadogan, the British military observer in Italy, that Cavour bungled the Romagnol revolution. (Cadogan to Russell, Milan, 14 July 1859, private, *Gran Bretagna e Sardegna*, vol. VII, 386.) See Mack Smith, *Making of Italy*, 285–92.

the foreign troops for them to rise and throw off the priestly power. That had not happened. Cavour complained about the feebleness of the revolution to Farini, the author of the history of the Roman States so influential in England, and now the *de facto* Piedmontese governor of Emilia, which included the Romagna:

> The people of the Romagna in their behaviour toward the pontifical troops have made me depressed and despairing. You yourself, like Beltrani and Minghetti, used to repeat every time the subject came up that there was no need to worry, since an insurrection would at once break out when the right opportunity presented itself. But now the Austrians have gone, leaving only three thousand f... Swiss soldiers, and these are enough to terrorize three million individuals. This gives the direct lie to our statements about the conditions of the Romagna. It puts both the Emperor and ourselves in a completely false position.[10]

Cavour was not ready to speak so frankly in public; instead, he would behave as if the revolution were a success. The practical reality was that the partisans of the National Society in the Romagna had succeeded in seizing power at the opportune moment. Cavour could act as if the mere existence of a provisional government was evidence in favour of his argument, and he hoped his supporters in the outside world, especially the English, would believe his propaganda. Events at Perugia during the seven days from 14 to 20 June helped serve him, too. In many towns throughout the papal provinces of the Marches and Umbria people loyal to Piedmont seized political power and proclaimed the end of papal rule in their areas. Their success was brief, however. In every place outside the Romagna, papal authorities and troops managed without much bloodshed to restore papal government, largely because the insurgents were not given armed backing by Piedmont or Tuscan nationalists from across the border.[11] The exception to this pattern of quiet restoration was Perugia. There on 14 June insurgents overthrew papal temporal power and established a provisional government loyal to Victor Emmanuel which controlled the city for almost a week. On 20 June, after negotiations between a papal representative and the provisional government failed, papal troops composed mostly of Swiss recruits tried to regain the city by direct assault. The battle for Perugia was bloody and ferocious although it lasted only a few hours. In the end the papal troops succeeded in restoring the city to papal authority. Italian nationalists regarded Perugia as no less than a 'massacre' of innocent, freedom-loving citizens by bloodthirsty mercenaries at papal command. The papal government would acknowledge only that intense and bloody fighting occurred during a civil war in which some soldiers may have temporarily gone out of control in the heat of the battle. In any case, while deploring the excesses, the papal government was unapologetic about its right to restore the 'rebellious' city to proper order, by

10 Cavour to Farini, Turin, 3 July 1859, *La liberazione del mezzagiorno e la formazione del Regno d'Italia* (5 vols., Bologna: Zanichelli, 1949–54), vol. v, 434–5; translated in Mack Smith, *Making of Italy*, 283–4.
11 Grew, 215–16.

force if necessary.[12] Cavour was delighted with the events in Perugia, and wanted the nationalist version of the Perugia 'massacre' widely publicized, for the picture of papal troops committing atrocities against 'the Italian people' would, he believed, be a great propaganda benefit to the cause.[13]

Cavour named a special commissioner to begin the process of absorbing the Romagna without technically doing so. He again turned to Massimo d'Azeglio, his special instrument to mollify England. He had used him on the delicate mission to the Prince of Wales in Rome in March, then sent him to London in April, and now to the Romagna in June. He was to be 'the vice-antipope', as Cavour's confidant Massari called him.[14] Hudson helped Cavour by assuring Russell that Sardinia was not annexing the Romagna, but merely assisting 'in maintaining the public peace should it ever be seriously endangered'.[15]

Pius IX battled the revolution with both ecclesiastical and political-military weapons. To the bishops and faithful of the church, including the English and Irish, he directed an encyclical, followed by an allocution to the Roman Consistory of the Sacred College of Cardinals. To the governments of the world, including the English, his secretary of state addressed a note via the diplomatic corps in Rome.[16] To Sacconi, the nuncio in Paris, he sent instructions to arouse the French bishops and faithful to pray and put political pressure on Napoleon. The action of the French Catholics in defence of the pope served as an example to Catholics in England and Ireland.[17] Against the revolutionaries, meanwhile, his armed forces performed their duties, culminating in the events at Perugia.

Pius IX claimed that the revolution was the work of only a small number of his subjects, led by a revolutionary club, and supported by outside activists and materiel. He called it an offence against lawful authority and public justice which all should condemn, but also a sinful act which brought harm to the Roman Catholic Church and the spiritual work of the Holy See. This was the moment

12 The Perugian nationalist version of the events may be found in a statement by the provisional government of Perugia, a declaration by Perugian refugees at Florence, enclosed in Hudson to Russell, Turin, 30 July 1859, no. 46, PRO, FO, 67/246/134–244, and in newspapers such as the *Monitore Toscano* and *Monitore Bolognese*. The papal version was presented in the report of the papal troops' commanding officer, Col. Schmid, and the official papal government reply to the descriptions of the event as a 'massacre', *Giornale di Roma*, 27 June and 4 July 1859. See Romano Ugolini, 'Perugia 1859: l'ordine di saccheggio', *Rassegna storia del Risorgimento* 59 (1972), 353–9; and Ugolini, *Cavour e Napoleone III nell'Italia centrale: il sacrificio di Perugia*, passim.
13 Massari, *Diario*, 22 June 1859, 278.
14 Massari, *Diario*, 15 and 18 June 1859, 272 and 274. Cavour to Massimo d'Azeglio, 5 July 1859, Chiala, *Cavour*, clxxxii. Marshall, *Massimo d'Azeglio*, 261–8.
15 Hudson to Russell, Turin, 1 July 1859, no. 14, *Gran Bretagna e Sardegna*, vol. VII, 126.
16 The encyclical, 18 June 1859, and the allocution, 18 June 1859, were enclosed in Odo Russell to Russell, Rome, 1 July 1859; the circular, Antonelli to the diplomatic corps, 18 June 1859, was communicated to Odo by Antonelli to Odo Russell, Rome, 18 June 1859, and enclosed in Odo Russell to Malmesbury, Rome, 21 June 1859, PRO, FO, 43/71.
17 Antonelli to Sacconi, Rome, 17 June 1859, no. 4241, ASV, ASdS, 1859, 165/3/192–3, and *Antonelli*, vol. I, 140. The *Tablet* understood this point and urged English and Irish Catholics to follow the lead of the French (*Tablet*, 1 and 8 Oct. 1859).

when he clearly defined the papal temporal power and declared that 'the civil power is necessary to the Holy See in order that it may be able, without any impediment, to exercise its sacred duties for the benefit of Religion'. He called upon the governments of the world to defend his sovereign authority and independence, upon the faithful to pray, and upon the rebels to desist and repent of their evil ways. To accentuate his appeals he declared that all those who had participated in the revolution had automatically incurred the ecclesiastical penalties of excommunication. He also asserted, through Antonelli, the right of the papal government to use political and military means to preserve the temporal power unimpaired. As the pope's and the cardinal's actions revealed, to them state and church, politics and religion, were inseparable in the States of the Church. Hereafter, any view of the Papal States which denied the bond of state and church offended papal orthodoxy.

The pope made it unmistakably clear that he refused to acknowledge the loss of the Romagna, that he intended to do everything within his power to restore the Romagna fully under papal authority, and that he expected the European powers to support the papacy in this as they had each time before. In the week-and-a-half following the revolution, the pope and Antonelli did all they could in defence of the papal temporal power. They could do no more now. It was the turn of the powers, especially England and Napoleon, to act.[18]

The events in the Papal States and the duchies occurred so quickly, one after another, that Palmerston and Russell had no time to settle into office before they had to formulate their Italian and papal policy. By 22 June, within ten days of taking office, they had a policy statement ready to send James Hudson in Turin for him to use with Cavour. They sent a copy to Rome to guide Odo Russell in his relations with Cardinal Antonelli. What Palmerston and Russell had decided was that as long as the war was on everything that happened in the Romagna and the duchies would be considered by Britain officially to be only provisional. The British vice-consul at Ancona, for example, should have only such unofficial relations with the provisional government in the Romagna as were necessary to protect British commercial interests there. However, the weight of British support would be given implicitly to the provisional government if it were successful in maintaining 'order' and preventing the 'disorder' of 1848 and 1849. They expected questions of territory and sovereignty to be settled by 'the will of the Italian people, the fortune of war, and finally a European treaty'. In a supplementary letter to Hudson, Lord John Russell enunciated what came to be the Palmerston government's most central and enduring principle throughout the entire Italian and papal crisis: 'I do not wish to see either the Tedescho or Gallic armenti drinking the waters of the Po. Let the Italians govern their own

18   Antonelli to the nuncios, Rome, 21 June 1859, ASV, ANParigi, 1859, SdS, AD/P, and Antonelli to Sacconi, Rome, 1 July 1859, no. 4438, draft, ASV, ASdS, 1859, 165/4/14, and *Antonelli*, vol. 1, 144 and 154–5.

affairs: that is my motto.'[19] Russell meant for Hudson to interpret the official despatch, generally phrased as it was, in the light of the private letter which accompanied it. In this manner, right from the start, he operated on two levels. The official statement which had to be approved by Queen Victoria and the whole Cabinet, and would probably be published in the Blue Books, worded things to get past these stages of approval while still heading in the desired direction. Russell's private letters to the diplomats, or his conversations, revealed the way in which the official statements should be understood. By this double-tiered method, Palmerston and Russell, in their personal foreign policy, could unabashedly support Cavour when they wanted and work against the papacy, without the fear of restraint.

Cavour had no difficulty, through Hudson, in catching Russell's intent: Piedmont and the liberal nationalists in central Italy had England's support so long as they kept the revolution 'respectable', and the French and Austrians away. Massari reflected Cavour's appreciation in his diary: 'This despatch is excellent, since it proves that the present English government understands the situation wonderfully. It is a consoling fact.'[20]

In a parallel private letter to Cowley in Paris Russell disclosed what he thought was the superior solution of the Papal Question: 'The Pope has claim on France to protect his person. But Rome and fifteen miles around is quite as much territory as he can manage. Even to do that he should have the assistance of a municipal corporation.'[21] Russell had no desire to see Pius IX personally humiliated or endangered, but he was very definitely prepared to encourage the end of the temporal power outside Rome and its environs. This solution repeated what he proposed unofficially in December 1858 and remained a central tenet of Russell's and Palmerston's personal foreign policy throughout the crisis of those years. Russell's two phrases summarized it all: 'Let the Italians govern their own affairs', and 'Rome and fifteen miles around'. Pius IX was nearly right when he told Odo that 'they want to see the Pope deprived of his temporal power'. Russell had none of Malmesbury's caution on the subject.

In the complexities of day-to-day diplomacy during the coming months, Russell and Palmerston, with Gladstone's advice, continued to look for intermediate, if second best, solutions to the Papal Question. Some of these Russell expressed to Cowley even now: 'I should be glad to see a lay viceroy for the Roman States. If he cannot be found the Kingdom of Sardinia has stomach enough for one half of Italy.' A similar suggestion was made by Gladstone in a lengthy memorandum on Italy on 30 June. In one sense it made little difference to the government whether Sardinia absorbed the Papal States outright or exercised control of them *de facto* through a lay viceroy under the pope's nominal

19 Russell to Hudson, 22 June 1859, no. 1, and 23 June 1859, private, *Gran Bretagna e Sardegna*, vol. VII, 120–1. Scarlett to Gaggiotti, Florence, 22 June 1859, PRO, FO, 79/205.
20 Massari, *Diario*, 1 July 1859, 286.
21 Russell to Cowley, 23 June 1859, private, Russell papers, PRO, 30/22/103.

sovereignty. In either case effective political control of the region would belong to Sardinia. Another conceivable solution was to attach the Legations to Tuscany or Venice – anywhere, it seemed, just so the Romagnols no longer endured papal rule.[22] He tried to obtain the queen's approval for an official despatch to Cowley, dated 1 July, endorsing a scheme he attributed to Count Persigny for the disposal of the papal territory as part of a reorganization of Italy: place the Legations under a viceroy, assign the Marches and Umbria to Tuscany to administer, and leave the pope ruling in Rome. Russell thought 'his plan had great merit' and wanted to see if Napoleon and Francis Joseph could be led to adopt it. The queen objected, however, and the despatch was never sent.[23]

It was the events at Perugia that permitted Russell to secure the queen's and the Cabinet's approval of some aggressive criticism of the papal government as well as of a sweeping official recommendation for the treatment of the papal temporal power. He prepared official instructions to Odo Russell, which the queen approved, telling him to protest the 'butcheries' by the papal troops. Actually Odo had already taken a private letter from Lord John to mean that he should protest 'the Perugia massacre', which he did in the strongest language.[24] The queen approved an even more vigorous attack sent to Cowley in Paris which charged that these 'unchristian outrages' flowed inescapably from a government run by priests. He asserted that calamities comparable to Perugia had been going on a long time: 'The disorders, the robberies, the insecurity which have been characteristic of the condition of the Legations for many years, the corruption which has prevailed in the central Government, and the authority used to prevent the progress of secular knowledge, and general education, have rendered the Papal government one of the most crying evils of Italy.' Russell reached a conclusion which was comprehensive in its implications: '[N]o hope remains for the people under the sway of His Holiness.' His proposal was for the European powers to force the pope to 'divest himself of the actual administration of temporal power'. Russell had in mind something like the viceroy arrangement he had mentioned privately to Cowley earlier. This solution was less satisfactory to Russell than 'Rome and fifteen miles around', but it was one that Napoleon, who had to move carefully around the Catholics of France, might be able to approve publicly. It would entail the end of the *exercise* of papal temporal power and not the end of the temporal power itself. This policy statement was the

22   Russell to Cowley, 20 June 1859, private, Cowley papers, PRO, FO, 519/197, and Russell to Cowley, 28 June 1859, private, copy, Russell papers, PRO, 30/22/103. *The Gladstone diaries*, 30 June 1859.
23   Russell to Cowley, 1 July 1859, no. 48, PRO, FO, 27/1284.
24   Russell to Odo Russell, 1 July 1859, no. 2, draft, PRO, FO, 43/69. Russell to Odo Russell, 23 June 1859, private, Ampthill papers, PRO, FO, 918/7/5–8, and Odo Russell to Russell, Rome, 1 July 1859, no. 80, PRO, FO, 43/71, and *Odo Russell*, 27 and 29. The Swiss consul in London objected to labelling the pope's troops at Perugia as 'Swiss'. They were not Swiss troops, he said, although some Swiss citizens may be enrolled in the papal army without Swiss government authorization (John Rapp to *The Times*, 4 July 1859, in *The Times*, 6 July 1859).

announcement that from now on England was committed to work for the *de facto* end of papal temporal power in the Romagna, and perhaps in other papal territories as well.[25]

Russell's diplomatic move achieved nothing, however. Walewski neutralized Russell's outrage by replying straightforwardly that the English had believed completely inaccurate information about Perugia and that the actual course of events was not as heinous as the English depicted. On top of this, while lamenting any excesses committed by the troops, Walewski stated that the pope had the right to use all necessary military force to restore his legitimate authority. Walewski refused to accept a copy of Russell's protest.[26] Odo Russell did no better with Antonelli in Rome. The cardinal told him simply that the accounts the English believed concerning Perugia were grossly exaggerated, and any protest was without foundation.[27]

Antonelli and Walewski, it turned out, were substantially correct in their criticism of the English version of the events. Odo's first protest to Antonelli and his report of Perugia dated 24 June, upon which Russell had based the vigorous English protest to the French government on 1 July, derived essentially from a second-hand account of the testimony of one family. Edward Newton Perkins and his sister, Americans from Boston, were trapped in their Perugia hotel when the fighting began. They saw some killing and looting by the papal troops, then went into hiding in their hotel where they remained for the duration of the episode. Their personal experience was horrendous, and their reports vivid, but necessarily very limited. Odo had been told about their experience by someone who had met them after the events, and he had taken what he heard by such a medium to be a definitive representation of the entire conflict. He had added to this the impressions he received from partisans of the nationalist cause. When later questioned by Lord John, Odo admitted that his version was 'incomplete', and although he stood by his basic judgment against the papal troops, he was glad Lord John did not publish it in the parliamentary Blue Books later.[28]

A second despatch on Perugia that Russell received came from Hudson at Turin, but arrived after Russell's protests to Antonelli and Walewski. Hudson's version rested on even less secure ground than Odo's. It was based on material supplied by Cavour, via Massari, in response to Hudson's request to Cavour for

25   Russell to Cowley, 1 July 1859, no. 47, PRO, FO, 27/1284.
26   Cowley to Russell, Paris, 5 July, no. 112; 4 July, no. 104; and 1 July 1859, no. 75, PRO, FO, 27/1299.
27   Odo Russell to Russell, Rome, 7 July 1859, no. 82, PRO, FO, 43/71, and *Odo Russell*, 32–3.
28   Odo's account of Perugia is in his despatch to Malmesbury, Rome, 24 June 1859, no. 76, PRO, FO, 43/71, and *Odo Russell*, 28. See Russell to Odo Russell, 9 July 1859, private, draft, Russell papers, PRO, 30/22/11, and Odo Russell to Russell, 15 July 1859, no. 87, PRO, FO, 43/71. Perkins' sister's report (signed 'S.P.C.') apeared in *The Times*, 2 July 1859, and his own (signed 'Boston, USA') was printed in *The Times*, 13 July 1859. See also Perkins' letter, from Villa Capponi, near Florence, 24 July 1859, in Galignani's *Messenger*, 30 July 1859. Perkins was awarded full indemnity by the papal government for his losses at Perugia (Corbett to Russell, Florence, 4 Aug. 1859, no. 95, PRO, FO, 79/206).

information on Perugia. Hudson's Perugia despatch was probably the most important item in Cavour's propaganda about the 'papal massacre'.[29]

Lord John admitted in the House of Commons on 7 July that the information in the despatches on Perugia he had received from Odo and Hudson were disputed and that he could not therefore make the reports public 'until the real facts have been ascertained'. He wrote to Odo and Corbett in Florence for further information.[30] In fact, Odo, Hudson and Lord John had been a little too ready to believe bad news about the papal government.

Russell's effort to gather more information on Perugia was perfunctory, and he never had to talk about it again in Parliament. He, Odo Russell, and the mass of the English reading public continued to think the most horrific things about the pope because of the battle of Perugia. The event passed into the store of English anti-papal legends.

The pope and Antonelli, on their side, hoped Perugia would provide convincing proof that the papacy intended to let none of the temporal power go without a fight. Antonelli explained this to Odo:

> Of course we deplore the necessity to employ force and we feel for those who have suffered . . . But on the other hand the moral effect produced by the conduct of our troops at Perugia has proved most beneficial, for Ancona and all the other towns we sent detachments to, submitted without resistance. Unfortunately we have not troops enough to enter the Legations at present and retake Bologna, Ferrara, and Ravenna.[31]

Antonelli left no doubt in Odo's mind that one day the papal army would act once again if it could. The cardinal gave Odo the papal government's protest against Sardinia's incursion into the Romagna. Antonelli asked Odo for England's help in restoring the Romagna if the pope's rights were ever discussed in a congress.[32]

Soon after this Odo was summoned to a private audience with Pius IX, his second since his arrival in Rome. Pius was anxious to talk. The main topic was the influence of England in the revolution and Italy. Pius told Odo that he regarded Sardinia to be the principal culprit in the revolution, but, he said, behind Sardinia lay England, and, for example, Russell's doctrine, now widely reported, 'Let the Italians govern their own affairs.' As Odo retold it, Pius went on to say:

> Now the Italians are a dissatisfied, interfering, turbulent, and intriguing race, they can never learn to govern themselves. It is impossible . . . A hotheaded people

29 Hudson to Russell, Turin, 3 July 1859, no. 16, *Gran Bretagna e Sardegna*, vol. VII, 127–8. Massari, *Diario*, 2 and 3 July 1859, 288–90.
30 Hansard's, CLIV, col. 795, 7 July 1859. Russell to Odo Russell, 9 July 1859, private, Ampthill papers, PRO, FO, 918/7/9–11; Corbett to Russell, Florence, 11 July 1859, no. 55, PRO, FO, 79/206.
31 Odo Russell to Russell, Rome, 7 July 1859, no. 82, PRO, FO, 43/71, and *Odo Russell*, 33.
32 Antonelli to the diplomatic corps, Vatican, 12 July 1859, enclosed in Odo Russell to Russell, Rome, 14 July 1859, no. 88, PRO, FO, 43/71, and *Odo Russell*, 35.

> like the Italians require a firm and just Government to guide and take care of them and Italy might have continued tranquil and contented had not the ambition of Sardinia led her to revolutionize the whole country . . . I often wonder at the language your statesmen hold about us in the Houses of Parliament. I always read their speeches. Lord Palmerston, Lord John Russell and Mr. Gladstone do not know us . . .

Pius was, no doubt, correct in believing that the English understood him poorly, but he was unaware of how poorly he understood the liberal nationalists in the Romagna. His paternalistic ultramontanism was not able to cope with the aspirations of some Italians for independence and English style institutions. Pius foresaw that when the war was over a congress on Italian affairs would convene. This, he said, 'is even worse for us than war', for a congress would try to force changes on the papacy. But, he assured Odo, the papacy would endure even if the pope must live in the catacombs. Then the pope paused. Odo described what happened next: 'The Pope then beckoned to me to approach and making the sign of the cross he gave me his blessing in Latin, then with both his hands he took one of mine, pressed it and said with great warmth: "Be our friend in the hour of need!"' The plea demonstrated benevolence as well as pathos as the pope asked his enemy to be his friend. Like Antonelli, Pius requested that England help the pope. When Lord John read of this episode he wrote on the despatch, 'Very curious.' Lord John's mind could not fathom what Pius had done.[33]

The pope's and Antonelli's appeals for England's help were rather hopeless. While Napoleon played double with the pope, England became the one great power now publicly committed to prevent the restoration of the pope's temporal power in the Romagna. The Palmerston–Russell government was the first one in Europe to accept the revolution in the Romagna, the first to support Sardinia's controlling influence there, and the first to offer a definite plan for the separation of Romagna, and perhaps more, from direct papal rule. Moreover, the Russell doctrine, 'Let the Italians govern their own affairs', was available for use in abetting the cause of Piedmont and inhibiting the cause of the pope. One day, perhaps, the Romagna might be returned to papal authority, as was Perugia, but not if the English government could help it.

Villafranca and the confederation

The build-up of Piedmontese troops in the Romagna constituted, in effect, a Piedmontese military occupation in place of the Austrian one. Since the war was still on, this development meant that the resources of the Romagna might be thrown into the conflict against Austria and the rest of the pope's territory. Suddenly, on 11 July, one month after the Bologna revolution began, Napoleon

---

[33] Odo Russell to Russell, Rome, 17 July 1859, no. 89, secret, PRO, FO, 43/71, and *Odo Russell*, 36–9. Odo does not identify the date of this audience, but it evidently took place before the Villafranca peace became known in Rome on 13 July.

arranged a peace with the Austrian emperor at Villafranca on the plains of the Po. Victor Emmanuel had to go along with the move.

Cavour and his supporters were completely upset by the timing of the peace. They had fully expected Napoleon to continue the war until Austria was expelled from Italy and, perhaps, until papal rule was overturned in more provinces. Hudson and Cowley both suggested that Napoleon had finally come to believe that the worse things became for the pope in the Romagna, the more pressure he himself would feel from French Catholics because of the continuation of the war. Of course, Napoleon had many grounds for stopping the war, but this was probably one of them.[34]

The contents of the peace were an even greater shock to Cavour and the liberal nationalists. Cavour resigned outright. In Bologna the nationalists felt betrayed. Marquis Pepoli, a leading member of the ruling junta, rushed to Turin to appeal to the king to reject the peace for the sake of the Romagna revolution.[35]

Lord John Russell, on 12 July, read to the House of Commons the terms of Villafranca as summarized by Napoleon's telegram to Empress Eugenie:

> Peace is signed between the Emperor of Austria and me. The bases of the Peace are: Italian Confederation under the honorary Presidency of the Pope. The Emperor of Austria cedes his rights to Lombardy to the Emperor of the French, who transfers them to the King of Sardinia. The Emperor of Austria preserves Venice but she will form an integral part of the Italian Confederation. General Amnesty.

Cowley reported two other provisions pertaining to the pope and central Italy:

> Tuscany and Modena to be restored to their rightful Sovereigns with a general amnesty. The two Sovereigns engage to use all their influence with the Pope to obtain a large measure of reform.[36]

Palmerston and Russell, together with Gladstone,[37] expressed both incredulity and outrage that Napoleon would try to force such terms upon Italy and the powers of Europe. Their complaint against Villafranca was essentially the same as that of Cavour and Romagnol nationalists. They were appalled by the provision for a confederation with the pope at its head and the Emperor of Austria as one of its members. Austria and the pope, plus the two restored dukes

34   Hudson to Russell, Turin, 13 July 1859, private, *Gran Bretagna e Sardegna*, vol. VII, 140. Cowley to Hudson, Paris, 29 July 1859, Cowley papers, PRO, FO, 519/226. Antonelli to Sacconi, Rome, 24 June 1859, no. 4316, ASV, ANParigi, 1859, SdS, AD/P, and *Antonelli*, vol. I, 145–8. Mack Smith, *Victor Emanuel, Cavour*, 104–5. Other grounds included the fear that Prussia would join the war on Austria's side and extend the conflict along the Rhine, and genuine revulsion at the carnage of the war.
35   Hudson to Russell, Turin, 12 July 1859, no. 19, confidential, and 16 July 1859, no. 33, *Gran Bretagna e Sardegna*, vol. VII, 139 and 174.
36   Hansard's, CLIV, col. 1051–2, 12 July 1859. Cowley to Russell, Paris, 13 July 1859, no. 196, confidential, PRO, FO, 27/1300. See A.J.P. Taylor, 'English mediation and the agreement of Villafranca, 1859', *English historical review* 51 (1936), 52–78.
37   Gladstone to Carlo Poerio, 15 July 1859, Morley, *Gladstone*, vol. II, 13.

of Tuscany and Modena, together with the king of Naples, would give the Austro-papal forces a majority. It was 'surely a strange monster', Russell said, that would be nothing but 'an instrument of Austrian and Papal despotism'.[38] Such a confederation, added Palmerston, would be 'a model machine for rivetting the yoke of slavery on Italy'.[39] Even Queen Victoria agreed. She wrote to Lord John, 'How Italy is to prosper under the Pope's presidency the Queen is at a loss to conceive.'[40] Russell surmised that Napoleon had been caught between his contradictory promises to Cavour to liberate Italy and to Pius IX to defend the temporal power; in order to compensate for the revolution in the Papal States the emperor had committed himself to set up a confederation favourable to papal interests.[41]

The English government heard through Walewski at Paris that Pius IX generally approved Villafranca and the confederation, and consented to be the honorary president.[42] Odo Russell appeared to confirm the news with his own conjecture that the Vatican was 'not unfavourable to the idea, the more so as it seems to have been sanctioned by Austria'. Gramont had got the impression from the pope that he would accept the confederation. According to Odo, Antonelli told him that 'the idea of an Italian confederation filled him with "national pride and enthusiasm"'.[43] Hudson contributed the observation, 'It is a remarkable symptom that the priests throughout Italy are in extreme good spirits – all this means that the Peace of Villafranca is a catholic league.'[44]

Russell had as yet issued no official statement against Villafranca, but news of English reaction spread quickly in diplomatic circles and through the newspapers. With Napoleon now discredited, England achieved new status in Italy. Odo Russell happily reported that among the liberals of Rome 'the old sympathies for England which had vanished since the beginning of the year have returned with extraordinary suddenness'. Hudson recounted a long conversation with Victor Emmanuel, now compelled to work without Cavour and Cavour's conspiracy with Napoleon. Feeling the burden of Villafranca, especially of the confederation and the disaster he thought it would bring to Italy, the king told Hudson: 'I have only one hope – that is England. It is always

38   Russell to Cowley, 16 July 1859, private, copy, and 19 July 1859, private, copy, Russell papers, PRO, 30/22/103. Persigny to Walewski, London, 17 July 1859, *Le conferenze e la pace di Zurigo nei documenti diplomatici francesi*, ed. Armando Saitta (Rome: Istituto storico italiano per l'età moderna e contemporanea, 1965), 329–30.
39   Palmerston to Russell, 19 July 1859, Russell papers, PRO, 30/22/20.
40   Queen Victoria to Russell, 14 July 1859, copy, Russell papers, PRO, 30/22/13G.
41   See Russell to Palmerston, 17 July 1859, Palmerston papers, 1859, GC/RU/507. *Punch* (23 July 1859), shared the Palmerston–Russell view of Villafranca, showing Francis Joseph shackling the maiden Italia to Austrian Venetia, and Napoleon III blind-folding her with the papal tiara. Italia holds a staff bearing Garibaldi's cap of liberty.
42   Cowley to Russell, Paris, 15 July 1859, no. 215, PRO, FO, 27/1300.
43   Odo Russell to Russell, Rome, 18 July 1859, no. 91, and 22 July 1859, no. 97, PRO, FO, 43/71, and *Odo Russell*, 39, 41–2. Gramont to Walewski, Rome, 22 July 1859, AMAE, CP, 1011/99–100. See Scott, 134–5.
44   Hudson to Russell, Galignani, 30 July 1859, private, *Gran Bretagna e Sardegna*, vol. VII, 175.

just. I commission you to write what I have said to you to your Government. But what shall I do?' The king repeated, 'I have no hope save in England, if she does not interfere Italy must become a foyer d'anarchie.' Cavour himself talked to Hudson just before leaving Turin and put the point even more candidly. The Derby government, he said, had failed Italy at the crucial moment of struggle, but Italy can recover, even from the troubles of Villafranca, if only the new English government will lead the constitutional cause.[45]

Russell and Palmerston could hope for no more direct mandate from the Italian nationalists. They privately debated between themselves how best to use England's favoured standing to give shape to the course of events in Italy and the Papal States. One thing they were sure of was that no confederation could be formed without English approval.[46] Perhaps the most suitable thing to do would be to convene a congress of the European powers, provided it were not designed merely to rubber stamp the terms of Villafranca. Palmerston argued this way: 'If we and other Powers interfere by means of a Congress or Conference, much of that Evil may possibly be prevented; and is it not right that we should do what we can to mitigate if not entirely to prevent mischief, instead of saying, we have been no Parties to the mischief and wash our hands of it.' Palmerston and Russell, with Gladstone's prodding, refused to accept the role that Malmesbury had claimed officially for England as a Protestant state – of retiring, at least in policy if not in practice, from active involvement in the settlement of papal affairs in Italy.[47] To Palmerston the course to pursue was obvious. The English government should work actively to defeat the whole confederation project; failing that, it should insure that the pope not be made president, that Rome not be made the headquarters, and that Austria not be a member. If the confederation were defeated, he would be content with one of the half-way measures, like a lay viceroy, that he and Russell had entertained earlier. He added, 'Alas for the poor People in the purely Roman State, what could be done for them. Perhaps nothing more effectual than to withdraw all foreign troops including the Swiss.'[48]

Palmerston and Russell decided to prepare a major policy statement, dated 25 July, to be sent to Lord Cowley and designed to influence the French government. The French were, after all, the crucial power for papal affairs. The draft, written by Russell, incorporated the objections to the confederation which Palmerston, Russell and the queen had expressed, and added a new argument against its Austrian–papal character. The confederation, the statement said,

45   Odo Russell, Rome, 18 July 1859, no. 91, PRO, FO, 43/71, and *Odo Russell*, 39. Hudson to Russell, Turin, 17 and 20 July 1859, private, *Gran Bretagna e Sardegna*, vol. VII, 162–3, and 166.
46   Russell to Cowley, 16 and 19 July 1859, private, copies, Russell papers, PRO, 30/22/103.
47   Palmerston to Russell, 18 and 19 July 1859, and Russell's 'Memorandum for Lord Palmerston', n.d., Russell papers, PRO, 30/22/20. See *Gladstone diaries*, 30 June 1859.
48   Palmerston to Russell, 15 July 1859, Russell papers, PRO, 30/22/20.

would quench not only Italian independence but also Italian liberties: 'For instance, the laws of Piedmont of late years have favoured liberty of worship, liberty of education, liberty of the press. But what hope would there be of maintaining these liberties before a tribunal presided over by His Holiness the Pope, and where the Emperor of Austria and two Archdukes of Austria would have a certain majority?' He referred to the anticlerical Siccardi laws, the laws most offensive to Catholic sensitivities, but most appealing to the English. The statement called for the confederation project either to be abandoned or entirely reorganized to exclude Austria from its membership. The first step, in either case, would be 'to free Italy as soon as possible from the presence of foreign troops, whether French or Austrian'.[49]

The queen approved the despatch, after rejecting an earlier draft, but demanded that it not be given to the French government until after England knew the outcome of the negotiations for a peace treaty between the two emperors to be held at Zurich. She thought that to try to influence the negotiations constituted improper interference in Italian affairs.[50]

Russell and Palmerston acquiesced in the queen's restriction, but they could not refrain from finding another means of proclaiming English policy so that the French and the Austrians would indeed feel England's influence during the Zurich conference. Russell chose the House of Commons as the forum, on 28 July, for a lengthy address on foreign policy. The Commons was a freer medium than a diplomatic despatch. Russell spoke against Villafranca and the confederation, raising the same objections that he had put in the 25 July despatch. Then he continued for a time to speak against the papal government, asserting that the question of the pope's temporal government 'is now, and has been for centuries, perhaps the most difficult of all in Italy'. His provocative comments stimulated a major debate on the pope's temporal power in which the leading figures of both main party groupings and of the Roman Catholics in Parliament participated.[51]

George Bowyer, the principal Catholic spokesman in the Commons, could not allow Russell's remarks to pass. He defended the papal government as a progressive and enlightened one which should not be attacked simply because it had chosen a different pattern of development than the English or Piedmontese. His point was that the confederation might work very well in Italy where there was no tradition of a unitary state as in England, but where numerous smaller states coexisted, each with different kinds of institutions. Bowyer argued that Russell was historically mistaken to think of Italy according to the model of Whig politics in England. Given Italian politics, there was no figure more

---

[49] Russell to Cowley, 25 July 1859, no. 177, *Gran Bretagna e Sardegna*, vol. VII, 224–7.
[50] Queen Victoria to Russell, 24 July 1859, copy, Russell papers, PRO, 30/22/13G. On the preparation of this despatch, see Gladstone to the Duke of Argyll, 31 Aug. 1859, in *Gladstone diaries*, 31 Aug. 1859.
[51] What follows on the Commons debate is drawn from Hansard's, CLV, col. 543–628, 28 July 1859.

eminent and more cosmopolitan than the pope to act as head of the confederation. Palmerston rejected Bowyer's historical argument. He insisted it *was* legitimate to think of Italy according to English political patterns – there was a Whig party in Italy and a Tory party too. He was convinced that Italy *could* be given the same institutions which had developed in England, and he hoped to use the influence of the English government to do so. The debate carried on into the night.

To the surprise of the English, including Bowyer, it was the pope who took the next step to quash the confederation project. On the same day as the debate in the Commons a congregation of cardinals convened at the Vatican to discuss a position paper drafted by Antonelli. The paper argued against accepting the confederation and the honorary presidency. It seemed to represent second thoughts on the subject, but it also seemed to suggest that Gramont and Odo and their governments had been overly anxious to interpret the pope as favourable to the project. The cardinals agreed with the argument that the confederation, however innocuous it might appear, would require certain papal interests to be subordinated to the whole organization, and would wrongly place the States of the Church in a position of equality with the other states as if it were merely another temporal state. The effect of this would be to compromise the absolute independence of the Holy See and to channel all kinds of troubles into the Papal States. In general, Antonelli argued, the office of the pope as common father of all the faithful would be incompatible with the military obligations, even defensive ones, of membership in the confederation. With the approval of the pope and the cardinals, Antonelli prepared a policy statement sent to the nuncio at Vienna on 29 July which rejected the confederation. It too was intended to influence the conference at Zurich.[52]

With the pope, the intended president, and England, a major power, both firmly opposed to the Villafranca project, Russell concluded by the end of August that 'the Confederation is nearly given up'. Russell and Palmerston were impatient for the queen to lift her embargo against officially stating their views during the Zurich talks. Russell drafted a new despatch against the confederation which proposed an alternative territorial rearrangement of Italy. The queen adamantly refused to give it her approval, but because the talks were dragging on, she decided to allow the 25 July despatch to be given to the French government while the Zurich sessions were still in progress.[53]

When Cowley did finally deliver the 25 July despatch to the French

52 'Posizione da servire per una Congregazione cardinalizia in data 28 luglio 1859', and Antonelli to DeLuca, Rome, 29 July 1859, Pirri, vol. II, part 2, 101–4, 108–10. Pirri, vol. II, part 1, 112–28.
53 Russell to Palmerston, 24 Aug. 1859, Palmerston papers, 1859, GC/RU/520. Russell to Cowley, n.d. (c. 21 Aug. 1859), draft, marked 'This despatch was stopped by the Queen's direction and cancelled', Russell papers, PRO, 30/22/13H. Queen Victoria to Russell, 21, 23, 24 and 26 Aug. 1859, copies, Russell papers, PRO, 30/22/13G. Russell to Cowley, 30 August 1859, no. 295, PRO, FO, 425/54. This episode with the queen caused Russell to consider

government, Walewski responded, ironically, that he could not reply to it as long as the Zurich talks were in progress. It was not until 19 October, after the text of the Treaty of Zurich was released, that Walewski gave an answer to Persigny to pass on to Russell in London. The treaty, following Villafranca, committed the two emperors 'to encourage with all their efforts the creation of a Confederation between the Italian States, which will be placed under the honorary Presidency of the Holy Father'. Austrian Venetia would be a member. In the hopes of mollifying papal resistance, article 18 stressed that the pact would 'maintain the independence and inviolability of the confederated States'. It would also 'assure the development of their moral and material interests'. It was to this clause that Walewski probably referred when he told Russell, via Persigny, that the French government expected the member states, including the Papal States, to profoundly modify their institutions to bring their governments into accord with 'the national spirit'. Walewski promised that if the project could not be achieved without the Austrian and papal predominance England feared, then they would consider organizing it without Austria. In any case, said Walewski, Napoleon was resolved to evacuate his troops from Italy and the Roman States as soon as the Italian confederation was established. He hoped this intention would satisfy England.[54]

Russell was not very pleased. He told Cowley, 'The Treaty of Zurich is bad as possible, especially the parts relating to the Duchies and the Pope.' Russell's position remained that as long as any confederation resembling the Villafranca one were put forward the English government was bound to oppose it.[55] By contrast, the papal government made very little immediate, direct public comment on the Zurich treaty. Antonelli simply continued to argue against the confederation proposal on the same grounds he had articulated in July and August. The confederation idea was stalled.

The papacy: first restoration, then reform

Right after the peace of Villafranca was signed in July, Napoleon informed Pius IX of its terms, notably the clauses on confederation and papal reforms. He went further and urged the pope to accept a separate administration for the Romagna and the Marches under a lay governor named by the pope and supported by an elected council. This was not far from what Russell was advocating at the moment. As precedent for such an arrangement Napoleon cited the relationship

---

resignation. Her stand, he told Palmerston, 'seems to place an interdict on any advice, or execution of the influence of England till the peace of Zurich is finally concluded' (Russell to Palmerston, 23 Aug. 1859, Palmerston papers, 1859, GC/RU/518).

54 Walewski to Persigny, Paris, 19 Oct. 1859, no. 136, *La questione italiana dalle annessioni al Regno d'Italia nei rapporti fra la Francia e l'Europa*, ed. Armando Saitta (Rome: Istituto storico italiano per l'età moderna e contemporanea, 1968), vol. II, 1–4.

55 Russell to Cowley, 20 Oct. 1859, private, copy, Russell papers, PRO, 30/22/103, and Russell to Palmerston, 21 Oct. 1859, copy, Russell papers, PRO, 30/22/30.

of Scotland and Ireland to England. The analogy could hardly be expected to appeal very strongly to the pope. Napoleon impressed upon the pope the advantage of agreeing now to this recommendation, since it was made by the two major Catholic states who, he claimed, both had the pope's interest at heart. If the pope refused, a congress of all the powers would probably have to be convened. Reiterating a point made many times by the papal government, he reminded the pope that a congress would unhappily contain a majority of 'Protestant and schismatic' states whose kindliness toward the head of the Roman Catholic Church could not be relied upon.[56]

Pius assured the emperor, in reply, that he was always ready to conciliate his subjects provided it could be done in a manner appropriate to the character of the papal temporal power. However, he said, Napoleon should be aware that most of the talk about papal reforms was raised by those who had the ulterior motive of attacking the temporal power of the pope – that is, by 'all the Protestant bigots, all the ambitious schismatics, and all the unbelieving revolutionaries'.[57]

What the papal government was interested in was not reforms or confederation, but the restoration of the Romagna to papal authority. Antonelli stated categorically on 15 July that the papal government intended to ask some foreign Catholic power for troops 'to reestablish order and the legitimate government' in the Romagna. He now asked Gramont what France would do in such an event. He especially wanted to know whether Sardinia would go to war if such troops marched against the rebel government. Gramont said he would have to consult his government before replying. When after a while Gramont still did not reply, Antonelli complained that the delay 'has entirely paralysed our efforts'.[58]

The cardinal drew Odo Russell into the problem on 21 July and described what the papal government expected the scenario to look like during the next few months. He pictured papal authorities engaging in a vigorous recruiting programme to build the papal army, Piedmont withdrawing its troops from the Legations under French pressure, while French troops continued to keep order west of the Apennines. Then, said Antonelli, he 'foresaw no difficulty in attacking and reconquering those rebellious provinces'. Odo listened closely to Antonelli and sought to impress Lord John with the seriousness of the pope's intention not to lose the Romagna, whatever the cost.[59]

Two things contributed to a very different course of events from what Antonelli had imagined. In the first place, after talks with the Marquis Pepoli, Napoleon gave the Romagnol rebel government a secret guarantee that if no further disturbances to social order occurred, France would allow no outside

---

56   Napoleon III to Pius IX, Desenzano, 14 July 1859, Pirri, vol. II, part 2, 90–2.
57   Pius IX to Napoleon III, 22 July 1859, Pirri, vol. II, part 2, 93—4.
58   Antonelli to Sacconi, Rome, 15 July 1859, no. 4930, ASV, ANParigi, 1859, SdS, AD/P.
59   Odo Russell to Russell, Rome, 22 July 1859, no. 94, PRO, FO, 43/71, and *Odo Russell*, 40.

intervention to restore papal authority in the Romagna.⁶⁰ Napoleon intended to let the revolution in the Romagna stand; the omission of direct reference to the pope in the Villafranca clause on the restoration of the dukes was not an oversight, and the idea of a lay governor under nominal papal authority was not intended as a restoration of papal authority. The Romagnol nationalists now knew that Napoleon as well as England accepted the overthrow of papal rule. However, since the English government did not know of Napoleon's pledge to the Romagnols, Russell and Palmerston could not be certain that the emperor would not support the restoration of the pope along with the dukes. Secondly, the Piedmontese, with French and English allowance, solidified their intention not to withdraw from the Romagna. Massimo d'Azeglio boasted to Hudson that one of his greatest accomplishments at Bologna was to prevent the pope's Swiss troops from crossing the border into the Romagna. General Dabormida, the successor of Cavour as Sardinian prime minister, told Hudson that Sardinian troops would stay in the Papal States as long as necessary to 'assist in maintaining order and preventing anarchy'.⁶¹ In other words, Antonelli would have to fight Sardinian troops if the papal army tried anything in the lost province.

The papal government did actively begin looking around for troops with which to regain the Romagna.⁶² The two most likely sources were Austria and Spain. The Austrian government had reason to be reluctant to contribute troops, due to her tenuous position in Italy and Europe after her defeat in the war. Spain might not feel quite so restrained. Queen Isabella wrote to Pius IX on 1 July to say that she was deeply troubled by the latest attacks on the temporal power and that she wanted God to relieve the Holy Father of his tribulations. On 9 July Antonelli then asked the nuncio in Madrid, Mgr Lorenzo Barili, to sound out the Spanish government about sending 'material aid' as in 1849. Antonelli pursued the inquiry for several weeks. On 26 July Pius hinted to the Spanish queen in writing that he could use some troops. Odo Russell picked up news of all this and reported that there were secret negotiations between the Vatican and Spain to arrange troops for His Holiness.⁶³ Another source of papal troops might be the enlistment of volunteers from among the Catholic faithful outside the Papal

---

60   Marian Swann Miller, 'Europe and the Sardinian annexations of the duchies, Tuscany and the Romagna, 1859–1860' (Ph.D. Thesis, University of Pennsylvania, 1965), 18–19.
61   Hudson to Russell, Turin, 20 July 1859, private, and 4 Aug. 1859, no. 52, *Gran Bretagna e Sardegna*, vol. VII, 165 and 181–2.
62   Sacconi to Antonelli, Paris, 29 July 1859, no. 1321, and Antonelli to Sacconi, Rome, 2 Aug. 1859, no. 5269, ASV, ANParigi, 1859, SdS, AD/P, and *Antonelli*, vol. I, 178–82, 192.
63   Queen Isabella II to Pius IX, Aranjuez, 1 July 1859, and Piux IX to Queen Isabella, 26 July 1859, Pirri, vol. II, part 2, 97–8, and 124–5. Antonelli to Barili, Rome, 9 July 1859, no. 4806, in *Il carteggio Antonelli–Barili, 1859–1861*, ed. Carla Meneguzzi Rostagni (Rome: Istituto per la storia del Risorgimento italiano, 1973), 72. Odo Russell to Russell, Rome, 22 July 1859, no. 94, PRO, FO, 43/71 and *Odo Russell*, 40.

States. Antonelli told Odo of offers of recruits from Ireland, but indicated he was hesitant to encourage them since, he said, 'the laws of England might involve the Pope in difficulties with Her Majesty's Government if he accepted the offers made by these Irish volunteers'.[64] In any case, the pope seemed to have actual prospects of bodies of fighting men to use in trying to retake the Romagna.

The provisional governments of central Italy took the initiative themselves by forming a military league on 10 August which the Romagna joined on 24 August. The league's purposes included maintaining order, opposing restorations, and specifically defending the Romagna against papal military attack. Garibaldi left the Sardinian army to become one of the generals of the league, and was stationed at Rimini, near the Marches border, with orders to repulse any papal attack and to stir up and assist insurrection in the remaining papal territory.[65]

This new and dangerous situation induced the English government to get even more involved in the Papal Question. Russell told Emanuel d'Azeglio in London that he expected the future of Italy to be decided during the coming months.[66] The immediate threat the English foresaw was that Austria might intervene to restore the archdukes as proposed by the terms of Villafranca; this might involve an attempt to restore the pope's authority in the Romagna. They did not know what the French would do. To resist this possibility, Russell and Palmerston gradually developed a doctrine which flatly opposed the use of armed force by any foreign power to effect the restoration of any overthrown rulers in central Italy. They asked the French and Austrians to support the renunciation of armed force.[67] Two policy statements sent to Cowley, on 16 August and 17 September, put their position most clearly. In addition to their doctrine 'Let the Italians govern their own affairs', there was, as they saw it, a related principle of international politics at issue which they introduced for the first time during these years of crisis: 'non-intervention'.[68] Russell and Palmerston construed 'non-intervention' narrowly to cover primarily the exclusion of armed force, such as France's, Austria's, or Spain's, in support of the restoration of papal and ducal territory. It did not prohibit the use of 'advice', that is, active diplomatic and political influence, particularly England's, in opposition to papal restoration, nor did it rule out the surrounding armed presence of the British Mediterranean fleet in support of British policy against papal restoration. The doctrine did not mean to prevent Piedmont from using armed force to uphold the pro-Piedmontese provisional government in the Romagna against all attack. Neither did it oppose armed force by the central

64   Odo Russell to Russell, Rome, 30 July 1859, no. 100, PRO, FO, 43/71, and *Odo Russell*, 44.
65   Giuseppi Garibaldi, *Memorie*, ed. Ugoberti Alfassio Grimaldi (Verona: Bertani, 1972), 356–70. Miller, 50–2.
66   Emmanuel d'Azeglio to Dabormida, London, 10 and 24 Aug. 1859, telegram, copies, ASMAE, Londra, LXXXVIII.
67   Russell to Cowley, 26 July 1859, private, Russell papers, PRO, 30/22/103.
68   Russell to Cowley, 16 Aug. 1859, no. 258, and 17 Sept. 1859, no. 329, *Gran Bretagna e Sardegna*, vol. VII, 227–8, and 229.

Italian league.⁶⁹ Once again English policy supported the consolidation of the new order of things in the Romagna and sought to prevent the return of the old papal régime.

The French government did not reply to Russell's inquiry about the use of force in central Italy, claiming again the need to wait until after the completion of the Zurich negotiations. In the meantime, Walewski regularly told Cowley, 'we cannot abandon the Pope'.⁷⁰ The English government could not be confident that it knew what Napoleon intended to do. If France would not resort to armed force to help the pope, Russell wondered, 'what will these great Catholic Powers [do] to put the Pope together again?'⁷¹

Austria categorically refused to renounce the right to intervene militarily in Italy. Count Rechberg, the new Austrian prime minister, responded to Russell with an argument which the papal government and Catholics in England and Ireland found agreeable: the English government should only advocate the principles of 'non-intervention' and 'the will of the people' for Italian and papal affairs if it were prepared to apply them as well to British India and Ireland. In both areas, Austria contended, England intervened with military power to deny the will of the people for independence.⁷² Russell bristled at the suggestion. India and Ireland, he said, were internal portions of Great Britain. 'Non-intervention' did not apply to them.⁷³ 'Intervention', he replied, was defined by what Austria had been doing in Italy, and Austria had better not try it anymore. Great Britain, Russell declared, would view any attempt by Austrian troops to impose a government in the duchies, or to restore the pope's authority in Bologna 'as the commencement of fresh troubles in Italy, and possibly the precursor of a war in Europe'. Behind this declaration lay the British fleet in the Adriatic.⁷⁴

Palmerston and Russell were sure they would have no difficulty preventing the use of Irish troops in the papal army. Palmerston remarked that Antonelli correctly understood English laws on this point: 'It is true that no Irish force could enter into the Pope's Service without permission which would probably not be given.'⁷⁵

Spain was another problem. Palmerston could think of nothing worse than

69 Miller, 52, Emanuel d'Azeglio to Dabormida, London, 20 and 27 Aug. 1859, telegram, copy, ASMAE, Londra, LXXXVIII. Russell to Queen Victoria, 23 Aug. 1859, RA J22/58.
70 Scott, 140. Cowley to Russell, Paris, 27 July 1859, private, copy, Cowley papers, PRO, FO, 519/226/30–1.
71 Russell to Cowley, 8 Sept. 1859, private, Cowley papers, PRO, FO, 519/197.
72 Rechberg to Apponyi, Vienna, 25 Aug. 1859, *Gran Bretagna e Sardegna*, vol. VII, 232–3. DeLuca to Antonelli, Vienna, 27 Aug. 1859, no. 764, ASV, ASdS, 1859, 165/5/59–60. Antonelli earlier confronted Odo with the claim that the British suppression of the India mutiny was analogous to the papal suppression of the Perugian revolt (Massari, *Diario*, 22 Aug. 1859, 344). Russell to Queen Victoria, 3 Sept. 1859, RA J23/3.
73 Russell to Fane, 14 Sept. 1859, no. 74, *Gran Bretagna e Sardegna*, vol. VII, 234–5.
74 Russell to Loftus, 27 July 1859, PRO, FO, 425/54/46.
75 Palmerston to Russell, 7 Aug. 1859, Russell papers, PRO, 30/22/20.

Spanish troops replacing the French at Rome. By comparison with the French, he told Russell, they would be 'more bigotted, Priest obeying, cruel and prone to violence'. Palmerston and Russell decided to let the French and Spanish governments know that England would oppose Spanish intervention of any kind. The French supported the English move. Queen Isabella was inclined to consider sending troops, and the prime minister, Leopoldo O'Donnell, had no immediate opinion, but as soon as they learned of English and French opposition, the government told the papal nuncio they would not do it. Spain would, however, undertake diplomatic action in Paris to induce Napoleon to behave more consistently toward the pope, and less receptively to English influence. Lord John was quickly satisfied that the Spanish government would not give the pope any troops.[76] The French government, meanwhile, finally responded in August to Antonelli's inquiry to Gramont several weeks earlier about the pope's use of the troops of another Catholic power, meaning Spain. Citing English pressure, Walewski told Sacconi, that while acknowledging in principle the pope's right to call for military assistance from Catholic powers, the French could not participate in or countenance any such plan which involved armed intervention. Sacconi asked why the French paid attention to English policy now if earlier they had not listened to English protests against French support of Piedmont in the war against Austria. English policy, observed Sacconi, worked to solidify the rebel governments and undermine the pope's temporal power; France should not listen to it. The French government remained unmoved, and its stand, together with England, prevented the papal government from making any further attempts to secure Spanish troops.

Meanwhile, the English decided to go along with a new French campaign to persuade the pope to adopt governmental reforms. Russell thought he might for the time being support Napoleon's efforts to establish a separate administration for the Romagna and the Marches under a lay governor. It corresponded, at least superficially, with the general proposal Russell had advocated after the Perugia affair in June to divest the pope of the *exercise* of his temporal power.[77] On 28 July Lord John instructed Odo Russell to work in every way possible with Gramont, the French ambassador in Rome, to win the pope's approval of the French recommendation. He asked Odo to speak to Antonelli in favour of the proposal of a lay governor, as the arrangement that 'would seem to Her Majesty's Government to afford the best chance of maintaining the Pope's temporal

---

76 Palmerston to Russell, 2 Aug. 1859, Russell papers, PRO, 30/22/20. Russell to Andrew Buchanan (English minister in Madrid), 26 July 1859, no. 18, confidential, PRO, FO, 72/952. Barili to Antonelli, 2 Aug. 1859, no. 387; 18 Aug. 1859, no. 398; and 24 Sept. 1859, no. 422, in *Antonelli–Barili*, 88, 91–3, and 100–3. Russell to Cowley, 9 Aug. 1859, private, copy, Russell papers, PRO, 30/22/103, and Russell to Queen Victoria, 9 Aug. 1859, RA J22/23.

77 Sacconi to Antonelli, Paris, 5 Aug. 1859, no. 1326, and 19 Aug. 1859, no. 1336, ASV, ASdS, 1859, 165/5/6–7, and 32–9, and *Antonelli*, vol. I, 195, 208–12. Cowley to Russell, Paris, 27 July 1859, no. 300, confidential, PRO, FO, 425/54/50–1.

sovereignty'.⁷⁸ Such a comment involved considerable compromise on Palmerston's and Russell's part. To keep the principles clear, he wanted Odo to tell Antonelli that the English government believed that 'the People are the best judges of the institutions under which they live', and that 'the readiness of the People of Romagna to rise when the weight of Foreign troops was removed affords to our minds a presumption against the administration of the Papal Legate'. Russell, in other words, accepted the propaganda Cavour had been anxious for the English to believe about the revolution in the Romagna.

The Austrians declined to join France in presenting the reform proposals, so that the plan came to the papal government as, in effect, a combined French–English project, as Sacconi, in alarm, correctly noted.⁷⁹ Gramont submitted to the pope and Antonelli in July virtually the same reform plan that the French had composed in 1857, together with the plan for a lay governor. At the end of July, Walewski believed, as he reported to Cowley, that the pope seemed disposed to grant all the changes asked, except the separate administration for the Legations. Antonelli, however, denied any willingness to institute the proposed changes, and claimed that Gramont had misunderstood the pope.⁸⁰ When Odo talked with the cardinal later, he found Antonelli immovable on reforms, and completely determined to use the force of arms to compel the Romagna to submit to papal authority. Palmerston remarked: 'It is very clear from Odo Russell's letters that the Pope will procrastinate and will grant no real reforms; you might as well ask a crab to walk straight.'⁸¹

This was Russell's and Palmerston's last attempt to consider favourably a compromise with the pope concerning the Romagna. They were becoming convinced that it had been a mistake to give serious attention to the idea of nominal papal sovereignty there. A despatch from Hudson helped them reach this conclusion. Hudson's despatch dated 5 August testified that the Romagna under the provisional government was tranquil; public order reigned everywhere without the need to repress any opposition; the people were determined never to accept papal rule again, and they yearned for political liberties similar to England's and Piedmont's. Above all, the despatch continued, the people were entirely ready to govern themselves and only awaited the opportunity to do so. The despatch said exactly what Russell wanted to hear about the Romagna. He

---

78 Russell's instructions were put in two separate despatches with the same date, Russell to Odo Russell, 28 July 1859, no. 8 and no. 9, PRO, FO, 43/69.
79 Sacconi to Antonelli, Paris, 31 July 1859, no. 1324, and 4 Aug. 1859, no. 1325, ASV, ASdS, 1859, 165/4/147–52, and 165/5/2–5, and *Antonelli*, vol. I, 189–91, 193–4.
80 Pirri, vol. II, part 1, 129–44. Cowley to Russell, Paris, 29 July 1859, no. 307, PRO, FO, 425/54/53. Antonelli to Sacconi, Rome, 30 July 1859, no. 5222, ASV, ANParigi, 1859, SdS, AD/P; and *Antonelli*, vol. II, 182–8. The text of the 1857 project is in Pirri, vol. II, part 2, 104–8.
81 Russell to Cowley, 6 Aug. 1859, private, copy, Russell papers, PRO, 30/22/103. Odo Russell to Russell, Rome, 10 Sept. 1859, no. 105, confidential, PRO, FO, 43/72.

did not know that Cavour's confidant, Massari, had written it at Hudson's request and that it was another important item in Cavour's propaganda campaign to win English support of pro-Piedmontese activity in central Italy.[82]

Russell and Pamerston began looking about for a plan for the political settlement of the Romagna. The difference now was that they no longer considered whether the pope would accept it, but only whether it was acceptable to the Romagnol nationalists and in keeping with their principles. In the process they flipped from an attempt at compromise with Napoleon and the pope to very nearly the opposite side of the conflict. Russell suggested that any settlement of the Papal Question would have to satisfy two points: 'To make the Pope anything less than a Sovereign would degrade him in the eyes of Europe. To leave him unprotected at Rome would separate him from his throne and the time-hallowed seat of his power.'[83] In their new frame of mind, Palmerston at first challenged these assumptions, thinking they should go all the way against the pope:

> Is it necessary to admit that the Pope must be a Temporal Prince and that the test of his authority must be Rome? The early history of the Popes scarcely bears out this position, and there seems no necessity for such a state of things in the doctrine and tenets of the Catholic Religion. At all events we are not called upon to record our admission of it.

Russell responded, 'Well, – this is a compromise with the Catholic Powers.'[84]

Palmerston and Russell eventually settled on an agreement to put forward publicly the proposal they favoured all along, but had only stated privately as their personal foreign policy. In a despatch to the Austrians on 24 August, Russell argued with great vigour for the reduction of the pope's temporal power to the city of Rome and some neighbouring territory. It was a strong, heroic-sounding, public statement of the Whig–Liberal policy of 'Rome and fifteen miles around', and Russell this time got Queen Victoria to approve it. Russell's description of the Romagna reflected Massari's version in Hudson's despatch of 5 August. He spoke of the papacy as 'an effete despotism', and the people of the Papal States as '2,000,000 to 3,000,000 ... discontented priestridden subjects' who were 'smarting from the ignorance, tyranny, and corruption of ecclesiastical rule' and were 'panting for secular government'. The purpose of the despatch with respect to the Roman States was, in Palmerston's words, 'to try to persuade the Pope to give the Legations a government similar to that of Wallachia and Moldavia, and to induce the Pope to give up his temporal Power in the rest of his dominions'.[85]

---

82   Massari, *Diario*, 5 Aug. 1859, 329. Hudson to Russell, Turin, 5 Aug. 1859, no. 54, *Gran Bretagna e Sardegna*, vol. VII, 183–4.
83   Russell to Cowley, Rome, 13 Aug. 1859, private, Russell papers, copy, PRO, 30/22/103.
84   Palmerston's comments are contained in 'Remarks and Suggestions on Draft', dated 15 Aug. 1859, with marginal replies by Russell, Russell papers, PRO, 30/22/20.
85   The final version of the despatch is Russell to Fance, 24 Aug. 1859, no. 66, *Gran Bretagna e Sardegna*, vol. VII, 230–1.

The papacy: first restoration, then reform

Russell and Palmerston considered a number of options for the Papal States and central Italy during August and September. Early in August Palmerston expressed that he would prefer that the Romagna and the duchies be taken over and incorporated into Sardinia, since 'the stronger and larger the Kingdom of Piedmont could be, the better'. It would endanger no British naval or commercial interests. He did not believe such a thing possible, but he thought that if Piedmont went ahead and took charge of troops in the Romagna, the powers would have to accept it.[86] Palmerston repeated this to Count Emanuel Marliani who came to London in mid-August on a mission from the Romagna to secure English support of the annexation of the Legations to Sardinia. Marliani recalled that Palmerston encouraged him with the saying, 'Heaven helps them who help themselves.'[87] Palmerston also spoke in support of annexation to Emanuel d'Azeglio, the Sardinian minister in London, although Palmerston warned Azeglio that this view was his personal, and not the official, policy. After talking with Palmerston, Azeglio told Dabormida, 'England will not support us with arms, but diplomatically it will give us all the moral support possible.' Dabormida was pleased, even though he hoped for more. The English prime minister advised Sardinia to act 'quickly, decisively, prudently' in the Romagna and the duchies.[88] Marquis Pepoli claimed that Palmerston urged him in London: 'Do it, do it, do it, and leave to others the task of undoing it.'

If annexation were not possible, Russell and Palmerston would consider other plans. One idea was a hereditary viceroy for the Papal States, perhaps Duke Robert of Parma. Another was the formation of a kingdom of central Italy, in addition to either a kingdom of northern Italy or an enlarged Piedmont in north Italy. Hudson and Cowley were alarmed at this one for they considered a kingdom of central Italy, or a kingdom of Etruria, as some called it, a napoleonic ploy to give Prince Napoleon, known as Plon Plon, a kingship and to place central Italy under Bonapartist influence.[89]

---

86 Palmerston to Russell, 9 Aug. 1859, copy, Cowley papers, PRO, FO, 519/197. See Palmerston, Cabinet Memorandum, 28 June 1859, in Blakiston, 'L'opinione pubblica inglese', 142.

87 Miller, 64–6. Massari, *Diario*, 19 Aug. 1859, 339: 'Aide-toi le ciel t'aidra.' Hudson to Russell, Turin, 5 Aug. 1859, private, *Gran Bretagna e Sardegna*, vol. VII, 185–6; this letter was in fact carried by Marliani to Russell.

88 The original wording was 'promptement, résolument, prudemment'. Emanuel d'Azeglio to Dabormida, London, 23/24, 28 and 29 Aug. 1859, telegram, ASMAE, Londra, LXXXVIII, and Dabormida to Emanuel d'Azeglio, Turin, 24 Aug. 1859, telegram, Colombo, vol. II, 224–5. Massari, *Diario*, 11 Sept. 1859, 360: 'Faites, faites, faites, et laissez aux autres le soin de defaire.'

89 Russell to Palmerston, 18 Aug. 1859, Palmerston papers, 1859, GC/RU/516. Russell to Cowley, n.d., draft, marked 'This despatch was stopped by the Queen's direction and cancelled', Russell papers, PRO, 30/12/13H. Palmerston to Russell, 5 Aug. 1859, Russell papers, PRO, 30/22/20. Hudson to Russell, Turin, 20 Aug. 1859, private, *Gran Bretagna e Sardegna*, vol. VII, 203–5; Cowley to Russell, Paris, 9 Sept. 1859, private, copy, Cowley papers, PRO, FO, 519/226/101. *Punch* (1 Oct. 1859) caught the point in a cartoon showing Napoleon unveiling Italian liberty and revealing – surprise! – Plon Plon.

Liberals and the revolution in the Romagna

Early in September the French ambassador in London, County Persigny, offered still another plan which Palmerston told Persigny he liked, and which he called 'a very good one no doubt if it could be carried into execution'. The count proposed taking away all of the pope's territory and giving him 'his Palace and gardens and residence as Head of the Church' within the city of Rome. Rome would be governed by a municipality as a free city like Frankfurt or Hamburg and the remainder of the States of the Church would be divided between Sardinia and Naples.[90] The queen was enraged that Palmerston had spoken to Persigny as he did without authorization. She could not abide this exercise of a personal foreign policy. She explained her position to Russell:

> What she objects to is binding beforehand the Government by expressions opinion of its leading members to the French Government, and thus bringing about those French proposals which it will be most embarrassing to the Cabinet either to reject or adopt.

This time Palmerston and Russell backed down and told Persigny that his plan was 'a scheme we had nothing to do with'. Actually the important consideration to them was that the plan would be impossible to effect, since Napoleon would be unable to accept such a sweeping solution to the Papal Question.[91] Cowley commented that if the plan were adopted for Italy, Persigny 'will have conferred a greater blessing on humanity and have proved himself a greater real friend to the Roman Catholic Church than any man living'.[92]

In the final analysis it was not the English or the French who determined what to do next in the Romagna. Knowing in advance that neither Napoleon nor the English would resist, it was the liberal Romagnols themselves, together with their counterparts in Tuscany, Modena and Parma, who took decisive action and opted for annexation.[93] On 1 September, the Romagna assembly convened and elected Marco Minghetti president. On the 6th it proclaimed officially the end of papal temporal power in the Romagna and the next day it declared for annexation to Sardinia. On the 24th a delegation from the Romagna went to Monza and presented the declaration to King Victor Emmanuel, who was obliged for strategic reasons to decline annexation at this time.

Pius IX prepared his own response to these events in the Romagna. On 26 September he delivered another major allocution in the Sacred Consistory at the Vatican denouncing the latest actions of the anti-papal Romagnols. The pope

---

90   Palmerston to Russell, 4 Sept. 1859, Russell papers, PRO, 30/22/20. Persigny to Napoleon III, London, 4 Sept. 1859, private, *Conferenze di Zurigo*, 359–61.
91   Queen Victoria to Russell, Balmoral, 6 and 7 Sept. 1859, copies, Russell papers, PRO, 30/22/13G. Russell to Queen Victoria, 7 Sept. 1859, RA J23/21. Palmerston to Russell, 10 Sept. 1859, Russell papers, PRO, 30/22/20.
92   Cowley to Russell, Chantilly, 18 Sept. 1859, private, copy, Cowley papers, PRO, FO, 519/226/111.
93   Miller, 105–7. Miller's study convincingly establishes the thesis that the Italian nationalists themselves were the decisive actors in determining which arrangement of central Italy would be adopted.

condemned their presumption in usurping the rights of temporal sovereignty which belonged only to the Vicar of Christ and declared all who performed these acts or abetted them would incur the ecclesiastical penalty of excommunication.[94] The Archbishop of Genoa hinted that the warning applied to Victor Emmanuel, and some in France were confident it applied to Napoleon.[95]

Pius did not stop there, for he too was aware that the threat of excommunication meant little to the anti-papal nationalists who led the Romagnol revolution. The pope broke diplomatic relations with Sardinia in protest at Victor Emmanuel's reception of the Romagnol delegation. The diplomatic break also terminated all ecclesiastical relations between the Holy See and the church in Piedmont.[96] Finally, on 27 September, Antonelli abruptly terminated all talks with France about papal reforms and enunciated an important new policy. Odo Russell paraphrased it:

> until the Legations returned to their lawful sovereign the Pope, nothing could be done in Rome or the rest of the Papal States in the shape of administrative reforms and . . . the French Government should have patience until the States of the Church are in their normal condition when the subject of reforms can again be taken into serious consideration by His Holiness.

Or as Odo put it elsewhere, 'Give me back my lost Legations and in return I will proclaim to the world that I have adopted your plan for reforming my temporal government.'[97] For the pope and Antonelli, it had to be first restoration, then reform.

By October 1859, the Romagna seemed less and less restorable to papal rule, although no party to the conflict could consider anything very settled. Antonelli and the pope were occupied primarily with their relations with France and Sardinia and with the turmoil in the Romagna. Nevertheless, everywhere they turned they found England in the background – supporting aggressive French actions, encouraging hostile Sardinian and Romagnol initiatives. As Pius IX came to see, it was the English government that was his most consistent opponent on the European scene.

94 Allocution, 26 Sept. 1859, enclosed in Odo Russell to Russell, Rome, 1 Oct. 1859, no. 111, PRO, FO, 43/72.
95 See 'Note by Archbishop Charvaz of Genoa, on a conversation with King Victor Emmanuel, October 15, 1859', trans. Mack Smith, *Making of Italy*, 296–7.
96 Antonelli to Sacconi, Rome, 1 Oct. 1859, no. 6595, ASV, ANParigi, 1859, SdS, AD/P, and *Antonelli*, vol. 1, 244–5. Odo Russell to Russell, Rome, 1 Oct. 1859, no. 112, 4 Oct. 1859, no. 114; and 10 Oct. 1859, no. 116, PRO, FO, 43/72, and *Odo Russell*, 50–5.
97 Antonelli to Gramont, Rome, 27 Sept. 1859, confidential, *Antonelli*, vol. 1, 242–4. Odo Russell to Russell, Rome, 1 Oct. 1859, no. 112, and 15 Oct. 1859, no. 117, PRO, FO, 43/72, and *Odo Russell*, 51, 55–6.

6 Liberals, the congress and the Romagna

Another proposed congress and the pope

The text of the treaty of Zurich was released in mid-October and immediately the attention of the European powers turned toward a congress. The idea of a congress system, at least, was not dead. Formally, the congress agenda would have to consider the Zurich treaty. Relevant to the Papal Question, the most difficult issue would be the organization, or reorganization, of central Italy, especially of the Romagna. During the autumn of 1859 and the winter of 1859–60, questions pertaining to the congress, central Italy, and the pope were the concern of all those involved with Italian and papal affairs.

The situation in the Romagna itself was extremely inflammable. Having voted in September to overthrow the pope's authority and to seek annexation to Piedmont, it was crucial for the liberal Romagnols to move cautiously and prove to the European powers that they could keep order, run an effective government, and prevent the spread of revolution against the pope. They had to switch quickly from revolution to establishment. The English, looking on approvingly, tended to stress how tranquil and settled the civil order was there, while the papal side looked hopefully for any sign of the failure of the government of rebels.[1]

Garibaldi and the Italian National Society threatened to upset the peace and quiet of the area, however. During October, the Italian National Society was reorganized, after its discontinuation in April, to lead the fight for annexation. Garibaldi became its president, and many local chapters proved to be so insistent in their endeavours that they embarrassed the Romagnol government and the Piedmontese.[2] Garibaldi was also second in command of the army of the league of central Italy. Poised at Rimini, he introduced arms into the Marches and Umbria, and was ready to move into the remaining papal territory at any time. He and his supporters were impatient for a national revolution stimulated by a

---

1   See, for example, Odo Russell to Lady William Russell, Rome, 19 Sept. 1859, copy, Ampthill papers, PRO, FO, 918/85/207–8; and Massari, *Diario*, 9 and 13 Sept. 1859, 358 and 360: 'they have not killed even one priest'.
2   Grew, 221–3, 226. The National Society was officially reorganized on 1 November.

Another proposed congress and the pope

network of revolutionary committees in the Papal States and Naples. On 22 October he issued a proclamation to the people of Naples calling on them to revolt. The difficulties were about to escalate. First Piedmont and then Austria declared their intentions to intervene with force, if necessary. King Victor Emmanuel met with Garibaldi in Turin on 29 October to dissuade him from the enterprise. The king then told the French of a plan to move Piedmontese troops into the Papal States 'for the purpose of maintaining order' if Garibaldi did march southward. Prince Metternich, the Austrian ambassador in Paris, informed the French that Austria was resolved to send its troops after the Piedmontese if they crossed the papal border, or any other frontier, for whatever purpose. Walewski claimed that France would not intervene in any case, but Napoleon secretly told Victor Emmanuel that he would support, at least diplomatically, whatever the king did.[3] The Piedmontese party in Italy feared, however, that France would intervene against Piedmont and not for it.[4]

Russell threw his support behind Victor Emmanuel's efforts to restrain Garibaldi, although he confessed to Hudson that he feared the king would be unsuccessful. Russell may have been preparing the way for the English government to approve a Piedmontese military move into the Papal States in order to stop Garibaldi. Hudson was alarmist about the whole matter.[5] At the same time, Russell allowed his thoughts to consider the pope's welfare. He realized that, if the revolution broke into the rest of the Papal States, the pope could be pushed into the sea. Russell was not ready for this to happen, and proposed that, at least for now, England should 'come forward for his remaining a Sovereign Prince'. That failing, England was still ready to help. He informed Napoleon privately that 'our Admiral is instructed, in case the Pope should wish to embark, to convey him anywhere he pleases'.[6]

In mid-November, Garibaldi suddenly resigned his command, gave up his plans to invade the Papal States, and announced that he would retire to his country house near Genoa. The Piedmontese and the English government were relieved, and Russell ecstatically called it 'heroic'.[7]

There remained another threat to the new *status quo* in the Romagna. The pope and his government decided to build the papal army with the aim of

3   Garibaldi, *Memorie*, 361–3. Giorgio Asproni, *Diario politico, 1855–1876* (Milan: Giuffré, 1976), vol. II, 11 Oct. 1859. Sackville West (*chargé d'affaires* in Turin) to Russell, Turin, 27 Oct. 1859, private, *Gran Bretagna e Sardegna*, vol. VII, 240. Cowley to Russell, Paris, 2 Nov. 1859, no. 720, and 15 Nov. 1859, no. 768, PRO, FO, 425/57/15 and 57–8. Russell to Odo Russell, 5 Nov. 1859, private, Ampthill papers, PRO, FO, 918/7. Miller, 163–7.
4   Hudson to Russell, Turin, 10 Nov. 1859, no. 90, *Gran Bretagna e Sardegna*, vol. VII, 245.
5   Russell to Hudson, 11 Nov. 1859, telegram, and 16 Nov. 1859, no. 36, *Gran Bretagna e Sardegna*, vol. VII, 246 and 249. Hudson to Russell, Turin, 16 Nov. 1859, no. 96, *Gran Bretagna e Sardegna*, vol. VII, 248.
6   Russell and Palmerston, 2 Nov. 1859, Palmerston papers, 1859, GC/RU/549; Russell to Cowley, Aberdeen, 11 Oct. 1859, private draft, Russell papers, PRO, 30/22/103.
7   Hudson to Russell, Turin, 16 Nov. 1859, telegram, no. 95, and Russell to Hudson, 17 Nov. 1859, private, *Gran Bretagna e Sardegna*, vol. VII, 247 and 250.

reclaiming the Romagna by force. The papal government was just as relieved as everybody else, except the Mazzinians, that Garibaldi abandoned his project of revolutionizing the rest of the Papal States. In the autumn of 1859, out of the 16,000 troops that papal plans called for, only about 8000 were ready for duty under General Kalbermatten. They could not have resisted Garibaldi, and they were nowhere near ready to march into the Romagna.[8]

The time had come to add new recruits to the papal army, and during the autumn many were attracted, mostly Swiss and Austrian. A recruiting office opened for a time at Vienna.[9] As early as mid-September Odo expressed the fear that enrolments in the army were increasing rapidly, and that Antonelli's will to use the army to recapture the Legations was becoming stronger.[10] Antonelli and the pope did look around again for outside military assistance. The Austrians offered them no hope, unless Piedmont sent its army against the Papal States, which Piedmont would not now consider doing.[11] The Spanish told the nuncio in Madrid that they could still do nothing because of English and French opposition, and besides, their troops were busy in Morocco.[12] The Naples government would give no help either, although Odo was certain the pope had succeeded in making secret arrangements for troops.[13] With military aid from the Catholic powers falling through, the pope knew he had no option other than to rely on his own papal army, which he and Antonelli were not hesitant to do. The prospect of the papal army, no matter how weak it was, throwing itself against Bologna continued to figure in the English government's calculations of the affairs of Italy.[14] At the same time, the situation looked sufficiently bleak to the pope and Antonelli that they began to reconsider some policy positions they had taken since the start of the crisis.

During the autumn, as the powers talked about a congress, there were three principal options available for the political settlement of the Romagna and the duchies. First, the liberal nationalists in the Romagna and the duchies insisted on annexation to the Kingdom of Piedmont-Sardinia. The English government unquestionably preferred annexation, while Napoleon secretly supported it. Victor Emmanuel naturally favoured annexation as well, but, out of fear of

8   Isastia, 40–2. Odo Russell to Russell, Rome, 10 Sept. 1859, no. 105, and 1 Oct. 1859, no. 112, PRO, FO, 43/72, and *Odo Russell*, 46 and 51.
9   Loftus to Russell, Vienna, 24 Nov. 1859, no. 790, and 25 Nov. 1859, no. 797, PRO, FO, 45/57/74 and 77.
10   Odo Russell to Russell, Rome, 16 Sept. 1859, no. 107, PRO, FO, 43/72, and *Odo Russell*, 49–50.
11   Baron Ottenfels (interim Austrian ambassador in Rome) to Rechberg, Rome, 2 Sept. 1859, no. 50B, HHSA, PA, XI, 200/502–4.
12   Barili to Antonelli, 15 Oct. 1859, no. 449, *Antonelli–Barili*, 109–10. Russell to Odo Russell, 6 Oct. 1859, private, Ampthill papers, PRO, FO, 918/7.
13   Antonelli to Sacconi, Rome, 19 Nov. 1859, no. 7259, ASV, ANParigi, 1859, SdS, AD/P, and *Antonelli*, vol. I, 288–9. Odo Russell to Russell, Rome, 20 Nov. 1859, no. 127, PRO, FO, 43/72.
14   Russell to Hudson, 28 Nov. 1859, private, *Gran Bretagna e Sardegna*, vol. VII, 264–5.

proceeding too quickly for the powers, had officially refused the request for annexation made to him by the liberal Romagnols. Second, the pope and the papal party insisted on the restoration of the *status quo ante bellum* in the Romagna. England, Piedmont and the liberal nationalists were adamantly opposed to this. Napoleon was secretly opposed to it, but until mid-October gave no public signs of being for or against it, other than failing to act upon the pope's wishes for restoration. Third, Napoleon and Austria, in the Zurich treaty, officially advocated confederation. This was Napoleon's public face, which England, Piedmont and the liberal nationalists categorically opposed. The pope and Antonelli, at first, firmly resisted it as well.

A break in the situation came in mid-October, about the same time as the release of the text of the Zurich treaty. *En route* to Paris from a holiday at Biarritz, Napoleon stopped at Bordeaux and exchanged speeches with Archbishop Donnet. Napoleon's remarks were his first public statement since the pope's allocution of 28 September condemning the revolution in the Romagna and appealing to all Catholics to come to the Holy Father's side. When given the opportunity to speak unequivocally in support of the pope and against the revolution, he did not. Instead, he spoke approvingly of 'the liberation and independence of Italy', and indicated his intention to evacuate his French troops from Rome. In the current international situation, such talk was tantamount to supporting the rebels in the Romagna and abandoning the pope.[15]

No one missed the significance of the occasion. Cavour believed it marked a new stage in Napoleon's public policy.[16] Lord John Russell praised the emperor's address.[17] Antonelli and Sacconi understood it as a distinct sign that Napoleon was ready to alter publicly his commitment to the pope and to put up less resistance to, even give public support to the liberal Romagnols. The way was now open for a significant *rapprochement* of English and French policies toward Italy and the pope.[18]

An immediate effect was that Napoleon stopped pushing the confederation plan for Italy. He drew closer to England on that issue. Simultaneously, the pope and Antonelli reversed themselves, and began to think that confederation, which the congress would consider, was not a bad idea after all. They began to see confederation as potentially compatible with papal restoration in Romagna. Antonelli, in November, revealed his change of mind to Odo Russell, and spoke

15   *Le Moniteur Universel*, 12 Oct. 1859, in *Antonelli*, vol. I, 252–3. See Case, *French opinion*, 105, and *Tablet*, 15 Oct. 1859.
16   Sacconi to Antonelli, Paris, 13 Oct. 1859, no. 1365, and 13 Oct. 1859, no. 1367, ASV, ASdS, 1859, 165/5/149–54, and *Antonelli*, vol. I, 250 and 255. Miller, 168–9. *Punch* (15 Oct. 1859) interpreted the Bordeaux speech as Napoleon politely shoving the papal tiara down over the pope's face, his response to the threat of excommunication in the pope's allocution of 28 September.
17   Persigny to Walewski, London, 15 Oct. 1859, no. 85, *Conferenze di Zurigo*, 369–70.
18   Sacconi to Antonelli, Paris, 16 Oct. 1859, no. 1370, ASV, ASdS, 1859, 165/5/159–64, and *Antonelli*, vol. I, 261–2.

of confederation as an idea which had originated, not with Napoleon, but the pope, back in 1846. The difficulties involved in organizing a confederation and making it work were stupendous, he acknowledged. Now, however, Antonelli came to a different conclusion about them than he had after Villafranca in the summer. As Odo reported, 'His Holiness is ready to accept the Protectorate if the Confederation can be organized.'[19]

In a parallel move, Antonelli and the pope decided to take a slightly more positive approach to reforms than the policy 'first restoration, then reforms' implied. They made a public offer to adopt reforms in the papal government. Sacconi suggested the strategy: the papal government should neutralize criticism from England and France by announcing that the pope would grant reforms, while, at the same time, it should keep things fluid by assuring the powers that the pope would use force if necessary to restore papal rule in the Romagna.[20] Antonelli fully approved Sacconi's strategy. Antonelli briefly resumed secret talks with Gramont in September, and indicated that some reforms were plausible, provided the pope would make them of his own free will and without pressure.[21] Lord John said Odo should continue to stick by the French in Rome and support Gramont's activity to secure papal reform. This Odo endeavoured to do, 'so far as Whiggism and conscience will allow of my doing so'.[22] On 12 November, Antonelli publicized a list of reforms the pope had in mind to give to his subjects. Odo congratulated Antonelli on the list, and the cardinal assured him that the Holy Father would implement these and the other measures embodied in the *Motu proprio* issued at Portici in 1849, as soon as 'the Pontifical State is entirely restored to order'.[23] Papal policy remained 'first restoration, then reform', but the pope and Antonelli had made some gesture toward reform before achieving restoration. This episode about reforms helped promote English–French *rapprochement* over the Papal Question.

The papal government's attitude toward the congress was the greatest turnabout of all in papal policy. Antonelli's initial response to a congress had been the same as that expressed in opposition to the earlier congress so energetically promoted by Lord Malmesbury in the spring – it would be a tribunal of Protestants, schismatics, and quarrelling Catholics sitting in judgment upon the pope. In September Walewski even used the threat of a

19 Odo Russell to Russell, Rome, 23 Nov. 1859, no. 128, PRO, FO, 43/72, and *Odo Russell*, 63–4.
20 Sacconi to Antonelli, Paris, 4 Sept. 1859, no. 1346, ASV, ASdS, 1859, 165/5/73–8, and *Antonelli*, vol. I, 223–4.
21 Antonelli to Sacconi, Rome, 20 Sept. 1859, no. 6238, ASV, ANParigi, 1859, SdS, AD/P, and *Antonelli*, vol. I, 232–3. Pirri, vol. II, part 1, 150–3.
22 Russell to Odo Russell, 5 Nov. 1859, private, Ampthill papers, PRO, FO, 918/7. Odo Russell to Russell, Rome, 19 Nov. 1859, private, Russell papers, PRO, 30/22/75, and excerpted in *Odo Russell*, 58–60.
23 Antonelli to Sacconi, Rome, 12 Nov. 1859, no. 7088–9, ASV, ANParigi, 1859, SdS, AD/P, and *Antonelli*, vol. I, 279–81. Odo Russell to Russell, Rome, 23 Nov. 1859, no. 128, PRO, FO, 43/72, and *Odo Russell*, 60–3.

congress so composed to try to coerce the papal government into making major concessions on reform before the congress convened. Then Antonelli resented the idea of such a congress.[24] Antonelli and the pope began to change their attitude in October when they realized that the papal army would be isolated in its attempts to restore the Romagna, and when Napoleon at Bordeaux appeared to weaken his public commitment to the pope. A congress looked more and more like the means by which the Romagna could be returned to papal authority. What led the pope and Antonelli actually to accept the congress was the provision that all the signatories of the Vienna treaty of 1815 possessed the right of participation in a new European congress which would undertake amendments to that treaty. This meant that in addition to the five major powers, Spain, Portugal and Sweden would join in. Furthermore, France and Austria agreed to invite the three Italian courts of Piedmont, Naples and Rome. All would have equal status. Counting heads, this meant a solid majority would be reliably Catholic – Austria, Spain, Portugal, Naples, Rome. An even bigger majority would be defenders of order and dynastic rights – Russia, possibly Prussia and Sweden. France, although a Catholic power, was, of course, a big question. England and Piedmont would be the pope's only straightforward opponents, but they would be overwhelmed by the other states.

Pius IX discussed congress strategy with the Austrian ambassador, Baron Bach, at Castel Gandolfo on 21 October. The pope would rely upon the Catholic powers, led by Austria and Spain, and augmented by the other conservative powers, to arrange an *entente* prior to the congress specifying a common course of action. The axis of the agreement would be Rome and Austria. Based on the *entente*, Pius thought the congress could beneficially decide upon the restoration of the dukes and the pope's authority in the Romagna, the organization of the confederation, and reforms to be introduced in the several Italian states. The details of the confederation and reform would, of course, be left to the states involved to work out. In addition to all this, Antonelli wanted the Catholic powers to provide armed intervention if necessary to implement the congress decisions.[25]

There was a phenomenon developing in the background which strengthened the pope's resolve to go to the congress. The clergy and the Catholic faithful, first in France, then in England and Ireland, and elsewhere, began to form a movement of support for the pope's temporal power. They constituted a source of spiritual consolation for the pope, but they also served as a political force that, in different ways, the governments of France and England would have to reckon with.

24 Sacconi to Antonelli, Paris, 4 Sept. 1859, no. 1346, ASV, ASdS, 1859, 165/5/73–8, and Antonelli to Sacconi, Rome, ASV, ANParigi, 1859, SdS, AD/P, and *Antonelli*, vol. 1, 225 and 229.
25 Bach to Rechberg, Rome, 21 Oct. 1859, no. 59A–H, HHSA, PA, XI, 200/698/705. See Gramont to Walewski, Rome, 22 Oct. 1859, no. 104, AMAE, CP, 1012/110. Antonelli to Barili, 29 Nov. 1859, no. 7454, *Antonelli–Barili*, 120–1.

The awakening of the clergy and the faithful was a tangible response to the pope's allocution of 28 September. In France a wave of addresses by bishops, pastoral letters, and articles began in October. Their content included support of the pope, indirect criticism of Napoleon's policy, and opposition to the English government. Bishop Dupanloup, Bishop of Orleans, singled out England as the culprit among the great powers responsible for leading a vendetta against the pope.[26] Napoleon's government tried to quash the political force of the French Catholics by means of a severe press censorship.[27]

The movement also developed in England and Ireland. An address by the Irish clergy assembled in Dublin on 5 August began things in Ireland. Later Archbishop Cullen, primate of Ireland, and Cardinal Wiseman, primate of England, both made public statements in defence of the temporal power. Throughout October, November and December, mass public meetings were held in England and Ireland, statements of support were gathered and sent to the pope, petitions and letters were presented to Lord Palmerston. Two giant meetings were held in Dublin in November, and on 15 December a 'Declaration of Catholic Laity of Great Britain' was published.[28] The statement pledged utter loyalty to the pope and support of the temporal power, and then bluntly criticized the policy of the Liberal government:

> We protest against the power or influence of our country being used – whether in a Congress of European States, or separately – in favour of the Holy Father's rebel subjects; or to despoil him of his dominions; or to interfere with his independent Sovereignty, by imposing any conditions upon him. And we hereby make known our determination to resist and resent, in the spirit of the Constitution, any such course on the part of the responsible advisors of the Crown, to whatever party in the State they may belong.[29].

The declaration may have reflected the opinion of all Catholics. The public press in England editorialized against the declaration. *The Times* labelled it 'a disgraceful monument of the bigotry and ignorance of Ultramontane Catholicism', and all the leading papers, including *The Times*, the *Standard*, the *Morning Post* and the *Daily News*, cited it as evidence that Catholics put loyalty to the pope above loyalty to the queen and the English constitution. Cardinal Wiseman showed the declaration to Pius IX personally. The pope approved it and ordered it to be printed in the *Giornale di Roma*.[30]

26   Cowley to Russell, Paris, 10 Oct. 1859, no. 615, PRO, FO, 425/56/30–7. Dupanloup's article appeared in the *Journal des Debates* (7 Oct. 1859) and was dated 30 September 1859. See Case, *French Opinion*, 1048.
27   See Sacconi to Antonelli, Paris, 16 Oct. 1859, no. 1370, 19 Oct. 1859, no. 1373, 23 Oct. 1859, no. 1374, and so on, ASV, ASdS, 165/5/159–64, 169–74, 192–3, etc., and *Antonelli*, vol. I, 259–61, 264–5, 267–8, etc.
28   The *Tablet* gives complete coverage of all the meetings, pastorals, letters and statements.
29   *Tablet*, 17 Dec. 1859. The chairman of the declaration organizers was Hon. Charles Langdale; the street address given was the Stafford Club, 18 Clifford Street, London.
30   Reprints of editorials from other papers were carried in the *Tablet*, 24 Dec. 1859. Wiseman to Charles Langdale, Rome, 26 Dec. 1859, reported by Langdale to the *Tablet*, 4 Jan. 1859, published in the *Tablet*, 7 Jan. 1860. *Giornale di Roma*, 28 Dec. 1859.

England: 'non-intervention' and annexation

The *Tablet* identified two ways English and Irish Catholics could help the pope politically: by helping to impress upon Napoleon that if he hurts the pope he hurts himself, and by persuading the Whig–Liberal ministry 'that, no matter what their wishes might be, they must abstain from carrying their hostility to the Holy Father into practice, under pain of forfeiting their places'.[31] Odo Russell heard from some priests in Rome 'that the Pope had caused a league to be formed in Ireland under the direction of forty-two Priests with a view to influence the next general elections in the interest of the conservative party'. He asked Antonelli about it. The cardinal denied any knowledge of it and claimed it was quite unfounded. Antonelli did acknowledge that his private opinion was that Lord Derby's government was more favourable than Lord Palmerston's to the unimpaired continuation of the temporal power. Then he added, 'but the Government of His Holiness always deprecated any interference in secular politics on the part of the priesthood of foreign countries and greatly regretted it when it occurred.'[32] The cardinal did not choose to recall his own intervention, at Malmesbury's request, in the English parliamentary elections in Ireland in the spring. Whether Antonelli or the pope exercised any such direct influence during the autumn is not known. Nevertheless the possibility of such priestly politics in Ireland was real. Sackville West told the Sardinians, in Massari's words, 'that Lord John will be cautious on the Roman question because of the Irish, for he would lose the majority in Commons'.[33] If the 'no confidence' vote in the early morning of 11 June were held now, the Liberals might have completely lost Catholic support, and might not have come to power.

In December, the pope was, surprisingly, in a relatively strong position. When France and Austria issued the official invitations to the congress the pope, on 10 December, accepted immediately and Antonelli was delegated to be the papal representative.[34] The numbers were on his side, and it was not completely unrealistic for him to think that the congress could vote to restore the Romagna and the duchies to their traditional rulers. The pope had an undivided Catholic Church behind him, clergy and laity. For the first time during the international crisis, the pope was able to take some initiative.

England: 'non-intervention' and annexation

The English government, during November and December, definitely feared that the congress might indeed vote to restore the pope and the archdukes, and then allow some power, or powers, to march their armies into the Romagna. Austria and France were the powers to fear, and the English government worked hard to secure their endorsement of a policy of 'non-intervention' in Central Italy.

31 *Tablet*, 24 Dec. 1859.
32 Odo Russell to Russell, Rome, 18 Nov. 1859, no. 124, PRO, FO, 43/72.
33 Massari, *Diario*, 9 Dec. 1859, 435.
34 Antonelli to Sacconi, Rome, 10 Dec. 1859, s.n., ASV, ANParigi, 1859, SdS, AD/P, and *Antonelli*, vol. II, 304.

Liberals, the congress and the Romagna

English policy on the congress and the 'no force' question remained the same in the autumn and winter as it had been in the summer. Russell reiterated his point numerous times in despatches to Cowley: 'Her Majesty cannot send a Minister to a congress where any sanction is to be given or required to a proposal to impose by force a government or constitution on Tuscany or Modena, or any part of Central Italy.'[35] The corollary was to 'let the Italians decide' what government they wished to live under.

When the Zurich negotiations ended, the French government finally replied to the inquiry Russell had made in the summer about whether France would renounce the use of armed force in Italy. Walewski declared that France would not use force to restore the dukes of Tuscany and Modena, but he made no explicit comment about the Romagna. In fact, during November and December, while often professing the policy of 'non-intervention', neither Napoleon or Walewski would say to England that they would not use force in the Romagna – Napoleon did not want to give French Catholics something specific to protest against, and he wanted to keep his actions toward the pope ambiguous.[36]

Austria was the real problem, however. Austria continued to decline to state that it would not use force to restore the pope and the archdukes. Count Rechberg's invitation to England to participate in a congress said that one of the purposes of the meeting of the European powers would be to decide upon 'the most appropriate means to pacify Italy'.[37] To the Austrian government this language assumed unequivocally that the congress would arrange the return of the duchies and the Romagna to their traditional rulers. Loftus reported Rechberg's views on the Romagna to Russell: 'His Excellency then states that it will be the duty of the Congress to restore to the authority of the Pope those provinces which are in rebellion against him, on the grounds of the urgent necessity of providing for the protection of legitimate rights against revolutionary inroads, and of defending the cause of social order and of religion.' How to achieve this objective Rechberg left wide open. Russell interpreted Rechberg's views to include the possibility of Austria using military force in the Romagna. At the very minimum, Austria would allow Austrian subjects to continue to enlist in the papal army, forming, in effect, Austrian battalions under papal command.[38]

Russell was determined to keep Austrian troops from invading the Romagna

---

35 Russell to Cowley, 17 Sept. 1859, no. 329, PRO, FO, 425/55/28—9.
36 Walewski to Persigny, Paris, 19 Oct. 1859, no. 136, *Annessioni al Regno d'Italia*, vol. II, 1–4. *Le Moniteur Universel* (9 Sept. 1859) had said the restoration of the dukes was not to be effected by force.
37 'les moyens les plus propres à pacifier l'Italie'. Rechberg to Apponyi, Vienna, 14 Nov. 1859, *Gran Bretagna e Sardegna*, vol. VII, 275. Apponyi communicated this note to Russell on 1 December.
38 Loftus to Russell, Vienna, Dec. 1859, no. 811, PRO, FO, 425/57/88. Loftus to Russell, Vienna, 1 Dec. 1859, no. 805, and 13 Dec. 1859, no. 830, PRO, FO, 425/57/86–7, 111, and 29 Dec. 1859, no. 855, PRO, FO, 425/58/37.

and the duchies. It was to him 'the most important and the most pressing part of the whole question'.[39] As early as 26 November he expressed to Lord Cowley his opinion of the extent to which England should go to stop it: 'I have no doubt in my mind that if the war were to be renewed in Italy, England would be found by the side of France in favour of Italian independence.'[40] This he boldly stated to Queen Victoria several times during the first week of December, for as he wrote to Palmerston, 'I have thought it my duty not to conceal my opinion from the Queen, viz–. . . that if Austria tried restoration in Tuscany or Romagna we must join France.' He explained to Queen Victoria, 'Lord John Russell feels that while it is a great advantage, to prevail by moral influence, yet if moral influence should not prevail, and at length war is probable, it becomes a great power like Great Britain to preserve the peace of Europe by throwing her great weight into the scale which has justice on its side.'[41] The queen would not hear of such talk, and declared that she could countenance no other position in the event of war in Italy than neutrality. Certainly she could never support Napoleon's cause against Austria.[42] A breach between the queen and her two chief ministers was developing. It was a case, said Palmerston, of 'her German policy' against 'our Italian policy', and 'we must maintain our own policy *coute que coute*'.[43] With the Mediterranean fleet in their minds, Russell and Palmerston wanted to take the ultimate step in *rapprochement* with France over Italy. Such was the 'force' side of their policy of 'no force' and 'non-intervention'.

The other side of English policy against outside military intervention in central Italy was Russell's and Palmerston's increasing determination to promote the annexation of the Romagna and the duchies to Piedmont-Sardinia. This would involve active British 'intervention' in support of the policy of 'non-intervention'. Russell explained to Cowley that the way he interpreted English diplomatic history since 1815 it would be consistent with British practice to use 'our influence to maintain and consolidate any regular and orderly Government which the Italians may form for themselves'.[44] This would rule out three options that some Italians wanted: a Mazzinian revolution, which would be 'anarchy'; the enlargement of Sardinia in Central Italy, if it entailed expansion of French influence and thereby threatened the balance of power in Europe; and, the return to 'the sacerdo-military rule of the Pope and Austria' through reconquest by the papal army or restoration by Austrian force. What this left, for Russell, was the annexation of central Italy to Piedmont with Piedmont

39   Russell to Lord Bloomfield (ambassador in Berlin), 7 Dec. 1859, no. 50, *Gran Bretagna e Sardegna*, vol. VII, 284.
40   Russell to Cowley, 26 Nov. 1859, private, copy, Russell papers, PRO, 30/22/103.
41   Russell to Palmerston, 6 Dec. 1859, Palmerston papers, 1859, GC/RU/560. Russell to Queen Victoria, 1 Dec. 1859, copy, Russell papers, PRO, 30/22/13H, and Russell to Queen Victoria, 3, 5 and 6 Dec. 1859, RA J24/12, 25 and 30.
42   Queen Victoria to Russell, 2, 6 and 7 Dec. 1859, copies, Russell papers, PRO, 30/22/13G.
43   Palmerston to Russell, 6 Dec. 1859, Russell papers, PRO, 30/22/20.
44   Russell to Cowley, 15 Nov. 1859, no. 498, PRO, FO, 425/57/39.

spreading English-style constitutional liberty and religious policy while being amenable to British commercial and naval interests.⁴⁵

In a letter to Queen Victoria, which he never sent, he stated his belief about the solution of the crisis in Italy this way:

> ... that an independent Italy resting on constitutional monarchies would be the best remedy, would afford repose to Europe, satisfaction to Italy, and would thereby promote English interests... that a renewal of Austrian supremacy in Italy accompanied by persecution of Protestants, and the use of torture in criminal cases would be a calamity for Italy, a danger for Europe, and a blow to that influence for good which is one of the sources of our power, and the best guarantee for its preservation.⁴⁶

Russell had put the matter succinctly in a sensational speech before 3000 people in Aberdeen, in Scotland, on 28 September. 'England', he proclaimed, 'held a beacon on high which might yet save the rest of the world.'⁴⁷ In the Cabinet, the Duke of Argyll and Gladstone stood fully on Russell and Palmerston's side against the queen's interpretation of 'non-intervention'. Argyll opposed 'undue interference' when the interests and honour of the country are not concerned, but he equally opposed 'selfish isolation, which would deprive us of our just influence in the counsels of the world'. He wanted the English government to exercise its influence with propriety 'in favour of the principles of justice, of humanity, and of freedom, which are the mainsprings of all our blessings'.⁴⁸

During October and November, Russell and Palmerston supported a plan which they saw as a good transition to annexation – a regency in the name of Victor Emmanuel in central Italy. The idea originated in a conversation between Cavour, Hudson and Marliani in September, and it became Hudson's assignment to obtain the backing of Russell and Palmerston.⁴⁹ The idea was for Tuscany, Parma, Modena and the Romagna each to vote to invite Prince Carignano, a cousin of Victor Emmanuel, to become regent in central Italy. In

45   Russell to Cowley, 15 Nov. 1859, private, copy, Russell papers, PRO, 30/22/103.
46   Russell wrote this to the queen as a defence of Sir James Hudson's beliefs, with which he said he 'entirely agrees'. He did not send the letter because he decided not to press for Hudson's appointment as British plenipotentiary to the congress. Russell to Queen Victoria, 8 Dec. 1859, incompleted draft, Russell papers, PRO, 30/22/13H.
47   *Tablet*, 1 Oct. 1859.
48   Duke of Argyll, Address in Edinburgh, 29 Oct. 1859, in George Douglas, Eighth Duke of Argyll, *Autobiography and Memoirs* (2 vols., London: John Murray, 1906), vol. II, 146. While they were working out 'non-intervention' for Italy, English naval vessels and troops joined with those of several countries to force China to open its ports to foreign trade and then to admit foreign diplomats to Peking. Argyll commented to Gladstone about the Chinese:
> We must, I suppose, fight those rascals. But at the same time I don't think our proceedings will stand the test of international law, as applicable between civilized states. But it would be madness to be bound on our side by that code with a barbarous people, to whom it is unknown, and, if known, would not be followed.

(Argyll to Gladstone, 23 Sept. 1859, in Argyll, *Memoirs*, 149–50). 17,000 English and French troops finally occupied Peking in October 1860 and burned the Summer Palace.
49   Hudson to Russell, Turin, 28 Nov. 1859, private, *Gran Bretagna e Sardegna*, vol. VII, 261–4. This despatch was based on a version written by Massari (*Diario*, 26 Nov. 1859, 425).

England: 'non-intervention' and annexation

this manner the states would remain technically independent, yet bind themselves dynastically to Piedmont. Hudson journeyed to London in October to introduce the idea to Russell and Palmerston. Soon afterward the two English ministers gave the Sardinians their personal encouragement, although officially they said they could give no 'advice'. With that news, the four assemblies in central Italy went ahead early in November and voted for the Carignano regency.[50]

Napoleon put a stop to the regency by threatening to withdraw his backing of Victor Emmanuel. The emperor disapproved the plan because it would embrace the pope's Romagna, and would move things too quickly toward annexation. Accordingly, Carignano declined the invitations to take up the regency personally, but as a compromise, designated Count Carlo Buoncompagni as governor-general to act in his place. Napoleon did not like the Buoncompagni arrangement either, but eventually let the plan go through. On 21 December the count finally took up his post in Florence.[51]

The papal government opposed the regency all along, and eventually issued an official protest on 7 December to the governments of Europe. Odo Russell conveyed the protest to Lord John.[52] The English government had decided not to press for the Carignano regency, but not out of any consideration of Antonelli's views. Austria's threat of withdrawing from the congress had some influence, as Sacconi noted. What mattered most to the English, however, was Napoleon's opposition. On the regency question, Russell and Palmerston decided to conform their policy to Napoleon's, and to permit Napoleon to reduce the speed of the movement toward annexation.[53] When Napoleon allowed Buoncompagni to proceed to central Italy, Russell was pleased, and congratulated Hudson on his role in arranging the regency.[54]

On 26 November, Lord John released a major policy statement to Cowley announcing that the English government officially endorsed the annexation of all of central Italy, including the Romagna, to Piedmont. Its general purpose was to shift the attention of the European powers away from mere resistance to restoration, and from the confederation idea of Zurich, toward annexation. He

50 'You know that it is essentially the letters of the Marquis Lajatico [reporting Palmerston's views] that have given the Assemblies the determination to vote the Regency' (Dabormida to Emanuel d'Azeglio, Turin, 16 Nov. 1859, telegram, Colombo, vol. II, 245. Miller, 180–90: 'The impetus, therefore, to the enactment of the regency came essentially from encouragement... from England' (190). Russell to Cowley, 8 Nov. 1859, private, copy, Russell papers, PRO, 30/22/103. Emanuel d'Azeglio to Dabormida, London, 10 Nov. 1859, ASMAE, Londra, LXVII.
51 Miller, ch. 5.
52 Antonelli to diplomatic corps, Vatican, 7 Dec. 1859, translated by Odo Russell, and enclosed in Odo Russell to Russell, Rome, 9 Dec. 1859, no. 134, PRO, FO, 43/72.
53 Russell to Hudson, 17 Nov. 1859, private, *Gran Bretagna e Sardegna*, vol. VII, 249–50. Miller, 100ff. Sacconi to Antonelli, Paris, 17 and 18 Nov. 1859, no. 1388, ASV, ASdS, 1859, 165/5/45–52, and *Antonelli*, vol. I, 284–5.
54 Russell to Hudson, 12 Dec. 1859, private, *Gran Bretagna e Sardegna*, vol. VII, 271. Emanuel d'Azeglio to Dabormida, London, 15 Nov. 1859, telegram, Colombo, vol. II, 241.

declared, 'The future position of Tuscany, Modena, Parma, and Romagna, is, however, the chief subject for our present consideration. It is a question not determined by the Treaty of Zurich; and we propose to enter on it with perfect freedom, for the purpose of discovering the true interests of Italy and of Europe.' For England the starting point in the forthcoming congress had to be 'the state of things which actually exists'. The 'people of central Italy' had clearly expressed their will: 'They, one and all, have proposed annexation to Sardinia. Their National Assemblies have voted that annexation, and their governments are now carried on in the name of King Victor Emmanuel.' Russell declared that in the opinion of the English government 'this solution would be perfectly satisfactory'. However, the statement went on to note that since both Austria and France officially opposed annexation, England wished to call attention to a 'modified proposition' for the arrangement of central Italy: Parma and a couple of smaller territories could be annexed to Sardinia; then Tuscany, Modena, and, 'should it be found practicable', the Romagna could form a separate kingdom in central Italy under a prince of the House of Savoy or another minor house of Europe.[55] It was one of those ideas which would satisfy no one, but with a congress coming up, Russell and Palmerston were tossing about for the formula which would keep events moving in Piedmont's favour, and against any attempts to restore papal temporal power in the Romagna.[56] There was the small possibility that Napoleon, unable to accept annexation publicly, might be able to approve such an intermediate kingdom, which, humble as the step was, would entail the giant result of abandoning the pope's rule in the Romagna.

Two rival strategies

On 3 December, the English government officially accepted the French and Austrian invitation to a congress, called to convene in Paris early in January. England agreed to enter a congress in which its point of view was in a decided minority. The papal government, statistically, had the advantage over England. During the month of December, two parallel and opposing strategies for the congress were plotted and organized. On one side were the pope and Austria, while on the other were England and Piedmont. The key power in between was France. On the issue at hand – the political settlement of the Romagna and the duchies – England had the practical advantage. The situation was that papal authority in the Romagna and the authority of the dukes were, in fact, overthrown, and the liberal nationalists in central Italy actively pushed for annexation to Sardinia. Nevertheless, even though the papal hope for restoration was more difficult to achieve than non-restoration, the English hope for annexation was more difficult to achieve than non-annexation. Once again,

55 Russell to Cowley, 26 Nov. 1859, no. 512, *Gran Bretagna e Sardegna*, vol. VII, 276–8.
56 Russell to Palmerston, 19 Nov. 1859, Palmerston papers, 1859, GC/RU/554. Russell to Queen Victoria, 24 Nov. 1859, RA J23/138.

France was crucial in between. How to relate to France, particularly Napoleon, was a central problem of both strategies.

The pope and Antonelli were becoming increasingly exasperated with Napoleon. The more Napoleon seemed willing to forsake the pope and draw closer to the English, the greater became the estrangement between Napoleon and the pope. Lord John reported to Hudson gleefully: 'Pius IX is very angry with Napoleon, calls him freely "a traitor" and "a liar" and other forms of papal benedictions. This I have from Rome.'[57] The pope held one major weapon over Napoleon, and Napoleon knew it. Odo quoted a Benedictine close to the pope: ' I will tell you, . . . The Pope is fully determined if the Emperor does not restore the Legations to him to use the power he has over the French clergy, and France will soon be made too hot to hold his Majesty much longer.'[58] Pius IX, on 2 December, appealed to Napoleon, as 'head of a Catholic People who take so much interest in the present events in Italy', to act in the forthcoming congress to restore the Romagna to papal authority. The letter was both a plea for help and a small hint of a threat.[59] The pope addressed a parallel letter to King Victor Emmanuel to ask him to reject the evils carried on by others in his name in the Romagna. In the congress, wrote Pius, the king ought to declare openly that he 'did not want to be covered by another's spoils much less by a portion of the robe of Jesus Christ, which remained untorn even on Calvary'.[60] Next the pope wrote a common letter to his friends who formed the core of his support, Francis Joseph of Austria, Peter V of Portugal, and Queen Isabella II of Spain. His letters were a direct reply to England. He appealed to the monarchs, on the basis of their Catholic faith and their legitimate authority, to join him in combating the new and very subversive principle,

> that the people can by their own will overturn their legitimate Sovereign, as has happened in Italy, not even by the people but by the revolutionaries, strongly supported by one who fears revolutionaries, and by one who is carried away by blind ambition; under such circumstances there will be no throne able to rule in Europe or elsewhere.[61]

With Austria came the real work of organizing a common strategy for the congress which the other conservative powers could endorse. Baron Bach, the Austrian ambassador in Rome, and Antonelli held talks which, Odo said, were 'veiled in mystery'.[62] Odo ferreted out the details of an Austro-papal agreement, and sent an extensive report on it to Lord John. In Turin, Hudson

---

57 Russell to Hudson, 28 Nov. 1859, private, *Gran Bretagna e Sardegna*, vol. VII, 265.
58 Odo Russell to Russell, Rome, 10 Dec. 1859, no. 138, most confidential, PRO, FO, 43/72, and *Odo Russell*, 65–6.
59 Pius IX to Napoleon III, Vatican, 2 Dec. 1859, Pirri, vol. II, part 2, 133–4.
60 Pius IX to Victor Emmanuel II, Vatican, 3 Dec. 1859, Pirri, vol. II, part 2, 135–6.
61 Pius IX to Francis Joseph, Peter V and Isabella II, Vatican, 5 Dec. 1859, Pirri, vol. II, part 2, 137–8. The reference is to Napoleon.
62 Odo Russell to Russell, Rome, 20 Dec. 1859, no. 744, secret, PRO, FO, 43/72, and *Odo Russell*, 69–72. The details which follow are from this document.

arranged for Cavour to see it.[63] Odo did not reveal how he obtained the information, but its authenticity was undeniable. The common aims of the two governments, Odo discovered, would be to restore the pope in the Romagna and the dukes in the duchies, to re-establish Austria's influence in Italy, and to organize a confederation of all the states of the peninsula. In order to overcome the opposition of England, Sardinia, and possibly France, the conservative powers would all have to act together. Then the crucial first manoeuvre would be to confine the congress to the basis established by the Zurich treaty, forcing the congress to deal only with restoration and a confederation. England would be prevented from introducing proposals for annexation or a kingdom in central Italy. The agreement included this agenda: recognizing the sovereign rights of the pope in the Romagna and the dukes in their states; seating the dukes' representatives, thereby enlarging the conservative majority; demanding the immediate resignation of the 'revolutionary governments of central Italy', and determining 'the best means of coercion' if they refuse to resign; establishing a confederation in principle, whose details would be worked out subsequently by the member states; and affirming the right of each state to establish its own internal administrations, thereby terminating all outside pressures for reforms. It was, observed Odo, a 'cunning policy', and Austria and the pope were confident of success.

Foremost in the English strategy was *rapprochement* with France, especially on the question of the Romagna. Sacconi had been warning Antonelli since early in November that Napoleon was gravitating toward England, specifically in anticipation of the congress. Barili in Madrid had been raising the same warning. Early in December, after a lengthy interview with Napoleon at Compiègne, Sacconi was convinced that the emperor was becoming dominated by the hope of *rapprochement* with the Palmerston–Russell government.[64] Later in December, Sacconi suspected that Napoleon and Cowley, who had spent several days together at Chantilly, had agreed upon a common strategy for the congress. The way Sacconi pieced it together, he imagined almost all the powers – England, France, Russia, Prussia, Sweden, Portugal and Piedmont – gradually coalescing around the English suggestion of a kingdom of central Italy as a compromise. Sacconi concluded: 'I maintain, therefore, that there is no reason to hope for any good coming to us from the congress, notwithstanding that the majority of the powers composing it will be inclined to favour the Holy See.'[65] In reality, the

63 Massari, *Diario*, 27 Dec. 1859, 450.
64 Sacconi to Antonelli, Paris, 4 Nov. 1859, no. 1380; 17 Nov. 1859, no. 1388; and 1 Dec. 1859, no. 1393; ASV, ASdS, 1859, 165/6/16–23, 45–52 and 86–93, and *Antonelli*, vol. I, 273 and 283. Barili to Antonelli, Madrid, 15 Nov. 1859, no. 480; and 22 Nov. 1859, no. 482; and 23 Dec. 1859, no. 506, *Antonelli–Barili*, 118–19, 136–7.
65 Sacconi to Antonelli, Paris, 16 Dec. 1859, no. 1399, ASV, ASdS, 1859, 165/6/134–9, and *Antonelli*, vol. II, 300–1, and 313. See Cowley to Russell, Paris, 29 Nov. 1859, no. 815, *Gran Bretagna e Sardegna*, vol. VII, 278–9.

English never made a firm agreement with Napoleon, although Palmerston and Russell surely would have liked an arrangement with the emperor before the congress.[66]

Russell, through Panizzi at the British Museum, did seek Cavour's advice on Italy and the congress. It was Russell's way of insuring that England stayed close to Piedmont's expectations, even though Cavour was not in office. Cavour essentially confirmed that Russell was proceeding in the manner best calculated to lead to annexation – 'non-intervention', opposition to the restoration of the pope and the dukes, support for the assemblies in the Romagna and the duchies. Cavour stressed that if the pope achieved a victory in the Romagna, the most difficult, yet the most important issue, it would give strength to the Ultramontane Catholics in all countries: 'Europe would be threatened in no distant future by the dangers of religious struggles like those of bygone centuries. Let all be yielded rather than Romagna be sacrificed. Her cause, I repeat it, is the cause of civilization.' Russell liked Cavour's advice, and told the queen that it was true 'that a fresh triumph of the Papacy would be a fresh blow to England and Prussia'.[67]

In designing English strategy in the congress, Russell, like Antonelli and Bach, knew that the decision about what to allow to come up for discussion would shape the entire congress. Russell continued to insist upon an 'open' agenda which was not limited to the Zurich treaty. The treaty, he argued, concerned only the war and the territories of the belligerents in the war; central Italy lay outside the war and should be treated as an additional question not properly covered by the peace treaty.[68] The next big point would be for the congress to establish its commitment to the principle of 'non-intervention', albeit as interpreted by England. All of Russell's diplomacy to secure Austria's and France's agreement not to use force was directed to this end. Once these two points were achieved, and if Napoleon would abandon the pope on the Romagna, the English would be free to face a variety of compromise proposals, like a kingdom of central Italy. Hudson wanted the congress to adopt the principle of 'universal suffrage', but Russell knew that was hopeless.[69] England's strategy could hardly be more completely opposite to the pope's and Austria's.

Sacconi wrote to Antonelli on 16 December about something very unsettling. After discussion of Pius' letter to Napoleon dated 2 December, the nuncio came to this perceptive conclusion: 'I am afraid that in his mind, and perhaps even in some communications with others, he has already made a decision unfavourable

---

66 Palmerston to Russell, 18 Nov. 1859, Russell papers, PRO, 30/22/20.
67 Russell to Queen Victoria, 13 Nov. 1859, RA J23/109; which enclosed Cavour to Antonio Panizzi, Leri, 24 Oct. 1859, RA J23/110, translation provided by Panizzi.
68 Russell to Cowley, 26 Nov. 1859, no. 512, *Gran Bretagna e Sardegna*, vol. VII, 276–7. See Sacconi to Antonelli, Paris, 1 Dec. 1859, no. 1393, ASV, ASdS, 1859, 165/6/86–93, and *Antonelli*, vol. II, 297–302.
69 Hudson to Russell, Turin, 25 Dec. 1859, private, *Gran Bretagna e Sardegna*, vol. VII, 292.

to us, and that we cannot expect anything very satisfying, or any real support, from him.'⁷⁰

Napoleon had indeed made a decision – to abandon publicly the pope's claims to authority in the Romagna. Lord John found this out from Cowley by 12 December and wrote an important letter to Odo Russell in Rome:

> Things are approaching their end, tho' very slowly. The Emperor N says he will ask the Pope to consent to the separation of Romagna, and I imagine will take no denial. That is to say, if the Pope refuses, as he is sure to do, Buoncompagni and Farini will rule without his Papal benediction.
>
> The French troops will stay till the settlement of the affairs of Italy. How long this may be no one can tell. But the Emperor has by this means a powerful club in his hand . . .
>
> In the meantime you have only to listen and report. I have a great respect for the virtues of Pius IX and hope he may be left undisturbed at Rome, but he must not seek to govern three millions of people for their perpetual misery, even though the pride of the Church may require it. In fact Italy has outgrown the Papacy. The Pope would be a saint at Madrid, Valencia or Majorca. In Italy he is only an anachronism.⁷¹

Antonelli learned indirectly of this letter. His information about its contents was garbled, but the essential point came through rather accurately. Antonelli prepared a despatch which he sent to his nuncios in Paris, Vienna and Madrid on 17 December. Antonelli informed them that Odo Russell had received a letter from his uncle which indicated that England and France were reaching agreement for the congress. Antonelli continued,

> And although it did not go into exact details, the letter did say that the Holy Father will lose the Legations.
>
> Such is the seriousness of these things, that although one does not want to believe all of it, they nonetheless give material for serious consideration as well as for advance warning to all those governments who cannot and do not wish to share with these two powers their way of seeing things.⁷²

70 Sacconi to Antonelli, Paris, 16 Dec. 1859, no. 1399, ASV, ASdS, 1859, 165/6/134–9, and *Antonelli*, vol. II, 315.
71 Russell to Odo Russell, 12 Dec. 1859, private, Ampthill papers, PRO, FO, 918/7. *Punch* (3 Dec. 1859) had a feeling that the trend of events in Italy could lead to the pope's complete expulsion from Italy. Where would Pius IX go? Why, to England, of course! Along with the other Italian refugees past and future. *Punch* imagined Pius IX, speaking in a heavy accent and carrying all his earthly possessions, asking a London hansom cab driver to take him to Leicester Square, then the centre of the Italian refugee community. There he and Mazzini could, no doubt, lament together the successes of Cavour.
72 Antonelli to Sacconi, Rome, 17 Dec. 1859, s.n., very confidential, ASV, ANParigi, 1859, SdS, AD/P, and *Antonelli*, vol. II, 317. Antonelli to Barili, Rome, 17 Dec. 1859, s.n. *Antonelli–Barili*, 135. Antonelli said Russell's letter reported an English–French agreement that France would support England's policy in Italy if England would not oppose the French over building a Suez canal. Russell's letter said nothing about that, of course. The thought that there was such an agreement probably reflected Antonelli's anxieties and the speculations of the person, or persons, who passed along the news of Russell's letter. See the editor's note, *Antonelli*, vol. II, 317, which rightly says there is no letter about the Suez canal,

Antonelli knew that if Napoleon had decided to give up the Romagna and move his policy toward England on that point, the pope would have a very hard time in the congress.

On 22 December, Napoleon removed all remaining doubt about his intentions toward the Romagna. A pamphlet written anonymously by the Viscomte de la Guéronnière, entitled *Le pape et le congrès*, appeared simultaneously in Paris and London. It transformed the situation entirely. Cowley said the pamphlet originated with Napoleon, although he did not write it. The ideas were unquestionably Napoleon's, as the emperor readily admitted. With Napoleon's approval the author had worked on the pamphlet throughout the month of December.[73]

Le pape et le congrès was a very careful and thoughtful discussion of the temporal power of the pope and its relation to both the pope's spiritual office and the actualities of Italian politics in central Italy. It analysed the problems of authority arising in an ecclesiastically integrated state and society. It identified some of the difficulties which befell both the state and the church when the needs of justice and order were subordinated to the requirements of the church and the papal office. At the same time it acknowledged the needs of the pope to be politically independent and completely free to make spiritual decisions. The pamphlet's conclusion was sweeping, especially in view of Napoleon's commitment to its ideas: 'Thus, then, the temporal power of the Pope is necessary and legitimate, but it is incompatible with a state of any size.' The way to fit both parts of the conclusion together, proposed the pamphlet, was to maintain the temporal power, but to limit its extent to Rome. The pope should have Rome entirely to himself. The city should be governed by a separate municipal administration, with no army, no press, no civic courts. Rome belonged to the pope – 'It is the decree of civilization, of history, of God himself.' The congress had the authority to act and it ought to take steps to achieve this arrangement. In no case should the Romagna be restored to papal authority. The pamphlet ended with the comment, 'The question is not that of diminishing the patrimony of St. Peter, but of saving it.'

Le pape et le congrès was the emperor's preferred answer to Pius IX's plea for help in restoring the lost Legations. On 27 December he wrote to the pope suggesting a solution less drastic than the pamphlet:

> I tell you with sincere and painful regret that ... the solution which seems to me to fit best with the true interests of the Holy See would be to sacrifice the provinces which are in revolt. If for the repose of Europe the Holy Father renounced these provinces ..., and in exchange he asked the powers to guarantee the rest of his

but which leaves the impression that Antonelli's news of a Russell to Odo Russell letter is completely erroneous.

73   An English translation of *Le pape et le congrès* was published in *The Times*, 22 Dec. 1859. The quotations used are from that translation. Cowley to Russell, Paris, 25 Dec. 1859, private, Cowley papers, PRO, FO, 519/226/224.

possessions intact, I do not doubt that on the immediate return of order the Holy Father would assure to a watching Italy peace for many years to come, and to the Holy See the peaceful possession of the states of the Church.[74]

The pamphlet caused an immense stir. Napoleon's real views about the temporal power and the revolution, partly expressed in the Plombières pact with Cavour in July 1858, were now clearly out in the open. Lord John remarked, 'What the nuncio will say to the Church's eldest son I cannot imagine, nor what the eldest son will reply. Anathema... will be the secret ejaculation of the Holy Father.' He asked Odo to tell him what they say about it in Rome.[75]

Taking the pamphlet and Napoleon's letter to the pope together, the implications of the emperor's position were significant. In the first place, the pope and the Catholic clergy and faithful now knew the emperor had given up on the temporal power except for Rome. The estrangement between the pope and Napoleon, which had been coming for months, was complete. Pius IX replied to Napoleon that he could not relinquish the Legations, and that he would have to turn elsewhere for help in restoring them.[76] Secondly, Napoleon's new stand was, indeed, as Pius perceived, an invitation to further revolution in the Papal States. Thirdly, the *rapprochement* between England and Napoleon with respect to Italy and the pope was also nearly complete. Both the Whig–Liberal leaders and Napoleon were now publicly committed to the loss of the Romagna, as well as to the reduction of the temporal power to 'Rome and fifteen miles around' or merely to Rome itself. Both England and Napoleon were anxious, for the time being, to prevent any further revolution. What lay immediately ahead was the question of what to do with Romagna, particularly whether to pursue, or at least permit, annexation.

On the level of European diplomacy, Napoleon's public decision to let the revolution stand and to abandon the pope's claims to temporal power in the Romagna was probably the crucial point determining the future of the States of the Church. From this point on, the situation was changed. Cowley expressed his sense of the historical moment to Odo Russell: 'Happen what may at present, it seems to me that a blow has been struck at the Popedom from which it can never recover.'[77]

The major influence on the European level inducing Napoleon to act as he did was England. The papal government recognized this immediately. Sacconi commented that 'England and the party now dominant in Italy' had nearly

74 Napoleon III to Pius IX, 27 Dec. 1859, Pirri, vol. II, part 2, 146–8.
75 Russell to Cowley, 24 Dec. 1859, private, Cowley papers, PRO, FO, 519/197. Russell to Odo Russell, 26 Dec. 1859, private, copy, Russell papers, PRO, 30/22/111. *Punch* (7 Jan. 1860) saw *Le pape et le congrès* as Napoleon blind-folding the pope with his own tiara and dragging him kicking and screaming into the congress to an unhappy fate.
76 Pius IX to Napoleon III, 8 Jan. 1860, Pirri, vol. II, part 2, 149–53. See also *Giornale di Roma*, 30 Dec. 1859.
77 Cowley to Odo Russell, Paris, 26 Dec. 1859, copy, Cowley papers, PRO, FO, 519/226/240.

succeeded in 'binding' Napoleon to their side.[78] After a lengthy interview with Napoleon on New Year's day, 1860, Cowley reported that in Paris 'the change in the Emperor's Italian policy, or rather the new knowledge of his true sentiments, is widely attributed to England's influence'. The same thing was said in Vienna. Cowley thought that Napoleon's future action toward the pope would depend on England too: 'Then again it is more than probable that the degree of development which the Emperor may give to his present policy will depend on the encouragement he may receive from Her Majesty's Government. His position is a very critical one – backed by Great Britain, it becomes strong; looked upon by her with indifference, it may become untenable.'[79]

Even though Napoleon had come out against the pope as he did, there was still Austria to worry about, and, of course, the pope's own army. Early in December, Queen Victoria had temporarily prevented Russell from talking further about England going to war on France's side against Austria, but the new circumstances created by *Le pape et le congrès* resurrected the question of stopping Austria at all costs. On 20 December, even before the pamphlet appeared, Russell had mentioned to Cowley privately the idea of a triple alliance of England, France and Sardinia against Austria and the pope.[80] Explicit in the alliance would be the threat of armed force to prevent Austria and the pope from regaining their positions in the Romagna and the duchies. In effect, the British navy and the French army would guarantee the triumph of Piedmont in northern and central Italy. On the 26th, after the pamphlet, the need for a triple alliance seemed greater. Russell explained this to Cowley:

> Whatever Walewski may say the blow to the Pope's authority in Romagna is struck, and he will not recover from it. Possibly the Pope from un peu d'espoir et beaucoup de desespoir ... may with his bran[d] new Austrian troops attack Bologna. I suppose Fanti could repel him, but the King of Sardinia would assist, Napoleon would assist [the] king of Sardinia. I trust Austria will be prudent enough not to allow her puppet the Pope to play this desperate game.[81]

Lord John told Odo the same day that Austria was perhaps not in a condition to go to war, but the threat was there.[82] He bade Lord Augustus Loftus 'to protect against the Austrian recruiting for the Pope'.[83] Palmerston agreed to Russell's triple alliance which he saw as offering the threat of going to war as a

78 Sacconi to Antonelli, Paris, 5 Jan. 1850, no. 1407, ASV, ASdS, 1860, 165/43/30–6, and *Antonelli*, vol. II, 337–46. Bach to Rechberg, Rome, 6 Jan. 1860, no. 1 A–F, HHSA, PA, XI, 201/17–19.
79 Cowley, 'Memo to a conversation with the Emperor, January 1, 1860', given to Russell in London, 6 Jan. 1850, copy, Cowley papers, PRO, FO, 519/226/250–6. Loftus to Russell, Vienna, 5 Jan. 1860, no. 4, PRO, FO, 425/58/43–4.
80 Russell to Cowley, 20 Dec. 1859, private, confidential, copy, Russell papers, PRO, 30/22/103.
81 Russell to Cowley, 26 Dec. 1859, private, copy, Russell papers, PRO, 30/22/103.
82 Russell to Odo Russell, 26 Dec. 1859, private, copy, Russell papers, PRO, 30/22/111.
83 Russell to Loftus, 28 Dec. 1859, private, copy, Russell papers, PRO, 30/22/98.

means of keeping Austria from contemplating another war with Sardinia. The alliance might also help keep the English and French together after a congress.[84] Both Palmerston and Russell were well aware that the gradual *rapprochement* between the two states was created by the convergence of their aims toward Italy and the pope, and that once the Papal Question seemed on its way to settlement it could dissipate rapidly.[85] Cowley hinted to Napoleon that England might be willing to back France against Austrian intervention in central Italy, and found Napoleon taking an interest in the idea.[86]

Palmerston and Russell proposed the triple alliance idea to a special cabinet meeting on 3 January. Lord Cowley was asked especially to come from Paris. The cabinet demurred. They were willing to press Austria to use no force, but were unwilling to get involved in a triple alliance which could implicate the British in a war over Italy and the pope. They decided to put the matter off for a while. The event moved Gladstone deeply. He spent the night at Windsor Castle drafting a giant letter to Russell which urged the foreign minister onward in his Italian policy.[87]

Le pape et le congrès created great uncertainty for three or four weeks after its publication; no one knew whether the congress would still meet. One day Russell felt it was still on, the next day he felt it was off. 'The congress seems to be hanging on the Pope's decision', he told Loftus.[88] At first the congress was postponed for a couple of weeks, and then, finally, indefinitely.

Odo reported from Rome, with Whiggish hyperbole, that 'the consternation it [the pamphlet] has struck in the Vatican is only equal to the joy and hope it has awakened in the street'.[89] In a lengthy interview Antonelli told Odo that the pamphlet's revolutionary principles would undermine every sovereign in Europe. As for the Romagna, said the cardinal, it was not a mere piece of territory that the pope could give away. The Romagna belonged to the entire church, even as the pope 'belongs to the Catholicks of England, Ireland, France, Germany, Austria, Spain, Portugal, to the Catholicks of all the world and to God whose vicar he is on Earth'.[90]

In spite of Antonelli's and the pope's obvious rejection of the pamphlet, they did not immediately reject the congress. Antonelli told Odo as late as 21 January that he was planning to attend the congress whenever it met. On 7 January Odo

---

84 Palmerston to Russell, 26 Dec. 1859, Russell papers, PRO, 30/22/20.
85 Russell to Cowley, 17 Dec. 1859, private, copy, Russell papers, PRO, 30/22/103.
86 Cowley, 'Memo . . ., January 1, 1860', copy, Cowley papers, PRO, FO, 519/226/250-6.
87 Russell to Queen Victoria, 3 Jan. 1860, RA J24/85. Russell to Palmerston, 3 Jan. 1860, Palmerston papers, 1860, GC/RU/71. Gladstone to Russell, 3 Jan. 1860, copy, Gladstone papers, British Museum, Add. Mss. 44291ff., 286–95. Also Beales, 'Gladstone on the Italian question', *Rassegna storica del Risorgimento* 41 (1954), 96–104. Russell threatened to resign over the affair. Mack Smith, *Victor Emanuel, Cavour*, 157.
88 Russell to Loftus, 4 Jan. 1860, private, copy, Russell papers, PRO, 30/22/98.
89 Odo Russell to Russell, Rome, 31 Dec. 1859, no. 150, PRO, FO, 43/72.
90 Odo Russell to Russell, Rome, 4 Jan. 1860, no. 4, PRO, FO, 43/76, and *Odo Russell*, 75.

Two rival strategies

supplied Lord John with an extensive account of the cardinal's biography.[91] It was not until 4 February that Antonelli finally told Sacconi that it would be 'unseemly' for the pope's representative to sit in a congress where the French government advocated the views expressed in *Le pape et le congrès*.[92] He believed that a congress no longer offered any hope of restoration of the lost Legations. Antonelli and the pope resolved that they would have to turn elsewhere for help – to God, to the faithful, to Austria perhaps, and to the papal army.

As it happened, after the pamphlet the congress was hanging, not on the pope's decision, but on England's. English diplomacy had created the environment in which Napoleon found the courage to publish the pamphlet which wounded the congress, and it was the English government which finally killed the congress by proposing a means other than a congress by which to settle the political outcome of the Romagna. Russell issued a new policy statement in two versions, one for Austria on 14 January and one for France on the 15th, which offered four propositions as a basis for solving the problems of Italy. Explaining his action, Russell told Cowley on 19 January, 'As to the meeting of the congress now that the Pope has declared he will not yield Romagna, I do not see how we can attend one – at all events it can do no good.'[93] Russell, of course, had known since June 1859 that the pope would not yield Romagna. The point is that Russell and Palmerston believed that unilateral action by England held better prospects of achieving a solution than a congress under the existing circumstances. As a result of Russell's four points, followed later by the papal government's rejection of the congress, the attention of the European governments turned away from a congress and, for a while, toward Russell's proposals.

From the summer onward into December, the English government had worked unsuccessfully to achieve a *rapprochement* of English and French policies toward Italy and the pope. It was their policies toward the pope which mattered most, for until Napoleon was willing publicly to abandon the pope over the Romagna the process of achieving 'Italian liberation and independence' remained at an *impasse*. It was English diplomacy which led to, or made possible, the *rapprochement* – against a confederation, for papal reform, against evacuation of Rome for now, against a Carignano regency, and, most important of all, against the restoration of the pope's authority in the Romagna.

As a result of these developments, England was in a new position of strength, and Austria and the pope in new positions of weakness. Russell recalled an observation by Count Apponyi, the Austrian ambassador in London, which described the change in international politics: '[Apponyi] said there were two

---

91   Odo Russell to Russell, Rome, 21 Jan. 1860, private, Russell papers, PRO, 30/22/75, and 7 Jan. 1860, no. 7, PRO, FO, 43/76.
92   Antonelli to Sacconi, Rome, 4 Feb. 1860, no. 8743, ASV, ANParigi, 1860, SdS, AD/P, and *Antonelli*, vol. II, 408.
93   Russell to Cowley, 19 Jan 1860, private, copy, Russell papers, PRO, 30/22/104.

powers of whose course no one could doubt – Austria and England, and this is true. But our [England's] star has risen, and that of Austria has declined since the Congress was first summoned.'[94] However weak this made the pope's position, Pius IX was a long way from being out of the picture. Odo remarked, 'At all events the Pope is going to give Europe a vast deal of trouble.'[95]

94 Russell to Cowley, 28 Dec. 1859, private, copy, Russell papers, PRO, 30/22/98.
95 Odo Russell to Cowley, Rome, 7 Jan. 1860, private, Cowley papers, PRO, FO, 519/205.

7 Liberals and the annexation of the Romagna

England's push for annexation

Lord John Russell acted in mid-January to end the uncertainty created by *Le pape et le congrès*. In policy statements addressed to Loftus and Cowley he explained that he believed a European congress no longer offered any hope of resolving the question of the Romagna and the duchies:

> It appears from the present aspect of affairs that either the Congress will not meet at all, or that, if it should meet, it must be divided by irreconcilable differences of opinion.
>
> Between the doctrine, that it will be the duty of a Congress to restore the authority of the Pope in Romagna, and the doctrine that no force ought to be used to impose a Government or Constitution on the people of Central Italy, there can be no agreement.

The English government, he said, aimed to provide another means of reaching a settlement of the crisis in central Italy.[1] With that he began the English push for annexation.

Both the English and papal governments, as principals of the opposing sides, found the waiting period after the publication of the pamphlet disturbing. For one thing Russell thought the pope could start a war. When the English cabinet, on 3 January, declined to endorse a triple alliance against Austria, Russell believed he had no adequate defence against the resumption of fighting in Italy. The day following this indecisive cabinet meeting Russell wrote to Loftus: 'I think the recruiting [for the papal army] at Vienna may bring affairs to a crisis.' The picture in his mind was very clear – 'the priests' throw their Austrian battalions against Bologna, Sardinia intervenes, then Austria intervenes, followed by the French. He lamented, 'It is a sad mess altogether and we must do the best we can. If the Pope will keep his hands off Bologna, all may go well, in spite of the pamphlet, and in spite of the congress.'[2]

1   Russell to Loftus, 14 Jan. 1859, no. 11, and Russell to Cowley, 15 Jan. 1859, no. 8, *Gran Bretagna e Sardegna*, vol. VII, 351–3, and 320–1. *Punch* (21 Jan. 1860) depicted Lord John and Lady Britannia ready to sit down with Napoleon at a banquet table to carve up Italia. There was ample fare, and no reason to wait any longer for the other guests to arrive.
2   Russell to Loftus, 4 Jan. 1860, private, copy, Russell papers, PRO, 30/22/98.

Liberals and the annexation of the Romagna

Russell's and Palmerston's related concern was that the *rapprochement* between England and France would collapse. They feared Napoleon could easily reverse his Italian and papal policy at any moment. In the country at large the fears of French expansionism in Europe and a French invasion of England increased. Queen Victoria and the majority of the cabinet resisted anything that appeared to help Napoleon.[3] Nevertheless, Russell and Palmerston, backed by Gladstone, reaffirmed their resolve not to lose the French relationship. Said Russell, 'The mistrust here of French designs is very great; but it is obviously our policy to draw near to France.'[4] Russell succinctly stated to Gladstone what to hope for: 'If the Emperor takes a Protestant view of Italy and a free trade view of Lancashire he will be popular again here, to his heart's content.'[5] On free trade, the English got their desire. Parallel with the Italian and papal crisis, France and England, with Richard Cobden as mediator, conducted negotiations for a new commercial treaty removing, or greatly lowering, tariffs on most English goods imported into France. On 21 December, the day before *Le pape et le congrès* appeared, Napoleon had told Cobden that he would go through with a freer trade treaty with England. The finished treaty was signed on 23 January, and became the centre of a new British network of freer trade treaties. On that level, at least, things looked good for the *entente*.[6] The English could only wish they had an unequivocal commitment from Napoleon against the pope.

The pope's and Antonelli's anxieties were, by contrast, more serious. Odo Russell wrote from Rome on 5 January that 'at present the Papacy is in a helpless and desponding condition'.[7] The pope's relations with France were a disaster. Napoleon had abandoned the pope. Count Walewski resigned in protest over *Le pape et le congrès*, and the papacy lost its best friend in the French government. The new foreign minister, Edouard-Antoine Thouvenel, formerly the French ambassador in Constantinople, would not be as sympathetic to the pope's defence.[8] The emperor's all-out campaign against the French Catholic press was crushing even the powerful *Univers*.[9] Then there were the English Whigs at the head of the Liberal government to contend with. Sacconi impressed on

3 Beales, *England and Italy*, 131–3.
4 Russell to Elliot, 9 Jan. 1860, *The later correspondence of Lord John Russell, 1840–1878*, ed. G.P. Gooch (London: Longmans, Green, 1925), vol. II, 253.
5 Russell to Gladstone, 23 Dec. 1859, Gladstone papers, British Museum, Add. Mss. 44291ff., 278.
6 See Arthur L. Dunham, *The Anglo-French treaty of commerce of 1860 and the progress of the industrial revolution in France* (New York: Russell and Russell, reprint 1971). There seems no doubt that Napoleon's decisions to desert the pope over the Romagna and to approve a freer trade treaty with England were linked in the Emperor's mind as two ways of pleasing the Whig–Liberal government.
7 Odo Russell to Russell, Rome, 5 Jan. 1860, no. 5, secret, PRO, FO, 43/76, and *Odo Russell*, 77.
8 See Lynn M. Case, *Edouard Thouvenel et la diplomatie du Second Empire*, tr. Guillaume de Bertier de Sauvigny (Paris: Pedone, 1976), esp. ch. 6–8. Walewski left office January 4, and Thouvenel entered office January 24.
9 See Louis Veuillot to Sacconi, 10 Jan. 1860, and Sacconi to Antonelli, Paris, 30 Jan. 1860, telegram, *Antonelli*, vol. II, 348 and 395. Case, *French opinion*, 112–14.

Antonelli the urgency of breaking the influence England had on the emperor.[10] Pius IX complained against the English government to Odo in a lengthy audience on 9 January, as Odo recounts it: 'But the truth is the French Emperor is now entirely in the hands of England. You are making use of him to carry out your policy, but that will not prevent him from turning against you too some day, and I do not think you have many friends in Europe to take your part when that moment comes.' Behind Napoleon's wiles, the pope believed, stood Palmerston and Russell, especially Russell.[11] Ironically, at this point in the events, both the papal and English governments were apprehensive of each other's actions as well as of Napoleon's.

The statements to Loftus and Cowley, dated 14 and 15 January, were the English government's attempt to get the situation under control. Count Persigny, the French ambassador in London, had originally suggested that, instead of a full-fledged triple alliance, England might once again ask France and Austria to renounce the use of military intervention in central Italy. Russell put the idea to the Cabinet on 10 January, which gladly adopted it.[12]

By the 14th Russell and Palmerston, in good English tradition, constructed a four point proposal which they sent to France and Austria. It constituted a compromise on their part with the queen and Cabinet, yet it did take them significantly farther in their support of Sardinia and the revolution in the Romagna and the duchies. In letters to the queen which she did not appreciate, Russell explicitly based his acceptance of the Italian revolution on the Whig doctrine of the validity of the English revolution of 1688–9.[13]

Three of their four points directly pertained to the pope and the Romagna. The remaining point was on Venetia. The general description of the troubles to which all four points were addressed concentrated entirely on the Papal Question – the unprecedented occupation of the Papal States by Austrian and French troops, the pope's rejection of reform, and the revolution against papal temporal power in the Romagna. The purpose of the four points was 'to let things take their course in Italy', provided they went in Piedmont's direction, and not the pope's.

Point one was the 'no force' proposal. In the version sent to Paris, Russell requested the French government explicitly and officially to declare that its renunciation of force in the duchies applied equally to the Romagna. The version sent to Vienna demanded from Austria a first-time declaration not to use force anywhere in central Italy. The second point called for the French to evacuate

---

10   Sacconi to Antonelli, Paris, 5 Jan. 1860, no. 1407, ASV, ASdS, 1860, 165/43/30–6, and *Antonelli*, vol. II, 338–9.
11   Odo Russell to Russell, Rome, 31 Jan. 1860, no. 19, secret, PRO, FO, 43/176, and *Odo Russell*, 85–6. Odo Russell to Lady William Russell, Rome, 24 Feb. 1860, copy, Ampthill papers, PRO, FO, 918/85/252. See Massari, *Diario*, 7 Feb. 1860, 484.
12   Palmerston to Russell, 8 Jan. 1860, copy, Russell papers, PRO, 30/22/14A. Russell to Queen Victoria, 10 Jan. 1860, RA J25/4. Beales, *England and Italy*, 124–5.
13   Russell to Queen Victoria, 12 Jan. 1860, RA J25/18.

Rome as soon as the papal government could arrange for its own internal security. Russell continued his view that the pope should be permitted to retain Rome, and to do so safely.[14] The fourth point proposed the annexation of the Romagna and the duchies to Sardinia. The queen and the Cabinet had added the proviso that new elections had to be held for new assemblies in those areas, and the assemblies had to express their wills in new votes. Then if they voted annexation, Sardinia could move its troops in without objection from France and England.[15] Russell said he would not seek Austria's assent to this final point. Taken together, the plan committed England to utilize the full force of its moral suasion and diplomacy to consolidate the revolution against the pope and the dukes, and to insure that central Italy would be annexed to Sardinia. No longer was there English talk about a kingdom of central Italy. Russell and Palmerston had found an annexation formula which the queen and cabinet and Napoleon might all accept. He told Hudson, 'The difficulty is Romagna. But with the help of *Le Pape et le congrès* I trust we shall get over it.'[16] If the proposal was rejected, he explained to Cowley, at least England openly disclosed its intentions to the European powers, and 'after that we are free to acknowledge the enlarged Sardinia and salute her flag without more ado'.[17]

It is important to note that the Tory opposition in Parliament advocated much the same view of the Papal Question at this conjuncture as the Liberals. When the new Parliament convened on 24 January, Queen Victoria forthrightly declared that her official policy would be to 'endeavour to obtain for the People of Italy freedom from foreign interference by force of arms in their internal concerns'.[18] Disraeli in the Commons and Derby in the House of Lords approved the queen's speech. Derby emphasized that the subjects of the pope should be 'free to choose their own government and their own constitution', and that the pope should be treated no differently than any other sovereign: 'Viewed in this light, his dynasty is capable of being overthrown, the constitution of his kingdom may be modified by the free will of his subjects, and no foreign Power has the right to interfere with the action of the Pope and his subjects.' The Tory leadership, in other words, also accepted the revolution in the Romagna, and perhaps even annexation to Sardinia, if the populations of the area wanted it.[19]

Palmerston had decided to push with new vigour for annexation right after *Le pape et le congrès* was released; Russell quickly agreed. On 31 December Palmerston suggested they might strike a bargain with Napoleon: 'We might even tell him that if he will support us as to annexation, we will back him up as to

14   Point two also mentioned the evacuation of French troops from northern Italy. The third point proposed to let Austria settle the internal government of Venetia without any intrusion from other European powers.
15   Russell to Queen Victoria, 13 Jan. 1860, RA J25/23.
16   Russell to Hudson, 9 Jan. 1860, private, *Gran Bretagna e Sardegna*, vol. VII, 302.
17   Russell to Cowley, 19 Jan. 1860, private, copy, Russell papers, PRO, 30/22/20.
18   Hansard's, CLVI, col. 2–3, 24 Jan. 1860.
19   Hansard's, CLVI, col. 60–2, and 103–4, 24 Jan. 1860.

any scheme he may have for arrangement of the Papal States.'[20] He was convinced annexation would be best for both England and Italy. He argued on 9 January that annexation would accord with the expressed wishes of central Italy while fostering the spread of 'constitutional institutions'. Moreover, it would avoid all the 'embarrassments' of a separate state in central Italy which might fall under Napoleon's influence,[21] and would create, instead, 'a state strong enough to be independent', and, hence, amenable to British interests.

Sardinia and the central Italians, meanwhile, began a campaign to persuade England to drop the idea of a central Italian kingdom and to accept annexation. In Sardinia's interest Hudson wrote Cowley a long argument for annexation on 5 January, and Count Emanuel Marliani, now the 'extraordinary envoy of the government of Emilia', set out from Bologna via Turin for London and Paris in the middle of January to convince the English to act for annexation.[22] Count Cavour returned to office on 16 January after a six-month absence and devoted himself to annexation. Hudson, Marliani and Cavour were all gratified to discover that Palmerston and Russell had already begun to work unilaterally among the European powers for annexation. As a matter of fact, with Russell's tacit approval, Hudson had actually helped to topple the Rattazzi government of Sardinia and bring Cavour back to power so he could work for annexation. The way Hudson saw it, the Rattazzi government deserved to fall because, among many other defects, it was 'vacillating with regard to Central Italy, undecided as to its conduct with regard to Rome, . . . and detested in the Legations'.[23]

Thouvenel discussed the French reply to the English four points with Cowley on 27 January. Thouvenel told Cowley that Napoleon 'agreed entirely in the principle' of the first point, but that since he had often renounced any intention to intervene by force 'in the internal affairs of Italy', he needed to make no further declaration now. This ambiguous mode of reply was a way of acknowledging Russell's assumption that the Romagna was included in the emperor's 'non-intervention' declaration without Napoleon actually saying so. Thouvenel said the emperor accepted the second point, but that 'he did not think the present moment opportune for mooting this question at Rome'. He hoped, nevertheless, to bring it up at Rome soon. Cowley pressed Thouvenel to try to fix a date for evacuation. The fourth point, Thouvenel commented, was 'the most difficult'. The emperor personally thought the idea of new votes seemed 'equitable and practical', but he would have to inform the Austrian government of this before giving the English a firm reply. Thouvenel intimated that the emperor, while being willing to invite the duchies to elect new

---

20 Palmerston to Russell, 31 Dec. 1859, Russell papers, PRO, 30/22/20.
21 Palmerston to Russell, 9 Jan. 1860, Russell papers, PRO, 30/22/21. Russell to Queen Victoria, 9 Jan. 1860, copy, Russell papers, PRO, 30/22/14A.
22 Hudson to Cowley, Turin, 5 Jan. 1860, Cowley papers, PRO, FO, 519/194. Hudson to Russell, Turin, 11 Jan. 1860, private, *Gran Bretagna e Sardegna*, vol. VII, 303.
23 Hudson to Russell, Turin, 9 and 16 Jan. 1860, private, *Gran Bretagna e Sardegna*, vol. VII, 299–301, and 305–7.

assemblies, may have to abstain from asking the Romagna to do the same. But Thouvenel added knowingly, 'the Romagna would probably of her own accord follow the example of the Duchies, and declare an annexation to Sardinia, and we could accept as "un fait accompli" without us that which we could not instigate ourselves.' Again, Napoleon might support what England wanted without actually saying so.[24]

Russell thought Thouvenel's official response to Persigny on 30 January looked good. Perhaps the English had found the device Napoleon could use to release himself from the Zurich treaty.[25] Thouvenel added an important stipulation which came to exercise crucial influence over England's, Piedmont's, and the Romagnol's behaviour during the coming weeks. England, he said, to get what it wanted in the Romagna, would have to help insure that no revolution occurred in the remainder of the Papal States. If Sardinian troops or agents caused a revolution in the Marches against the pope, 'either the Emperor must interfere, or his position in France might become critical'. A few days later Cowley argued insistently to Thouvenel in favour of letting revolution spread in the Marches. Thouvenel was quite candid that the emperor had to oppose further revolution against the pope out of 'political necessity' in Catholic France.[26]

The answer from Austria was significant as well. The response to point one was the important thing. Russell had received intimations earlier in the month indicating that Austria may be ready to let things take their course in Italy.[27] Loftus saw Count Rechberg on 24 January and again on the 30th after the count had spoken with Francis Joseph, and both times Rechberg conveyed the reply that Austria would not be bound by any agreement not to use its army in Italy again. But what followed was crucial, as Loftus recounted it: 'At the same time his Excellency assured me that the Imperial Cabinet entertained no intention of interfering by force of arms in Italy. "If we should be attacked – said his Excellency – we shall, of course, defend our territory, but we have no intention or wish to interfere by force beyond our frontiers."'[28] In Rechberg's reply to Russell via Count Apponyi in London he added a dimension to what Loftus reported. He confirmed that he had implied to Loftus in mid-December that Austria regarded its military occupation of the Papal States to be a fruitless experience:

> Austria, I observed to Lord Loftus, in times past was burdened by immense sacrifices in the interest of maintaining and reestablishing order and tranquility in

24 Cowley had to wait until Thouvenel took office on 24 January to give him the despatch. Cowley to Russell, Paris, 27 Jan. 1860, no. 42 and no. 43, confidential, *Gran Bretagna e Sardegna*, vol. VII, 321–4.
25 Thouvenel to Persigny, Paris, 30 Jan. 1860, no. 6, *Annessioni al Regno d'Italia*, 50–3. Case, *Thouvenel*, 148–52.
26 Cowley to Russell, Paris, 30 Jan. 1860, no. 53, confidential, *Gran Bretagna e Sardegna*, vol. VII, 325–6.
27 Russell to Queen Victoria, 9 Jan. 1860, copy, Russell papers, PRO, 30/22/14A.
28 The statement from Russell arrived on 24 January via messenger from Cowley in Paris. Loftus to Russell, Vienna, 24 Jan. 1860, no. 36, and 30 Jan. 1860, no. 51, *Gran Bretagna e Sardegna*, vol. VII, 353–6.

the different Italian states. In spite of the intentions of these sacrifices, the end result did not respond to our efforts. That is for us a powerful reason not to want to continue the same system into the future.

Austria was tired of the burden of the affairs of Italy.[29]

Russell's diplomatic initiative in January had succeeded, so far, remarkably well. He secured from Austria a very clear statement that it had no intention of exercising its military force in central Italy. From France he obtained a virtually explicit approval of new elections in the Romagna as well as in the duchies. With these two responses in hand, the way was open for things 'to take their course in Italy'. It was a course directed toward annexation. Mack Smith has observed correctly, 'This was the moment, rather than any other, when it was settled that Italy would be a unitary and not in any sense a federal kingdom and British policy here had a distinct contribution to make.'[30]

The faithful and the papal army

While England promoted annexation, the papal government re-invigorated its determination to achieve restoration in the lost Legations. *Le pape et le congrès* and Napoleon's letter to Pius IX on 27 December had removed all doubt in the pope's mind that Napoleon was his adversary. The pope, and Antonelli, in January turned toward other sources of support. They found Naples still unwilling to help. Francis II continued to express devotion to the pope but declined to offer any material assistance. Spain was still involved in Morocco, and still unwilling to encounter British and French opposition in Italy. Cowley reported rumours in Paris that Queen Isabella was ready to send the pope troops, but they were unfounded.[31]

Then there was Austria. Antonelli believed that the only reason Austria did not provide direct military help to the pope was, as Sacconi worded it, because 'the Emperor of Austria is not at the present time in a position to resort to arms to enforce respect for treaties'. It did not even occur to him that Austria would tell the pope's enemy that it would not use its troops to restore the pope. Consequently, Baron Bach had no trouble assuring the Cardinal that Rechberg's response to the English four points was a defence of the papacy.[32] The cardinal thought the four points so destructive of papal rights that he refused even to comment on the first three. He was especially outraged by the fourth point which

29 Rechberg to Apponyi, Vienna, 30 Jan. 1860, *Gran Bretagna e Sardegna*, vol. VII, 358.
30 Mack Smith, *Victor Emanuel, Cavour*, 159.
31 Barili to Antonelli, Madrid, 19 Jan. 1860, no. 522, and Antonelli to Barili, Rome, 30 Jan. 1860, no. 8628, *Antonelli–Barili*, 159–60, 162. Odo Russell to Russell, Rome, 8 Jan. 1860, no. 8, PRO, FO, 43/76, and *Odo Russell*, 81. Cowley to Russell, Paris, 29 Jan. 1860, private, copy, Cowley papers, PRO, FO, 519/227/4.
32 Sacconi to Antonelli, Paris, 3 Feb. 1860, no. 1431, ASV, ASdS, 1860, 165/43/103–12, and *Antonelli*, vol. II, 403–4. Bach to Rechberg, Rome, 17 Feb. 1860, no. 7 A–E, HHSA, PA, XI, 201/141. DeLuca to Antonelli, Rome, 5 Feb. 1860, no. 896, ASV, ASdS, 1860, 165/43/83–4. Sacconi to Antonelli, Paris, 3 Feb. 1860, 1431, ASV, ASdS, 1860, 165/43/103–12, and *Antonelli*, vol. II, 402–6.

assumed the Whig version of the will of the people, so essential to Russell's approach. Antonelli believed it was dangerous and outrageous to propose that by the mere casting of votes a population could overthrow the ancient and sacred rights of the Holy See:

> On the fourth proposition it is impossible to keep silent and not to declare right now how unacceptable and inappropriate it is, whether one wishes to consider it in relation to the principles of justice and legitimacy, or whether one reflects on the exceptional circumstances of the government of the Holy See in relation to the oaths which bind the Holy Father and to the violent state of affairs which characterize such a rebellious people.

Antonelli expected Austria to persist in defending the pope's rights against point four. He also let himself imagine Prussia and Russia, as conservative powers, joining the defence. Together, the three conservative courts would be able to spoil the plans of England and France and erect a solid barrier against the onslaughts of revolution. He instructed DeLuca to work to that end.[33]

If Austria did not send its army to help the pope, the papal government had to build its own. Antonelli asked the Austrian government to continue to permit Austrian subjects to enlist in the papal army.[34] The Austrian government decided to give this kind of tangible military help as well as to resist English pressures to stop it. In November when Loftus had questioned Rechberg about papal recruiting in Vienna, the count claimed ignorance of it, but saw nothing wrong with it. When the recruiting continued in December, Russell instructed Loftus to protest against it. Then when Austrian troops kept arriving at Ancona during January, Russell became more alarmed. He asked Edwin Corbett in Florence to learn from Ancona how many Austrian recruits were landing there. The English vice-consul in Ancona, Gaggiotti, began sending regular reports cataloguing each new shipload of Austrian soldiers for the papal army. The recruits included both men and officers, greatly supplementing the Swiss and native troops in the Marches.[35]

Palmerston and Russell were fearful of this flow of troops. They regarded it as an *Austrian* military intervention in the Marches. Palmerston insisted to Russell that 'a change of uniform did not change nationality'. He proposed that England press Austria 'not to furnish any of the Italian governments with Troops who by putting on an Italian uniform should be called Italian'.[36] On 12 January in Vienna, Loftus formally protested the Austrian enlistments in the papal army.

33 Bach to Rechberg, Rome, 10 Feb. 1860, no. 6, H–D, HHSA, PA, XI, 201/123–5. Antonelli to DeLuca, Rome, 13 Feb. 1860, no. 8963, ASV, ANVienna, 376/510–11. On the conservative powers, see Katherine Schach Cook, 'Russia, Austria, and the question of Italy, 1859–1862', *International history review* 2 (1980), 542–65.
34 Bach to Rechberg, Rome, 3 Feb. 1860, no. 5C, HHSA, PA, XI, 201/117–18.
35 Russell to Corbett, 7 Jan. 1860, (telegram), no. 1, PRO, FO, 79/212. Gaggiotti to Corbett, Ancona, 5, 12, 13, 13, 17, etc., Jan. 1860. No. 1, 2, 3, 4, 5, etc., PRO, FO, 70/213. Gaggiotti's reports continued until the English mission in Tuscany was closed in April after the annexation of Tuscany to Sardinia.
36 Palmerston to Russell, 8 Jan. 1860, Russell papers, PRO, 30/22/21.

Not only did the Austrian troops buoy up the papal cause and thereby increase the possibility of a papal attack on Bologna, but, argued Loftus, they might also alarm Sardinia who could view their presence as 'a masked intervention', affording that power 'a pretext for marching into the Legations, in defence of the army of Central Italy'. Rechberg belittled the danger and disclaimed any Austrian government responsibility for the enlistments. He affirmed the pope's right to recruit troops from wherever he could find them. He thought the English would do better to urge the Sardinians not to get involved in the troubles between the pope and his rebellious province. Mgr DeLuca told Antonelli about Loftus' protest and Rechberg's reply. Antonelli was entirely satisfied with what Rechberg said.[37]

After Russell received this report from Loftus, he conceived another line of approach. Through Persigny he urged Napoleon to warn the pope that the French government would immediately withdraw its troops from Rome if the pope authorized an expedition into the Romagna.[38] Napoleon was in no position to fulfill Russell's request, but Thouvenel did speak to Sacconi several times against the Austrian enlistments. He also applied some pressure on Sacconi against accepting French recruits in the papal army.[39] The English protests had no effect on the flow of Austrian soldiers.

Pius IX simultaneously turned to the clergy and faithful of the church. On 19 January he issued an encyclical thanking them for their movement of support – the addresses, declarations, the pastorals, the meetings. He told them of Napoleon's abandonment of his cause, and promised that he would leave nothing untried to preserve the church's temporal sovereignty inviolate. Then he challenged the bishops to inflame the faithful to defend the Church and maintain the 'civil sovereignty of the Holy See'.[40] It was a call to battle, making use of the strongest weapon the pope still possessed – the millions of Catholics of France, Ireland, England, Austria, and elsewhere throughout the world.

The pope still regarded the French Catholic faithful as his most strategic allies, which they no doubt were. Napoleon still had to act cautiously because of them, as Thouvenel admitted on 30 January. Nevertheless, there was evidence that the emperor was gaining public support for his side at least about the Romagna, as presented in *Le pape et le congrès*.[41]

37   Loftus to Russell, Vienna, 12 Jan. 1860, no. 19, PRO, FO, 425/59/3-4. DeLuca to Antonelli, Vienna, 19 Jan. 1860, no. 882, ASV, ASdS, 1860, 165/41/24. Bach to Rechberg, Rome, 3 Feb. 1860, no. 5C, HHSA, PA, XI, 201/117-18.
38   Persigny to Napoleon, London, 19 Jan. 1860, *Annessioni al Regno d'Italia*, 46-7.
39   Sacconi to Antonelli, Paris, 12 Feb. 1860, no. 1437, ASV, ASdS, 1860, 165/30/31-8, and *Antonelli*, vol. II, 420-1. Thouvenel to Sacconi, 10 Feb. 1860, *Antonelli*, vol. II, 416.
40   Encyclical, 19 Jan. 1860; translation published in *Tablet*, 4 Feb. 1860. Two prelates of the pope's private chamber sent out copies prematurely, one to England, one to France. George Talbot could have been one of them (Gramont to Thouvenel, Rome, 7 Feb. 1860, no. 12, AMAE, CP, 1013/113-15). Odo Russell had thought the pope was hesitant to appeal openly to the faithful: Odo Russell to Russell, Rome, 10 Jan. 1860, no. 10, PRO, FO, 43/76.
41   Case, *French opinion*, 115-17.

Liberals and the annexation of the Romagna

Among the Irish and English Catholics the pope added new support daily. The movement of mass meetings, addresses, and pastoral letters continued to build into January and February. During his stay in Rome in January Cardinal Wiseman personally presented two statements of devotion to the pope, one signed by the English Catholic clergy and one by 14,000 English Catholic laity. On 17 February he led a delegation of 150 English people to see the pope. Some 1500 Catholics rallied in London on 3 January with hundreds reportedly turned away, and on 14 February Catholics filled Birmingham Town Hall to hear a defence of the temporal power by Bishop Ullathorne, fresh from Rome. During February, the Lenten pastorals of virtually all the English and Irish bishops were devoted in part to the temporal power. Henry Edward Manning delivered three important discourses on the temporal power in London during February. The movement of the faithful continued unabated.[42]

There were some attempts to turn this Irish and English Catholic resurgence behind the pope into immediate political impact. Cardinal Cullen, who had supported the Liberals in the spring 1859 elections, now cautiously criticized the Palmerston–Russell government. He noted on 24 December that Irish Catholics were achieving unity on the point since the last elections. On 9 January a delegation of Irish Liberals presented Palmerston a declaration in support of the pope's temporal power.[43] Of special significance was the visit of George Bowyer to Rome during the Christmas and New Year period. He met frequently with Antonelli and at least once with the pope, and no doubt spoke with them about English politics. Odo Russell reported that during Bowyer's visit there was talk at the Vatican about the Catholic members of the English Parliament banding together to vote Palmerston and Russell out of office. Bowyer wrote a letter from Rome to *The Times* chastizing the Liberals for their policy against the pope.[44] Sacconi commented from Paris that if the Catholic M.P.s did help overturn the Palmerston government 'our cause would become improved'.[45] The *Tablet*, on 21 January, began urging Catholic M.P.s to oust the Liberals, later suggesting that a forthcoming vote on Gladstone's budget in February would be the time to do it. The liberal press spoke anxiously of a 'Tory–Papist coalition'. Henry Elliot, the English minister in Naples, wrote to Odo, 'There are some alarming accounts of the government being not unlikely to be beaten in the H. of Commons by the Tories backed by the Catholics, which I do not believe.'[46] The

42   The *Tablet* gives full reports of the movement during January and February. Odo Russell to Russell, Rome, 30 Jan. 1860, no. 17, PRO, FO, 43/76, and *Odo Russell*, 83.
43   Paul Cullen to Dr Gillooly, Dublin, 24 Dec. 1859, *Paul Cullen*, vol. III, 274. *Tablet*, 28 Jan. 1860. *The Times*, 9 Jan. 1860.
44   Odo Russell to Russell, Rome, 5 Jan. 1860, no. 4, secret, PRO, FO, 43/76, and 7 Jan. 1860, private, Russell papers, PRO, 30/22/75, and *Odo Russell*, 77 and 80–1. Bowyer to the editor, Rome, 5 Jan. 1860, *The Times*, 13 Jan. 1860. The pope demonstrated his gratitude to Bowyer by awarding him the Grand Cross of the Pontifical Order of St Gregory, and giving him a ride home on the papal ship, *The Immaculate Conception* (*Tablet*, 14 Jan. 1860).
45   Sacconi to Antonelli, Paris, 20 Jan. 1860, no. 1419, *Antonelli*, vol. II, 371.
46   Henry Elliot to Odo Russell, Naples, 18 Jan. 1860, Ampthill papers, PRO, FO, 918/29.

trend of Catholics away from the Liberals and toward the Conservatives, begun the previous spring, continued with a rush, in spite of the fact that Catholics, Malmesbury's despatches in hand, now knew that the Tories had been just as anti-papal as the Liberals. Derby's speech in Parliament left no doubt that the Tories had not mellowed. The *Tablet* continued to argue that Tories, nonetheless, were still relatively better than Liberals.[47] Cardinal Cullen warned Catholics that either way, Liberal or Conservative, England would be an opponent of the pope. Even Queen Victoria's role was unsettling to the papal supporters. Odo reported, 'Cavour's accession to power and the Queen's speech (in Parliament) have been severe blows to the Vatican. Both were unexpected here and it will take them some time to recover.'[48] Palmerston, Russell and Gladstone, took the Catholic political threat seriously. Gladstone wrote:

> I cannot but think that the most recent conduct and declarations of the Papal party throughout Europe, and particularly the declarations and threats in this country from the Roman Catholics generally to be governed in their conduct upon civil and domestic questions by our conduct if we presume to concur in any measure of interference with the Papal States (except of course keeping him by force upon his throne) constitutes something of a challenge to all governments as such.[49]

Russell mentioned the insecurity of the Whig-Liberal government to Odo Russell and added, 'But I believe we shall pull thro' in spite of Bowyer's Papal Guard.'[50]

With the faithful in England and Ireland exercising their political muscles, Antonelli ventured to inquire, cautiously, about help from the English. Napoleon had suggested in his letter to Pius IX on 27 December that the pope should ask the powers of Europe to guarantee the remainder of his states in exchange for renouncing his claims to the Romagna. Pius knew that such a guarantee would require the powers to intervene by armed force to protect the Marches and Umbria. He doubted the powers would consider it.[51] Nevertheless, as Odo reported it, Antonelli hesitatingly asked Odo, 'after demonstrations of increasing cordiality, ... what I thought of the Emperor's offer to guarantee the integrity of the remaining possessions of the Holy See'. Odo noted that he had no official word on the subject from his government, but that privately he could be sure 'England would not be a party to any new treaty engagements to guarantee the possessions of any foreign sovereign.' On this Antonelli commented that such an answer was 'not a very generous policy'.[52]

47   *Tablet*, 21 Jan., 4 and 11 Feb. 1860. The *Manchester Review* published an article entitled 'The Tory–Papist coalition', reprinted by the *Tablet*, 4 Feb. 1860.
48   Odo Russell to Russell, Rome, 31 Jan. 1860, private, Russell papers, PRO, 30/22/75, and excerpted in *Odo Russell*, 88.
49   *The Gladstone diaries*, 7 Jan. 1860.
50   Russell to Odo Russell, 6 Feb. 1860, private, Ampthill papers, PRO, FO, 918/7.
51   Pius IX to Napoleon, 8 Jan. 1860, Pirri, vol. II, part 2, 150.
52   'une politique peu genereuse'. Odo Russell to Russell, Rome, 21 Jan. 1860, private and secret, Russell papers, PRO, 30/22/75, and *Odo Russell*, 81–2.

Disraeli, in Parliament, asked Palmerston about Napoleon's suggestion, to which the prime minister replied with evident understatement, 'It is not a guarantee, I think, which this country would be disposed to enter into.'[53] Earlier, in response to an anxious inquiry from the Sardinians, Russell had assured Emanuel d'Azeglio that England would not guarantee the pope's territory under any circumstances.[54] Russell expressed his opinion to Persigny, however, that if Pius were wise, he would pressure Napoleon to help him obtain the guarantee from the powers of Europe. The pope should be content to hold on to what he still controlled, for 'in the state of things it is impossible even to dream of reconquering [the Romagna] whether by France, or Austria, or in the last resort by papal troops'.[55]

Antonelli had another very delicate matter to raise with Odo Russell. After *Le pape et le congrès* there was talk in Paris and Rome about whether the pope might even be forced personally to flee from Rome. When the cardinal had finished asking about the guarantee, he changed the subject, and 'after beating about the bush for some time', asked whether any English ships were near Civita Vecchia. Odo feigned not to understand, until Antonelli asked explicitly whether the English government 'would afford the Pope personal protection should he require it'. Odo replied, speaking unofficially, that England always granted asylum to all who sought it, and that 'if a foreign sovereign applied to us for personal protection on board one of our ships, we would undoubtedly grant it'. Odo recounted what happened next:

> His Eminence thanked me and a few days later he took me aside and told me in a low whisper that he had communicated our conversation to the Pope, who desired him to thank me for the 'bonnes dispositions' I attributed to my Government; ... in these critical times it was difficult to foresee how far the Emperor might go, and it was therefore a comfort to the Holy Father to think that the strong arm of England would afford him personal protection if things came to the worst.[56]

Lord John gladly assured Odo that 'His Holiness will have a ship at Civita Vecchia, whenever he wanted it.'[57] For the pope, however bizarre it seemed, England might serve as a consolation in the last resort.

The pope explicitly rejected the suggestion of giving up his claims to the Romagna in exchange for a guarantee to guard his rights to the rest of his territory. There was no practical possibility of any government providing such a guarantee, but more important to the pope, the Romagna was not his to

---

53   Hansard's, CLVI, col. 105–6, and 114, 24 Jan. 1860. See Derby's comments at col. 60–1. There was some confusion over whether Napoleon offered a guarantee, or merely suggested that the pope inquire about a guarantee. The second was correct.
54   Emanuel d'Azeglio to Dabormida, London, 12 Jan. 1860, *Cavour e l'Inghilterra*, vol. II, part 2, 2.
55   Persigny to Thouvenel, London, 31 Jan. 1860, no. 7, *Annessioni al Regno d'Italia*, 54–5.
56   Odo Russell to Russell, Rome, 21 Jan. 1860, private and secret, Russell papers, PRO, 30/22/75. See 'Notes' by Sacconi, Paris, 12 Jan. 1860, *Antonelli*, vol. II, 350–1.
57   Russell to Odo Russell, 6 Feb. 1860, private, Ampthill papers, PRO, FO, 918/7.

relinquish; Pius had his duty to God and the Church to uphold. With the clergy and the faithful as a source of spiritual and psychological comfort, the pope could persist in what he understood as his responsibility to regain the Romagna. He would do it by means of the papal army, and without the assistance of the troops of any foreign power. In pursuing this resolve, the pope and Antonelli had to disregard the judgment of Sacconi that 'it was not possible to restore papal authority in the Romagna without foreign intervention'. Sacconi, it would appear, was in touch with the new political situation – the pope was isolated, and now no power would come to his aid, although all, including the English, would treat him with caution. As with annexation, January and early February was the moment when the pope lost all realistic possibility of regaining the Romagna. But to the pope and Antonelli, that did not matter. They continued to believe in the reconquest of Bologna.[58]

Annexation, not vicariat

When Russell and Palmerston received the French and Austrian replies to their four points, Russell began actively to implement the English plan, including the three provisions relevant to the pope.

The French implicit and the Austrian explicit acceptances of the 'no force' stipulation for the Romagna took care of point one. Russell relaxed and expressed no further protest of the Austrian enlistments in the papal army as long as they constituted genuinely *papal* activity and not direct Austrian military intervention. On 1 February he asked Loftus to authenticate a report by Odo Russell that Austrian soldiers in the Marches were financed by the Austrian government. Loftus called the story unfounded. He thought the government may have financed a papal recruiting officer in Vienna, but not the troops. They were maintained by private subscriptions from the faithful, he said.[59] Russell then checked on a complaint by Cavour that the Austrian government conveyed the recruits from Trieste to Ancona in an Austrian warship. Loftus denied this report as well. The volunteers, he said, travelled on a papal steamer or commercial packets. Russell was satisfied.[60] Antonelli defended the papal use of foreign enlistments by recalling that England had employed them during the Crimean War when English troops were insufficient.[61]

Russell made firm England's position on evacuation by deciding as official policy to let Napoleon determine the pace of withdrawing his troops from Rome.

---

58   Sacconi to Antonelli, Paris, 3 Feb. 1860, no. 1431, ASV, ASdS, 1860, 165/43/103–12, and *Antonelli*, vol. II, 403–4. At the top of the despatch was handwritten 'importante'.
59   Odo Russell to Russell, Rome, 10 Jan. 1860, no. 10, PRO, FO, 43/76. Loftus to Russell, Vienna, 9 Feb. 1860, no. 71, PRO, FO, 425/59/47–8.
60   Loftus to Russell, Vienna, 16 Feb. 1860, no. 84, and Russell to Hudson, 21 Feb. 1860, no. 31, *Gran Bretagna e Sardegna*, vol. VII, 362.
61   Antonelli to DeLuca, Rome, 2 March 1860, no. 9391, ASV, ANVienna, 376/556–7.

Liberals and the annexation of the Romagna

He suggested merely that a date be set, subject to postponement if need be. The significant feature of this policy on evacuation was the reason he gave for it:

> You will take care to repeat to Thouvenel what I have so often told you, that we have no desire to press France as to the time of leaving Rome. It would injure the British government almost as much as that of the Emperor, if we were to expose the Pope to any personal outrage by urging a hasty evacuation of Rome.[62]

Russell and Palmerston, like Napoleon, had to tip-toe around the pope, lest the Catholics of Ireland and England cause the Liberals real political trouble. Russell now consciously adjusted his behaviour out of consideration of Catholic political pressure.

On 6 February, Russell notified Hudson that the English government was ready for Sardinia to proceed with new elections in the Romagna and the duchies, in keeping with point four. Cavour had already indicated his willingness to do so. Russell favoured the strategy suggested by the central Italians themselves of having the electors in the Romagna and the duchies vote simultaneously with the Sardinian elections and send deputies to the Sardinian parliament; the king merely had to sanction their admission and 'then the whole thing is finished, so far as Central Italy is concerned'. He disliked using universal suffrage, but would accept it if the central Italians decided it was necessary to appease Napoleon.[63] Cavour was prepared to act quickly, but France and Austria needed time to come to agreement on the matter. At Thouvenel's request, Russell reluctantly cabled Hudson to persuade Cavour 'to avoid precipitation' and postpone calling the elections. Russell knew that at this conjunction in the events, the English had much more influence over the Piedmontese than the French.

Russell disliked having to wait for Napoleon this time,[64] but he waited anyway because he himself continued to hold the view that a revolution in the remaining Papal States, or in Austrian Venetia, 'would renew the war and bring great armies again into the field'.[65] On 29 January Russell met in London with Count Marliani, the envoy from Bologna, and, while affirming his complete support of annexation, impressed upon Marliani the need to be cautious and prudent in order not to stir the revolution again. Marliani assured Russell that the government in the Romagna and the duchies would do nothing insurrectionary in the Marches and Umbria. Russell was pleased and added that 'time will be the real liberator of the provinces still under the pope'.[66] Immediately

---

62   Russell to Cowley, 26 Jan. 1860, private, copy, Russell papers, PRO, 30/22/104.
63   Hudson to Russell, Turin, 3 Feb. 1860, no. 28, and Russell to Hudson, 6 Feb. 1860, no. 15, *Gran Bretagna e Sardegna*, vol. VII, 328 and 334. Russell to Cowley, 26 Jan. 1860, private, copy, Russell papers, PRO, 30/22/104.
64   Hudson to Russell, Turin, 10 Feb. 1860, (telegram), no. 46, *Gran Bretagna e Sardegna*, vol. VII, 341. Cowley to Russell, Paris, 10 Feb. 1860, no. 103, confidential, PRO, FO, 425/59/45. Russell to Hudson; 11 Feb. 1860, (telegram), no. 19, *Gran Bretagna e Sardegna*, vol. VII, 342. Russell to Cowley, 11 Feb. 1860, no. 113, PRO, FO, 425/59/46.
65   Russell to Hudson, 31 Jan. 1860, private, *Gran Bretagna e Sardegna*, vol. VII, 318–19.
66   Marliani to Cavour, London, 30 Jan. 1860, *Cavour e l'Inghilterra*, vol. II, part 2, 8–10.

Annexation, not vicariat

after this interview, Russell again telegraphed to Hudson to get Cavour 'not to precipitate and to keep matters quiet'. Russell was convinced that if the Piedmontese and Romagnols gave no armed assistance to stir revolution in the Marches and Umbria, 'the Pope's troops will probably keep all quiet'.[67] Russell and Palmerston gave the same message to the Sardinian ambassador in London, Emanuel d'Azeglio.[68]

While in London Marliani became aware of the political threat that English and Irish Catholics were to the Liberal Government. He explained to Cavour, 'The Italian question, and especially that of the Pope, overagitated by the Catholic clergy, is taking away from the Cabinet the votes of many Irish and even English Catholics who in a sectarian spirit sacrifice the most cherished interests of the country.' Marliani estimated that a Tory–Catholic challenge would be insufficient to overturn the Liberals, but it could be close. He urged Cavour to be cautious so that his activity detrimental to the pope would not contribute to the erosion of Catholic support for the Palmerston government.[69]

During February Russell received conflicting information and appeared uncertain about whether there existed a possibility of revolution or war in the Papal States. At one point, for example, Hudson assured him things were well under control. Later the same day, after receiving new information, Hudson sounded the alarm about a counter-revolution by the exiled duke of Modena in league with papal troops in the Marches and Umbria.[70] On another occasion, Russell warned Hudson to be sure General Fanti kept the army of central Italy from lending its aid across the border in the Marches. Not long before, Russell had commented privately to Hudson that since 'there does not appear much danger of a renewal of war' the mission of George Cadogan, England's special military observer in central Italy, could be terminated. Colonel Cadogan had gone to the duchies and the Romagna at Russell's request in October 1859 and had continued throughout the winter sending periodic reports to London on the military situation. He assured Russell that General Fanti's army was strong enough to repel any attack by the papal and ducal armies. Hudson wanted Cadogan's mission extended so he could observe the movement of papal and Austrian troops, but Russell did not agree to it.[71]

In any case, the English government's efforts to discourage the spread of revolution into the Marches and Umbria no doubt contributed to preventing it.

67   Russell to Hudson, 29 Jan. 1860, (telegram), no. 7, Hudson to Russell, Turin, 30 Jan. 1860, (telegram), private, and Russell to Hudson, 31 Jan. 1860, private, *Gran Bretagna e Sardegna*, vol. VII, 317–19.
68   Emanuel d'Azeglio to Cavour, 1 and 2 Feb. 1860, telegrams, *Cavour e l'Inghilterra*, vol. II, part 2, 13.
69   Marliani to Cavour, London, 4 Feb. 1860, *Cavour e l'Inghilterra*, vol. II, part 2, 16–17.
70   Hudson to Russell, Milan, 15 Feb. 1860, private, and Turin, 15 Feb. 1860, no. 50, secret, *Gran Bretagna e Sardegna*, vol. VII, 348–9.
71   Russell to Hudson, 14 Feb. 1860, no. 20, and 31 Jan. 1860, private, *Gran Bretagna e Sardegna*, vol. VII, 346 and 318. Cadogan's reports between October 1859 and January 1860 are published in *Gran Bretagna e Sardegna*, vol. VII, 389–420. Hudson to Russell, Turin, 9 March 1860, private, *Gran Bretagna e Sardegna*, vol. VII, 43–4.

Liberals and the annexation of the Romagna

All sides of the struggle ended up benefiting from this pause in revolution. In particular it enabled the papal army to cope, for the time being, with a potentially inflammable situation. Palmerston and Russell did not forget their idea that the Marches and Umbria might one day join the Romagna, but for now they had to be content to counsel the Sardinians to be satisfied with one piece of the pope's territory at a time.

Thouvenel may have expressed Napoleon's agreement to England's four points, but no such statement prevented the emperor from having another idea on his mind. On 27 January, unknown to the English, and while Thouvenel was busy accepting the English four points, Napoleon proposed to Victor Emmanuel a four point plan of his own which came to be called the vicariat plan. The first three points were consistent with Thouvenel's reply to the English – non-intervention in Italy, a new general vote in central Italy, and no extension of revolution to the Marches and Umbria. It was the emperor's fourth point and an unnumbered fifth which, when made public later, shocked the English government. As his point four Napoleon proposed holding a vote in Savoy and Nice to determine whether those provinces would be annexed to France. Then he further proposed naming a vice-regent, or vicar, for the Romagna under the suzerainty of the pope 'until the Holy Father has given his consent to the separation of his provinces'.[72] On the 29th Thouvenel and Napoleon devised a strategy by which, after it seemed that annexation of the Romagna to Sardinia could not be prevented, the French government would suggest the vicariat publicly. The French would also endorse employing universal suffrage in the Romagna, which undoubtedly would result in a vote for annexation. By such a strategy Thouvenel thought they could insure annexation while appearing to oppose it, possibly thereby neutralizing the political force of the militant Catholics.[73]

There seems no doubt that what interested Napoleon most at this moment was not Italy or the Romagna, but Savoy and Nice.[74] Napoleon's idea was to arrange a simple exchange – he would agree to the annexation of the Romagna and the duchies to Sardinia if Sardinia could give Savoy and Nice to France. The Savoy question, on one level of treatment, was a straightforward problem of balance of power – if Sardinia got substantial new territory, France had to get some too in order to stay ahead as a great power. The trade had been discussed at Plombières by Napoleon and Cavour nearly two years earlier and was included

---

72 Napoleon III to Victor Emmanuel, 27 Jan. 1860, *Cavour–Nigra*, vol. III, 25.
73 Edouard-Antoine Thouvenel, *Le secret de l'empereur: correspondance confidentielle et inédite échangée entre M. Thouvenel, le Duc de Gramont, et le Général Comte de Flahault, 1860–1863*, ed. Louis Thouvenel (Paris: Calmann-Levy, 1889), vol. I, 7–12. Scott, 164.
74 Case, *Thouvenel*, 152–4, and 166–70. In general, see Paul Scherer, 'British reaction to French annexation of Nice and Savoy', *International review of history and political science* 2 (1965), 31–40.
75 Russell to Cowley, 8 Nov. 1859, private, copy, Russell papers, PRO, 30/22/103.

in the secret French–Sardinian treaty of December 1858–January 1859. Public talk about France acquiring at least Savoy had been around since the war in 1859. Palmerston and Russell privately acknowledged all along that the exchange was probably necessary diplomatically.[75] However, by the end of January 1860, when Cowley reported the likelihood of the Savoy deal, they were without hesitation adamant against it. During February spokesmen of virtually all political viewpoints in England opposed the Savoy annexation, and the parliamentary debates and the press reflected this. Images of French expansionism to the 'natural frontiers' of the Rhine and the Alps seemed threatening.[76]

Deciphering Napoleon's intentions on the matter was not easy for the English government. All along the emperor, as well as Cavour, publicly denied any intention of making a deal on Savoy. However, at least twice in the first ten days of February Cowley reported that Napoleon and Thouvenel tacitly offered to drop all objections to the annexation of the Romagna if England would acquiesce in the Savoy annexation to France. Russell and Palmerston wanted the Romagna annexation so badly that they were close to letting Napoleon proceed on Savoy. Russell even wrote to Queen Victoria to that effect on 9 February.[77]

Then came news of Napoleon's vicariat proposal. The situation was complicated considerably.[78] The English government did not learn of it until Thouvenel discussed the idea with Cowley on 17 February. The papal government heard intimations of it somewhat earlier, although Sacconi did not receive firm news of the vicariat until the 17th, the same day as Cowley.[79] As Thouvenel disclosed it to Cowley, the French plan entailed annexing Parma and Modena to Sardinia, maintaining a separate Tuscany under a prince of the House of Savoy, and, as the crucial point, naming Victor Emmanuel as vicar of the pope for the separate government of the Legations, 'holding them in fief for the pope, until the Sardinian Government could come to an understanding with the Court of Rome'. Thouvenel said it was only an idea, but he hoped England could endorse it.[80] Actually, as Cowley detected, Thouvenel knew that the pope and Sardinia would reject the proposal out-of-hand.[81] Under Cowley's

76   Russell to Cowley, 28 Jan. 1860, no. 62, *Gran Bretagna e Sardegna*, vol. VII, 326–7. See Hansard's, CLVI, 10, 14, 16 and 17 Feb. 1860, *passim*. Beales, *England and Italy*, 134ff.

77   Cowley to Russell, Paris, 3 and 10 Feb. 1860, private, copies, Cowley papers, PRO, FO, 519/227/7–9, and 21–4. Russell to Queen Victoria, 9 Feb. 1860, *Letters of Queen Victoria*, vol. III, 387–9.

78   See Michael J. McDonald, 'The vicariat proposals: a crisis in Napoleon III's Italian confederative designs', *Diplomacy in an age of nationalism: essays in honor of Lynn Marshall Case* (The Hague: Martinus Nijhoff, 1971), 86–108.

79   Odo Russell to Russell, Rome, 4 Feb. 1860, no. 24, PRO, FO, 43/76, and *Odo Russell*, 88–9. Sacconi to Antonelli, Paris, 12 Feb. 1860, no. 1437, ASV, ASdS, 1860, 165/30/31–8, and *Antonelli*, vol. II, 417–18. Sacconi to Antonelli, Paris, 17 Feb. 1860, telegram, *Antonelli*, vol. II, 433.

80   Cowley to Russell, Paris, 17 Feb. 1860, secret and confidential, and 21 Feb. 1860, no. 158, PRO, FO, 425/59/55–7, and 71.

81   Cowley to Russell, Paris, 22 Feb. 1860, no. 169, PRO, FO, 425/59/78, and 28 Feb. 1860, private, copy, Cowley papers, PRO, FO, 519/227/46.

Liberals and the annexation of the Romagna

questioning, Thouvenel offered the explanation that the plan was devised because of two considerations. First was the need to avoid further confrontation with the Austrian government, who opposed outright annexation and popular sovereignty.[82] Second and more important was the French Catholic movement. Napoleon had to find some measure which would convince the French Catholics that he 'has done all in his power to save, as much as possible, the temporal powers of the Pope'.[83]

In an ironic way, the introduction of the vicariat plan helped the papal cause, not by satisfying the French Catholics, but by confusing the situation and thwarting thereby the easy fulfilment of the British–Sardinian–Romagnol hopes for annexation. The English government had no way of telling whether Napoleon intended the vicariat plan as a serious proposition or merely as a diversion to pacify Catholic opinion.[84] The English did consider it rather absurd to imagine Victor Emmanuel as a vicar for the pope. Russell remarked, 'Harnessing such a slow mule as the Pope with such a frisky kicking pony as Cavour would hardly make a good team. Nor do I see that the main object, that of pleasing the Catholics of France, will be obtained.'[85] Cowley advised Russell that the best reponse to give the plan was not protest, but calm rejection. What Russell wrote officially on 20 February was a mild reaffirmation of his own proposal of new elections, saying that the English point four was already on the table and 'virtually' accepted by Turin, Modena, Florence and Bologna.[86] Actually, Russell and Palmerston were furious with the idea. They felt that Napoleon was hitting them with destructive plans on both sides of the Savoy–Romagna exchange.

On 1 March Napoleon implied in a speech to the French Senate that he intended to annex Savoy. On 24 March the deed was accomplished by the signing of a French–Sardinian treaty which threw in the province of Nice. Russell denounced the arrangement in an angry speech in the House of Commons on the 26th. He considered the inclusion of Nice to be especially treacherous of both Napoleon and Cavour since that province included Italian towns.[87] The English felt completely deceived in the matter. The Savoy affair marked a major break in the English *rapprochement* with Napoleon over Italy and the pope.[88]

---

82 McDonald, 92. See Crampton (English ambassador in St Petersburg) to Russell, 11 Feb. 1860, no. 18, PRO, FO, 425/59/66–7, for an excellent statement of the conservative criticism of popular sovereignty.
83 Cowley to Russell, Paris, 22 Feb. 1860, no. 169, PRO, FO, 425/59/78.
84 McDonald (104–8) argues unconvincingly that the vicariat plan was a genuine offer of compromise by Napoleon.
85 Russell to Cowley, 25 Feb. 1860, private, copy, Russell papers, PRO, 30/22/104.
86 Russell to Cowley, 20 Feb. 1860, no. 141, confidential, PRO, FO, 425/59/57–8. Cowley had written that 'the Emperor is so tormented he does not know which way to turn' (Cowley to Russell, Paris, 17 Feb. 1860, private, copy, Cowley papers, PRO, FO, 519/227/30).
87 Hansard's, CLVII, col. 1255–8, 26 March 1869. Russell to Hudson, 29 April 1860, private, *Gran Bretagna e Sardegna*, vol. VIII, 86.
88 Mack Smith, *Victor Emanuel, Cavour*, 158–62. Scherer, *passim*.

Annexation, not vicariat

The prospect of the Savoy deal shook the English–French *rapprochement*; the vicariat plan broke it. The very day that Thouvenel first discussed the vicariat idea with Cowley – 17 February – he also suggested forming an *entente cordiale* with England. Russell declined the suggestion immediately, saying that the English government's position with respect to Italy and the pope was too different from the emperor's to allow it to enter into an alliance for uncertain purposes. England's intentions were friendly, he assured the French, and the situation could change, but for now, no alliance.[89]

Russell then set out to oppose the vicariat. For the first time since beginning their *rapprochement* with France in June 1859 Palmerston and Russell deliberately separated their Italian and papal policy from the emperor's. On 20 February, the day Russell wrote the 'mild' reply to France against the vicariat, he wrote two letters to Hudson. One notified Hudson of the vicariat plan and the other gave England's consent for Cavour to proceed without further delay to call the elections for the Sardinian parliament. Russell decided not to wait for France any longer. He mentioned merely that Cavour should inform the French about the elections.[90] He explained his strategy to Cowley:

> I begin to see land in the Italian question. I take for granted that Cavour will advise the King of Sardinia to refuse the new French propositions. The King of Sardinia as Vicar of the Pope would be a sort of mayor of the Palace. If he went to the Vatican he might be so entirely. If Cavour summons the new Assemblies, if they conform their votes and then proceed to Turin, the whole matter is effected, and the King of Sardinia may wait quietly for Northern recognition.[91]

Russell counted on the Sardinians and the nationalists of the Romagna and the duchies to force the situation by simply going ahead with annexation.

Next Russell told Emanuel d'Azeglio in London on 21 February that the English government had switched its position and decided to let the Sardinians determine what mode of elections to use. Palmerston added his personal advice that the Italians would be wise to adopt universal suffrage, and they should do it quickly.[92] Within a few days Cavour, Farini and Ricasoli agreed to hold plebiscites for annexation in the duchies and the Romagna, using verbatim the decree for universal suffrage by which Napoleon was elected emperor. Simultaneously, Cavour prepared to hold the elections for the Sardinian parliament, and the officials in Tuscany and the Romagna did the same. As a precaution in the Romagna and the duchies General Fanti called up extra men for the army of central Italy, aiming for a total of 160,000 men-at-arms during the elections.[93]

89   Russell to Cowley, no. 164, 22 Feb. 1860, PRO, FO, 425/59/72–3.
90   Russell to Hudson, 20 Feb. 1860, no. 25, confidential, and no. 26, *Gran Bretagna e Sardegna*, vol. VII, 350.
91   Russell to Cowley, 22 Feb. 1860, private, copy, Russell papers, PRO, 30/22/104.
92   Emanuel d'Azeglio to Cavour, London, 21 Feb. 1860, telegram, *Cavour e l'Inghilterra*, vol. II, part 2, 33.
93   Hudson to Russell, Turin, 27 Feb. 1860, s.n., secret, and no. 69, *Gran Bretagna e Sardegna*, vol. VII, 368.

Liberals and the annexation of the Romagna

On 24 February Thouvenel formally proposed the vicariat plan to the Sardinians, calling it a way for Sardinia to gain effective control of the Romagna. Simultaneously he issued another despatch endorsing universal suffrage.[94] Thouvenel and Napoleon were implementing their strategy. Persigny presented the proposal officially to Russell in London. At first Russell commented in reply that the vicariat might have been a plausible proposal six months earlier when England had been willing to endorse a lay governor for the Romagna under the pope's nominal sovereignty, but 'it was now too late'. He told Hudson what transpired next:

> But thinking over the matter it struck me that if adopted there would be such a jumble with the infant Prince of 5 years old in Tuscany, and the old Priest reigning but not governing in Romagna that Italy must go to the dogs . . .
>
> Palmerston said, 'If you think so and you think rightly so you ought to tell Sardinia. It will be too late when the mischief is done.'[95]

Russell then wrote to Cowley officially that England regarded the vicariat plan as 'entirely subversive of the independence of Italy'.[96] The Romagnol nationalists were exceedingly grateful to Russell for his letter against the vicariat. Marco Minghetti in Bologna exclaimed, 'Lord John has acted as a great gentleman, and our friend.'[97]

Sardinia rejected the vicariat. Cavour drafted an extensive diplomatic memorandum to Nigra in Paris which sought to demonstrate how wrong and impractical the idea was. Russell called it 'a masterpiece' and congratulated Hudson on his role in the whole matter. Thouvenel acknowledged that Cavour's arguments were excellent, but unnecessary, since the French already knew the vicariat would not work. They had only proposed it, he reiterated, out of deference to Catholic opinion.[98]

The papal government, of course, rejected the vicariat as well. The Duc de Gramont formally presented the proposition to Antonelli on 1 March, calling it a way for the pope to retain his temporal sovereignty in the Romagna. Antonelli responded that the pope's position on any scheme which fell short of total restoration of the *status quo ante bellum*, whether a vicariat or something else, was already stated in the encyclical of 19 January.[99] Just to make sure the powers all

---

94 Thouvenel to Baron Talleyrand (French ambassador in Turin), Paris, 24 Feb. 1860, PRO, FO, 425/59/81–3. In this version Thouvenel even proposed to re-establish the duke of Tuscany. Thouvenel to Persigny, Paris, 24 Feb. 1860, *Gran Bretagna e Sardegna*, vol. VII, 369–73.
95 Russell to Hudson, 5 March 1860, private, *Gran Bretagna e Sardegna*, vol. VIII, 38.
96 Russell to Cowley, 27 Feb. 1860, no. 180, and Russell to Hudson, 27 Feb. 1860, (telegram), no. 34, *Gran Bretagna e Sardegna*, vol. VII, 373 and 377.
97 Marco Minghetti to Count Pasolini, Bologna, 1 March 1860, *Carteggio tra Marco Minghetti e Giuseppe Pasolini*, ed. Guido Pasolini (Turin: Bocca, 1929), vol. III, 29.
98 Cavour to Nigra, Turin, 29 Feb. 1860, *Cavour–Nigra*, vol. III, 122–30. Cowley to Russell, Paris, 5 March 1860, no. 143, confidential, PRO, FO, 425/59/108–9.
99 Antonelli to Sacconi, Rome, 3 March 1860, no. 9490, ASV, ANParigi, 1860, SdS, AD/P, and

understood this, Antonelli composed a lengthy statement to Sacconi in defence of the temporal power and had it reprinted as a pamphlet for general distribution. George Bowyer referred to the statement in Parliament a few weeks later.[100]

Antonelli did have one concrete suggestion of a papal alternative in the European diplomatic theatre to the English four points or the French vicariat plan. That was to convene a conference of the smaller Catholic powers, probably to include Spain, Portugal, Naples and Bavaria. They in turn would invite the great powers to support the pope's claims to restoration in the Romagna.[101] Antonelli had followed with some interest a suggestion made during February by Prussia and Russia, with French approval, to convene a conference of the five major powers to discuss the English four points. Since the three conservative powers would hold the majority, he did not fear it terribly. But the idea eventually failed because of Austrian opposition, and England's unwillingness to participate – England thought it would hinder annexation.[102]

The pope received support in the English Parliament from Catholic M.P.s, but not enough to influence the government or to affect any vote. On 24 February Gladstone easily passed his budget with its provisions for the commercial treaty with France; only one Catholic objection to the government was raised, by Edward McEvoy, member for Meath in Ireland.[103] But four days later a major Catholic protest in Parliament came over the Savoy question. The Liberals were heavily criticized by Tories and Catholics. George Bowyer formulated the Catholic critique most succinctly by showing how he understood the papal and Savoy questions to be related: 'if Her Majesty's Government had not encouraged rebellion, annexation, demonstration, and schemes of settlement in different countries by upsetting the treaties on which international law had previously been based, nothing would ever have been heard of this proposal for annexing Savoy to France'. Russell and Palmerston, in other words, by actively interfering in papal and Italian affairs, had caused great turmoil in Italy and played into Napoleon's hands in Savoy. In his opinion they deserved to reap the whirlwind of Napoleon's expansionism, and to be overturned in Parliament.[104]

Russell this time did not let the Catholic criticism pass. He publicly displayed

---

Antonelli, vol. II, 463. Bach to Rechberg, Rome, 2 March 1860, no. 9 A–G and no. 9 D, HHSA, PA, XI, 201/167 and 175. Odo Russell to Russell, Rome, 6 March 1860, private, Russell papers, PRO, 30/22/75, and excerpted in *Odo Russell*, 92.

[100] Antonelli to Sacconi, Rome, 29 Feb. 1860, ASV, ANParigi, 1860, SdS, AD/P, and *Antonelli*, vol. II, 452–61. The pamphlet version was published 17 March 1860. Hansard's, CLVII, col. 1330 and 1493, 27 and 29 March 1860.

[101] Antonelli to Sacconi, Rome, 3 March 1860, no. 9490, ASV, ANParigi, 1860, SdS, AD/P, and *Antonelli*, vol. II, 464. See Scott, 167.

[102] Loftus to Russell, Vienna, 1 March 1860, no. 119, confidential, PRO, FO, 425/60/17–18, and Russell to Loftus, 7 March 1860, no. 66, PRO, FO, 425/59/110. Cook, 460–3.

[103] Hansard's, CLVI, col. 1711–13 and 1718–19, 24 Feb. 1860. Dunham, *Anglo-French treaty*, 117–21.

[104] Hansard's, CLVI, col. 1961–5, 28 Feb. 1860.

evidence of frustration with the Catholics by treating Bowyer with ridicule, as if to get back at him:

> The hon. and learned Member for Dundalk [Mr Bowyer], I am happy to see, has been able to speak his mind tonight. It must have been very painful to him, charged as he was with the whole sentiments of the Pope and the Cardinal, not to have been able to express his views before this time. We have now heard those opinions ...

Russell labelled Bowyer a poor advisor of the pope for not warning His Holiness that the revolutionary manifestations in the Romagna were not merely performances by outside agitators, but also genuine reflexes of a people suffering under bad papal government. As for Savoy, Russell was certain that the emperor would realize the unwisdom of annexing that area, for such an act would generate great distrust of the emperor's intentions in Europe.[105]

After 1 March, when Napoleon publicized his intention to annex Savoy, the debates in Parliament on the Savoy question continued intermittently for weeks. For almost two weeks the Papal Question and the annexation of the Romagna received little attention. Russell, for his part, was beginning to understand that on Savoy he had been taken by the emperor.

The plebiscites in the Romagna and the duchies were set for 11 and 12 March. The pope's rejection of the vicariat freed Napoleon to accept the vote for the annexation of the Romagna to Sardinia. On one level, England and France were reunited in support of the plebiscites and annexation, while on another, they became daily more estranged over Savoy and Nice. The plebiscite by which the Romagna voted for annexation took place at the very same moment that Cavour signed a secret treaty giving up Savoy and Nice to Napoleon. Plombières was fulfilled.[106]

The plebiscite in the Romagna was a choice between annexation to Sardinia or formation of a separate kingdom in central Italy. Restoration of papal authority was not given as an option. When the tabulation was completed annexation had won by 202,659 votes to 244. The *Tablet* calculated that probably 80 per cent of the males over 21 years of age voted for annexation. Similar majorities for annexation were obtained in the duchies of Tuscany, Parma and Modena.[107] In Savoy and Nice, one month later, on 15 April, the plebiscites produced great majorities for annexation to France.

The voting in central Italy violated two criteria Russell had established to achieve an authentic balloting – freedom from outside intimidation and from excessive fanfare. The Sardinian-dominated army of central Italy, with its

---

105 Hansard's, CLVI, col. 1968–70, 28 Feb. 1860.
106 Miller, 409.
107 *Tablet*, 24 March 1860. The statistics were reprinted from the *Allgemeine Zeitung*. *Punch* (7 April 1860) thought the votes augured the expulsion of papal tyranny from Italy. One day the pope and two other despots, Napoleon and King Bomba of Naples, might land in England, ragged and unheralded.

Annexation, not vicariat

160,000 troops, stood by. The Italian National Society organized the actual voting as a carnival under strict control – 'yes' ballots for annexation were distributed by the tens of thousands, 'no' ballots were not printed, peasants who had not the slightest understanding of what a plebiscite meant were told how to vote, influential people stood next to the ballot boxes to observe how each person voted, polling stations were festooned with Sardinia's red, white and green, and voters were marched to the polls in groups accompanied by bands.[108]

The National Society proclaimed that the vote demonstrated the true will of the Italian people. Yet it retained deep doubts about the devotion of the masses of peasants to 'Italy', and in the weeks ahead argued against suffrage for any but the 'respectable' classes. On the other side, the *Tablet* denied that the balloting was a valid gauge of the wishes of the population. And it chastized the masses of the people in the most severe language for not rallying to the pope's defence at the crucial moment.[109] These opposing attitudes were an indication of one of the prime realities of the Risorgimento – the apolitical outlook of the masses of the population of the peninsula.

Russell and Palmerston accepted the voting as valid nevertheless.[110] England immediately granted official recognition of the votes by formally abolishing its diplomatic mission in Tuscany. Russell consciously did so in order to help consolidate the vote for annexation and to support Cavour.[111] With the closure of the Florence mission, Odo Russell's official diplomatic affiliation was transferred from Florence to the English mission in Naples. Odo had requested the attachment to Naples in order not to offend the papal government by an affiliation with the English mission in Turin. This, Odo reported with delight, 'has given great satisfaction at the Vatican, as I expected'.[112] As a bonus, the English envoy in Florence, Edwin Corbett, left Italy. For the papal party it was good riddance: 'What he has done in Florence for the national party is incredible. Lord Russell cannot have had a more active and zealous agent than him to revolutionize a country. He is an enemy of Catholicism and a coadjutor of Protestant propaganda.'[113]

On 24 March Antonelli formally protested the plebiscite in a statement to the diplomatic corps in Rome. He gave Odo Russell a copy. He rejected the validity

---

108   Grew, 273–6.
109   Grew, 276–8. *Tablet*, 17 March 1860: 'If they are attached to their Sovereign, and faithful to their Church, they are the most white-livered set of cravens that ever disgraced humanity. It is probably that the great majority of them are simply unable to form a vigorous resolution on either side.'
110   Russell to Queen Victoria, 14 March 1860, RA J27/40. Count Corti to Cavour, London, 16 March 1860, *Cavour e l'Inghilterra*, vol. II, part 2, 54.
111   See Hudson to Russell, Turin, 9 March 1860, private, *Gran Bretagna e Sardegna*, vol. VIII, 42.
112   Odo Russell to Russell, Rome, 18 March 1860, and 1 May 1860, private, Russell papers, PRO, 30/22/75. E. Hammond to Odo Russell, 25 March 1860, draft, PRO, FO, 43/75.
113   Anon. to Alexander Franchi, Pisa, 6 April 1860, ASV, ASdS, 1860, 165/45/74, forwarded by Lorenzo Bruschi to Franchi in Rome for communication to Antonelli.

and authority of the plebiscite, and announced that the papal government would not recognize Piedmont's claim to the Legations. He called on the European governments to stop Sardinia's encroachments upon papal territory. He warned that the movements of Catholic faithful would 'further prevent the sovereigns from recognizing this sacrilegious and fraudulent act of usurped sovereignty'.[114] In a parallel letter to Barili in Madrid he suggested rather plaintively that the Catholic courts might jointly declare their desire to maintain papal territory unbroken. Antonelli later put some of the blame for the annexation squarely upon France and England who supported 'the gluttonous cupidity of the aggrandisement of Piedmont'.[115]

On 26 March, acting in what Antonelli understood as the way of the glorious popes of the past, Pius pronounced the major excommunication 'against the Invaders and Usurpers of some Provinces of the Pontifical States'. The letter of excommunication restated the necessity of the temporal power to the spiritual mission of the church. As such it was the pope's reply to those in France, Italy and England who asserted that the two facets of the church's life could and ought to be separated. Thouvenel had written such an opinion to the English government in February which Russell thought was masterful, and the English repeatedly said such things. No one was named in the excommunication, but Victor Emmanuel was commonly identified as the chief offender.[116] Hudson reported with great satisfaction that the excommunication had no effect on anyone in Turin. 'No one seems to care a straw for these harmless curses...', he said. Lord John wrote to Odo, 'His Excommunication is probably the last shot to be fired from that gun. Next time it will burst.' The pope and Antonelli were sorely disappointed. No Catholic power, not even Spain, came to the pope's side. Antonelli lamented to Barili that, by their inaction, the Catholic powers seemed to sanction the sacrilege.[117]

On 13 March, the day after the plebiscite in the Romagna, Lord John delivered a major address to the House of Commons on the revolution in central

[114] Antonelli to diplomatic corps, Vatican, 24 March 1860, no. 10035, translated by Odo Russell and sent to Lord John, Odo Russell to Russell, Rome, 3 April 1860, no. 49, PRO, FO, 43/76. Pius IX rejected Victor Emmanuel's proposal to open negotiations on the transfer of the Romagna to Sardinia (Pius IX to Victor Emmanuel, 2 April 1860, Pirri, vol. II, part 2, 163–5).

[115] Antonelli to Barili, 24 March 1860, no. 9893, *Antonelli–Barili*, 189. Antonelli to Sacconi, Rome, 3 April 1860, no. 10217, ASV, ANParigi, 1860, SdS, AD/P, and *Antonelli*, vol. II, 486.

[116] Antonelli to Barili, 30 March 1860, no. 10143, *Antonelli–Barili*, 191. The letter of excommunication, 26 March 1860, was translated by Odo Russell and sent to London, Odo Russell to Russell, Rome, 6 April 1860, no. 52, PRO, FO, 43/76. Thouvenel to Persigny, Paris, 8 Feb. 1860, PRO, FO, 425/59/42–5. Odo Russell to Russell, Rome, 20 March 1860, private, Russell papers, PRO, 30/22/75.

[117] Hudson to Odo Russell, Turin, 17 April 1860, Ampthill papers, PRO, FO, 918/42. Russell to Odo Russell, 16 April 1860, private, Ampthill papers, PRO, FO, 918/7. *Punch* (21 April 1860) reflected the common English view of the ineffectiveness of the excommunication. *Punch* showed Pius IX pushing a scary papal Bull mask at Victor Emmanuel and Napoleon, who respond to it with sophisticated boredom. Antonelli to Barili, 6 April 1860, no. 10360, *Antonelli–Barili*, 196–7.

Italy. It was his own summary of his action and accomplishments. He denied the Catholic charge that his diplomatic involvement in Italian and papal affairs had necessitated the French acquisition of Savoy and Nice. He asserted that he had always opposed the annexation of Savoy to France, and that he had never 'required' the annexation of the Romagna and the duchies to Piedmont. What the English government had done, he explained, was to employ all its diplomatic power to secure two things – that the people of central Italy would determine for themselves what their political outcome would be, and that the powers of Europe, particularly France and Austria, would not interfere by military force to determine the affairs of central Italy. He claimed that his government had been willing to accept a central Italian kingdom and even papal restoration, if that were what the central Italians wanted and if they effected it themselves. But, he continued, he worked for the annexation of the Romagna and duchies to Piedmont, because he was convinced by 'the leading people of Italy' that the populations of those regions unequivocally desired it. It was, his opponents might say, a way of 'insisting' on annexation without 'requiring' it. Russell, in any case, was pleased with the outcome of England's endeavours:

> ... if, consulting at once the interests of Great Britain and those of Europe, it should have been our fate at the same time to contribute in any way, even in the smallest degree, to the permanent independence of Italy, to the raising up a people who have been long sunk, and enabling men of the most cultivated intellect, and possessed of every gift of knowledge, to exercise their minds free of a censor ..., so far from shrinking from any responsibility, I shall, on the contrary, take pride to myself that I have been able, in any degree, to contribute to that result.[118]

Russell summarized his accomplishment more bluntly to Cowley privately. His words recalled the affair of Felice Orsini with which the current series of events opened two years before: 'The poignard, of course, plays its part, and I think the Emperor ought to bless his stars that we have relieved him from his obligation to restore the Pope and the Grand Duke Leopold. He will not be assassinated by a Romagnol.'[119] Mgr Sacconi told Antonelli that as a result of the annexations, England's influence in Italy was replacing that of France and Austria.[120]

The annexation of the Romagna to Sardinia completed the revolution against papal temporal power in the Romagna which began in June 1859. Russell's own summary in Parliament of his diplomatic action rightly emphasized that the Liberal government did not take the lead in deciding what should be done with the Romagna; they did follow the liberal Romagnols who, much earlier, had formalized their desire for annexation by the vote of September 1859, and they did look around for other solutions that might be possible to obtain.

Nevertheless, after *Le pape et le congrès*, Russell and Palmerston worked

118 Hansard's, CLVII, col. 450–6, 13 March 1860.
119 Russell to Cowley, 10 March 1860, private, copy, Russell papers, PRO, FO, 30/22/104.
120 Sacconi to Antonelli, Paris, 20 March 1860, no. 1467, ASV, ASdS, 1860, 165/43/237–9, and *Antonelli*, vol. II, 477.

incessantly in the diplomatic theatre to make annexation possible and to remove any impediments to it. Their relationship with Napoleon regarding annexation was the crucial one. They were his support, and his prod, and probably also his front. So long as they believed the emperor's diplomacy served the nationalist cause they nurtured *rapprochement* with him. But the moment they believed he subverted the nationalist cause – the vicariat proposal – they broke with him. In this, it seems plausible to conclude, they promoted the things he was unable to promote and they opposed what he was not free to oppose. It seems that by February 1860, Napoleon allowed them, even wanted them, to push for the annexation of the Romagna to Sardinia. In this way his overweening desire to annex Savoy and Nice to France enabled Russell and Palmerston to give Cavour the diplomatic assistance necessary to acquire the Romagna. George Bowyer's charge was not entirely unfounded – the Liberal government's push for the annexation of the Romagna did help make it possible for Napoleon to annex Savoy and Nice.

The annexation of the Romagna while completing one revolution was the opening of another. All parties involved knew in their different ways that the Marches and Umbria were next. Said Palmerston to Lord John, in a moment of historical reflection, 'it is imposible not to see that the present annexation of Romagna is only the beginning of "The Decay and Fall of the Roman Empire".'[121]

[121] Palmerston to Russell, 3 March 1860, Russell papers, PRO, 30/22/21.

8 Liberals and the annexation of the Marches and Umbria

Next the Marches and Umbria

The feeling that the Marches and Umbria were next in the progress of revolution in Italy was powerful among virtually all the parties to the conflict. Whether to regard the prospect with dread or joy depended on one's allegiances. How it might happen no one knew. The expectation itself was to have an influence on the course of events.

The Italian National Society issued a proclamation on 22 March to papal and Neapolitan troops urging them not to resist the movement to liberate Italy, and inviting them to defect to Sardinia's side. Tens of thousands of copies were distributed throughout the Papal States. Some small demonstrations were held. Odo Russell reported low-key and well-disciplined demonstrations in Rome itself. The National Society was in direct and regular communication with Cavour on the matter.[1]

Napoleon continued for the time being to desire no further revolution to break out in the Papal States.[2] What Napoleon now wanted most was to take his troops out of Rome. Annexing Savoy and Nice appeared to be satiating him, and he could concentrate on extricating himself from his papal difficulty. Even before the plebiscites in the Romagna, the French government had reopened the topic of evacuation, suggesting to the papal government that troops from the king of Naples might replace the French in the Papal States. Antonelli did not oppose the idea.[3] Palmerston and Russell actually welcomed the proposal at first. Their policy was still to let Napoleon set the timing and mode of evacuation, and they were glad for almost any plan that could achieve French withdrawal. Naples was not Palmerston's and Russell's first choice for a substitute, but Russell officially

---

1   Grew, 282–5. Odo Russell to Russell, Rome, 16 March 1860, no. 39, and 20 March 1860, no. 41, PRO, FO, 43/76, and *Odo Russell*, 93–5. Odo Russell to Lady William Russell, Rome, 6 and 20 March 1860, Ampthill papers, PRO, FO, 918/85/256 and 261. Gregorovius, 20 March 1860, 79.
2   Cowley to Russell, Paris, 23 March 1860, private, copy, Cowley papers, PRO, FO, 519/227/76.
3   Odo Russell to Russell, Rome, 13 March 1860, no. 35, PRO, FO, 43/76, and *Odo Russell*, 92. See Scott, 170–2.

indicated that England would permit the Neapolitan occupation of the Papal States if the pope and the king of Naples arranged it.[4] Cavour saw the suggestion as a great opportunity to place his troops in the Marches. When Russell asked him what he thought of replacing the French with Neapolitan troops, Cavour replied immediately with an offer to accept it, on the condition that Sardinian troops occupy Ancona.[5] Russell did not like that prospect, and was much relieved when the king of Naples settled the question by unequivocally declining the French suggestion.[6] Russell now expressed to the French that the English would not object to prolonging the French occupation of Rome 'for the present moment' so long as its purpose was merely 'the personal protection of His Holiness the Pope'.[7]

Cavour was already set with his old strategy to get Sardinian troops into the Papal States. On 25 March, James Hudson explained Cavour's thinking and intentions: 'an outbreak in the Marches will lead the Piedmontese to the assistance of their brethren in distress. There can be no repetition of the massacre in Perugia: Italy won't stand that, and so Victor Emmanuel *must* march sooner or later whether he likes it or not.' What this meant, which Hudson did not say, was that Cavour believed he was in a position more or less to determine when and where 'an outbreak in the Marches' would occur. And even if the radicals — the Mazzinians or Garibaldini — stirred insurrection, he thought he could still use the need to assist the 'brethren in distress' as his excuse to invade papal territory. Hudson ended his explanation on Cavour's behalf with a rousing appeal to Russell to support Cavour to the full: 'Cavour from the very necessities of his position is now more than ever thrown into your hands; if your policy in Southern Italy is vigorous and armed, you will then hold the scales.' Hudson recommended doubling the British navy in the Mediterranean to neutralize the French, arguing that if they helped Cavour in this way now, they could expect a strong Italy as an ally in the future.[8]

Russell's reply was conditioned by the fact that his trust in Cavour had been deeply shaken by the Savoy and Nice affair. Russell told Hudson that Sardinia ought to concentrate on consolidating the government in central Italy and laying 'the foundations of a free representative Monarchy', especially now that the

4   Palmerston to Russell, 3 March 1860, Russell papers, PRO, 30/22/21. Russell to Cowley, 27 March 1860, no. 309, PRO, FO, 425/60/160.
5   Corti to Cavour, London, 28 March 1860, telegram, and Cavour to Corti, Turin, 30 March 1860, *Cavour e l'Inghilterra*, vol. II, part 2, 57–8. See Hudson to Russell, Turin, 29 March 1860, private, *Gran Bretagna e Sardegna*, vol. VIII, 58–9.
6   Elliot to Russell, Naples, 23 March 1860, no. 103, secret, and Russell to Elliot, 31 March 1860, no. 38, PRO, FO, 425/60/170 and 189.
7   Russell to Cowley, 31 March 1860, no. 334, PRO, FO, 425/60/198.
8   Hudson to Russell, Turin, 25 March 1860, private, *Gran Bretagna e Sardegna*, vol. VIII, 56–7. I have slightly altered the punctuation as shown in the printed text to more closely accord with the meaning of the original manuscript. As elsewhere in this study, I have modernized the punctuation.

Sardinian parliament was soon to convene.[9] He added, 'Sardinia ought not to attack either Pope or Caesar. I hope she will have the prudence to refrain.' In any case, he reminded Hudson, his support of Sardinia was not an endorsement of Cavour as such, but of 'the welfare and liberty of Italy'.[10]

Russell explained to Count Apponyi, the Austrian ambassador, that English opposition to a Sardinian attack on the Papal States was based partly on a Whig doctrinal distinction between a war of aggression and an internal revolution. The overthrow of the pope in the Romagna he defined as an internal revolution against papal oppression after which the Romagnols asked for Sardinian protection. But a straightforward Piedmontese military invasion of papal or Neapolitan territory would be regarded as aggression. Without doubt, said Russell, England would condemn it and even look for a way to prevent such a thing.[11] Given the nature of Cavour's relations with liberal revolutionary organizations in the Papal States, such a distinction would be difficult to make in the course of events, and almost anything could be labelled an invitation to keep order. Of this Cavour was well aware.

The papal government responded to the new circumstances by more earnestly building the papal army. Antonelli told Odo Russell just after the plebiscite in the Romagna that recruits from other states were joining the papal army, but much too slowly. Only about 1500 foreign volunteers had arrived by mid-March.[12] What offered new hope to the papal government was the appointment of General Christophe de Lamoricière as commander-in-chief of the papal forces, sanctioned by Napoleon. Lamoricière was a former French general, a one-time republican, but now a devout Ultramontane who lived in Belgium in exile from the Second Empire. He had the reputation of being a competent organizer and strategist and a daring officer. *The Times* acknowledged that Lamoricière's acceptance of the post rendered the papal army a serious thing.[13] Lamoricière arrived in Rome on 2 April. In his first order of the day on 11 April the new general declared his work to be a new crusade: 'Catholic Christianity is the life of civilization. Europe is threatened by revolution as it formerly was by Islamism. The cause of the Pope is that of civilization and liberty.'[14] Part of Lamoricière's task would be to develop the papal army to such a strength that it could allow the French troops to withdraw from Rome. Napoleon indicated that the reason he approved the general, and, for that matter, did not prevent other

9   Russell to Hudson, 31 March 1860, no. 66, *Gran Bretagna e Sardegna*, vol. VIII, 62–3.
10 Russell to Hudson, 2 April 1860, private, *Gran Bretagna e Sardegna*, vol. VIII, 68.
11 Apponyi to Rechberg, London, 6 April 1860, no. 14C, HHSA, PA, VIII, 52/637–8.
12 Odo Russell to Russell, Rome, 16 March 1860, no. 37, confidential, PRO, FO, 43/76, and *Odo Russell*, 93.
13 Antonelli to Sacconi, Rome, 3 April 1860, telegram, ASV ANParigi, 1860, SdS, and *Antonelli*, vol. II, 486–7. Odo Russell to Russell, Rome, 3 April 1860, no. 48, PRO, FO, 43/76, and *Odo Russell*, 96–7. *The Times*, 31 Dec. 1860.
14 *Tablet*, 7 and 14 April 1860.

French volunteers from enlisting in the papal army, was his hope of evacuating Rome soon.[15]

Cowley warned Lord John not to regard the appointment of Lamoricière lightly. Many among the papal party had hopes that the general's appointment foreshadowed an attempt to reconquer the Romagna.[16] However, everything seemed to indicate, as Russell believed, that the most the papal government could expect was to maintain order in the Marches and Umbria, and, if nothing unusual happened, to fill the void left by an evacuation of the French troops from Rome.[17] By Lamoricière's count, he found 16,000 to 18,000 ill-equipped troops waiting for him on his arrival; he wanted to raise it to perhaps 25,000 men. The Sardinian army, according to Hudson, was ten times larger.[18]

It was the pope himself who settled the question at the end of April. The Duc de la Rochefoucauld arrived in Rome with a gift of a million francs to finance 'a crusade against illegitimate sovereigns'. Pius IX kindly rejected the money, saying that he had no idea of using military force for such a campaign against the Romagna, but that if attacked in the other parts of his states he would defend himself. Cowley learned about the pope's declaration via Lamoricière's reports to friends in Paris, and relayed the news to Lord John in London.[19] It was significant news. It meant that hereafter the English government did not need to fear that the papal army would attack Bologna. Indeed, the English could regard the papal army with indifference. For the papal government it meant a *de facto*, if not *de jure*, recognition that the Romagna was lost and that the pope would need all the help he could get merely to hold on to what remained.

Anticipating Garibaldi in the Papal States

The event that seems to have forced this new awareness on the pope and Antonelli was a revolt in Palermo in Sicily on 4 April against the authority of the king of Naples. The revolt was a strictly local movement in response to local issues, but it was enough to arouse fear in the papal party.[20] It suggested how imminent a revolution in the Marches and Umbria could be.

The Palermo revolt gave Cavour something to say to Lord John Russell. He wrote to Emanuel d'Azeglio in London on 6 April:

15   Cowley to Russell, Paris, 5 April 1860, no. 408, confidential, PRO, FO, 425/60/241–2.
16   Cowley to Russell, Paris, 6 April 1860, private, copy, Cowley papers, PRO, FO, 519/227/91.
     Odo Russell to Russell, Rome, 17 April 1860, private, Russell papers, PRO, 30/22/75, and *Odo Russell*, 99.
17   Russell to Odo Russell, 16 April 1860, private, Ampthill papers, PRO, FO, 918/7.
18   Cowley to Russell, Paris, 6 April 1860, no. 416, most confidential, PRO, FO, 425/60/246–7.
     Hudson to Russell, Turin, 25 March 1860, private, *Gran Bretagna e Sardegna*, vol. VIII, 56.
     Odo reported the papal army had 17,000 when Lamoricière arrived (Odo Russell to Russell, Rome, 7 April 1860, private, Russell papers, PRO, 30/22/75, and *Odo Russell*, 98).
19   Cowley to Russell, Paris, 27 April 1860, private, copy, Cowley papers, PRO, FO, 519/227/114–15. Scott, 176.
20   Mack Smith, *Cavour and Garibaldi*, 4.

> Each day brings new complications. Umbria and the Marches are in such a state that one cannot pretend to maintain tranquillity there. At the same time a new insurrection breaks out in Sicily. Make the English government understand that whatever may be our intention to devote all our care to the internal organization of our new kingdom, we cannot remain indifferent in the face of such developments.[21]

Shortly after this, Emanuel d'Azeglio spent a couple of days with Palmerston in the country, and on 14 April wrote to Cavour about something significant he had learned. Palmerston told him, in effect, that there was a way that Sardinia could invade papal territory without protest from the English government. D'Azeglio summarized what Palmerston said: 'The occupation of Umbria and the Marches appears a very simple and natural thing to do, provided we cannot be accused of serious provocation and provided it comes as a result of insurrectionary movements independent of us.'[22] Palmerston, at least, gave his implicit support of Cavour's formula for conquest.

Russell was still unmoved, however. It was Russell's view of Cavour, readily approved by the queen and the Cabinet, that underlay official English policy. Hudson wrote a stirring appeal to Lord John, reminding him of all Cavour had done to accomplish what England desired most in Italy – building a constitutional system, promoting free trade and material prosperity, and resisting the pope and priests. Hudson pleaded with Russell:

> But I can't throw a stone at him: I have been here 8 years and I have seen him fight single-handed Pope and Caesar (both Gallic and Teutonic) in many a long fight for liberty of conscience and liberty of commerce . . .
>
> Who on the Continent has done 1/10th part for free trade that he has done, who has broke down so many customs barriers? He has done the same for men's consciences. He has liberated millions from the thraldom of priests and if supported (properly supported) will reduce that great lever of iniquity to its proper place and level.[23]

Hudson's appeals did not change Russell's opinion about Cavour. 'I quite agree with you as to Cavour's past services', he replied to Hudson, 'but it appears to me he has cancelled them, and placed his country in the hands of France by the Treaty of Turin.'[24] Russell consistently enunciated a policy which opposed Sardinian intervention in any of the remaining parts of Italy – Sicily, Naples and the Papal States. Repeatedly he urged that 'it would be wisdom to consolidate what has been obtained, rather than to seek for new acquisitions'.[25] Russell demanded the same non-intervention from France and Austria, and pledged that England would observe it as well:

21 Cavour to Emanuel d'Azeglio, Turin, 6 April 1860, no. 88, *Cavour e l'Inghilterra*, vol. II, part 2, 63.
22 Emanuel d'Azeglio to Cavour, London, 14 April 1860, *Cavour e l'Inghilterra*, vol. II, part 2, 64–7.
23 Hudson to Russell, Turin, 20 April 1860, private, *Gran Bretagna e Sardegna*, vol. VIII, 80–1.
24 Russell to Hudson, 29 April 1860, private, *Gran Bretagna e Sardegna*, vol. VIII, 86.
25 Russell to Hudson, 30 April 1860, no. 86, *Gran Bretagna e Sardegna*, vol. VIII, 87.

Liberals and the annexation of the Marches and Umbria

> I do not want to have anything to do with the affairs of the south of Italy, with the occupation of Ancona or the insurrection in Sicily. Italian affairs ought now to be left to settle themselves, and Great Britain ought not to interfere any more than Austria or France. But I do not believe either Austria or France are ready to keep their fingers out of the pie.[26]

For the moment, Russell's estrangement from Cavour assisted the pope in retaining the Marches and Umbria.

On 1 May, Odo Russell wrote to Lord John saying that matters were at a standstill in Rome. Easter had passed, the social season was over, and nothing at all political was happening:

> I have literally nothing wherewith to trouble you today. I have called on my diplomatic friends and have found them idle and their chancelleries deserted. Baron Bach had retained his messenger in Rome for another week having nothing to say, the Duc de Gramont was planning a day at the quails, and Cardinal Antonelli, ever cheerful and pleasant, finding I had no news to give him, talked for an hour about his flower garden and the fish in the Lake of Albans.[27].

It was a lull that English diplomacy had helped to create.

Then the storm began. On 6 May, Giuseppe Garibaldi and about a thousand volunteer fighters sailed from Genoa harbour for the Papal States and Sicily. Cavour's earnest efforts to stop them had failed. On the 7th Garibaldi's forces landed at Talamone on the south Tuscan coast a few miles from the papal border.[28] There he issued a proclamation calling on the Papal States and Naples to revolt: 'May the Marches, Umbria, Sabina, Rome, the Neapolitans all arise in rebellion in order to divide the forces of our enemies.'[29] A company of about 60 men, joined by another 170 coming from Tuscany, were despatched to invade the Papal States on a route passing through Orvieto and Perugia into the Marches. All the rest of the forces sailed for Marsala on the western tip of Sicily where they landed on 11 May. Garibaldi declared that their purpose was to support 'the gallant sons of Sicily' who might soon have to fight 'not only the mercenaries of the Bourbons, but those of Austria and of the Priests in Rome'. The plan corresponded with a general strategy conceived by Mazzini in February. The idea was to squeeze the Papal States and the Kingdom of Naples between two guerrilla forces. From the north the volunteers led by Zambianchi were to move from the Marches and Umbria into Naples territory, picking up recruits along the way as each city and town overthrew papal rule. Garibaldi was

---

26   Russell to Hudson, 18 April 1860, private, *Gran Bretagna e Sardegna*, vol. VIII, 80.
27   Odo Russell to Russell, Rome, 1 May 1860, private, Russell papers, PRO, 30/22/75, and *Odo Russell*, 100–1.
28   For the following details of the Talamone events and the invasion of papal territory I have relied upon G.M. Trevelyan, *Garibaldi and the Thousand* (London: Longmans, Green, 1909), ch. 11 and 12.
29   Giuseppe Garibaldi, *Edizione nazionale degli scritti di Giuseppe Garibaldi* (Bologna: Zanichelli, 1932), vol. I, 239–41.

to do the same from the south, moving across Sicily to the mainland and north to the city of Naples. Dr Agostino Bertani, Garibaldi's organizer in Genoa, was to send new recruits to support Zambianchi in the Papal States. For the time being, at least, Rome was not to be revolutionized.

The papal government, according to Odo Russell's accounts, was severely alarmed by news of the guerrilla bands on the papal–Tuscan border. The rumour in Rome was that Garibaldi himself was in command. Lamoricière despatched a small number of mounted soldiers who met the guerrillas on 19 May at Grotto di Castro near Lake Bolsena, and scattered them. About 3000 papal soldiers, meanwhile, moved into Viterbo a little to the south. The disarrayed Garibaldini were seized by Piedmontese troops who were waiting at the papal border. The papal army succeeded this round in thwarting the revolution and maintaining its own defence.[30]

Although the northern half of the Garibaldi strategy failed, Garibaldi's movements in the south fared differently. The French–papal talks about troop evacuation stopped abruptly, and Russell reaffirmed England's willingness for the French to remain in Rome 'as long as he [the pope] requires it, and the Emperor grants it'.[31] Once they were sure Garibaldi acted independently of Cavour, Russell and Palmerston decided not to consider Garibaldi's guerrilla invasion of Sicily to be 'armed intervention' in violation of the doctrine of 'non-intervention'. In fact, the English moved the British fleet to Marsala to give Garibaldi tacit assistance, and English consuls helped him unofficially at Genoa, Palermo, and later, Catania. Russell justified Garibaldi's actions to Queen Victoria by once again citing the Whig interpretation of the 1688–9 revolution. Garibaldi provided the unexpected source of outside support which carried the Palermo revolt across Sicily and eventually to the mainland. What Russell would have protested in Cavour, he applauded in Garibaldi. By contrast, the papal government was terrified.[32]

Both the English and the papal governments adopted an overview of the future movements of events in Italy which assumed that an attack by Garibaldi on Naples and the Papal States was virtually inevitable. Initially Russell stated his belief to Odo Russell on 14 May that 'Garibaldi I expect will not succeed', but after a few days observation of Garibaldi's exploits he changed his mind totally. He told Palmerston on 18 May, 'One must expect that Umbria and the Marches as well as Naples will fall and proclaim Victor Emmanuel.'[33] By the time Garibaldi conquered Palermo and established a provisional government on 27

30   See Odo Russell to Russell, Rome, 15, 17 and 26 May 1860, no. 69, no. 70 and no. 71, PRO, FO, 43/77, and *Odo Russell*, 104–7. Antonelli to the diplomatic corps, Vatican, 21 May 1860, ASV, ANParigi, 1860, SdS, AD/P, and *Antonelli*, vol. II, 518–19.
31   Antonelli to Sacconi, Rome, 21 May 1860, no. 11393, *Antonelli*, vol. II, 517. Russell to Cowley, 5 June 1860, private, copy, Russell papers, PRO, 30/22/104.
32   Case, *Thouvenel*, 182. Mack Smith, *Victor Emanuel, Cavour*, 164–5. Russell to Queen Victoria, 30 April and 1 May 1860, RA J28/61 and 66.
33   Russell to Odo Russell, 14 May 1860, private, Ampthill papers, PRO, FO, 918/7. Russell to Palmerston, 18 May 1860, copy, Russell papers, PRO, 30/22/30.

Liberals and the annexation of the Marches and Umbria

May, Odo reported that the pope and Antonelli had no doubts that Garibaldi was headed not merely for the Marches and Umbria, but especially for Rome.[34] Russell came to the same conclusion. He stated this to Cowley on 5 June:

> There can be no doubt that Garibaldi once in possession of Sicily will cross the strait, and beat up the quarters of the king of Naples. The next point is Rome, and here I think the Emperor's honor and reputation are concerned in protecting the Pope's person in Rome while a dangerous crisis is hanging over the Holy see.[35]

On the northern papal border, after the papal army defeated the Garibaldini, the Sardinian army and the local revolutionaries became the threat to fear instead. Odo reported that the Sardinians began to station soldiers along the entire length of the papal frontier from Orbetello on the Tyrrhenian to Cattolica on the Adriatic. Odo assured Lord John that the Sardinians' purpose was purely 'to guarantee the Papal Territory from all future violation'.[36] The arrangement was not unlike having the wolf protect little Red Riding Hood. With Garibaldi active in the south and the Sardinians tensed on the northern papal border, both the English and the papal governments understood that the pope was about to be caught, or as Lord John expressed it to Odo, 'if the candle is burning at both ends the fire will reach the middle before long'.[37] Lord John took one precaution just to make certain that the papal army would not complicate matters unexpectedly. He telegraphed Odo in Rome, 'Ask Cardinal Antonelli whether the Roman Government contemplate any attack on Tuscany or Romagna.' Odo replied reassuringly, 'Certainly not. The Rome Government have no aggressive intention, but they fear an attack on the part of Garibaldi in the Marches or elsewhere.'[38]

With Garibaldi on the move, Russell again worried that Cavour might plot a Piedmontese attack on the pope and Naples, or, as it now appeared, even on Austria in Venetia. He had begun to fear that Cavour and Napoleon had a secret deal for France to annex Genoa, or even Sicily or the island of Sardinia. Russell proposed to Palmerston that they compel Cavour to make a choice: either renounce all intentions to attack anyone and trade away any territory, and then receive an English guarantee to defend by armed force all existing Sardinian possessions; or refuse to do so, and be faced by an English alliance with Austria to defend Venetia by armed force against Sardinia. Russell felt the British fleet could help settle his frustration with Cavour.[39] The despatch that Russell finally

---

34 Odo Russell to Russell, Rome, 1 June 1860, private, Russell papers, PRO, 30/22/75, and *Odo Russell*, 108.
35 Russell to Cowley, 5 June 1860, private, copy, Russell papers, PRO, 30/22/104. *Punch* (29 Sept. 1860) thought Garibaldi would be the best way to settle the Papal Question, and pictured him offering an ailing Pius IX the cap of liberty in place of the papal tiara.
36 Odo Russell to Russell, Rome, 27 May 1860, no. 74, PRO, FO, 43/77.
37 Russell to Odo Russell, 14 May 1860, private, Ampthill papers, PRO, FO, 918/7.
38 Russell to Odo Russell, Rome, 14 May 1860, no. 21, PRO, FO, 43/75 (Russell's telegram was dated 13 May 1860). Odo Russell to Russell, Rome, 14 May 1860, telegram, no. 61, PRO, FO, 43/77.
39 Russell to Palmerston, 18 May 1860, copy, Russell papers, PRO, 30/22/30.

sent Hudson on 22 May was relatively tame. He was content to repeat his statement that Cavour should consolidate his existing acquisitions, and forswear all intentions to cede Italian territory to France or to attack any other ruler on the peninsula. He did inform Hudson unofficially that he might use the British navy to stop Sardinian aggression against Venetia. He mentioned nothing about preventing aggression against the pope, saying only that he expected Cavour 'to maintain a defensive attitude' toward the pope. His strategic advice to Cavour was simple enough: 'He will do well to be quiet and leave that great innovator [Garibaldi] to do his work. Garibaldi seems to be successful and no one will be sorry for it . . . But we cannot give him any support till the course of events is pretty clear.'[40]

In a speech to the Sardinian parliament Cavour denied any intention to cede any further territory, but made no comments about aggression against Venetia or the Papal States. As a matter of fact, Cavour did hope to seize both states whenever it was feasible. Russell refused to accept Cavour's denial as adequate, and he continued to worry about Cavour's untrustworthiness.[41] Because of the English and the uncertainty created by Garibaldi, Cavour did send out word for the Italian National Society to stop trying to revolutionize the Marches and Umbria for the time being. The National Society itself became divided over the issue, with the Romagna branch continuing to plot revolution in the Marches, smuggling arms into the Papal States, and collecting funds from sources within papal territory. Simultaneously, Bertani continued planning an expedition into the Papal States, even though the first band of volunteers had failed. Now Cavour was in trouble.[42]

The French government had its own problem with Garibaldi. Thouvenel and Napoleon, like the English and papal governments, realized Garibaldi could be headed for Rome. As long as the French troops remained in Rome, the pope was still Napoleon's responsibility. Russell, early in June, even cautioned the French government not to endanger the pope's security in Rome; the English government would feel the ire of the Catholic faithful if the pope were endangered or insulted severely in the Holy City.[43] Napoleon underscored his determination to protect the pope at Rome, but hinted to the English more openly that he did not intend to defend papal authority in the Marches and Umbria.[44] The emperor thought this stand might please the English, and enable

40 Russell to Hudson, 22 May 1860, no. 107, and 22 May 1860, private, *Gran Bretagna e Sardegna*, vol. VIII, 115–16.
41 Mack Smith, *Victor Emanuel, Cavour*, 162–3. Russell to Hudson, 28 May 1860, private, *Gran Bretagna e Sardegna*, vol. VIII, 123.
42 Grew, 307–8, 327–4. Hudson to Russell, Turin, 2 June 1860, private, *Gran Bretagna e Sardegna*, vol. VIII, 128.
43 Cowley to Russell, Paris, 2 and 4 June 1860, private, copies, Cowley papers, PRO, FO, 519/227/169 and 171. Persigny to Thouvenel, London, 5 June 1860, no. 64, *Annessioni al Regno d'Italia*, vol. II, 240–1. Case, *Thouvenel*, 183–98.
44 Cowley to Russell, Paris, 6 June 1860, private, copy, Cowley papers, PRO, FO, 519/227/175–6.

the English once again to act in unison with him with respect to Italian and papal affairs.[45]

Unfortunately for the papacy, Garibaldi's successes multiplied in Sicily during June and July, and Piedmont's presence on the papal border solidified. Napoleon refrained from giving an unambiguous declaration that he would protect the pope in Rome, and he left unclear whether he would or would not defend the pope in the Marches and Umbria. The pope and Antonelli were left quite uninformed and insecure.[46] Napoleon did keep Cavour apprized of his intentions, however. On 13 July, through Nigra in Paris, he gave Cavour his tacit approval of a Sardinian invasion of the Marches and Umbria, on the condition that Piedmont leave Rome alone. Simultaneously, Prince Napoleon urged Cavour to act quickly to take the initiative from Garibaldi and seize the Papal States.[47] Even James Hudson, according to Cavour, went against the policy of the English government and secretly urged Cavour to invade the Papal States in order to pre-empt Garibaldi.[48]

The English government acted to help Garibaldi all the more. Lord Palmerston used the forum of the House of Commons on 12 June to make the English position utterly plain. He warned the pope and the king of Naples that the English government would do nothing to help them against Garibaldi. He declared that the pope and the king of Naples brought the revolution upon themselves 'by the cruelties and atrocities committed under their authority'. The only way to stop the revolution, he observed ironically, would be to deal with its real 'authors and instigators' and remove the pope and the king from their thrones. The speech, for all to hear, was an unqualified public invitation to Garibaldi to proceed with English blessing.[49]

Pius IX was not, of course, persuaded by Palmerston's clever point. He met Odo Russell in a special audience on 12 July at the Vatican. The pope affirmed his resolve to resist all who caused him troubles – Piedmont, foreign agents, a 'small and criminal minority' in the Romagna, Napoleon, and 'the revolutionary

45   See Napoleon to Persigny, 25 July 1860, quoted in Case, *Franco-Italian relations*, 7–8. Case incorrectly states that this letter was the emperor's answer to new English pressure to evacuate Rome just as Garibaldi seemed bent on attacking. Throughout 1860 the English consistently maintained their policy of letting the emperor decide when and even whether to withdraw his troops from Rome; Russell in fact, explicitly said he wanted Napoleon not to do anything to endanger the pope in Rome.
46   Antonelli to Sacconi, Rome, 3 July 1860, no. 12288; 7 July 1860, no. 12433; and 21 July 1860, no. 12756, ASV, ANParigi, 1860, SdS, AD/P, and *Antonelli*, vol. II, 541, 543–4, and 552–3. *Punch* (18 August 1860) could sympathize with the pope. Napoleon's protection over the years probably caused Pius more anguish than comfort.
47   Nigra to Cavour, Paris, 13 July 1860, *Cavour–Nigra*, vol. IV, 75–8. See Case, 'Thouvenel et la rupture des relations diplomatiques franco-sardes en 1860', *Revue d'histoire moderne et contemporaire* 8 (1960), 149–77.
48   Mack Smith, 'L'Inghilterra di fronte agli eventi italiano del 1860', *Atti del XXXIX congresso di storia del Risorgimento italiano* (1961), 429.
49   Hansard's, CLIX, col. 329–30, 12 June 1860. Sacconi to Antonelli, Paris, 5 June 1860, no. 1533, *Antonelli*, vol. II, 527–8.

policy of England'. Pius trusted all the more in God to protect his church and relied on devout Catholics the world over to rally to his side.⁵⁰

Russell and Palmerston considered during July how Italy might be organized after Garibaldi's expected triumph. It was now evident that because of Garibaldi's announced allegiance to Victor Emmanuel, the annexation of nearly the whole of Italy to Piedmont was a possibility. For the first time they considered the merits of the unification of the peninsula. Russell believed the impediments to constitutional government over such vast and diverse areas were many. Hence, he definitely preferred the formation of *two* kingdoms of Italy, one in the north under Victor Emmanuel and one in the south under a regenerated throne of Naples, with a cordial alliance between the two states.⁵¹ Palmerston and Russell did not consider what to do with the pope. The pope would be left somehow in the middle. On 26 July, however, Palmerston talked with Emanuel d'Azeglio in London about the pros and cons of Sardinian annexation of the Papal States, except for Rome. Palmerston spoke against such an annexation, but the implication seemed clear enough that he regarded Sardinian acquisition of the Marches and Umbria as a serious possibility.⁵² He did specify that Rome was absolutely untouchable, in his view, since the French army was there, and since the Catholic states generally could not permit the pope to be molested in the Holy City.⁵³ Palmerston in this way again gave Cavour the clue that England would not oppose him in the Marches and Umbria if he handled it carefully. Meanwhile, Hudson and Odo Russell both contributed their assessments in favour of one kingdom in Italy.⁵⁴ By the beginning of August, Lord John no longer thought it worthwhile to dispute about unity or duality, for he conjectured that 'Garibaldi's sword will cut the Gordian knot.' His policy was to allow Garibaldi to proceed. His expectations drove him again to contemplate the unification of the peninsula. He wrote to Odo on 6 August, 'The spectacle of the papacy with Victor Emmanuel on one side and Garibaldi on the other will be curious. I conclude with you that the unity of Italy under one sceptre will come to pass.'⁵⁵

The pieces of a new English policy toward the Marches and Umbria were slowly fitting together under the impact of Garibaldi's successes. On 14 August

50 Odo Russell to Russell, Rome, 12 July 1860, no. 103, secret, PRO, FO, 43/77, and *Odo Russell*, 118–21.
51 Russell to Hudson, 23 July 1860, no. 148, confidential, *Gran Bretagna e Sardegna*, vol. VIII, 150–1.
52 Emanuel d'Azeglio to Cavour, London, 26 July 1860, no. 189, confidential, *Cavour e l'Inghilterra*, vol. II, part 2, 112–14.
53 Emanuel d'Azeglio to Cavour, London, 29 July 1860, *Cavour e l'Inghilterra*, vol. II, part 2, 116.
54 Hudson to Russell, Turin, 31 July 1860, private, *Gran Bretagna e Sardegna*, vol. VIII, 155–9. Odo Russell to Russell, Naples, 28 July 1860, private, Russell papers, PRO, 30/22/75.
55 Russell to Odo Russell, 6 August 1860, private, Russell papers, PRO, 30/22/111, and excerpted in *Odo Russell*, 122. Russell to Hudson, 6 August 1860, private, *Gran Bretagna e Sardegna*, vol. VIII, 162.

Liberals and the annexation of the Marches and Umbria

Russell responded formally to a query by Thouvenel about whether the English and French might together prevent Garibaldi from entering papal territory. Russell rejected the suggestion outright, declaring that under no circumstances would England endorse such an action. The English government, he said, would support French protection of the pope in Rome and no more. He advocated allowing the Marches and Umbria to follow the Romagna in overthrowing the temporal power of the pope. Russell's was a policy of revolution in the Papal States in which the mode of revolution was left deliberately unspecified.[56]

By mid-August Garibaldi approached Messina where a narrow body of water separated his triumph in Sicily from his hoped-for conquest of Naples and the Papal States. Cavour and Napoleon had already agreed secretly upon a Piedmontese invasion of the Marches and Umbria. Russell and Palmerston had officially sanctioned an attack by Garibaldi on the Marches and Umbria, and Palmerston implied to Sardinia that England would not disapprove a Sardinian attack upon the Papal States if it came in response to a revolutionary initiative from within papal territory. Moreover, Russell had accepted as historically likely that Piedmont would annex the whole peninsula, except for Rome and Venetia. To activate all this, Garibaldi simply had to cross the straits of Messina.

Peter's Pence and the Irish Brigade

The papal government was not entirely passive while Garibaldi conquered Sicily during the spring and summer. As Odo Russell discovered on 12 July, Pius IX possessed an intense feeling of political isolation – all but God and the faithful had abandoned him. But he also had developed an optimistic reliance on General Lamoricière and the papal army.

Odo Russell hoped the English government would not hinder recruitments for the papal army, 'so that the French army may *really* withdraw altogether and the Temporal Power of the Pope rest solely on its own merits'. Irish Catholics, and English Catholics, too, had begun to volunteer for military service in the Papal States as well as to send money to Rome. The public meetings, petitions and declarations by Irish and English Catholics during the winter had been a boon to the pope. With the loss of the Romagna in March, however, the papal government and the clergy in all countries, including England and Ireland, realized that meetings and declarations were not enough. For one thing, the pope needed money. When Sardinia annexed the Romagna the pope lost a major source of tax revenue for his government, and the turmoil kept English and other visitors away from Rome, reducing that source of income as well.[57] Furthermore, when it became obvious that the Marches and Umbria were next,

---

56 Russell to Cowley, 15 August 1860, no. 809, PRO, FO, 425/62/66.
57 Isastia, 248–50.

Peter's Pence and the Irish Brigade

the pope needed foreign volunteers for his army. The clergy and faithful had to transmute speeches into money and men from all over Europe.

The money came first. It had already started to arrive before March, but within days of the annexation of the Romagna the first of several organized channels of giving was announced. On 14 March Viscount Feidling, a prominent English Catholic nobleman, publicized plans to re-establish the medieval institution of St Peter's Pence which had been banned under Henry VIII. It would be a voluntary confraternity for regular giving to Rome sanctioned by the Vatican. Catholic believers were urged to give at least a penny a week to keep the pope on his throne.[58] Two weeks later Cardinal Wiseman, in his Lenten pastoral, enjoined Catholics to contribute toward a 'benevolence' for the pope and designated Sunday, 15 April, for a collection in every church and chapel in the diocese of Westminster. Other bishops did the same. He also endorsed the papal bond drive to raise a loan for the pope from among the faithful of the church.[59] Similar actions were taken in Ireland. On 16 May a Papal Fund Committee met in London and issued a statement to Catholics of England and Ireland soliciting contributions for the pope.[60] Through such means money reached the Vatican, often passing via the rectors of the English and Irish Colleges in Rome. Odo Russell, referring to the boycott of the papal lottery in Rome, commented to his mother: 'it is of no use, for money is pouring in from all parts of the Catholic world and even poor Paddy I see is contributing his mite to enable the Pope to continue his misgovernment of this fair spot of the world'.[61] Parallel to Catholic giving, enthusiasts for Garibaldi collected money in England for the Garibaldi Fund from May onward.[62]

Next came the men. When Lamoricière arrived in Rome in April the foreign regiments in the papal army were either Swiss or Austrian. The pope now needed recruits from the whole Catholic world, especially from France, Belgium, Bavaria, Spain and Ireland. In July 1859 Antonelli had mentioned to Odo offers of Irish recruits which he had declined out of deference to the English government. By January 1860 Pius IX expressed new interest in receiving Irish enlistments, if the English would not object.

Nothing was done about it until March, however, just prior to the annexation of the Romagna. Count Charles MacDonnell, an Austrian of Irish descent and

---

58   Viscount Feidling to the editor, 14 March 1860, *Tablet*, 17 March 1860. See 25 H8.c.21. ss. 1, 17; and 1 Eliz. c.1.s.2.
59   Wiseman's pastoral, 25 March 1860, published in *Tablet*, 21 April 1860. The loan was announced in *Giornale di Roma*, 3 May 1860. The quota for England and Ireland combined was £80,000, which represented 4 per cent of the total papal bond issue of £2 million (*Tablet*, 9 June 1860).
60   *Tablet*, 19 May 1860.
61   Odo Russell to Lady William Russell, Rome, 6 March 1860, copy, Ampthill papers, PRO, FO, 918/85/256.
62   *The Times*, 6 and 9 May 1860.

a chamberlain of Pius IX, visited Ireland and suggested the project to A.M. Sullivan, editor of *The Nation*, a leading newspaper in Dublin.[63] The *Nation* immediately promoted Irish enlistments in the papal army, and Cardinal Cullen endorsed them. Recruiting stations were opened throughout Ireland and parish clergy directed men to them. Strictly speaking, the volunteers were not called 'recruits', but 'pilgrims' or 'emigrants', since there was some doubt about the legality of enlistments in a foreign army. As one enthusiast put it: 'But then there is no law which forbids any number of able-bodied Pilgrims from going to Rome to kiss His foot and get His blessing.'[64] The official enlistment in the army occurred after arrival in the Papal States. Antonelli explained to Odo that this method was used in order not to violate English law. He hoped 'Her Majesty's Government would generously throw no impediments in the way of such of her Roman Catholic subjects, who, of their own free will, proceeded to Rome to offer their services to the Pope.'[65] This was the message Odo urged upon Lord John on 10 May.

The first volunteers left Ireland in April and arrived in the Papal States on 26 May. The first Irish were received by the pope in early June.[66] They travelled by two main routes – most went via Malines in Belgium, Vienna, and Trieste to Ancona, and some via Paris, Marseilles, and Civita Vecchia to Rome. About 1300 men of all social classes arrived in the Papal States. They were eventually formed into eight companies as part of one battalion, called the Battalion of St Patrick. They wore green uniforms with yellow and black. About half were based in the citadel of Ancona and the rest in Spoleto.[67] Their commander was Major Myles O'Reilly, a country gentleman whom Cardinal Cullen introduced to Antonelli as a very devout person of a good family.[68] A small number of English Catholics volunteered as well, and were assigned to the Franco-Belgian Tirailleurs or the Irish brigade.[69]

Like the money, the Irish Catholic men were matched by English volunteers for Garibaldi's forces. About 200 Englishmen went to Sicily in the spring, and another 500 were recruited in London in August by Captain Edward Styles, an English *aide-de-camp* of Garibaldi. Colonel F.W. Peard and a few other officers were already serving Garibaldi. One band of 145 Englishmen captured the island

---

63 G.F.-H. Berkeley, *The Irish battalion in the papal army of 1860* (Dublin: Talbot, 1929), 19–21. In general see also Norman, *Catholic church and Ireland*, 49–51; and Anthony P. Campanella, 'Il battaglione di San Patrizio e la mitica crociata per salvare lo Stato Pontificio nel 1860', *Risorgimento* 22 (1970), 117–34.
64 *The Nation*, from March 1860 onward. Article signed 'C', *Tablet*, 14 April 1860.
65 Odo Russell to Russell, Rome, 10 May 1860, no. 65, PRO, FO, 43/77, and *Odo Russell*, 102.
66 *The Nation*, April and May, *passim*. Apostolic delegate in Ancona to Antonelli, 26 May 1860, ASV, ASdS, 1860, 165/50. *Tablet*, 9 June 1860.
67 Berkeley, *Irish battalion*, 22. By June 25, 1100 volunteers had passed through Malines, Belgium (*Tablet*, 7 July 1860).
68 Cullen to Antonelli, Dublin, 9 June 1860, ASV, ASdS, 1860, 165/50.
69 *Tablet*, 14 July 1860.

Peter's Pence and the Irish Brigade

of Monte Cristo in the Tyrrhenian sea in August *en route* to invade the Papal States.[70]

British subjects, thus, fought for and financed opposing sides of the papal conflict in Italy. The legality of the Irish enlistments was questioned in the House of Commons on 11 May by Grant Duff, member for Elgin. As far as he was concerned, the Irish recruitments for the pope were 'perfectly illegal' while the English enlistments and money for Garibaldi's 'noble cause' were not. The solicitor general made no comment about the troops, but stated that the funds for Garibaldi were not illegal. On the 14th the chief secretary for Ireland said steps would be taken to prevent 'any illegal proceedings' pertaining to Irish enlistments for papal service. A heated debate erupted in the Commons on the 17th in which partisans of Garibaldi and the pope exchanged charges. Soon afterward the government in Dublin issued a police notice listing the provisions of the Foreign Enlistments Act.[71]

On 14 May Charles Newton, the English consul in Rome, requested a ruling from his government on the legal status of the Irish recruits. Officially Russell replied that by enlisting in the papal army they forfeited their rights to British protection, but that the rights would return upon their resignation from papal service. Simultaneously, however, he told Odo to let the Irish use the foreign office mail service to protect their mail to and from Ireland.[72] When the Irish left the papal army in the autumn, Russell arranged free passage back to Ireland, a precedent which worried Gladstone. He did the same for Garibaldi's English volunteers, which upset the queen.[73]

Actually the English government did nothing whatsoever to hinder the enlistments. It was a marked reversal of policy compared to the winter days when Russell worried about and protested against the Austrian recruits for the pope. Cavour tried to provoke Palmerston and Russell into either stopping them or giving counterbalancing support to Sardinia. Palmerston told him not to be concerned.[74] By the time the first Irish arrived in the Papal States, Russell and Palmerston knew that the papal army was no threat to Cavour or Garibaldi.

---

70   Mack Smith, 'L'Inghilterra', 426–7; Mack Smith, *Victor Emmanuel, Cavour*, 164–5; and Mack Smith, *Cavour and Garibaldi*, 224. *Tablet*, 25 August 1860.
71   Hansard's, CLVIII, col. 1128–30, 11 May 1860; col. 1206, 14 May 1860; and col. 1367–412, 17 May 1860. See the subsequent debates, Hansard's, CLVIII, col. 1766–73, 25 May 1860, and CLIX, col. 571–80, 18 June 1860.
72   Newton to Russell, Rome, 14 May 1860, no. 38, PRO, FO, 43/79B. Russell to Odo Russell, 9 July 1860, no. 30 and no. 31, PRO, FO, 43/75.
73   Norman, *Catholic church and Ireland*, 51. Gladstone to Palmerston, 7 and 16 Oct. 1860, *Gladstone and Palmerston, being the correspondence of Lord Palmerston with Mr. Gladstone, 1851–1865*, ed. Philip Guedalla (London: G.P. Putnam's, 1928), 152–3. Queen Victoria to Russell, 26 Jan. 1861, copy, Russell papers, PRO, 30/22/14B.
74   Cavour to Emanuel d'Azeglio, Turin, 4 June 1860, and Emanuel d'Azeglio to Cavour, London, 9 June 1860, *Cavour e l'Inghilterra*, vol. II, part 2, 74–5. PRO, FO, 43/77, and *Odo Russell*, 1–2.

Liberals and the annexation of the Marches and Umbria

They knew as well that their numbers would be strictly limited by the papal government. Antonelli explained to Odo that the pope intentionally declined offers for large numbers of Irish, on the grounds that he needed not an army of conquest but of self-defence, strong enough to allow the French to leave Rome.[75] This was a purpose the English heartily approved. A small number of Irish was all the papal government even wanted to handle. No sooner did the first shipload land than discontent and disorders began among them. Both the papal government and the English consul in Rome and vice-consul in Ancona were kept busy sorting out their complaints. As many as a hundred or more returned home.[76] On 14 July, Antonelli finally pleaded with Cardinal Cullen to stop the departure of any more Irish for Rome and Ancona. They had such a good religious spirit, he said, and the pope was deeply grateful for them, but the pope had enough of them. It would be a drain on papal finances to receive any more. Cullen agreed to do what he could.[77] Russell and Palmerston had no need or wish to infuriate Irish Catholics by interfering with the Irish enlistments. Their political relations with the Irish in Parliament were sensitive already. Besides, the Irish recruits for the pope were a *quid pro quo* for English recruits for Garibaldi. In any case, the disgruntled Irish volunteers were good anti-papal propagandists when they returned to Ireland.[78] Whatever the difficulties with the Irish volunteers, by the time Garibaldi reached the straits of Messina at the end of August, Major O'Reilly and his officers had succeeded in transforming over a thousand of St Patrick's battalion into a fairly well trained organization. On the whole they were crusaders, not mere mercenaries. Lamoricière called them 'magnificent troops', and tried to secure more equipment and materiel for them. The Irish remained at Ancona and Spoleto, but one company was transferred to Perugia in preparation for the coming storm.[79]

The conquest of the Marches and Umbria

Garibaldi crossed the straits of Messina to the boot of Italy on 19 August. He and his Red Shirts moved deliberately up the peninsula toward Naples and Rome, gathering vast popular support and large numbers of recruits along the way. His forces numbered 40,000 by the time he reached Naples on 7 September.

---

75   Odo Russell to Russell, Rome, 10 May 1860, no. 65, PRO, FO, 43/77, and *Odo Russell*, 102.
76   Apostolic delegate in Ancona to Antonelli, 26 May 1860; Apostolic delegate in Macerata to Antonelli, 7, 12, 18 and 24 June 1860; and G. Gaggiotti to Antonelli, Ancona, 11 July 1860, ASV, ASdS, 1860, 165/50. DeLuca to Antonelli, Vienna, 24 June 1860, no. 1038, ASV, ASdS, 1860, 165/42.
77   Antonelli to Cullen, Rome, 14 July 1860, draft, and Cullen to Antonelli, Dublin, 20 July 1860, ASV, ASdS, 1860, 165/50.
78   *Punch* (2 March 1861) imagined the pope reprimanding one of his foreign recruits, a bad little boy who promised never, never, never to do anything bad again.
79   Berkeley, *Irish battalion*, 67 and 90–2. Trevelyan, *Garibaldi and the making of Italy* (London: Longmans, 1911), 207–9.

The conquest of the Marches and Umbria

Calabrian peasants, like their counterparts in Sicily, regarded him with semi-religious awe; many placed his picture in their cottages, shrine-like.

Garibaldi was pledged to King Victor Emmanuel, having publicly declared that his cause was 'Italy and Victor Emmanuel'. He had addressed a proclamation to 'the Romans' which promised to liberate Italy from 'the double tyranny of foreigners and the priests'.[80] The king responded warmly to Garibaldi according to a policy of his own, while Cavour manoeuvred erratically to pre-empt Garibaldi. Early in August the king had sent Garibaldi a message encouraging him to advance toward Naples, and even the Papal States. Contrary to this, Cavour worked to prevent any revolutionary movement against the pope until he could plot his own with Napoleon's permission. Accordingly by 2 August he had successfully stymied an attempt by Bertani, Garibaldi's back-up in Genoa, to begin a new guerrilla invasion of the Papal States from the north, a move Garibaldi desired as a complement to his own from the south. Cavour had not wanted Garibaldi to cross the straits.[81]

Late in July, the French Government, thinking of Rome and the pope, had asked the English to join them in blocking Garibaldi at the straits. Queen Victoria certainly hoped for a way to stop him, and even Lord John would not have minded if he remained in Sicily for now.[82] Garibaldi, however, was confident England would assist him along his way. He wrote to 'the people of Sheffield' in England, in response to their resolution encouraging his campaign,

> England, country of true liberty, cannot be unsympathetic with a people oppressed by a fierce tyranny, now intent on obtaining their proper rights among the free nations ... Sicily is now free ... Protected by God, we will progress on our way. You will not permit the intervention of foreign diplomacy, and Italy will be created by Italians. Italy will be one, independent, free, and worthy of having England for a sister.[83]

Lord John did not disappoint Garibaldi. With the endorsement of the cabinet, he flatly declined to co-operate with the French against Garibaldi, and instead the English fleet permitted Garibaldi to cross the straits. He knew this was a key decision that meant accepting the risk that Garibaldi might attack Rome and eventually Venetia, although he told the French that he was confident Garibaldi would not. By refusing to join with the French Russell insured that they could do nothing to stop Garibaldi's march to Naples and the Papal States.[84]

Russell next made sure the Austrians contemplated nothing drastic. He asked Count Apponyi what the Austrians intended to do as the Red Shirts neared papal

---

80   Proclamation to 'The Romans', 30 April 1860, *Scritti di Garibaldi*, vol. I, 237–8.
81   Mack Smith, *Cavour and Garibaldi*, 127, 143–5, 158.
82   Queen Victoria to Russell, 7 July 1860, copy, Russell papers, PRO, 30/22/14B. Russell to Hudson, 23 July 1860, private, *Gran Bretagna e Sardegna*, vol. VIII, 149.
83   Garibaldi to the people of Sheffield, 13 July 1860, *Scritti di Garibaldi*, vol. I, 274–5.
84   Russell to Cowley, 26 July 1860, no. 741, PRO, FO, 425/62/45–6. Case, *Thouvenel*, 198–201. See the intriguing story of James Lacaita and Russell, in Lacaita, *An Italian Englishman*, 139–41.

territory. He specifically inquired whether they considered reoccupying the Romagna and even the Marches as a way of defending their border at Venetia or as a holy duty in protection of the pope. Apponyi assured him that they would do nothing of the kind. Palmerston conveyed this news to Thouvenel and Cavour. Russell warned Cavour not to provoke Austria over Venetia, because 'Great Britain has interests in the Adriatic which Her Majesty's Government must watch with careful attention.'[85]

Odo Russell observed that, as far as he could tell, Austria had already reoccupied the Marches *de facto* by means of volunteers in the papal army. By the first of September, he reported that more than 8000 Austrians had joined papal ranks, forming special Austrian regiments. Most of them, he said, were former Austrian soldiers, many of whom had served in the Austrian army in Bologna and Ancona before their evacuation in June 1859. They composed a significant portion of Lamoricière's total force which now numbered about 30,000 troops. By contrast, the French army in Rome had about 6000 men.

The papal government earnestly hoped for some direct intervention on its behalf by a Catholic power. Antonelli described his feeling that a storm was about to crash upon them in Rome from all sides. Sacconi held out hope that Austria might help, but he discovered Austria had agreed to abide by England's prohibition of military intervention.[86] Antonelli once again pleaded with Spain for intervention as in 1849. Barili again was told that English and French opposition made it impossible.[87]

Antonelli even tried to force Napoleon to commit himself to the defence of the Papal States, but failed. Thouvenel, on 14 August, gave Sacconi a calculatedly ambiguous statement saying that French troops were in Rome 'as much in defence of the person of the Holy Father as of his authority', and that they would 'combat and suppress any attack and disorder wherever they found it'.[88] Antonelli recognized the inadequacy of such a statement. He had never seriously doubted French protection of the pope in Rome; it was the Marches and Umbria he was anxious about.[89]

85 Russell to Apponyi, 18 August 1860, copy, and Apponyi to Rechberg, London, 18 August 1860, no. 74A–E, HHSA, PA, VIII, 53/38–40. Palmerston to Russell, 21 August 1860, Russell papers, PRO, 30/22/21. Russell to Hudson, 31 Aug. 1860, no. 161, *Gran Bretagna e Sardegna*, vol. VIII, 170. In general on the Venetian question, see Noel Blakiston, ed., *Il problema veneto e l'Europa, 1859–1866* (Venice: Istituto veneto di scienza, lettere, ed arti, 1966), vol. II ('Inghilterra').
86 Sacconi to Antonelli, Paris, 17 August 1860, no. 1586, and 26 August 1860, no. 1591, ASV, ASdS, 1860, 165/44/116–20, and 125–30, and *Antonelli*, vol. II, 568–9 and 574.
87 Queen Isabella to Pius IX, 9 August 1860, Pirri, vol. II, part 2, 166. Antonelli to Barili, 18 Aug. 1860, no. 13338, and Barili to Antonelli, 30 Aug. 1860, no. 638, *Antonelli–Barili*, 225–6 and 228. Sacconi to Antonelli, Paris, 26 August 1860, no. 1591, ASV, ASdS, 1860, 165/44/125, and *Antonelli*, vol. II, 574.
88 Sacconi to Antonelli, Paris, 14 August 1860, no. 1585, ASV, ASdS, 1860, 165/44/112–13, and *Antonelli*, vol. II, 565. Thouvenel to Gramont, Paris, 18 August 1860, AMAE, CP, 1015/108–9.
89 Antonelli to Sacconi, Rome, 24 August 1860, no. 13444, ASV, ANParigi, 1860, SdS, AD/P, and *Antonelli*, vol. II, 571–2.

The conquest of the Marches and Umbria

In the end the pope and Antonelli had only the papal army to rely upon to defend the Marches and Umbria. English diplomacy had helped keep the pope isolated, while Napoleon undermined him, and Cavour and Garibaldi looked for rival ways of overturning him.

After Garibaldi crossed the straits of Messina and began sweeping northward, events moved quickly. The day he learned of Garibaldi's success at Messina, Cavour decided that the time had come to have the Piedmontese army invade the Papal States. He had specifically entertained the idea at least since the annexation of the Romagna in March, and had maintained secret designs on Ancona since Plombières in July 1858. Now he resolved to act, risking everyone's anger. He felt he had to take the revolution away from Garibaldi. If he succeeded, 'the prospective winnings were enormous, nothing less than Sicily, Naples, and the papal provinces of Umbria and the Marches; in other words a half of the whole peninsula'.[90]

Cavour was already armed with Palmerston's unofficial promise not to oppose him, provided he met certain conditions, and Russell's doctrinal distinction between 'aggression' and 'responsive' action favoured him. Cavour simply had to arrange a revolutionary uprising, invade the Papal States, and be sure to stay away from the French and the pope in Rome, and from the Austrians in Venetia. Russell and Palmerston were open to the most far-reaching eventualities. Russell, on 29 August, told Cowley forthrightly, 'the Italians should be able to maintain or change the Governments of Naples and Sicily and of Rome, according to their wishes'.[91] Napoleon met secretly at Chambéry in the Savoy Alps with two representatives from Cavour – Luigi Carlo Farini, now minister of the interior, who earlier had written the history of the Roman States translated by Gladstone, and General Cialdini, chief of the Sardinian army on the papal frontier. Napoleon gave his approval for Sardinia to invade the Marches and Umbria on much the same conditions Palmerston had stated first back in April – provided a revolution broke out and provided the purpose of the invasion was 'to get the revolutionary movement under control'. The plan was to annex the Marches and Umbria to Piedmont and leave the Patrimony of St Peter for the pope. Upon learning the news from Chambéry, Cavour exclaimed, 'The supreme moment has arrived.'[92]

Garibaldi conquered the city of Naples on 7 September. Rome was only three days' march away, and he was ready, in Palmerston's phrase, 'to have dinner in Naples and go to bed in Rome'. The English government earnestly tried to stop Garibaldi from attacking Rome. Henry Elliot, the English ambassador in Naples, at Russell's request, met Garibaldi on the 10th on board a British flagship anchored in Naples Bay. Garibaldi resisted the English diplomat's pressure not to attack the French in Rome, and announced his intention to push on for Rome at once. He would conquer Rome readily, he thought, and offer the

90 Mack Smith, *Cavour and Garibaldi*, 151, 223.
91 Russell to Cowley, 29 August 1860, PRO, FO, 425/62/87.
92 Case, *Thouvenel*, 209–15, and Case, *Franco-Italian relations*, 10–14.

crown of a united Italy to Victor Emmanuel. He hoped the English would continue their diplomatic support.[93]

The English wanted the papal government to know of their efforts to prevent an attack on Rome. Odo gave Antonelli a report of Elliot's conversation with Garibaldi.[94]

The day Garibaldi conquered Naples, Cavour set his finale in motion. He sent Antonelli an ultimatum warning that King Victor Emmanuel could not be passive while foreign troops in the papal army repressed the just discontents and the feelings of nationality of the populations of the Marches and Umbria. Either dismiss the foreign mercenaries, Cavour demanded, or the king would have to intervene to prevent any further threat to the tranquillity of Italy. He could allow no more Perugias. The ultimatum did not cite an uprising as its justification, and that omission got Cavour into trouble with Thouvenel and contributed to restraint from Russell later on.[95]

Cavour's plan continued to unfold. Hudson's duty was to convince the English government that a Sardinian invasion met the conditions Russell and Palmerston had placed on Cavour. On 7 September Hudson informed Russell of the ultimatum, and explained that a revolutionary outbreak in the Marches and Umbria was imminent and could not be stopped – the people under papal tyranny could be kept silent no longer, especially with Garibaldi in Naples. The king of Sardinia intended to intervene, Hudson continued, in order to prevent the march of Garibaldi against the French at Rome and the Austrians at Venetia, and 'to prevent bloodshed and a repetition of the massacres of Perugia in the Papal States'. Hudson's letter read like a prepared script.[96] In fact, on 31 August Palmerston had learned of Cavour's invasion plans well before the ultimatum, through the Rothschild bankers whom Cavour had told confidentially in Turin.[97]

Cavour and the Italian National Society sought to arrange a general revolution in the Marches and Umbria for 8 September. Apparently some kind of demonstrations did occur around Orvieto and a few other places in Umbria. A band of nationalist volunteers secretly entered the Marches from the Romagna, stirred up some action at Montefeltro and captured Urbino. At Ancona the central committee of the National Society for the Marches refused to do anything, and reminded the leaders of the National Society who ordered the revolution that the Marches lacked the spirit for such a thing.[98]

On the 9th Antonelli pointed out that the agitation on the previous day was

93 Elliot to Russell, Naples, 10 Sept. 1860, no. 502, PRO, FO, 425/62/132–3. Emanuel d'Azeglio to Cavour, London, 26 July 1860, no. 189, *Cavour e l'Inghilterra*, vol. II, part 2, 114.
94 Bach to Rechberg, Rome, 22 Sept. 1860, no. 39 C, HHSA, PA, XI, 201/200–1.
95 Cavour to Antonelli, Turin, 7 Sept. 1860, copy, PRO, FO, 425/62/138. Case, *Thouvenel*, 215–18.
96 Hudson to Cavour, Turin, 7 Sept. 1860, no. 346, *Gran Bretagna e Sardegna*, vol. VIII, 174–6.
97 Mack Smith, *Victor Emanuel, Cavour*, 171.
98 Grew, 379–80.

stirred up by armed bands from across the border. Cavour complained on the 10th that Italians in the Marches and Umbria did not know how to sacrifice enough to gain their independence. General Fanti, all set to invade, remarked that the revolt in Umbria did not amount to much.[99]

Never mind. Hudson telegraphed Russell on the 9th, 'Insurrection in Umbria. Deputation from thence expected to arrive in Turin to demand intervention of Sardinia which I believe will be granted.' The delegation duly reached Turin on the 10th, and the next day, 11 September, the Sardinian army invaded the Marches and Umbria.[100] Victor Emmanuel proclaimed to the Sardinian troops, 'You are entering the Marches and Umbria to restore civil order in those desolate cities, and to give to the people the freedom to express their own wishes.' General Cialdini led one army of 25,000 down the Adriatic coast toward Ancona. General Fanti led another of equal strength into Umbria via the Tiber valley toward Perugia. Sardinia, not Garibaldi, invaded the Papal States. Cavour fulfilled his 'long premeditated plan'.[101]

Gramont, the French ambassador in Rome, gave the pope instant hope, and Odo Russell grave alarm, by announcing on the 11th that Napoleon would oppose any invasion and protect the pope not only in Rome, but also in the Marches and Umbria. Lord John refused to believe the news, but told Cowley to inquire about it and speak against it if need be. Meanwhile Cowley had already secured Thouvenel's explicit assurance that French troops would defend Rome only. In his excitement, Gramont, it seems, had made an egregious error, based on what he hoped would happen.[102]

Russell's other concerns were to keep the Austrians and Garibaldi out of the conflict. The English *chargé d'affaires* in Vienna, Julian Fane, reminded Count Rechberg of Austria's policy not to intervene in Italy unless its territory was attacked. Victor Emmanuel requested English assurance that Austria would not attack, and Russell gave it; Russell was looking after Piedmont's interests. In fact, just prior to the invasion Austria briefly contemplated some military intervention against Sardinia, but Napoleon had quashed it.[103] Elliot had already spoken to Garibaldi against attacking Rome. That English objection stood.

99 Antonelli to Sacconi, Rome, 9 Sept. 1860, telegram, *Antonelli*, vol. II, 583. Grew, 381.
100 Hudson to Russell, Turin, 9 and 10 Sept. 1860, telegram, no. 348 and no. 349, *Gran Bretagna e Sardegna*, vol. VIII, 177–8.
101 Victor Emanuel's proclamation, 11 Sept. 1860, translation provided by Hudson, in Hudson to Russell, Turin, 11 Sept. 1860, no. 354, PRO, FO, 425/62/126. The phrase 'long premeditated plan' is Cavour's (Cavour to Nigra, 12 Sept. 1860, *Cavour–Nigra*, vol. IV, 203).
102 Russell to Cowley, Abergeldie, 13 Sept. 1860, private, copy, Russell papers, PRO, 30/22/104. Odo Russell to Russell, Rome, 11 Sept. 1860, no. 119, PRO, FO, 43/77, and excerpted in *Odo Russell*, 124–5. Cowley to Russell, Paris, 11 Sept. 1860, no. 1200, PRO, FO, 425/62/119. Odo Russell to Russell, Rome, 25 Sept. 1860, private, Russell papers, PRO, 30/22/75, and *Odo Russell*, 130–1.
103 Fane to Russell, Vienna, 13 Sept. 1860, no. 96, PRO, FO, 425/62/136–7. Russell to Hudson, 20 Sept. 1860, telegram, no. 169, *Gran Bretagna e Sardegna*, vol. VIII, 184. Case, *Franco-Italian relations*, 23.

Russell summarized his concern: 'The steps Garibaldi has already made are wonderful and if he has but discretion enough to stop now and give up his mission to Victor Emmanuel he will be as great a statesman as he is a patriot and warrior.' Russell directed considerable diplomatic effort during the coming weeks to prevent any aggression against Rome and Venetia.[104]

Baron Bach apparently discussed Austrian intervention with Antonelli, and considered joint action by all the Catholic powers. French and English opposition would prevent it, however. This time Spain sent inquiries to Paris and Vienna to see whether some kind of joint action by Catholic powers might be plausible, but nothing came of it, again because England and France would oppose it. The French gave Antonelli the excuse that they did not resort to arms to defend the pope because England would oppose them.[105]

The enthusiasm among English people generally for the invasion was immense. What caused the joy was that Piedmont had attacked the pope's own territory. It was the most direct way there was of extending 'civil and religious liberty among that great and long oppressed People'. Virtually all but Catholics were thrilled by it.[106] The Liberal government, by contrast, was officially restrained. Personally, Russell and Palmerston immediately approved of the invasion, although they knew Cavour had contrived it. Russell ordered Hudson not to express any opinion to Cavour about it until instructed to do so; he wanted to see how the other powers would react.[107] Count Corti, the Sardinian *chargé d'affaires*, explained to Cavour his analysis of why the government was so reserved: 'The reason is that the present position of the parties in the House of Commons is such that voting of the "Irish brigade" sometimes decides the majority. For if they had encouraged in any way an attack against the Pope their hatred against it would become implacable.'[108]

Despite official restraint the English government's approval of the invasion was conspicuous. As Mgr DeLuca in Vienna noted, England was the only great power, including France, who did not protest the invasion. Sacconi observed

---

104   Russell to Palmerston, 11 Sept. 1860, Palmerston papers, 1860, GC/RU/622. Hudson to Russell, Turin, 15 Sept. 1860, telegram, no. 370, *Gran Bretagna e Sardegna*, vol. VIII, 370. When Garibaldi in October did just what Russell had hoped, and turned his conquests over to Victor Emanuel, *Punch* (27 Oct. 1860) likened it to a card game. Garibaldi was winning all the hands for the sake of Italy, while a crazed pope and a bewildered king of Naples kept losing. When the heroic and dashing Victor Emmanuel replaced Garibaldi they all knew the game would soon be over.

105   Bach to Rechberg, Rome, 22 Sept. 1860, no. 39B, HHSA, PA, XI, 201/190–5. Antonelli to DeLuca, Rome, 14 Sept. 1860, no. 13981, and 29 Sept. 1860, no. 14213, ASV, ANVienna, 376/770–1 and 796–7. Barili to Antonelli, 12 Sept. 1860, no. 643, *Antonelli–Barili*, 231–4.

106   Count Wimpflen to Rechberg, London, no. 83, 18 Sept. 1860, HHSA, PA, VIII, 53/214. The phrase in quotes is Lord Shaftesbury's (Shaftesbury to Cavour, Paris, 12 Sept. 1860, *Cavour e l'Inghilterra*, vol. II, part 2, 123).

107   See Russell to Cowley, Abergeldic, 13 Sept. 1860, private, copy, Russell papers, PRO, 30/22/104. Russell to Hudson, 14 Sept. 1860, telegram, no. 163, *Gran Bretagna e Sardegna*, vol. VIII, 182.

108   Corti to Cavour, London, 13 Sept. 1860, *Cavour e l'Inghilterra*, vol. II, part 2, 124.

The conquest of the Marches and Umbria

similarly that England was the only power not to break diplomatic relations with Piedmont. The papal government protested to the diplomatic corps in Rome, including Odo Russell, and Sacconi especially sought out Cowley to present the protest. England gave the pope no solace and was the only power not to do so. Loftus did express the opinion to DeLuca that Sardinia acted in a most uncivilized manner, but that was merely his personal view.[109] The French protest was a ruse, as Cowley sensed, a way for Napoleon to 'throw dirt into the eyes of his loving subjects' while rejoicing in his heart 'that between Sardinia and Garibaldi nothing but Rome will be left to His Holiness'. The papal government was not fooled by it.[110]

Meanwhile, the Piedmontese invasion became conquest as their armies pursued their parallel routes from town to town – though Città di Castello, Perugia and Spoleto in Umbria, and Pesaro, Urbino, Fano and Senigallia in the Marches. The army from Umbria advanced to Macerata. The Piedmontese navy moved a small fleet from the Tyrrhenian into the Adriatic, with the British fleet watching and letting it happen. Everything focussed on Ancona. The decisive battle occurred on 18 September a few miles south of Ancona, near Castelfidardo, where Lamoricière's troops were overwhelmed. A land siege and naval blockade of Ancona commenced in earnest thereafter and lasted until the city fell at the end of September. With that event the temporal power was ended in the Marches as well as Umbria.

Irish soldiers fought in the battles of Perugia, Spoleto, Castelfidardo and Ancona. Lamoricière spoke well of their service. They had worked hard with inadequate arms to uphold the temporal power of the pope.[111]

Before Sardinia's conquest was concluded, the French government ordered several thousand troops to reinforce the Rome garrison. During the first two weeks of October they occupied several major towns outside Rome – Viterbo, Tivoli, Frosinone, and others – in order to secure the Patrimony of St Peter for the pope. With that the boundaries of what remained of the temporal power were drawn for the next ten years.[112]

On 19 September, the day after the papal defeat at Castelfidardo, Palmerston finally informed Emanuel d'Azeglio officially that the English completely

109   Antonelli to the diplomatic corps, Vatican, 18 Sept. 1860, *Antonelli*, vol. II, 598–9. Antonelli to DeLuca, Rome, 19 Sept. 1860, no. 13981, ASV ANVienna, 376/770–1. DeLuca to Antonelli, Vienna, 25 Sept. 1860, no. 1125, ASV ASdS, 1860, 165/42/114–15. Sacconi to Antonelli, Paris, 5 Oct. 1860, no. 1622, ASV, ASdS, 1860, 165/44/177–81, and *Antonelli*, vol. II, 616.
110   Cowley to Russell, Paris, 11 Sept. 1860, private, copy, PRO, FO, 519/228/1–2. Case, *Thouvenel*, 215–25. Sacconi to Antonelli, Paris, 11 Sept. 1860, no. 1603, ASV, ASdS, 1860, 165/44/142–5, and *Antonelli*, vol. II, 585–6.
111   Hudson's despatches give Piedmontese progress reports during this period. On the Irish, see Berkeley, *The Irish battalion*, *passim*, who praises the Irish. Campanella (128, 131–2) claims the Irish did poorly. Odo Russell to Russell, Rome, 17 Nov. 1860, no. 172, PRO, FO, 43/78, and *Odo Russell*, 137–9.
112   Odo Russell to Russell, Rome, 5 and 13 Oct. 1860, private, Russell papers, PRO, 30/22/75, and excerpted in *Odo Russell*, 133–4.

approved the Piedmontese conquest of the Papal States. Russell approved the blockade of Ancona, even though it, as well as the whole invasion, spoiled British trade. He helped Cavour by reminding him to conduct the blockade according to international law. He and Palmerston were gratified at the fall of Ancona. On the 21st Russell told Austria that England approved the Piedmontese action. He followed Cavour's line about the conquest and justified it: ' It was the business of the king to command and regulate the movement; to put down anarchy by force; and to substitute orderly government for the oppression which crushed and the insurrection which convulsed the Italian provinces. The last hope for Italy lay in the success of the King of Sardinia.'[113] The conquest was a *fait accompli* which, for Russell and Palmerston, had the advantage of being right.

The annexation of the Marches and Umbria

The conquest of the Papal States in September was not the end of the matter. Sardinia had to annex the Marches and Umbria, and annexation was not to be taken for granted. Cavour and Victor Emmanuel faced solid opposition from Austria, Prussia, Russia, Spain, Portugal, and Bavaria. The French opposition, although a charade, complicated the situation; Napoleon's behaviour was unpredictable. All the powers, except England, thought instinctively of calling a congress of the European powers to treat Italian affairs. Cavour asked the English government to keep a congress from convening. He hoped Russell and Palmerston would overcome their hesitations toward him and give him their full moral support:

> ... we need the support of England. We ask not for material support but its 'moral support' to keep the other powers, whether friends or foes, from meddling in our affairs, as well as to encourage by its approval the efforts of the great national party to continue the Italian movement along the ways of order and moderation that it has followed up to now.[114]

Palmerston and Russell did provide support through their diplomacy, but still not without being slightly wary of Cavour. They urged Cavour to carry on from Ancona to Naples, to unite his conquests with Garibaldi's, but repeatedly warned him to remain clear of Rome.[115] Russell added that Cavour should convene 'a Parliament of all Italy, exclusive of Rome and Venetia, ... to settle the destiny of their country'.[116] Russell and Palmerston also specifically used

---

113   Emanuel d'Azeglio to Cavour, London, 19 Sept. 1860, *Cavour e l'Inghilterra*, vol. II, part 2, 125. Russell to Hudson, 18 Sept. 1860, telegram, no. 168, *Gran Bretagna e Sardegna*, vol. VIII, 184. Russell to Palmerston, 30 Sept. 1860, Palmerston papers, 1860, GC/RU/625. Russell to Fane, 21 Sept. 1860, no. 34, PRO, FO, 425/62/142.
114   Cavour to Lord Shaftesbury, Turin, 22 Sept. 1860, and Cavour to Emanuel d'Azeglio, Turin, 22 Sept. 1860, *Cavour e l'Inghilterra*, vol. II, part 2, 126–7.
115   Emanuel d'Azeglio to Cavour, London, 24 Sept. 1860 (two letters), and 29 Sept. 1860, *Cavour e l'Inghilterra*, vol. II, part 2, 129–31 and 134–6.
116   Russell to Palmerston, 27 Sept. 1860, Palmerston papers, 1860, GC/RU/624.

their influence to prevent a congress. At first they considered attending one in order to oppose armed intervention in the Marches and Umbria or Naples. In October, however, they decided the whole idea was harmful and supported France when Thouvenel said his government would not propose or endorse one. Then, at the end of October when Napoleon still toyed with the congress idea, Cowley argued against it once again. When Spain called for a conference of Catholic powers, Russell labelled the project 'absurd' and supported French rejection of it as well.[117] Sacconi was told that the reason a congress, which the papal government wanted, could not meet was because of the opposition by England and France to intervention in Italian affairs.[118]

On all these matters concerning the pope, England's policy coincided remarkably with the French. One point on which the two powers differed, however, was the French occupation of Rome. On 22 September, as soon as the English government learned of a plan to increase substantially the number of French troops in Rome, Russell objected emphatically. He decided to give the pope no respite. He issued an important policy despatch in which he asserted that the reinforcement of the garrison in Rome was an admission that if the Romans were left to themselves, together with 'such assistance as they might receive from their fellow countrymen in other parts of Italy', they would overthrow the papal monarchy. It was more evident than ever, he said, that the pope was entirely dependent upon the French for the very existence of the temporal power in Rome. It was a sham to claim that papal temporal power, as now constituted, rendered the pope independent of all political powers. Then Russell came to his conclusion: 'If such be the pope's condition, it would be far better that his person should be protected by the troops of an Italian Sovereign, who would respect his spiritual authority, and give relief to his temporal subjects.' On 15 October, Russell reiterated his conclusions in a despatch to Odo Russell in Rome.[119]

Thouvenel responded to Russell's statement by remarking that England needed to be patient with France and to understand the pope's tenacity of purpose. Thouvenel reminded Russell that the English government also had a

---

117   Russell to Palmerston, 30 Sept. 1860, Palmerston papers, 1860, GC/RU/625. Russell to Cowley, 13 Oct. 1860, no. 1007, PRO, FO, 425/62/208. Cowley to Russell, Paris, 25 Oct. 1860, private, copy, Cowley papers, PRO, FO, 519/228/41.
118   Sacconi to Antonelli, Paris, 12 Oct. 1860, no. 1628, ASV, ASdS, 1860, 165/44/193–4, and *Antonelli*, vol. II, 622–3.
119   Russell to Cowley, 22 Sept. 1860, no. 954, PRO, FO, 425/62/152. Russell to Odo Russell, 15 Oct. 1860, no. 35, PRO, FO, 43/75; the draft of this despatch was misdated 15 Feb. *Punch* had some fun with the notion that Napoleon was now 'solely responsible' for the pope's temporal power. In one cartoon (13 Oct. 1860) Napoleon consoled a very distraught pope by promising to 'look after your little temporal matters'. In another (8 Dec. 1860), the emperor as 'The Eldest Son of the Church' admired his handsome bearing as he tried on the papal tiara – reminiscent of the first Napoleon's self-coronation in Pius VII's presence in Paris in 1804.

Liberals and the annexation of the Marches and Umbria

political interest in the continued well-being of the pope. Reluctantly the English government accepted the perpetuation of the French occupation of Rome. Palmerston had suggested to Russell that the French occupation could be regarded as opportune, since it would give Cavour time to consolidate his vast conquests: 'Let him [Garibaldi] and let Cavour take possession of all the Roman States except the neighbourhood of Rome and the country between it and Civita Vecchia, and they may rest awhile and digest what they have swallowed up.' When the French not only reinforced their garrison but also extended their occupation to include most of the Patrimony of St Peter, Russell and Palmerston were angry.[120]

In spite of the French troop activity, there were recurrent rumours that the pope might voluntarily leave Rome. Spain, Bavaria, even Trieste were mentioned as hospitable places for his exile. Pius IX was indeed greatly troubled by the Piedmontese war against him and Napoleon's connivance with Cavour. Mgr George Talbot, the pope's English chamberlain, admitted to Cardinal Wiseman on 29 September that 'we are in a state of complete consternation'. Talbot himself believed the pope could very well decide to leave Rome.[121] Palmerston and Russell briefly enjoyed imagining a rapid finish to the papal question. Lord Cowley expressed it: 'I wish with all my heart he [the pope] would go, for I see little hope of tranquillity in Italy as long as Rome is in his hands.' They even told the Piedmontese that if such a thing happened Sardinia would be free, as far as England was concerned, to move in and take over the Holy City. Odo Russell, however, constantly advised Lord John that he did not believe the pope had any other thought than remaining in Rome until he died. The pope, said Odo, preferred martyrdom.[122]

Cavour proceeded to establish via the Sardinian parliament the means to annex the Marches, Umbria, Naples and Sicily – as in the case of the Romagna and the duchies, he would arrange plebiscites based on universal suffrage. Meanwhile Victor Emmanuel personally went to Ancona, arriving on 3 October, and arranged to advance with the Piedmontese troops into the territory of Naples to connect with Garibaldi. On Cavour's behalf, Hudson asked Russell to endorse the plebiscites. Russell had his reservations – the plebiscites could back-fire and the difficulties of amalgamating the south with the north would be great – but he agreed. His statement of approval had anti-Catholic overtones:

120   Cowley to Russell, Chantilly, 27 Sept. 1860, private, copy, Cowley papers, PRO, FO, 519/228/20. Emanuel d'Azeglio to Cavour, Broadlands, 29 Sept. 1860, *Cavour e l'Inghilterra*, vol. II, part 2, 136. Odo Russell to Russell, Rome, 29 Sept. 1860, no. 145, confidential, PRO, FO, 43/77, and 4 Dec. 1860, no. 183, PRO, FO, 43/78, and excerpted in *Odo Russell*, 131–2, and 142.
121   George Talbot to Wiseman, Vatican, 29 Sept. 1860, Wiseman papers, W3/20. George Talbot to George Paterson, Vatican, 29 Sept. 1860, copy, Wiseman papers, Pre-1865, 137/26.
122   Cowley to Russell, Paris, 25 Sept. 1860, no. 1250, and no. 1254, PRO, FO, 425/62/167 and 169. Palmerston to Russell, 19 Sept. 1860, Russell papers, PRO, 30/22/21. Emanuel d'Azeglio to Cavour, 1 Oct. 1860, *Cavour e l'Inghilterra*, vol. II, part 2, 139.

The annexation of the Marches and Umbria

> Universal suffrage is no favorite of mine, and I should be afraid that a few sweating madonnas and canting friars might pervert that mode of voting into a machinery for restoring Francis the 2nd of pious memory. However 'a fool knows more in his own house than a wise man in someone else's house', and as Cavour is no 'fool' and I am not 'wise' I bow readily to his authority. The project has indeed a Gallic taste in it which I do not fancy.

Russell was willing to overcome his hesitations about Cavour and universal suffrage in order to enable annexations to succeed. On 19 October, in reply, Hudson passionately appealed to Russell to give Cavour the unreserved moral support he desired. If England did this, he urged, it would rout the 'sweating madonnas' and 'canting friars' in Italy as well as the 'pious' conservative and Catholic powers in Europe. He continued, 'In point of fact, to sum up the "situation" into a phrase – if Italy is now to belong to the Italians, it will be by and through the British Government, and this Cavour and all Italians not only feel but say.'[123]

Two developments at the end of October impressed upon Palmerston and Russell the need to give Cavour more than restrained approval if the Piedmontese conquest of the Papal States and Garibaldi's conquest of Naples were to survive. The first was a forthcoming conference of the emperors of Austria, Prussia and Russia scheduled to meet at Warsaw on 22 October. The papal government had definite hopes that the three emperors would decide to intervene on its behalf. Napoleon was worried about such a possibility and sought to forestall it. The English government continued to hope that Austria would keep her commitment not to intervene and once again, on 16 October, and upon Cavour's request, assured Piedmont Austria would stay uninvolved. But Russell had some doubts.[124] Just before the Warsaw conference Russell had Lord Loftus speak to the Austrian government about it. Loftus, along with the French ambassador in Vienna, obtained a renewed pledge from Austria that it would not attack Sardinia. Russell earlier had instructed the English ambassadors in Berlin and St Petersburg to oppose intervention by those courts.[125] The other development was the news from Napoleon on 25 October that the queen of Spain was determined to send an expedition to aid the pope. Napoleon suggested a joint English–French naval action in the Mediterranean to prevent it if necessary.

123 The proverb Russell quoted was in Spanish: 'Mas sabe el necio en su casa que el cuerdo en la agena', Russell to Hudson, Mayence, 11 Oct. 1860, private, and Hudson to Russell, Turin, 19 Oct. 1860, private, *Gran Bretagna e Sardegna*, vol. VIII, 190–1, and 208.
124 Hudson to Russell, Turin, 15 Oct. 1860, telegram, private, and Russell to Hudson, 16 Oct. 1860, telegram, no. 184, *Gran Bretagna e Sardegna*, vol. VIII, 203.
125 Palmerston to Emanuel d'Azeglio, 21 Oct. 1860, *Cavour e l'Inghilterra*, vol. II, part 2, 148–9. Russell to Crampton, 4 Oct. 1860, no. 129, PRO, FO, 62/180 (an identical despatch was sent to Bloomfield in Berlin). English diplomacy had more of a role in discouraging intervention by the three emperors than is usually recognized, as, for example, by Case, *Franco-Italian relations*, 23–5.

Liberals and the annexation of the Marches and Umbria

As if the threats of Austrian and Spanish intervention were not enough, Cowley reported on 26 October his own uncertainty about Napoleon's intentions. Cowley admitted to Russell that he thought it possible that the emperor would 'play the game of the reactionary party, unless he is afraid of our assistance in defending the cause of the Italians'. By now Napoleon not only had his troops stationed throughout the Patrimony, but he had decided to situate the French fleet at Gaeta to protect the king of Naples from Garibaldi and Cavour.[126]

Palmerston was ready on 26 October to threaten Spain that England would use its fleet to stop a military expedition to support the pope. Simultaneously he wanted to pressure Napoleon to remove his troops from the newly occupied territory of the Patrimony and confine them to Rome and a few miles around. On the 27th Russell admitted he might be willing to make an armed threat against Austria, telling Cowley that England 'might I think very well defend Italy if Austria were so imprudent as to revive her views of supremacy and attack Italy'.[127]

Cowley concluded on 26 October that 'the moment is certainly critical'. Russell and Palmerston felt an urgent necessity to take decisive action. They wanted to preserve Cavour's victory over the pope and Garibaldi's over Naples, and simultaneously to prevent any armed interference by Spain, or Austria, or any other power in support of the pope.

In such a context, on 27 October, Russell sent Hudson a sensational despatch which had the character of a proclamation, and all the flourish of his letter to the Bishop of Durham in 1850. He believed Sardinia needed decisive help from England. He announced England's unqualified acceptance of the Sardinian conquest and the overthrow of the papal temporal power. He had wanted to threaten the use of English naval force against any interfering power, but Queen Victoria and Prince Albert would not hear of it. They approved what Russell did send because 'it was so much less bad than what they had been led to expect'.[128] Russell completely accepted Cavour's version of the events and adapted it, for England's sake, to a Whig interpretation of history. He categorically rejected every important point of the papal interpretation of the story. The events in the Papal States and Naples, Russell claimed, constituted a valid Italian revolution,

126   Cowley to Russell, Paris, 25 and 26 Oct. 1860, private, copies, Cowley papers, PRO, FO, 519/228/40–1 and 46.
127   Palmerston to Russell, 26 Oct. 1860, Russell papers, PRO, 30/22/21, and Russell to Cowley, 27 Oct. 1860, private, copy, Russell papers, PRO, 30/22/104.
128   Russell to Hudson, 27 Oct. 1860, no. 195, *Gran Bretagna e Sardegna*, vol. VIII, 217–20. Beales, *England and Italy*, 156. Beales interprets this despatch – I think incorrectly – as Russell's belated contrition for not supporting the annexationist movement more unquestioningly. In fact, the document is entirely consistent with Russell's and Palmerston's long-standing policy to endorse Cavour's action against the pope and to support Garibaldi's achievements. It is a rousing attempt to consolidate and preserve an outcome that neither the English nor Cavour anticipated in advance, and to do so against plausibly ominous threats by the other four great powers.

akin to England's own 'Glorious revolution' of 1688. He regarded it to be a genuine expression of the will of the people by which they arose to overthrow unjust governments, and to secure independence from foreign control by means of the formation of 'one, strong Government for the whole of Italy'. He rejected the pope's contention that the mass of his people were loyal to him and that the revolution was the product of outside agitators and foreign adventurers. The English government, said Russell, had decided 'that the Italians themselves are the best judge of their own interests', and so would not question their actions any further. They had succeeded in avoiding the 'extreme views of democrats' and vindicating 'Constitutional Monarchy'. As a result, he declared, England rejected the censures against the revolution made by Austria, France, Prussia and Russia: 'Her Majesty's Government will turn their eyes rather to the gratifying prospects of a people building up the edifice of their liberties, and consolidating the work of their independence, amid the sympathies and good wishes of Europe.'

Russell felt good about his despatch, but he and Palmerston did not consider it sufficient to cope with the tremendous danger they perceived from the other powers. They were ready to go further to preserve the Italian revolution. Their fears were mitigated, however, by the news they learned from around Europe. First, on 29 October, Russell received from Madrid a flat denial that the Spanish government would intervene – the queen of Spain might wish it, but her government would not allow it. From Paris, Cowley reported still another affirmation by the Austrian government that it would not under any circumstance intervene. From Warsaw came the news that none of the three emperors wished anything to do with armed intervention.[129] The papal government was as disappointed as the English were pleased.

Just to make sure, Russell still proposed, on 30 October, taking the ultimate step of threatening armed intervention to prevent armed intervention by any other power in defence of the pope or in opposition to Piedmont: 'I therefore propose a circular to all the 7 Powers of Vienna telling them that if beyond the excepted cases of Rome and its neighbourhood, and Venetia, the principle of nonintervention is infringed we shall hold ourselves free to act as etc., etc., etc.'[130] Russell prepared a draft by 2 November which disturbed the queen tremendously. Its wording was imprecise and vague, yet it said two things unmistakeably. It expressed the hope that Rome and Venice would follow the rest of Italy in overthrowing their sovereigns and uniting with Piedmont. Then it implied the threat to use English armed force against the other powers for Italy's

---

129 Sir A. Buchanan (English ambassador in Madrid) to Russell, Madrid, 29 Oct. 1860, telegram, and 30 Oct. 1860, no. 341, PRO, FO, 425/63/51. Cowley to Russell, Paris, 30 Oct. 1860, private, copy, Cowley papers, PRO, FO, 519/228/49–51. Loftus to Russell, Vienna, 1 Nov. 1860, no. 502, most confidential, PRO, FO, 425/63/48–9. Case, *Franco-Italian relations*, 23–6.
130 Russell to Palmerston, 30 Oct. 1860, Palmerston papers, 1860, GC/RU/631.

sake. Victoria commented, 'the Queen, for one, is not prepared to decide to go to war to secure the success of the Italian revolution'.[131]

The November diplomatic circular was never sent. In fact, it was unnecessary. The moment of perceived danger from the other powers of Europe had passed. Each power for its own reasons had decided against intervention in support of the pope.

The annexations in central and southern Italy proceeded along a rapid schedule. On 4 and 5 November plebiscites were conducted in the Marches and Umbria under the control of the Piedmontese, with the Piedmontese army on hand. A carnival atmosphere was again created around the polling stations. As in the Romagna, the vote overwhelmingly favoured annexation. It was marred, from Piedmont's point of view, by a reported boycott by peasants under the influence of their parish priests. The plebiscites in Naples and Sicily were held earlier on 21 Ocober. On 8 November Garibaldi officially handed over his power to Victor Emmanuel at Naples, as Russell and Palmerston had hoped, and retired to Caprera off the north-east tip of the island of Sardinia. Victor Emmanuel officially accepted the votes of the Marches and Umbria on 22 November.[132]

Russell's despatch of 27 October, even without hinting at English armed intervention, was accomplishing everything Russell and Palmerston hoped that a threat of armed force would achieve. Cavour had leaked a copy to the press immediately. It provided timely and decisive diplomatic support for Cavour, Garibaldi and Victor Emmanuel, and against the papacy. Both in Italy and among the powers everyone knew that England accepted the overthrow of papal temporal power and the concommitant aggrandizement of Piedmont, and that England would allow nothing to reverse those events.

The principals on all sides of the conflict recognized how decisive English diplomacy and particularly the 27 October despatch were. The discussion of the despatch extended into 1861. When Cavour first read the despatch, according to Hudson's account, 'he shouted, rubbed his hands, jumped up, sat down again; then he began to think, and when he looked up tears were standing in his eyes'. Cavour personally thanked Lord John for the despatch coming as it did just when Piedmont was being isolated from the rest of Europe. England's moral support, he said, will enable the Italians to build their national edifice as 'the splendid temple of civil and religious liberty on the continent', and to join

---

131 A draft copy of the circular is in Russell papers, PRO, 30/22/14B. Queen Victoria to Russell, 3 Nov. 1860, copy, Russell papers, PRO, 30/22/14B.
132 See Gaggiotti to Hudson, Ancona, 6 Nov. 1860, *Gran Bretagna e Sardegna*, vol. VIII, 234. Two other tiny and separate areas, both south of the Patrimony, also overthrew papal rule and joined to Piedmont – on October 25 the ancient papal duchy of Benevento, and on 25 and 26 December the area of Pontecorvo (Gregorovius, 11 Nov. 1860, and 6 Jan. 1861, 110, 119). Mack Smith, *Cavour and Garibaldi*, ch. 25 and 26. *Punch* (17 Nov. 1860) saw Garibaldi as the humble hero fitting the boot of Italy on the foot of gallant Victor Emanuel. If because of Rome and Venetia the boot will not quite go on, a little more gun powder will finish the job.

The annexation of the Marches and Umbria

England, that 'classical land of liberty'.[133] In a statement to the people of Glasgow who had supported him, Garibaldi confessed his belief that 'England was the representative of God' in the conflict against 'tyranny and evil priests'.[134] Victor Emmanuel, in his speech opening the new Piedmontese parliament on 18 February 1861, publicly thanked England, 'the long established land of liberty', for proclaiming aloud 'our right to be arbiters of our own destiny'.[135] Odo Russell described most dramatically and hyperbolically the impact of the despatch upon the liberal nationalists:

> Ever since your famous despatch to Sir James on the 27th, you are blessed night and morning by twenty millions of Italians. I could not read it myself without deep emotion and the moment it was published in Italian, thousands of people copied it from each other to carry it to their homes and weep over it for joy and gratitude in the bosom of their families, away from bruted mercenaries and greasy priests.[136]

On the other side of the conflict, George Talbot called Russell's despatch 'the most unprincipled document that ever was written by a Minister of any civilized court'.[137] The papal government officially condemned the Piedmontese conquest of the Papal States and on 17 December Pius IX delivered an allocution against it. He and Antonelli affirmed all the principles and all the interpretations of the course of events in the Marches and Umbria that Russell had denied. Mgr DeLuca in Vienna called Russell's policy an invitation 'to abandon Italy to the unbridled fury of impiety, of revolution, and of the most immodest perfidy'. Mgr Megli, auditor of the Paris nunciature, commented that Russell's doctrines 'justified the revolutionaries of every country' except in England itself – there Russell talked quite differently about the discontents of the Irish Catholics and their right of rebellion.[138]

Pius IX received Odo Russell in a special audience on 16 January 1861, and defended the papal temporal power against Russell's claims. It was a lively and spirited debate – the pope criticized the English government and Odo defended it. Pius reiterated his belief that his people still loved him and that they were not yet sufficiently mature to determine their own affairs. He charged that England was not animated by disinterested motives as it pretended, but was 'guided by commercial interests and selfish ends'. Above all, he said, England was motivated by profound abhorrence of the papacy and pursued a deliberate policy

---

133 Hudson to Russell, Turin, 2 Nov. 1860, private, *Gran Bretagna e Sardegna*, vol. VIII, 224–5. Cavour to Russell, Turin, 16 Nov. 1860, *Cavour e l'Inghilterra*, vol. II, part 2, 158.
134 Garibaldi to the Glasgow Committee, Caprera, 30 Nov. 1860, *Scritti di Garibaldi*, vol. I, 337–8.
135 Victor Emmanuel's speech, 18 Feb. 1861, translation provided by Hudson, PRO, FO, 425/64/99–100.
136 Odo Russell to Russell, Rome, 1 Dec. 1860, Spencer Walpole, *Life of Lord John Russell*, vol. II, 328.
137 George Talbot to Henry Edward Manning, Vatican, 3 Jan. 1860, Manning papers, Talbot–Manning correspondence.
138 DeLuca to Antonelli, Vienna, 7 Nov. 1860, no. 1146, ASV, ASdS, 1860, 165/42/137. Megli to Antonelli, Paris, 10 Nov. 1860, ASV, ASdS, 1860, 165/44/212.

of undermining papal authority. Odo paraphrased the pope's words: 'England is ever at work against us . . . favouring and assisting revolution. Your people hate the Pope, your Parliament hates the Pope, your ministers and especially your uncle hate the Pope.'[139]

Russell's and Palmerston's policy and the despatch of 27 October received wide acclaim in England itself. But there was surprisingly significant opposition to it. For weeks afterward, Queen Victoria and Prince Albert continued to be 'anything but pleased with the revolutionary doctrines' Russell had enunciated.[140] The Tories demonstrated that, close as they were to the Whig–Liberals in opposition to the papacy, their views on the Italian revolution were not identical. At the opening of the new session of Parliament on 5 February, Lord Derby in the House of Lords and Disraeli in the Commons called the Sardinian invasion of the Papal States strictly illegal. They charged that Russell's policy was 'to preach the principle of insurrection and promulgate a theory of revolution'.[141]

Immediately after the plebiscites in Naples and the Marches and Umbria, the English government indirectly accepted the votes by closing the English mission in Naples. Lord John planned to attach Odo to the English mission in Turin, but Antonelli requested some alternative arrangement. The cardinal suggested Paris, half tongue-in-cheek. On 17 November, Lord John instructed Odo to remain in Rome officially employed in 'special service under the immediate order of the Secretary of State for Foreign Affairs'. Antonelli was grateful for this small consideration of his desires amid overwhelming English opposition to the papal temporal power.[142]

On 11 November, from his retirement in Caprera, Garibaldi issued an address to the 'Italians of Naples'. He stated what virtually all parties to the conflict regarded as an obvious thought – Rome and Venetia were next. 'Rome and Venetia await my help. They too are part of Italy, their inhabitants are our brothers, and they now groan under the hard bondage of Austria and the Pope.'[143] Cavour and Garibaldi both believed that Rome had to be the capital of a new Italy. For the time being, however, no one was prepared to do anything to revolutionize Rome. Piedmont in less than two years had annexed vast territory – the duchies of Parma, Modena and Tuscany, the kingdom of Naples, as well as all of the States of the Church except for Rome and the Patrimony of St Peter. It

139   Odo Russell to Russell, Rome, 16 Jan. 1860, no. 5, secret, PRO, FO, 43/83A, and *Odo Russell*, 152–9.
140   Earl of Clarendon to Cowley, 24 Dec. 1860, Cowley papers, PRO, FO, 519/178.
141   Hansard's, CLIX, col. 21–30, and 67–81, 5 Feb. 1861.
142   Odo Russell to Russell, Rome, 6 Nov. 1860, private, Russell papers, PRO, 30/22/75, and excerpted in *Odo Russell*, 135–7. Russell to Odo Russell, 17 Nov. 1860, no. 38, PRO, FO, 43/75.
143   Garibaldi to the Italians of Naples, Caprera, 11 Nov. 1869, *Scritti di Garibaldi*, vol. I, 332–3.

The annexation of the Marches and Umbria

was time to pause, and as Russell was in the habit of saying to Cavour, time to consolidate the acquisitions already made.

On 11 November Russell anticipated Cavour. He wrote to Palmerston, 'We must recognize the New Kingdom of Italy, I think, without further delay.' Palmerston reminded him to be patient – the kingdom of Italy had to be established before England could recognize it. That culminating act came in March 1861. England was the first power to grant Italy diplomatic recognition.[144] The Marches and Umbria joined the Romagna in accepting Victor Emmanuel as the new king of Italy. Only in Rome and the Patrimony of St Peter was the pope still monarch.

144   Russell to Palmerston, 11 Nov. 1860, Palmerston papers, 1860, GC/RU/634. Palmerston to Russell, 11 Nov. 1860, Russell papers, PRO, 30/22/21. Russell to Queen Victoria, 13 Nov. 1860, RA J31/65. Emanuel d'Azeglio to Cavour, London, telegram, 30 March 1861, *Cavour e l'Inghilterra*, vol. II, part 2, 203.

Conclusion

The end of the papal temporal power outside the city and region of Rome, and the formation of the unified kingdom of Italy turned out to be two distinct sides of the same events between 1858 and 1861. What the pope lost, Italy gained. The process which yielded unification, rather than some other result, was not straightforward and not at all inevitable. The Tory government before June 1859 did not even consider the possibility of political unification of the whole peninsula. The Liberals only came to consider it as an option in the summer of 1860, and even then they regarded it as not unquestionably desirable. Unification was forced on England as well as Italy by Garibaldi, the annexationists among the liberal nationalists, and belatedly by Cavour. Russell's decisive 27 October despatch marked English acceptance of a *fait accompli*.

The overthrow of the pope was different, however. Both the Tory and the Liberal leadership envisioned and actually advocated the end of most of the temporal power from the very beginning of the new crisis in Italy. At the end of 1858, Malmesbury proposed a 'redistribution' of papal territory, while simultaneously Russell stated that all the pope should rule over was 'Rome with fifteen miles around.' With the approach of war in 1859, Malmesbury, for the time being, dropped open reference to his proposal in order to concentrate on maintaining the Vienna settlement and getting the powers together in a congress as a means of securing peace. Russell never gave up his formula throughout the entirety of the crisis. He and Palmerston were willing to accept something less in order to accommodate France and the changing circumstances, but they continued to regard 'Rome and fifteen miles around' as the best solution to the Papal Question. They demonstrated that the formula worked both against the pope and for him. When it appeared that Garibaldi or Cavour might take even Rome from the pope, Russell insisted that the pope needed at least Rome, certainly for now. This preference for ending the papal monarchy in most of the Papal States, rather than for papal reform, operated as a constant factor within the changes in Liberal policy toward Italy.

It is clear that the Papal Question was a far more central and persistent concern of English foreign policy and diplomacy toward Italy during these years

Conclusion

than has usually been recognized. The English government, whether Tory or Liberal, regarded the Papal Question as a crucial, if not *the* crucial dimension of every major phase of the events – during the crisis leading to war in northern Italy in 1859, during the time of revolution and its settlement in the Romagna and the duchies in 1859–60, and during the struggle between Garibaldi and Cavour in southern Italy and the Marches and Umbria in 1860. Malmesbury's four points in March 1859 and Russell's four points in January 1860, the two most comprehensive programmes the English governments created, both made papal issues the dominant ones. The English always regarded the Papal Question as the most difficult one they had to face.

Furthermore, the role of England in the overthrow of the papal temporal power was much more important and much more practically effective than has usually been acknowledged. England stood out among the great powers as the only one that consistently opposed the papal monarchy. It is true that, by means of his connivance with Cavour, beginning as early as Plombières in July 1858, Napoleon harmed the pope's interest more severely than any other great power. Yet, official French policy defended the pope, and Napoleon's own enigmatic policy and activity toward the pope were ambiguous and not consistently directed against papal interests. By contrast, both Malmesbury and Russell, each in his own way and in different times and circumstances, relentlessly pursued official policies and diplomatic action which consciously worked against papal interests. England's role was to make possible and to insure the ongoing, yet carefully regulated momentum of the attacks against the papal temporal power. England would only allow the attacks to proceed in stages: in 1859 in the Romagna, but not in the Marches and Umbria; in 1860 in the Marches and Umbria, but not in Rome. To the Piedmontese and especially to the liberal nationalists in the Papal States, England was the example, an inspiration, a diplomatic godfather, a guarantor of the results. To the French emperor, England was an assistant in exercising calculated negative impact on papal interests, or an explanation to French Catholics and the pope for Napoleon not coming to the pope's aid.

On the other side of the conflict, it is evident that the papal government believed much more than is usually noted that England was a decisive influence in the movement against the temporal power. Pius IX regarded Sardinia as his worst enemy in Italy and Napoleon as his greatest agony. But he considered England, especially the Palmerston and Russell government, to be his enemy in a more fundamental way. He was aware, even if only belatedly on occasion, that English diplomacy singled out his state as 'the plague spot of Europe', put pressure on the papacy among the governments of Europe, and sought to isolate him from his political support. However, he repeatedly acknowledged that the way England hurt him most was by providing the model in politics, religious policy, commerce, and social order for a new society in Italy which left no room for the papal temporal power. The papal government was helpless diplomatically to counteract England's activity and influence, so that England's role against the

Conclusion

papacy became all the more effective. The pope had no equivalent to Odo Russell in London who would express papal opinions to the English government, or would be able to demand an answer to any of his protests. In general, it had no choice other than to do nothing about English opposition. The pope's one means of political influence upon the English was his appeal to the Catholics of Ireland and England. It is evident that Catholic political action in England and Ireland during this period had more impact on the conduct of foreign affairs than is usually understood. The pope and Antonelli consciously relied upon it and included it in their strategies. English and Irish Catholic action did, indeed, help to restrain some of the diplomatic thrusts of the English government against the papacy.

The events in the Papal States and throughout the peninsula enabled the English to experience a happy convergence of their many pragmatic interests with their views of history and society. Their promotion of civil and religious liberty and material prosperity found a tangible outlet in the advancement of Piedmont, while their opposition to despotism, superstition, and economic stagnation had its object in the papacy and the papal society of the States of the Church. The Conservatives and the Liberals affirmed many times that no 'British interests' were threatened by the events in Italy. This meant that English concerns in commerce, finance, industry, naval affairs, social class, the arts, the church and religion all easily conjoined to promote the moral and material progress of Italy and to overcome the moral and material contagion of the papacy. For the English there was no inner tension among these factors in relation to Italy and the pope. English diplomacy pertaining to the papacy and the place of the Papal States in Italy did not proceed from any direct need to keep Britain secure, or to reap greater profits in London or Lancashire. The English, in this case, used their diplomacy to promote, as they understood it, the improvement of Italy. It was the sort of activity which drove the pope finally to accuse them either of self-righteousness or self-interest.

Thus, anti-Catholic, especially anti-papal, convictions explicitly motivated the principal English diplomats and statesmen in their diplomatic action concerning Italian affairs. In their endeavours, these men could rest upon the near-universal support of the non-Catholic English population. Derby, Malmesbury and Disraeli, Palmerston, Russell and Gladstone, Cowley, Hudson and Odo Russell all, with variations, expressed such convictions and acted upon them. Their anti-Catholicism was not rabid, but it was earnest nonetheless, and it was a long way from being dead. Anti-Catholicism was a powerful factor in British involvement in Italy, all the more so because it was not focussed narrowly on doctrine and ecclesiastical styles, but on the wide range of the religious, political, and socio-economic make-up and activity of the papacy in the Papal States. The English leaders of both party groupings sympathized with the liberal nationalists in the Papal States, small in number though they were, and took up their cry that something was deeply wrong about papal rule. Their

Conclusion

experience of injustice and economic and social repression in a society governed exclusively in the interests of the church must be recognized as perhaps the essential dynamic which kept the events going, and which attracted the committed involvement of the English. Anti-papal conviction and policy provided an underlying continuity between Malmesbury and Russell in the Papal Question. There were many discontinuities between them, but this was not one of them. When the Tories or the Liberals did restrain the anti-papal thrust of their diplomacy, they did so not due to any sweetening of their assessment of the papacy or any shift in their analysis about the papal problems being central to the troubles in Italy, but out of deference to other factors. The Tories exercised restraint toward the pope out of a desire to persuade him to adopt reforms which might prevent war, or to defend the Vienna settlement, or to attract Catholic votes. The Liberals were restrained, especially during 1860, in order to avoid driving the pope to drastic action over the Romagna, or to allow Garibaldi to proceed unimpaired, or to hold on to Catholic votes.

In the affairs of Italy, Liberal foreign policy was considerably more effective than the Tories' in achieving its aims. The Whigs at the head of the Liberal government were in touch in a fundamental way with the movement of events in Italy which prevailed during their time in office. Malmesbury's diplomacy had to resist a conspiracy by Napoleon and Cavour to provoke a war which he believed to be harmful. Russell and Palmerston, by contrast, had to facilitate activity by Cavour, the liberal nationalists in the Romagna, and Garibaldi which they fundamentally approved. The English for several months after the Savoy and Nice affair in 1860 pulled back their support from some of Cavour's activities, but they gave it all the more to Garibaldi, the one who held the formative power in that period anyway.

It is this underlying Whig–Liberal approval of the general trend of events against the papacy and in favour of the liberal Risorgimento which provides the key to understanding the application of Russell's twin doctrines summarized in his climactic despatch of 27 October 1860: let the people decide, and non-intervention. As long as 'the people' doing the deciding were the 'respectable classes' who looked to England, and who decided things that England fundamentally approved, the Whig–Liberals were happy to let 'the people' decide. If, however, either the Mazzinians or the *papalini* had taken the initiative, their approach no doubt would have been different. In any case, it did not concern Russell and Palmerston that 'the people' doing the deciding were a tiny percentage of the total population and only one party in the conflict. Nor did they care that, as Pius IX correctly charged, outside agents and money stirred up what unrest there was.

Similarly with non-intervention. That doctrine, in practice, meant preventing Austria, Spain, and the other conservative powers, from assisting the pope in material ways. It did not mean preventing Garibaldi from making an attack on the Papal States outside Rome or, in the end, preventing Cavour's army from

Conclusion

invading the Marches and Umbria even without the pretext of an insurrection. The doctrine did not mean keeping England from intervening fully in papal affairs in several ways – by its 'moral support', by direct diplomatic action, and even by considering or threatening frequently the armed intervention of the British fleet. The doctrine most likely would have meant British intervention, even armed intervention, if it were necessary to prevent the papal army from attempting the reconquest of Bologna. In fact, in January 1861, Russell did make a veiled threat to Antonelli to warn him against trying to regain the lost papal territory.[1] In other words, Russell's two doctrines were a means of assisting the political Risorgimento which the English generally approved, while harming the temporal power of the pope which they abhorred.

The English welcomed a solution in Italy whereby the Italian victors in the conflict against the Papal States immediately secularized the former papal territories: they abolished clerical civil government, introduced the Siccardi laws which subordinated the clergy and the church to civic law, suppressed religious orders, redistributed their buildings and lands, and removed public education from church control. The new Italian government sought to make the state, as sovereign and national, the decisive authority in the formation of the new society throughout Italy. Such a declericalization of the former Papal States necessitated the most radical political and social transformations of any of the regions of the Italian peninsula, and may have constituted the only revolution of the social structure in the whole Risorgimento.[2] The overthrow of papal temporal power was one manifestation of the secularization of modern society, in this case a reconstitution of the social structure according to secular convictions in opposition to the papal Christian convictions which once prevailed in the States of the Church.

In December 1858, near the beginning of the Italian crisis, Malmesbury had suggested fundamental papal reform and perhaps rearranging some papal territory to remove it from papal authority. By November 1860, the papal monarchy was overthrown in all of its areas except Rome and the surrounding region; the territory lost by the pope was transferred to Piedmont and in March 1861 officially became part of the Kingdom of Italy. What Malmesbury had only with trepidation suggested, was, in a way he himself never imagined or foresaw, fulfilled with a vengeance. Pius IX opposed these results with the spiritual weapons he had available. On 18 March 1861, in an allocution to the Sacred College of Cardinals, he protested at the absorption of the Papal States

[1] Russell to Odo Russell, 21 Jan. 1860, no. 2, PRO, FO, 43/82.
[2] The Gramsci thesis called attention to the absence of social revolution in the Risorgimento, meaning the absence of democratic or agrarian revolution; the aristocratic and upper bourgeois élites who controlled the political and social structures before unification continued in power afterward. But the thesis tends to overlook the declericalization of the government in the region of the former States of the Church where the clerical ruling élite was forcibly and totally removed from political authority: Antonio Gramsci, *Il Risorgimento* (Turin: Einaudi, 1949).

Conclusion

into the kingdom of Italy. He condemned the secular and anticlerical principles that motivated Piedmont and the Italian liberals, and which *they* said represented 'modern civilization'. He declared he would not be reconciled to such principles, nor to the kingdom they supported. The English misunderstood his protest and believed that an arrogant pope had sought to snuff out modern civilization itself.[3]

The pope continued to be monarch in Rome. Perhaps 650,000 people remained under his rule in the city and region of Rome. That reality made no one happy. The pope looked upon these people as his children who had lost the rest of their family. He thought of his lost provinces and talked of rebuilding his shattered papal army. Cavour declared that the glorious city of Rome must one day become the capital of Italy. Garibaldi promised to liberate the city. Napoleon's troops tenaciously occupied Rome, while the emperor searched for a way to withdraw. The English government declared its approval of the eventual overthrow of the temporal power in Rome.

These were the makings of the Roman Question, the next phase of papal and Italian affairs.[4] For a few months during the winter of 1860–1, while things were quiet in Rome, Pius IX allowed his representatives to negotiate secretly with Piedmont about the relation of Rome to the new political order. Odo Russell and Dr Pantaleoni, the physician favoured by the English, had a part in them. In January 1861, Odo appealed to Pius to reconcile the papacy to the new Italy, and to unite with England to promote Lord John's vision of 'the building up of the edifice' of the Italian nation. He encouraged Pius, 'With the Pope's blessing and England's moral support, Italy has nothing to fear.'[5] It was the kind of appeal a victor makes to the vanquished. Pius IX could not join the revolution, no matter how severely defeated he was. And as long as he did not, England could not mitigate its diplomacy against the papacy. It was an *impasse*. They, and everyone else, had to wait, knowing that Rome was next.

[3] *Punch*, 13 April 1861. Three of the major ecclesiastical events of the period 1860 to 1870 may be seen as continuations of Pius IX's use of spiritual weapons during 1859–61: the Syllabus of Errors of 1864, the Vatican Council of 1869–70, and the decree of papal infallibility of 1870. The events of 1858–70 still reverberate in the life of the Roman Catholic Church, as indicated by Hans Küng's *Infallible: an enquiry* (London: Collins, 1971); and August B. Hasler, *Pius IX (1846–78), päpistliche Unfehlbarkeit und 1-Vatikanisches Konzil* (Stuttgart: Anton Hiersemann, 1977). The journal *Pio IX* was founded in 1972 to concentrate on his pontificate. The Vatican published a volume of essays on Pius IX's pontificate on the hundredth anniversary of his death, *Pio IX nel primo centenario della sua morte* (Città del Vaticano: Libreria editrice Vaticana, 1978), in which the possibility of his beatification is considered.

[4] See Renato Mori, *La questione romana, 1861–1865* (Florence: Le Monnier, 1963); Bartoccini, ch. 4.

[5] Odo Russell to Russell, Rome, 16 Jan. 1861, no. 5, secret, PRO, FO, 43/83A, and *Odo Russell*, 157. Odo Russell to Lady William Russell, Rome, 15 Dec. 1860, Ampthill papers, PRO, FO, 918/85/228.

Select Bibliography

Archives
N.B. The letters and numbers in [brackets] give the abbreviation used in footnotes.

Austria
Politische Akten des Ministeriums des Aussen, 1848–1918. Haus-, Hof-, und Staatsarchivs, Vienna [HHSA PA].
    VIII, England (London).
    XI, Italienische Staaten. Papstlicher Stuhl (Vatikan).

France
Correspondance Politique du Ministère des Affaires Étrangères. Archives du Ministère des Affaires Étrangères, Paris [AMAE, CP].
    Angleterre, 712–19.
    Rome, 1009–17.
Papiers Gramont. Archives Nationales, Paris. Section des Microfilms Privés. 101 AP, Series E.
Papiers Persigny. Bibliothèque Nationale, Paris.
Papiers Thouvenel. Archives du Ministère des Affaires Étrangères, Paris. Unclassified Papers.
Papiers Walewski. Archives du Ministère des Affaires Étrangères, Paris. Unclassified Papers.

Great Britain
Ampthill Papers (Odo Russell). Public Record Office, London. Foreign Office, 918 [PRO, FO, 918].
Cowley Papers. Public Record Office, London. Foreign Office, 519 [PRO, FO, 519].
Derby Papers. Knowsley, Prescott, Lancashire, on loan to Lord Blake, The Queen's College, Oxford.
Foreign Office, Public Record Office, London [PRO, FO].
    7, Austria.
    27, France.
    43, Rome.
    70, Sicily and Naples.
    79, Tuscany.
    425, Confidential prints.
Gladstone Papers. British Museum, London. Department of Manuscripts.
Malmesbury Papers. Hampshire Record Office, Winchester.
Manning Papers. Oblates of St Charles, St Mary of the Angels, Bayswater, London.

Select Bibliography

Palmerston Papers. British Museum, London. Department of Manuscripts.
Palmerston Papers (Broadlands Papers). National Registry of Archives, London.
Royal Archives, Windsor Castle [RA].
Russell Papers. Public Record Office, London. 30/22 [PRO, 30/22].
Talbot Papers. Archives, The English College, Rome.
Wiseman Papers. Archives, Archbishop's House, Westminster Cathedral, London.

    Papal States (The Vatican)
Archivio Antonelli. Archivio di Stato di Roma. Carteggio personale del Cardinal Giacomo Antonelli.
Archivio della Nunziatura di Parigi. Archivio Segreto Vaticano [ASV, ANParigi].
    Monsignor Sacconi: Segretario di Stato [SdS].
    Monsignor Megli: Segretario di Stato [SdS].
Archivio della Nunziatura di Vienna. Archivio Segreto Vaticano [ASV, ANVienna].
    Cardinal DeLuca.
Archivio Personale di Pio IX. Archivio Segreto Vaticano [ASV].
    Inghilterra: Sovrani; Particolari.
    Oggetti vari.
Archivio delle Sacra Congregazione di Propaganda Fide, Rome.
    Le scritture originali riferite nele Congregazioni Generali. La seconda serie.
    Scritture riferite nei Congressi. La prima serie, Anglia.
Archivio Segreto del Segretario di Stato. Archivio Segreto Vaticano [ASV, ASdS].
    Rubrica 165   Arrollamento estero
                          Atti pontificii
                          Circolari
                          Corpo diplomatico
                          Nunziatura di Firenze
                                    Madrid
                                    Monaco
                                    Napoli
                                    Pargii
                                    Torino
                                    Vienna
    Rubrica 227   Viaggio di principi
    Rubrica 228   Commissioni
    Rubrica 247   Nunziatura di Vienna
    Rubrica 248   Parigi Nunzio
    Rubrica 249   Madrid Nunzio
    Rubrica 278   Inghilterra
    Rubrica 283   Vescovi esteri
    Rubrica 297   Console inglese
Carteggio Antonelli–Sacconi. Archivio di Stato di Roma. Miscellanea di Carte Politiche Riservate. Busta 136, Sottofascicolo 4895 a–c.

    Piedmont-Sardinia
Archivio Storico del Ministero degli Affari Esteri, Rome [ASMAE].
    La legazione sarda in Londra [Londra].
    La legazione sarda presso la Santa Sede.
Consolato in Roma. Le scritture della Segretaria di Stato degli Affari Esteri del Regno di Sardinia.
Consolato in Roma. Le scritture della Segretaria di Stato degli Affari Esteri del Regno d'Italia.

Select Bibliography

Published documents and contemporary writings

N.B. Entries are listed according to the name of the principal person in a collection, or of the state to which the diplomatic documents pertain, not according to title or editor's name. The brief titles in [brackets] give the abbreviation used in footnotes for the most common collections.

Acton, John Edward Dalberg, *The correspondence of Lord Acton and Richard Simpson*, vol. I. Edited by Joseph Altholz and Damian McElrath. Cambridge: Cambridge University Press, 1971.
Albert, Prince Consort, *Letters of the Prince Consort, 1831–1861*. Edited by Kurt Jagow. Translated by E.T.S. Dugdale. London: John Murray, 1938.
Antonelli, Giacomo, *Il carteggio Antonelli–Barili, 1859–1861*. Edited by Carla Meneguzzi Rostagni. Rome: Istituto per la storia del Risorgimento italiano, 1973 [*Antonelli–Barili*].
    Il carteggio Antonelli–Sacconi, 1858–1860. Edited by Mariano Gabriele. 2 vols. Rome: Istituto per la storia del Risorgimento italiano, 1962 [*Antonelli*].
Argyll, George Douglas, Eighth Duke of, *Autobiography and Memoirs*. Edited by the Dowager Duchess of Argyll. 2 vols. London: John Murray, 1906.
Asproni, Giorgio, *Diario politico, 1855–1876*, vol. II ('1858–60'). Edited by Carlino Sole and Tino Orrù. Milan: Giuffrè, 1976.
Austria, *Il problema Veneto e l'Europa, 1859–1866*, vol. I: 'Austria'. Edited by Richard Blaas. Venice: Istituto veneto di scienze, lettere, ed arti, 1966.
    Il tramonto del potere temporale nelle relazioni degli ambasciatori austriaci a Roma, 1860–1870. Edited by Stefano Jacini. Bari: Laterza, 1931.
Azeglio, Emanuele d', *Carteggi e documenti diplomatici inediti di Emanuele d' Azeglio*. Edited by Adolfo Colombo, 2 vols. Turin: Istituto per la storia del Risorgimento, 1920, 1935.
Azeglio, Massimo d', *La politica di Massimo d'Azeglio dal 1848 al 1859: documenti in continuazione alle lettere inedite di Massimo d'Azeglio al Marchese Emanuele d'Azeglio*. Edited by Nicomede Bianchi. Turin: Roux e Favale, 1884.
    L'Italie de 1847 à 1865: correspondance de Massimo d'Azeglio. Edited by Eugene Rendu. Paris: Didier, 1867.
Bennett, William, *Popery, as set forth in Scripture: its guilt and its doom*. London, 1850.
Blakeney, R.P., *Popery in its social aspect, being a complete exposure of the immorality and intolerance of Romanism*. London: Protestant Reformation Society, 1854.
Blewitt, Octavian, *Handbook for travellers in Central Italy*. 1st–5th ed. London: John Murray, 1843–61.
Cassell's illustrated family Bible. London and New York: Cassell, Petter and Calpin, 1860.
Cavour, Camillo Benso, conte di, *Il carteggio Cavour–Nigra dal 1858 al 1861*. 4 vols. Bologna: Zanichelli, 1926–9 [*Cavour–Nigra*].
    Carteggio Cavour–Salmour. Bologna: Zanichelli, 1936.
    Cavour e l'Inghilterra: carteggio con V.E. d'Azeglio. 2 vols. Bologna: Zanichelli, 1933 [*Cavour e l'Inghilterra*].
    Lettere edite ed inedite del conte Camillo di Cavour. Edited by Luigi Chiala. 6 vols. Turin: Roux e Favale, 1883–7.
    La liberazione del mezzogiorno e la formazione del Regno d'Italia: carteggi di Camillo Cavour con Villamarina, Scialoja, Cordova, Farini, ecc. 5 vols. Bologna: Zanichelli, 1949–54.

Select Bibliography

La questione Romana negli anni 1860–1861: carteggio del Conte di Cavour con D. Pantaleoni, C. Passaglia, O. Vimercati, 2 vols. Bologna: Zanichelli, 1929.

Tutti gli scritti di Camillo Cavour, vol. IV ('Scritti, 1850–1861'). Edited by Carlo Pischedda and Giuseppe Talamo. Turin: Centro studi piemontesi, 1978.

Clarendon, George William Frederick, fourth Earl of, *The life and letters of George William Frederick, fourth Earl of Clarendon*. 2 vols. London: Edward Arnold, 1913.

Cowley, Henry Richard Charles Wellesley, first Earl, *The Paris embassy during the Second Empire*. Edited by F.A. Wellesley. London: T. Butterworth, 1928.

Cullen, Paul, *Paul Cullen and his contemporaries, with their letters, 1820–1902*. Edited by Peadar MacSuibhne. 3 vols. Naas, Ireland: Leinster Leader, 1961–5 [*Paul Cullen*].

DeSanctis, Luigi, *Popery and Jesuitism at Rome*. London, 1852.

Elliot, Sir Henry G., *Some revolutions and other diplomatic experiences*. Edited by Gertrude Elliot. London: John Murray, 1922.

Farini, Luigi Carlo, *The Roman State from 1815 to 1850*. Translated by W.E. Gladstone. 4 vols. London: John Murray, 1851–4.

Fergusson, James, *The illustrated handbook of architecture*. 2 vols. London: John Murray, 1855.

France, *Le conferenze e la pace di Zurigo nei documenti diplomatici francesi*. Edited by Armando Saitta. Rome: Istituto storico italiano per l'età moderna e contemporanea, 1965.

La Guerra del 1859 nei rapporti fra la Francia e l'Europa. Edited by Armando Saitta. 5 vols. Rome: Istituto storico italiano per l'età moderna e contemporanea, 1961 [*La guerra del 1859*].

Il problema italiano nei testi di una battaglia pubblicistica: gli opuscoli del Viscomte de la Guérronnière. Edited by Armando Saitta. 4 vols. Rome: Istituto storico italiano per l'età moderna e contemporanea, 1963–4.

Il problema Veneto e l'Europa, 1859–1866. Vol. III: 'Francia'. Edited by Georges Dethan. Venice: Istituto veneto di scienze, lettere, ed arti, 1967.

La questione italiana dalle annessioni al Regno d'Italia nei rapporti fra la Francia e l'Europa. Edited by Armando Saitta. 4 vols. Rome: Istituto storico italiano per l'età moderna e contemporanea, 1968 [*Annessioni al Regno d'Italia*].

Garibaldi, Giuseppe, *Edizione nazionale degli scritti di Giuseppe Garibaldi*, vol. I. Bologna: Zanichelli, 1932.

Memorie. Edited by Ugoberto Alfassio Grimaldi. Verona: Bertani, 1972.

Gavazzi, Antonio, *My recollections of the last four popes, and of Rome in their times*. London, 1858.

Gladstone, William E., *The financial statements of 1853, 1860–1863*. London: John Murray, 1863.

The Gladstone diaries. 6 vols. Edited by M.R.D. Foote and H.C.G. Matthew. Oxford: Clarendon, 1968–78.

Two letters to the Earl of Aberdeen on the state prosecutions of the Neapolitan government. London: John Murray, 1851.

Great Britain, *Gran Bretagna e Italia nei documenti missione Minto*. Edited by Federico Curato. 2 vols. Rome: Istituto storico italiano per l'età moderna e contemporanea, 1970.

Parliament. *Hansard's parliamentary debates*. 3rd series. Vols. CLII–CLXI [Hansard's].

Parliament. *Parliamentary papers* (Commons). *Annual Statement of the trade and navigation of the United Kingdom with foreign countries and British possessions.* 1854 to 1880.

Parliament. *Parliamentary papers* (Commons). *Correspondence respecting the affairs of Rome. 1851*, vol. 57.

Select Bibliography

Parliament. *Parliamentary papers* (Commons). *Correspondence respecting the affairs of Italy. 1849*, vols. 57 and 58.
Parliament. *Parliamentary papers* (Commons). *Declarations exchanged between the governments of Great Britain and of the Roman State for securing national treatment to the vessels and commerce of the one country in the ports of the other. 1854*, vol. 72.
Parliament. *Parliamentary papers* (Commons). *Despatches from Mr. Lyons respecting the condition and administration of the Papal States. 1860*, vol. 68.
Parliament. *Parliamentary papers* (Lords). *Copies or extracts from the despatches of Her Majesty's minister in Tuscany, in 1855, 1856, and 1857, referring to the condition and administration of the Roman States. 1860*, vol. 22.
Parliament. *Parliamentary papers* (Commons). *Correspondence respecting the affairs of Italy, January to May 1859. 1859/2*, vol. 32.
Parliament. *Parliamentary papers* (Commons). *Statement exhibiting the moral and material progress and conditions of India during the year 1859–1860. 1861*, vol. 47.
Il problema Veneto e l'Europa, 1859–1866. Vol. II: 'Inghiltera'. Edited by Noel Blakiston. Venice: Istituto veneto di scienze, lettere, ed arti, 1966.
Le relazioni diplomatiche fra la Gran Bretagna e il Regno di Sardegna, vol. VI–IX. Edited by Giuseppe Giarrizzo. Rome: Istituto storico italiano per la età moderna e contemporanea, 1962–9 [*Gran Bretagna e Sardegna*].
The statutes of the United Kingdom (*Statutes at large*).
Gregorovius, Ferdinand, *The Roman journals of Gregorovius, 1852–1874*. Translated by G.W. Hamilton. London: G. Bell, 1911.
Greville, C.C.F., *The Greville memoirs, 1814–60*, vols. VI and VII. Edited by Lytton Strachey and Roger Fulford. London: MacMillan, 1938.
Hübner, Joseph, Count, *Neuf ans de souvenirs d'un ambassadeur d'Autriche à Paris sous le Second Empire, 1851–1859*, vol. II. Edited by Count Alexander de Hübner. Paris: Plon-Nourrit, 1904.
Ideville, Henri Amédée d', *Journal d'un diplomate en Italie, 1859–1862*. Paris: Librarie Hachette, 1873.
Italy: Classical, historical, and picturesque, illustrated in a series of views by the leading landscape painters of Great Britain with descriptions of the scenes. 2nd ed. Glasgow, Edinburgh, and London: Blackie, 1859 [New title: *Italy illustrated and described, with a review of its past condition and future prospects*. 3rd ed., 1864].
La Farina, Giuseppe, *Epistolario*. Edited by Ausonio Franchi. 2 vols. Milan: E. Treves, 1869.
Loftus, Augustus, Lord, *The diplomatic reminiscences of Lord Augustus Loftus, 1837–1862*. 1st series. 2 vols. London: Cassell, 1892.
Maguire, J.F., *Rome, its ruler and its institutions*. London: Longman's, 1857.
Malmesbury, J.H. Harris, third Earl, *Memoirs of an ex-minister*. 3rd ed. 2 vols. London: Longmans, Green, 1884.
Manning, Henry Edward, *The Temporal Power of the Vicar of Jesus Christ*. 2nd ed. London: Burns and Lambert, 1862.
Massari, Giuseppe, *Diario dalle cento voci, 1858–1860*. Edited by Emilia Morelli. Bologna: Cappelli, 1959.
Mayhew, Henry, *London labour and the London poor*. Enlarged edition. 4 vols. London: Griffin, Bohn, 1861–2.
McCulloch, J.R., *A description and statistical account of the British Empire*, vol. II. London: Longman, Brown, Green and Longmans, 1854.
Minghetti, Marco, *Carteggio tra Marco Minghetti e Giuseppe Pasolini*, vols. II–III. Edited by Guido Pasolini. Turin: Bocca, 1926, 1929.

Select Bibliography

Newman, John Henry, *The letters and diaries of John Henry Newman*, vol. XIX. Edited by Charles Stephen Dessain. London: Nelson, 1969.
The pope and the revolution. London: Longman, Green, Reader and Dyer, 1866.
Orsini, Felice, *Memoires and adventures, . . . containing unpublished state papers of the Roman Court*. Translated by George Carbonel. Edinburgh: Thomas Constable; London: Hamilton, Adams, 1857.
Palmerston, Henry John Temple, Lord, *Gladstone and Palmerston, being the correspondence of Lord Palmerston with Mr. Gladstone, 1851–1865*. Edited by Philip Guedalla. London: G.P. Putnam's and Sons, 1928.
Papal States, *Das Ende der Kirchenstaates*. Edited by Norbert Miko. 4 vols. Vienna: Herold, 1964.
Raccolta delle leggi e disposizioni di pubblica amministrazione nello Stato pontificio. Rome: Tipografia Rev. Camera Apostolica, 1847–61.
Statistica della popolazione dello Stato pontificio dell'anno 1853. Rome: 1857.
Stato dell'anime per l'alma città di Roma per l'anno 1859. Rome: 1860.
Pius IX, Pope, *Acta Pii IX, pontificis maximi*. Part 1: 7 vols; part 2: 2 vols, 1858–64. Reprint ed. Graz: Akademische Druck, 1971.
Pio IX e Leopoldo II. Edited by Giacomo Martina. Rome: Pontificia Università Gregoriana, 1967.
Pio IX e Vittorio Emanuele II dal loro carteggio privato. Vol. II: 'La questione romana, 1856–1864'. Part 2: 'I documenti'. Edited by Pietro Pirri. Rome: Pontificia Università Gregoriana, 1951 [Pirri].
La parole de Pie IX, ou recueil des paroles, discours, homélies allocutions . . . prononcés . . . par le Pape Pie IX depuis le commencement de son pontificat jusqu'à nos jours. Edited by Abbé Marcone. Translated by A. Richard. Paris: Victor Sarlit, 1866.
Rhodes, M.J., *His Holiness Pope Pius IX and the temporal rights of the Holy See as involving the religious, social, and political interests of the whole world*. London: Thomas Richardson, 1859.
Russell, Lord John, *The later correspondence of Lord John Russell, 1840–1878*. Edited by G.P. Gooch. 2 vols. London: Longmans, Green, 1925.
Russell, Odo, *The Roman question: extracts from the despatches of Odo Russell from Rome, 1858–1870*. Edited by Noel Blakiston. London: Chapman and Hall, 1962; reprint, Wilmington, Delaware: Michael Glazier, 1980 [*Odo Russell*].
Sardinia, et al, *Stato e chiesa: la legislazione ecclesiastica fino al 1867*. Edited by Guiliana d'Amelio. Milan: Giuffré, 1961.
Seymour, M. Hobart, *Evenings with Romanists*. London: Seeley's, 1854.
Thouvenel, Edouard-Antoine, *Le secret de l'empereur: correspondance confidentielle et inédite échangée entre M. Thouvenel, le Duc de Gramont, et le Général Comte de Flahault, 1860–1863*. Edited by Louis Thouvenel. 2 vols. Paris: Calmann-Levy, 1889.
Ullathorne, Archbishop, *Letters of Archbishop Ullathorne*. London: Burns and Oates, 1892.
The speech on the question of the Pontifical States, delivered . . . at the Town Hall, Birmingham, on Tuesday the 14th of February 1860. London: Burns and Lambert, 1860.
United States of America, *Consular relations between United States and the Papal States: instructions and despatches*. Edited by Leo Francis Stock. Washington: American Catholic Historical Association, 1945.
L'unificazione italiana vista dai diplomatici statunitensi, vol. III. Edited by Howard Marraro. Rome: Istituto per la storia del Risorgimento italiano, 1967.

Select Bibliography

United States ministers to the Papal States: instructions and despatches, 1848–1868. Edited by Leo Francis Stock. Washington: Catholic University of America Press, 1933.

Victoria, Queen, *Dearest child: letters between Queen Victoria and the Princess Royal, 1858–1861*. Edited by Roger Fulford. London: Evans, 1964.

The letters of Queen Victoria. 1st series, 1837–61. 3 vols. Edited by A.C. Benson and Lord Esher. London: Longmans, 1907 [*Letters of Queen Victoria*].

Letters of Queen Victoria: from the archives of the house of Brandenburg-Prussia. Edited by Hector Bolitho. Translated by Mrs J. Pudney and Lord Sudley. London: T. Butterworth, 1938.

Regina v. Palmerston: the correspondence between Queen Victoria and her foreign and prime minister, 1837–1865. Edited by Brian Connell. London: Evans, 1962.

Wiseman, Nicholas. *Recollections of the last four popes and of Rome in their times.* London: Hurst and Blackett, 1858, new revised ed. 1859.

Wylie, J.A., *Rome and the workings of Romanism in the Papal States.* London: Hamilton and Adams, 1854.

Contemporary periodicals and directories

Almanac de Gotha
Annual Register
Annuario Pontificio
British Almanac and Companion
Catholic Directory (London)
Catholic Directory, Almanac, and Registry of the Whole Catholic World (Dublin)
Civiltà Cattolica
Dublin Review
Eclectic Review
Edinburgh Review
Foreign Office List
Giornale di Roma
Illustrated London News
Le Moniteur Universel
Morning Post
The Nation (Dublin)
Punch
The Rambler
The Record
Tablet
The Times

Historical studies

Altholz, J.L., *The liberal Catholic movement in England: the 'Rambler' and its contributors, 1848–1864.* London: Burns and Oates, 1962.

'The political behavior of the English Catholics, 1850–1867'. *The journal of British studies* 4 (1964), 89–103.

Ashley, Anthony Evelyn, *The life and correspondence of Henry John Temple, Viscount Palmerston.* 2 vols. London: John Bentley, 1879.

Aubert, Roger, *Le pontificat de Pie IX, 1846–1878.* Paris: Bloud and Gay, 1952.

Barie, Ottavio, *L'Inghilterra e il problema italiano, 1846–1848.* Milan: Edizioni Universitarie, 1954.

'Palmerston, Russell e il primo progetto di "Regno dell'Italia settentrionale",' *Clio* 1 (1965), 25–53.
Bartoccini, Fiorella, *La 'Roma dei romani'*. Rome: Istituto per la storia del Risorgimento italiano, 1971.
Beales, Derek, *England and Italy, 1859–1860*. London: Thomas Nelson, 1961.
'Gladstone on the Italian question', *Rassegna storica del Risorgimento* 41 (1954), 96–104.
The Risorgimento and the unification of Italy. London: George Allen and Unwin, 1971.
Beck, George Andrew, ed., *The English Catholics, 1850–1950*. London: Burns and Oates, 1950.
Berkeley, G.F.-H., *The Irish battalion in the papal army of 1860*. Dublin: Talbot, 1929.
Italy in the making, 1815–1848. 3 vols. Cambridge: Cambridge University Press, 1932–40; reprint, 1968.
Best, G.F.A., 'Popular Protestantism in Victorian England', in *Ideas and institutions of Victorian Britain: essays in honour of George Kitson Clark*, ed. R. Robson, 115–42. London: G. Bell, 1967.
Blakiston, Georgiana, *Lord William Russell and his wife, 1815–1846*. London: John Murray, 1972.
Blakiston, Noel, *Inglesi e italiani nel Risorgimento*. Catania: Bonanno, 1973.
'Joseph Severn, consul in Rome, 1861–1871', *History today* 17 (1968), 329–36.
'Rome in 1860', *History today* 10 (1960), 488–95.
Blumberg, Arnold, 'The diplomacy of the Austro-Sardinian War of 1859'. Ph.D. thesis, University of Pennsylvania, 1952.
Bordonali, Salvatore, *Riflessi diplomatici e politici nella crisi del potere temporale negli anni formativi dell'Unità italiana, 1859–61*. Milan: Giuffré, 1979.
Bossey, John, *The English Catholic community, 1570–1850*. London: Darton, Longman and Todd, 1975.
Bowen, Desmond, *The Protestant crusade in Ireland, 1800–1870: a study of Protestant–Catholic relations between the Act of Union and Disestablishment*. Montreal: McGill-Queen's University Press, 1978.
Bury, J.P.T., 'England and the unification of Italy', *Atti del convegno internazionale sul tema 'Il risorgimento e l'Europa'*, 163–83. Rome: Accademia Nazionale dei Lincei, 1964.
Cahill, Gilbert A., 'Irish Catholicism and English Toryism', *Review of politics* 49 (1957), 62–76.
Cameron, R.E., 'Papal finance and the temporal power, 1815–1871', *Church history* 26 (1957).
Campanella, Anthony P., 'Il battaglione di S. Patrizio e la mitica crociata per salvare lo Stato pontificio nel 1860' *Risorgimento* 22 (1970), 117–34.
Case, Lynn M., 'Anticipating the death of Pius IX in 1861', *Catholic historical review* 43 (1957–8), 309–23.
Edouard Thouvenel et la diplomatie du Second Empire. Paris: Pedone, 1976.
Franco-Italian relations, 1860–1865: the Roman question and the convention of September. Philadelphia: University of Pennsylvania Press, 1932, 1955.
French opinion on war and diplomacy during the Second Empire. Philadelphia: University of Pennsylvania Press, 1954.
'Thouvenel et la rupture des relations diplomatiques franco-sardes en 1860', *Revue d'histoire moderne et contemporaine* 7 (1960), 149–77.
Castronovo, Valerio, 'The Italian take-off: a critical re-examination of the problem', *Journal of Italian history* 1 (1978), 492–510.
Chadwick, Owen, *The Victorian church*. 2 vols. London: Adam and Charles Black, 1966–70.

Select Bibliography

Colombo, Adolfo, *L'Inghilterra nel Risorgimento italiano*. Milan: Casa Editrice Risorgimento, 1917.
Cook, Katherine Schach, 'Russia, Austria, and the question of Italy, 1859–1862', *The international history review* 2 (1980), 542–65.
Courten, Giartosio de, 'La Gran Bretagna di fronte all'Italia, gennaio–aprile 1859', *Risorgimento* 11 (1959), 1–31.
Dasent, Arthur Irwin, *John Thadeus Delane, editor of 'The Times': his life and correspondence*. 2 vols. New York: Scribner, 1908.
Della Torre, Paolo, *L'opera riformatrice ed amministrativa di Pio IX fra il 1850 e il 1870*. Rome: Edizione A.V.E., 1945.
DeCesare, Raffaele, *The last days of papal Rome, 1850–1870*. Translated by Helen Zimmern. London: Constable, 1909.
DeRuggiero, Livia, 'L'Inghilterra e lo Stato pontificio nel primo triennio del pontificato di Pio IX', *Archivio della societa romana di storia patria* 76 (1953), 51–172.
Dunham, Arthur L., *The Anglo-French treaty of commerce of 1860 and the progress of the industrial revolution in France*. New York: Russell and Russell, 1930, 1971.
Ellis, John Tracy, *Cardinal Consalvi and Anglo-papal relations, 1814–1824*. Washington: Catholic University of America Press, 1942.
Engel-Janosi, Friedrich, 'Le potenze conservatrici e gli avvenimenti italiani del 1860', *Atti del XXXIX congresso di storia del Risorgimento italiano* (1961), 224–39.
Fernessole, Pierre, *Pie IX, pape, 1792–1878*. 2 vols. Paris: Lethielleux, 1960–3.
Ghisalberti, Alberto Maria, *Massimo d'Azeglio: un moderato realizzatore*. Rome: Edizioni dell'Ateneo, 1953.
Giangrasso, Letizia, 'La politica inglese e il piano di confederazione italiana dopo Villafranca', *Risorgimento* 22 (1970), 93–116.
'La politica inglese e il progetto di un congresso europeo dopo Villafranca', *Risorgimento* 21 (1969), 125–47.
Giarrizzo, Giuseppe, 'La politica inglese verso l'Italia e il Regno di Sardegna nel 1857–1861', *Critica Storica* 1 (1962), 399–420.
Gilley, Sheridan, 'Evangelical and Roman Catholic missions to the Irish in London, 1830–1870'. Ph.D. thesis, Cambridge University, 1970.
'Protestant London, no-popery, and the Irish poor, 1830–1860', *Recusant history* 10 (1969–70), 210–30, and 11 (1971–2), 21–46.
Graham, Robert A., *Vatican diplomacy: a study of church and state on the international plane*. Princeton: Princeton University Press, 1959.
Gramsci, Antonio, *Il Risorgimento*. Turin: Einaudi, 1949.
Grew, Raymond, *A sterner plan for Italian unity: the Italian National Society in the Risorgimento*. Princeton: Princeton University Press, 1963.
Hales, E.E.Y., *Pio Nono: a study in European politics and religion in the nineteenth century*. London: Eyre and Spottiswoode, 1954.
Hall, Basil, 'Alessandro Gavazzi: a Barnabite friar and the Risorgimento', *Studies in church history* 12 (1975), 303–56.
Hearder, Harry, 'Clarendon e l'Italia', in *Il Risorgimento e l'Europa*, ed. Vittorio Frosini, 173–86. Catania: Bonanno, 1969.
'The foreign policy of Lord Malmesbury, 1858–1859'. Ph.D. thesis, University of London, 1954.
'La politica di Lord Malmesbury verso l'Italia nella primavera del 1859', *Rassegna storica del Risorgimento* 43 (1956), 35–58.
'Politica e opinione pubblica inglese verso l'Italia dal luglio 1859 al marzo 1860', *Atti del XLII congresso di storia del Risorgimento italiano* (1966), 77–96.
'Queen Victoria and foreign policy: royal intervention in the Italian question,

Select Bibliography

1859–1860', *Studies in international history: essays presented to W. Norton Medlicott*, 172–88. Edited by Kenneth Bourne and D.C. Watt. London: Longmans, 1967.
Holmes, J. Derek, *The triumph of the Holy See: a short history of the papacy in the nineteenth century*. London: Burns and Oates, 1978.
Hopper, K. Theodore, 'Tories, Catholics and the general election of 1859', *The historical journal* 13 (1970), 48–67.
Ingram, Edward, *The beginning of the Great Game in Asia, 1828–1834*. Oxford: Clarendon Press, 1979.
Isastia, Anna Maria, *Roma nel 1859*. Roma: Istituto per la storia del Risorgimento italiano, 1978.
Jászay, Magda, 'La questione italiana nei rapporti anglo-austrici durante la crisi del 1859', *Rassegna storica del Risorgimento* 52 (1965), 557–78.
Jenks, L.H., *The migration of British capital to 1875*. New York: Knopf, 1927.
Kitson Clark, George, *Churchmen and the condition of England, 1832–1885*. London: Methuen, 1973.
   The making of Victorian England. London: Methuen, 1962.
Lacaita, Charles, *An Italian Englishman: Sir James Lacaita*. London: Grant Richards, 1933.
Larkin, Emmet, 'The devotional revolution in Ireland, 1850–1875', *American historical review* 77 (1972), 625–52.
   The making of the Roman Catholic Church in Ireland, 1850–1860. Chapel Hill: University of North Carolina Press, 1980.
Lesourd, Jean Alain, *Les Catholiques dans la société anglaise 1765–1865*. Paris: Honoré Champion, 1978.
Leti, Giuseppe, *Roma e lo Stato pontificio dal 1849 al 1870*. 2 vols. Ascoli Piceno: Giuseppe Cesari, 1911.
Ley, Horst, *Die italienische Einigung und die englische Politik, 1859–1861*. Leipzig: Noske, 1935.
Machin, G.I.T., *The Catholic question in English politics, 1820 to 1830*. Oxford: Clarendon, 1964.
   Politics and the Churches in Great Britain, 1832 to 1868. Oxford: Clarendon, 1977.
MacKay, D.F., 'British "public opinion" and the Italian "Risorgimento" with special reference to the period 1859–1861'. D.Phil. thesis, Oxford University, 1959.
Mack Smith, Denis, 'Cavour and Clarendon: English documents on the Italian question at the congress of Paris', *Atti del XXXV congresso di storia del Risorgimento italiano* (1957), 235–49.
   Cavour and Garibaldi, 1860. Cambridge: Cambridge University Press, 1954.
   'Cavour and Parliament', *Cambridge historical journal* 13 (1957), 37–57.
   'Cavour and the Tuscan revolution of 1859', *The diversity of history: essays in honor of Sir Herbert Butterfield*, 269–314. Edited by J.H. Elliot and H.G. Koenigsberger. London: Routledge and Kegan Paul, 1970.
   'L'Inghilterra di fronte agli eventi italiani del 1860', *Atti del XXXIX congresso di storia del Risorgimento italiano* (1961), 411–43.
   ed. *The making of Italy, 1796–1870*. New York: Harper and Row, 1968.
   'Palmerston and Cavour: some doubts about the Risorgimento, 1859–1960', *Italian studies presented to E.R. Vincent on his retirement from the chair of Italian at Cambridge*, 244–71. Edited by C.P. Brand, K. Foster and U. Limentani. Cambridge: Cambridge University Press, 1962.
   Victor Emanuel, Cavour, and the Risorgimento. London: Oxford University Press, 1971.
Magnus, Philip, *King Edward the Seventh*. London: John Murray, 1964.

Select Bibliography

Marshall, Ronald, *Massimo d'Azeglio: an artist in politics, 1798–1866*. London: Oxford University Press, 1966.
Martin, Theodore, *The life of the Prince Consort*. 5 vols. London: Smith, Elder, 1875–80.
Martina, Giacomo, *Pio IX, 1846–1850*. Rome: Università Gregoriana Editrice, 1974.
Maurain, Jean, *La politique ecclésiastique du Second Empire de 1852 à 1869*. Paris: Felix Alcan, 1930.
McDonald, Michael J., 'The vicariat proposals: a crisis in Napoleon III's Italian confederative designs', in *Diplomacy in an age of nationalism: essays in honor of Lynn Marshall Case*, ed. Nancy N. Barker and Marvin L. Brown, Jr, 86–108. The Hague: Martinus Nijhoff, 1971.
McIntire, C.T., 'Mid-Victorian anti-Catholicism, English diplomacy, and Odo Russell in Rome', *Fides et historia* 13 (1980), 13–23.
Miller, Marian Swann, 'Europe and the Sardinian annexations of the duchies, Tuscany and the Romagna, 1859–1860'. Ph.D. thesis, University of Pennsylvania, 1965.
Miko, Norbert, 'Die diplomatischen Beziehungen zwischen England und dem Heiligen Stuhl im 19. Jahrhundert', *Zeitschrift für katholische Theologie* 78 (1956), 206–25.
Monypenny, William Flavelle, and buckle, George Earle, *The life of Benjamin Disraeli, Earl of Beaconsfield*. 6 vols. London: John Murray, 1910–24.
Mooney, Gary, 'British diplomatic relations with the Holy See, 1793–1830', *Recusant history* 14 (1978), 193–210.
Morelli, Emilia, *1849–1859: I dieci anni che fecero l'Italia*. Florence: Le Monnier, 1977.
 Lo Stato Pontificio e l'Europa nel 1831–1832. Rome: Edizioni Ricerche, 1966.
Mori, Renato, *La questione romana, 1861–1865*. Florence: Le Monnier, 1963.
Morley, John, *The life of William Ewart Gladstone*. 2 vols. London: Macmillan, 1903.
Newton, Lord, *Lord Lyons: a record of British diplomacy*. 2 vols. London: Edward Arnold, 1913.
Norman, Edward Robert, *Anti-Catholicism in Victorian England*. London: George Allen and Unwin, 1968.
 The Catholic Church and Ireland in the age of rebellion, 1859–1873. Ithaca: Cornell University Press, 1965.
 Church and society in England, 1770–1970: a historical study. Oxford: Oxford University Press, 1976.
Packe, Michael St John, *The bombs of Orsini*. London: Secker and Warburg, 1957.
Partner, Peter, *The lands of St. Peter: the Papal States in the Middle Ages and early Renaissance*. London: Eyre Methuen, 1972.
Pine-Coffin, R.S., *Bibliography of British and American travel in Italy to 1860*. Florence: Leo S. Olschki, 1974.
Pio IX nel primo centenario della sua morte. Città del Vaticano: Libreria Editrice Vaticana, 1978.
Pirri, Pietro, *Pio IX e Vittorio Emanuele II dal loro carteggio privato*. Vol. II: 'La questione romana, 1856–1864'. Part 1: 'Testo'. Rome: Pontificia Università Gregoriana, 1951.
Platt, D.C.M., *Finance, trade, and politics: British foreign policy 1815–1914*. Oxford: Oxford University Press, 1968.
Popolazioni residente e presente dei communi al censimento dal 1861 to 1961. Rome: Istituto centrale di statistica, 1967.
Porter, Bernard, *The refugee question in mid-Victorian politics*. London: Cambridge University Press, 1979.
Prest, John, *Lord John Russell*. London: MacMillan, 1972.
Purcell, Edmund Sheridan, *The life of Cardinal Manning*. 2 vols. London: MacMillan, 1895.

Select Bibliography

Randall, Alec, 'A British agent at the Vatican: the mission of Odo Russell', *Dublin review* 479 (1959), 37–60.
'British diplomacy and the Holy See, 1555–1925', *Dublin review* 482 (1959–60), 291–303.
Richards, Jeffrey, *The popes and the papacy in the early Middle Ages, 476–752.* London: Routledge and Kegan Paul, 1979.
Romeo, Rosario, *Cavour e il suo tempo.* 2 vols. Rome and Bari: Laterza, 1969–77.
Rudman, Harry W., *Italian nationalism and English letters.* London: Allen and Unwin, 1940.
Scherer, Paul, 'British reaction to French annexation of Nice and Savoy', *International review of history and political science* 2 (1965), 31–40.
Schreuder, D.M., 'Gladstone and Italian unification, 1848–70: the making of a Liberal?' *English historical review* 84 (1970), 475–501.
Scott, Ivan, *The rise of the Italian state: a study of Italian politics during the period of unification.* Meerut: Sadha Prakashan, 1980.
The Roman question and the powers, 1848–1865. The Hague: Martinus Nijhoff, 1969.
Signoretti, A., *Italia e Inghilterra durante il Risorgimento.* Milan: A Nicola, 1940.
Simpson, F. A., 'England and the Italian war of 1859', *Historical journal* 5 (1962), 111–21.
Simpson, R., 'The Catholic Church in England in 1859', *Downside review* 84 (1966), 171–92.
Spini, Giorgio, *Risorgimento e protestanti.* Naples: Edizioni Scientifiche italiane, 1956.
Storia d'Italia, vol. III: 'Dal primo settecento all'Unità'. Turin: Einaudi, 1973.
Taylor, A.J.P., 'European mediation and the agreement of Villafranca, 1859', *English historical review* 51 (1936), 52–78.
The Italian problem in European diplomacy, 1847–1849. Manchester: Manchester University Press, 1934.
The struggle for mastery in Europe, 1848–1918. Oxford: Clarendon, 1954.
Tedeschi, Mario, *Cavour e la questione Romana, 1860–1861.* Milan: Giuffré, 1978.
Francia e Inghilterra di fronte alla questione romana, 1859–1860. Milan: Giuffré, 1978.
Thureau-Dangin, Paul, *The English Catholic revival in the nineteenth century.* Translated by Wilfred Wilberforce. 2 vols. London: Simpkin, Marshall, Hamilton and Kent, 1914.
Tremelloni, Roberto, *Storia dell'industria italiana contemporanea dalla fine del settecento all'unità italiana.* Turin: Einaudi, 1947.
Trevelyan, G.M., 'Englishmen and Italians', in *Clio a muse, and other essays.* 2nd ed. London: Longmans, Green, 1930, 1949.
Garibaldi and the making of Italy. London: Longmans, 1911.
Garibaldi and the Thousand. London: Longmans, Green, 1909.
Garibaldi's defence of the Roman Republic. London: Longmans, 1907.
Ugolini, Romano, *Cavour e Napoleone III nell'Italia centrale: il sacrificio di Perugia.* Rome: Istituto per la storia del Risorgimento italiano, 1973.
'Perugia 1859: l'ordine di saccheggio', *Rassegna storica del Risorgimento* 59 (1972), 353–9.
Ullmann, Walter, *The growth of papal government in the Middle Ages: a study in the ideological relation of clerical to lay power.* London: Methuen, 1970.
Urban, Miriam, *British opinion and policy on the unification of Italy, 1856–1861.* Scottsdale, Pennsylvania: Mennonite Press, 1938.
Valsecchi, Franco, 'European diplomacy and the expedition of the Thousand: the conservative power', *A century of conflict, 1850–1950: essays for A.J.P. Taylor*, 47–72. Edited by Martin Gilbert. London: Hamish Hamilton, 1966.

Select Bibliography

'L'Inghilterra e la questione italiana nel 1859: la missione Cowley', *Archivio storico italiano* 126 (1968), 479-94.

L'Italia del Risorgimento e l'Europa delle nazionalità: L'unificazione italiana nella politica europea. Milan: Giuffré, 1978.

'Le potenze europee e la questione romana nel periodo della unificazione italiana, 1859-70', *Storia e politica* 1 (1962), 177-95.

L'unificazione italiana e la politica europea dalla guerra di Crimea lla guerra di Lombardia, 1854-1859. Milan: Istituto per gli studi di politica internazionale, 1955.

Vaussard, Maurice, *La fin du pouvoir temporal des papes*. Paris: Spes, 1964.

Ventrome, A., *L'amministrazione dello Stato pontificio dal 1814 al 1870*. Rome: Edizioni Universitarie, 1946.

Verucci, Guido, *Il movimento cattolico italiano: dalla Restauazione al primo dopo guerra*. Messina and Florence: D'Anna, 1978.

Vincent, John, *The formation of the Liberal party, 1857-1868*. London: Constable, 1966, and Harmondsworth: Penguin, 1971.

Vinay, Valdo, *Evangelici italiani esuli a Londra durante il Risorgimento*. Turin: Claudiana, 1961.

Walpole, Spencer, *Life of Lord John Russell*. 2 vols. London: Longmans, Green, 1889.

Ward, Wilfred Philip, *The life and times of Cardinal Wiseman*. 2 vols. London: Longmans, Green, 1897.

Whyte, A.J., *The political life and letters of Cavour, 1848-1861*. Oxford: Oxford University Press, 1930, 1962.

Whyte, J.H., *The independent Irish party, 1850-1859*. Oxford: Oxford University Press, 1958.

Index

Achilli, Dr Giacinto, 32
Acton, Sir John Edward Dahlberg, 26, 27n
Albert Edward, Prince of Wales (Bertie), 41, 42, 48n, 70, 73–9, 81, 117
Albert, Prince Consort, 73–9, 103–4, 216, 220
Anti-Catholicism, anti-papalism, 3, 4, 8–11, 15–16, 29–38, 40, 43, 46–57, 73–9, 86–7, 107, 112, 122, 136, 138, 146–7, 150, 156, 173, 185, 193, 214–15, 219–20, 223–7
Antonelli, Giacomo, Cardinal (secretary of state to Pius IX), 5, 27–8, 142–3, 155, 160–1, 175, 182–3, 185–6, 198, 208–11; policy, 22–9, 68–9, 81–7, 99–101, 102–4, 117–18, 122–3, 128–9, 130, 139, 144–7, 151, 153–4, 160–1, 185–6, 189; and England, 20, 46, 48–9, 51–2, 61, 68–9, 72, 74, 86–7, 90–2, 97–101, 106–13, 122–3, 139, 145, 156–7, 169–70, 172–4, 204, 220, 224; see Russell, Odo; Pius IX
Apponyi, Count Rudolph (Austrian ambassador in London), 68, 95, 114, 161–2, 168, 191, 206
Argyll, George Douglas, Eighth Duke of, 150
Aristocrats, 5, 10–11, 28, 34–5, 40–2, 46–8, 71–2, 77, 225
Armed force, material force, 132–3, 147–52, 155, 159–60, 165, 167–9, 175, 176–7, 192, 225–6; British, 4, 7, 19–20, 36, 57–65, 137, 141, 159–60, 163, 173–5, 191, 196–7, 205, 209–10, 215–16, 225–6; Piedmont's, 193–200, 204–21, 225–6; Garibaldi's, 194–200, 204–10, 212; see non-intervention, intervention; navy, British; Austria; France

Art, Italian, British, 34–5, 45, 224
Aubin, Thomas (British representative in Rome, 1832–44), 47
Austria, 13, 14, 17, 18–21, 123–9, 145, 180, 183, 215; and the papacy, 6, 134–5, 145, 152–4, 210, 212; and the occupation of the Marches and Umbria, the Romagna, 6, 13, 15, 28, 48, 68–9, 79–87, 88–90, 92, 93–6, 102–5, 112–13, 114–16, 126–7, 130, 165, 168–9; and the restoration of the Romagna, 130, 132, 133, 141, 148–9, 159–60, 163, 168–70; and England, 6, 69, 88–93, 98–9, 155, 163, 165–6, 168–9, 205–6, 215, 225; see papal army
Austro-Sardinian War (1859), 49, 52, 77, 101–6, 123–4, 222; fear of outbreak of, 1, 13, 17–18, 22, 29, 36, 40, 67–70, 85, 87, 88, 89–90, 95–6, 101
Azeglio, Emanuel d' (Piedmontese Minister in London), 67, 132, 137, 174, 177, 181, 192–3, 199, 211–12
Azeglio, Massimo d' (Piedmontese diplomat, artist), 35, 78, 117, 131

Bach, Baron von (Austrian ambassador in Rome until August 1859), 48, 145, 153–5, 169, 194, 210
Barili, Monsignor Lorenzo (papal nuncio in Madrid), 131, 154, 156, 186, 206
Bavaria, 183, 201, 212, 214
Belgium, 75, 96, 191, 201–2
Bertani, Dr Agostino (Garibaldi's supporter), 195, 197, 205
Bloomfield, Lord John (British ambassador in Berlin), 18–20
Boncompagni, Count Carlo, 151, 156
Bowyer, Sir George (MP, Dundalk, Catholic leader in British parliament),

Index

41–2, 50, 106, 111, 127–8, 172–3, 183–4, 188
Bruce, Colonel (Prince of Wales' governor), 73–9
Buchanan, Sir A. (British ambassador in Madrid), 217n
Buol, Count Karl Buol-Schanenstein (Austrian prime minister), 20n, 69, 88, 91, 94–7

Cadogan, Colonel George (British Special Observer in Central Italy), 177
Capitalists, see Trade; Middle classes
Caraffa, Raffele, 85
Carignano, Prince Eugenio di, 150–1, 161
Carrara and Massa, 17
Castlereagh, Lord, 21
Catholic Powers, 183, 210, 212, 215; see Austria; France; Spain; Portugal; Naples; Bavaria
Cavour, Count Camillo Benso di (prime minister of Piedmont), 3, 5, 8, 13, 14–17, 20, 24, 52, 57, 85, 89, 94, 97, 101–6, 123–6, 167, 173, 178–82, 205–12; out of office, 124–6, 131, 143, 150, 155, 158, 167; and the Romagna, Marches and Umbria, 80, 85, 101, 104–6, 114–18, 135–6, 176–7, 189–91, 195, 197, 205–12, 212–21; and Rome, 227; and England, 35–6, 50, 66–7, 75–8, 119, 154–5, 167, 176–7, 192–4, 196–200, 203, 207–12, 212–21, 225; see Victor Emmanuel; Napoleon III; Piedmont–Sardinia
China, 150, 150n
Church of England, 8, 11, 30–8, 43, 68; see Protestants; English Chapel in Rome; Puseyites
Cialdini, General Enrico (Piedmontese General), 207, 209
Civil liberty, 3, 10n, 19–21, 29–30, 35–9, 59, 126–7, 149–50, 167, 191, 193, 205, 210, 216–17, 218–19, 223–5; see religious liberty; material prosperity; progress
Civiltà Cattolica, 28–9, 82
Clarendon, Lord George William Villiers, 20, 30–1, 35–6, 98, 101, 114
Cobden, Richard, 55, 164

Colloredo, Count (Austrian ambassador in Rome), 48, 68, 82–7, 100, 109
Confederation proposals, Italy, 15, 93–4, 123–9, 143–5, 151–2, 154, 161
Congress proposals, Congresses, for European powers (1859), 93–101, 126, 130, 140–7, 148, 151–2, 152–62, 163, 222; (1860), 183, 212–13; for Catholic powers (1860), 183, 213; Conference of Emperors in Warsaw (1860), 215, 217; Congress of Paris (1856), 20, 35–6; Congress of Vienna (1815), see Vienna, Treaty of; Congress of Laibach (1821), 97; Conference of London (1831), 96
Conservatives, see Tories
Corbett, Edwin (British *chargé d'affairs* in Florence), 47, 122, 170, 185
Corti, Count Luigi (Piedmontese *chargé d'affairs* in London), 210
Cowley, Lord Henry Richard Charles Wellesley (British ambassador in Paris), 17–19, 22, 50, 55, 66, 69–70, 102, 105, 119, 120, 124, 126–7, 128–9, 132, 137, 148–9, 151–2, 154, 163, 165, 166, 167–8, 169, 179–82, 187, 192, 209, 211, 213, 216–7; and the papacy, 50, 72, 138, 158, 168, 214, 224; mission to Vienna, 88–93, 98–9, 106
Cullen, John, Cardinal (Archbishop of Dublin), 7, 24, 34, 41, 43, 110–12, 146–7, 172–3, 202–4

Dabormida, General Giuseppe (Piedmontese Foreign Minister, July 1859 – January 1860), 131, 137, 151n
Daily News (London), 146
Delane, John (editor of *The Times*), 44
De Luca, Monsignor Antonino (papal nuncio in Vienna), 49, 90, 93, 98–9, 101, 103, 128, 156, 170, 210–11, 219
Derby, Fourteenth Earl (prime minister of Great Britain, 1858–9), 3, 14, 38, 57, 60, 79–81, 89, 102, 104–5, 106–12, 126, 147, 166, 173, 174n, 220, 224
DeSanctis, Luigi, 32
Disraeli, Benjamin (Tory Leader in The House of Commons), 17, 55, 80–5, 88, 101, 111, 166, 174, 224
Donnet, Archbishop (Archbishop of Bordeaux), 143

Index

Duff, Grant (MP, Elgin), 203
Dupanloup, Bishop (Bishop of Orleans), 146
Durham, Bishop of (Dr Edward Maltby), 30–1

Elliot, Henry (British Minister in Naples), 172, 207–8, 209
England as model, 3, 7, 11, 60–1, 67, 205, 223
English Chapel in Rome, 43; *see* Church of England
English College, Rome, 43, 77, 201; *see* Talbot, George
English in Rome and Italy, 32, 34–5, 40–6, 48, 60–1, 73–9, 81, 194, 200; *see* Russell, Odo
Ercole, A. (British consular official), 45
Errington, George (Co-Adjutor Bishop of Westminster), 41
Eugenie, Empress of France, 124
Evacuation of foreign troops, *see* Austria; France
Evangelicals, 30, 33–4, 67
Evangelical Alliance, 33

Fane, Julian (British *chargé d'affairs* in Vienna), 209
Fanti, General Manfredo (army of Central Italy), 159, 177, 181, 209
Farini, Luigi Carlo, 32–3, 80, 116, 156, 181, 207
Feidling, Viscount, 201
Ferdinand II, King of Naples, 44, 70–2
Ferretti, Salvatore, 32
France, 6, 67, 130, 148; and papal reform, 69, 134–5; and the occupation and evacuation of Rome, 6, 48, 52, 68–9, 79–87, 88–90, 92, 93–6, 102–5, 112, 126–7, 133–4, 156, 165–7, 175–7, 189–91, 195, 197–8, 200, 206, 208–12, 212–21, 227; and the Romagna, Marches and Umbria, 130, 132, 141, 212–16; and England, 6, 70–1, 143–4, 148–9, 151, 152–62, 164, 167–9, 178–82, 187–8, 189–90, 195–200, 205, 213–14, 223; *see* Napoleon III; Gramont; Walewski; Thouvenel
Franchi, Monsignor Alessandro (papal nuncio in Florence), 49
Francis II, King of Naples, 104, 169, 215

Francis Joseph, Emperor of Austria, 88, 91, 123–5, 135, 168–9, 215
Freeborn, John (British consul in Rome, 1831–59), 29, 40, 44–5
French Catholics, *see* Roman Catholics; papal army

Gaggiotti, Gustavus (British vice-consul at Ancona), 45–6, 64, 118, 170, 204
Gallenga, Antonio (correspondent for *The Times*), 32, 44–5
Garibaldi, Guiseppe, 6, 8, 13, 29, 57, 220, 222, 227; in Central Italy, 17, 88, 132, 140–2; moving toward Rome and the Papal States, 194–200, 204–10, 212; and England, 195, 198, 200–3, 205, 207–10, 214, 215, 219, 225
Gavazzi, Alessandro, 32–3n
Genoa, 194–6, 205
Gibson, John, 42
Gibson, Milner (president, Board of Trade), 114
Giornale di Roma (official papal newspaper in Rome), 49–50, 103, 110, 115, 117n, 146
Gladstone, Williams Ewart (Liberal Chancellor of the Exchequer), 32–3, 55, 61, 71–2, 80, 114, 119, 123, 124, 126, 150, 160, 164, 172–3, 183, 203, 224
Goyon, General (French Commander in Rome), 85
Gramont, Antoine, Duc de (French ambassador in Rome), 48, 67, 82–7, 100–1, 125, 128, 130, 134–5, 144, 182, 194, 209–10
Granville, Lord George, 41, 55, 80–1, 114
Gregory XVI, pope (1831–46), 20, 30
Gueronnière, Viscomte de la, 157–62

Hübner, Count Joseph von (Austrian ambassador in Paris), 18
Hudson, James (British Minister in Turin), 18, 38, 50, 66–7, 118–19, 124, 125–6, 131, 153, 166–7, 176–7, 181–2, 197–9, 210; supports Piedmont and Cavour, 67, 85–6, 104, 115, 117, 121–2, 135–6, 137, 141, 150–1, 153–4, 167, 182, 190–2, 193–4, 208–9, 214–15, 218; and the papacy, 50, 141, 224

243

Index

India, 4, 11, 59, 63, 133, 133n
Ireland, *see* Roman Catholics; papal army
Irish College, Rome, 43, 77, 201
Isabella II, Queen of Spain, 6, 131, 134, 153, 169, 215, 217
Italian National Society, 5–6, 16, 52, 88–9, 113, 115–16, 140–1, 185, 189, 197, 208
Italian, things Italian, 34–9, 73–9
Italy, Kingdom of, 1, 9–10, 221, 222, 226–7

Kalbermatten, General (papal General), 142

Lacaita, Giacomo, 32, 72
La Farina, Giuseppe, 16–17, 88
Lamoricière, General Christophe de (General in the papal army), 191–2, 195, 201, 204, 206, 211
Langdale, Charles, 146n
Leopold, Grand Duke of Tuscany, 102, 187
Lever, Charles (British vice-consul at La Spezia), 105
Lewis, Sir George (British home secretary), 45
Liberal nationalists, the national party in Italy, 5–6, 44, 51–2, 56–7, 67, 81, 105–6, 114, 124–6, 141, 212, 222–7; in the Romagna, Marches and Umbria, 113, 114–19, 124, 132, 135–6, 138, 142–3, 152, 167, 181–2, 187, 197, 208–12; in Rome, 51–2, 78, 85, 125, 189; and England, 224–6; *see* Cavour
Liberals, Whig–Liberals, Liberal Government (1859–65), 2, 3, 23, 30–1, 52–3, 113, 114–39, 140–62, 163–88, 189–221, 222; as opposition, 20–1, 79–87, 108, 110–13; and Roman Catholics, 30–1, 106–13, 146–7, 172–3, 175–7, 183–4, 186–7, 224–5; *see* Russell, Lord John; Palmerston; Gladstone
Loftus, Lord Augustus (British ambassador in Vienna), 18–19, 66, 94–6, 148, 159–60, 163, 165, 168, 170–1, 175, 211, 215
Lombardy, *see* Venetia and Lombardy
Lopez, Tito, 85

Lowe, John Thomas (British vice-consul at Civita Vecchia), 45
Lyons, Richard, also Lord (British representative in Rome, 1853–8), 20, 30, 36, 47

MacDonnell, Count Charles, 201–2
MacHale, Bishop, 110
MacPherson, R. 42
Maguire, John F. (MP, Dungarvan), 26n, 43, 106
Malmesbury, Third Earl (Foreign Minister of Great Britain, 1858–9), 3, 14, 38, 46–52, 60–1, 71–2, 88–113, 224–5; policy toward the papacy, 17–21, 66–70, 78, 89, 93–5, 96, 103, 110–11, 119, 126, 144, 173, 222–7; *see* Tories
Manning, Dr Henry Edward (Provost of Westminster), 26n, 41, 43, 50, 172
Mapei, Camillo, 32
Marches and Umbria, 1, 9, 13, 15–17, 116–18, 120–3, 140, 194, 223; anticipation of revolution in, 167, 176–8, 188, 189–200, 204–7; Piedmontese–Sardinian invasion and conquest of, 190–1, 199, 204–12; annexation to Piedmont–Sardinia, 12, 212–21; and England, 189–90, 192–4; *see* Austria; Perugia; Cavour; Liberal nationalists; Piedmont–Sardinia
Marliani, Count Emanuel (Romagnol diplomat), 137, 150, 167, 176–7
Massari, Giuseppe (confidant of Cavour), 50, 101–2, 117, 119, 121, 136, 147
Material prosperity, 3, 6, 29–30, 35–9, 59, 61–65, 193, 219, 223–5; *see* civil liberty; religious liberty; progress
Mazzini, Giuseppe, 5, 8, 13, 29, 32, 89, 194
Mazzinians, democrats, republicans, radicals, 5–6, 15, 19, 21, 32, 67, 88–9, 130, 149, 190, 217, 225
McEvoy, Edward (MP, Meath), 183
Megli, Monsignor (papal official in the Paris nunciature), 219
Method, 9–12, 222–7
Metternich, Prince Richard (Austrian ambassador in Paris), 141
Middle classes, bourgeois, 4–6, 11, 34–5, 37–8, 40–2, 61–5, 225

Minerva, Count della (Piedmontese envoy in Rome), 104
Minghetti, Marco (Romagnol leader), 114, 116, 138, 182
Minto, Lord (British diplomat), 30, 55
Modena, see Tuscany, Parma and Modena
Moniteur, Le (Official French government newspaper), 14
Moore, George (British consul at Ancona), 45
Moral influence, moral force, British, 2, 4, 7, 19, 60, 137, 149, 166, 210–13, 215, 218–19, 223–4, 226–7; see armed force; non-intervention
Morning Post (London), 146
Mortara, Edgar (Jewish boy in Romagna), 36–7

Naples (or Two Sicilies), Kingdom of, or city of, 2, 13, 20, 32–3, 124–5, 138, 141, 145, 169, 192, 194–6, 198, 204–5, 207–8, 212–21; and England, 36, 44, 70–2, 193–4, 212; and the papacy or Papal States, 70–2, 183, 189–90
Napoleon III, Emperor of France, 14, 17–21, 106, 123–9, 163, 197–8, 209, 227; and Cavour and Piedmont-Sardinia, 14–17, 20, 22, 101–2, 125, 141, 200, 205, 207, 225; and the Romagna, 118, 130–1, 134–5, 142–3, 148, 151–2, 178–84; and the Marches and Umbria, 197–8, 212–16; and England, 20, 69–70, 89, 93, 120, 143, 151–2, 152–62, 164, 166–8, 178–84, 187–8, 197–8, 198n; and the papacy, 6, 14–17, 78, 81, 86, 89, 94, 123–9, 129–30, 133, 139, 143–4, 146, 151, 152–62, 164–5, 169, 171, 173, 175–7, 189, 196–8, 206–7, 209, 211, 212–26, 223; see France
Napoleon, Prince, (Plon Plon), 137, 198
Nation, The (Dublin), 202
Navy, British, 7, 18, 36, 40, 57–65, 74, 77, 103, 132–3, 137, 141, 148–9, 149–50, 150n, 159–60, 163, 174, 190, 193–4, 195–7, 205–6, 207–8, 210–12, 215–18, 224–6; French, 205, 216; Piedmontese, 211–12; see armed force; non-intervention
Newman, John Henry, 26, 27n
Newton, Charles (British consul in Rome, 1859–61), 44–6, 203–4

Nigra, Constantino (Cavour's representative in Paris), 182, 198
Non-intervention, intervention, 7, 60, 132, 147–52, 155, 163, 165, 167, 175, 193–5, 207, 209–10, 212–21, 225–6; see armed force; navy, British
Normanby, Lord (British Minister at Florence), 50

O'Donnell, Leopoldo (Spanish prime minister), 134
O'Reilly, Major Myles (Commander of the Irish Brigade), 202, 204
Orsini, Felice, 13–14, 32, 187

Panizzi, Antonio (Head, British Museum), 32, 72, 155
Pantaleoni, Dr Diomede (physician in Rome), 42, 56, 227
Palmerston, Lord Henry John Temple (prime minister of Great Britain, 1859–65), 3, 14, 29, 52, 55, 61–2, 70, 107–10, 113, 114–15, 124, 126–9, 147, 163–4, 167, 172, 174, 179, 183, 185, 188, 189, 195, 206–7, 224–5; on the papacy and Papal States, 21, 35–6, 80–7, 118, 123, 126–9, 131–8, 148–52, 159–60, 175–8, 193, 198–200, 203–4, 210–12, 212–21; see Russell, Lord John; Liberals
Papal army, 68–9, 82, 122, 130–9, 141–2, 145, 149, 159, 163, 169–75, 177–8, 189, 191–2, 195–6, 206–12, 226–7; Irish and English, Irish Brigade, 45, 132–3, 200–4, 211; Austrians, 131, 142, 148, 170, 175, 201, 203, 206; French, 191–2, 201; Swiss, 48, 52, 55, 116, 120n, 126, 131, 142, 201
Papal asylum, 141, 174, 214; in Malta, 59–60; in Britain, 156n
Papalini, papal supporters in Italy, see Roman Catholics
Papal Question, 1, 4, 6, 9–12, 31, 50, 59, 67, 88, 95, 110, 119, 127, 132, 136, 138, 140, 144, 160, 165, 166, 184, 196n, 222–3; importance of, 222–3, 225; see Roman Question
Papal reform, 19–21, 22–3, 29, 35–6, 66, 68–70, 72, 82, 85–7, 89–92, 93–6, 98–9, 103, 112, 129–39, 144–5, 154, 161, 165, 226

245

Index

Papal restoration, in 1849, 6, 15, 20–1, 23, 29, 30–1, 59; in the Romagna, 122–3, 129–39, 143, 144–5, 147, 152–5, 158, 161, 163, 169–75, 182–3, 196, 226

Papal States (States of the Church), 2, 6, 9–10, 13, 157–8, 166, 189–92, 192–200, 201–4, 208–12, 212–21, 223–5; structure of, 1–2, 11, 27–29, 218n, 224–7; English diplomatic relations with, 9–10, 40, 46–57, 161, 220, 223–4; English consular relations with, 44–6, 203–4; English commercial relations with, 61–5, 164; see Russell, Odo; Newton, Charles; Romagna; Marches and Umbria; Rome, city of

Papal temporal power, 1–2, 4, 22–39, 117–18, 127–8, 157–62, 169–70, 174–5, 186, 200, 213; and redistribution of territory, 19–21, 66, 69, 86, 90, 94–6, 97, 112, 119, 120, 136, 138, 157, 166, 226–7; and papal sovereignty, 27n, 118–20, 135, 136, 141, 153–4, 157, 171, 182–3; end of, 2–3, 9–12, 21–3, 119–21, 123, 130–1, 134–9, 149, 151–2, 156, 158, 187–8, 200, 211–12, 216, 218, 222–7; importance of, 9–12, 19–20, 25–6, 38, 66, 70, 79, 84, 95–6, 127, 222–3; and England's role, 222–7; see Papal States; Papal Question

Pape et le Congrès, Le, 157–62, 163–4, 166, 169, 171, 174, 187

Parliament, British, on the papacy, 79–87, 88, 98, 101, 111–12, 122–3, 124, 127–8, 166, 172–3, 179, 180, 183–4, 186–7, 198, 203–4, 210, 220, 224; elections (1859), 106–13, 146–7

Parma, *see* Tuscany, Parma, Modena

Patrimony of St Peter (Rome and surrounding region, Latium), 2, 20–1, 119–20, 136, 138, 157–8, 208, 211, 212–21, 222; *see* Rome, city of

Peard, Colonel F.W., 202

Peasants, 27–9, 56–7

Pepoli, Marquis Gioacchino Napoleone (Romagnol official), 124, 130, 137

Perkins, Edward Newton, 121

Persigny, Count Jean de (French ambassador in London), 115, 120, 129, 138, 168, 174, 182

Perugia, revolt in, Perugia 'Massacre', 52–3, 55, 116–18, 120–3, 190, 208

Peter's Pence, 200–4

Petre, William (British representative in Rome, 1844–53), 47

Piedmont–Sardinia, Kingdom of, 2, 3, 5, 6, 14–17, 19–21, 22–3, 93–7, 101–6, 145, 154, 167–9, 178–82, 195–200, 222–7; and the Romagna, Marches and Umbria, 80, 85, 101, 104–6, 114–20, 123, 130–9, 141, 149–52, 163, 167, 184–5, 186, 189–91, 198, 204–12, 212–21; and England, 16, 31–8, 63–5, 75–8, 79, 93–4, 95–6, 114, 149–52, 152, 174, 176–8, 181–2, 193–4, 207–12, 212–21, 223; *see* Cavour; Victor Emmanuel; Romagna; Marches and Umbria

Pius VII, pope (1800–23), 21

Pius IX, pope (1846–78), 1, 2, 13, 34, 41, 124–5, 131, 153, 155, 157, 162, 164–5, 186, 192, 198, 200, 213–14; policy, 22–9, 84, 117–18, 122–3, 125, 128–9, 138–9, 143, 151, 171–5, 192, 223–4, 226–7; on the temporal power, 4, 22–9, 117–18, 139, 153, 171; on papal reform, 22–3, 129–39; on confederation, 128–9; and England and the English, 29, 39, 46, 49, 51–2, 60, 71–2, 73–9, 81, 86–7, 97–101, 112–13, 120, 122–3, 139, 145, 164–5, 198–9, 219–20, 223–7; *see* Russell, Odo; Napoleon III

Plebicites, 184–6, 218, 220

Plombières (July 1858), 14–17, 20, 94, 102, 158, 178, 184, 223

Poerio, Baron Carlo, 32–33, 71

Portugal (Peter V, King), 24, 145, 153–4, 160, 183, 212

Priests, 4–6, 27–9, 30–1, 41–3, 54, 56, 226

Progress, moral and material progress, 3, 4, 6, 35–9, 61–5, 224–5

Protestants, 6, 8–9, 11, 18–19, 30–38, 42, 54–5, 68, 70, 73, 94, 98, 126, 130, 144, 150, 164, 185; *see* Church of England; Evangelicals

Protestant Alliance, National, 33

Protestant Reformation Society, 33

Prussia, 6, 18, 20, 41, 71, 94, 124n, 145, 154, 170, 183, 212, 215, 217

Punch cartoons, 125n, 137n, 143n, 156n,

158n, 163n, 184n, 186n, 196n, 198n, 204n, 210n, 213n, 218n, 227n
Puseyites (Dr Edward Bouverie Pusey), 8, 36–7, 72

Rattazzi, Urbano (Leading member of Piedmontese Government, July 1859 – January 1860), 167
Rechberg, Count Johann von (Austrian prime minister from August 1859), 133, 148, 167, 169–71, 209
Record, The (Anglican newspaper, London), 33
Refugees, 13–14, 32–5, 59–60, 71–2
Religious liberty, 3, 7–8, 29–30, 35–9, 59, 126–7, 149–50, 193, 210, 216–17, 218–19, 223–5; *see* civil liberty; progress
Revolution, political, *passim*; social, 226–7
Ricasoli, Baron Bettino (Tuscan prime minister), 181
Romagna, the, 1, 9, 13, 15–17, 132, 138–9n, 167, 221, 223; revolution in, 1, 25, 113, 114–17, 140, 165–6, 186–8; restoration of papal authority in, 122–3, 129–39, 147–54, 161, 184; political settlement of, 113, 115–17, 129–33, 135–6, 137–9, 142–3, 147–52, 152–62, 163–9, 175–88; annexation to Piedmont, 163–88, 200, 201; and England, 137, 140, 151n, 154, 167, 223, 225; *see* Austria; France; Napoleon III; Liberal nationalists; Cavour
Roman Catholic Church, 2, 4, 11, 22–9, 30–1, 35, 38, 40–1, 53–4, 76, 117–18, 130, 138, 157, 171, 186, 226–7
Roman Catholics, faithful and clergy, 2, 131–2, 145–7, 155, 160, 169–75, 186, 191–2; of the Papal States and Italy (*papalini*), 4–5, 56, 85, 143, 185, 225; of France, 6, 15–16, 23–4, 110, 117, 120, 124, 145–6, 148, 153, 158, 160, 164–5, 168, 171, 176, 178, 180, 182, 197, 223; of Austria, 131, 142, 148, 170, 171, 175; of England and Ireland, 7–9, 11, 23–7, 29–38, 41–3, 72, 77, 106–13, 117, 132–3, 146–7, 160, 171–3, 176–7, 183–4, 197, 200–4, 210, 213–14, 219, 224; of Spain, 6, 160; *see* papal army; Tories; Liberals

Roman Question, 9, 227; *see* Papal Question
Roman Republic and Revolution of 1849, 5, 6, 15, 23, 29–30, 77, 118
Rome, city of, 1–2, 5, 20, 27–9, 34, 40–6, 46–50, 57, 73–9, 119–20, 136, 138, 157–8, 166, 194–200, 205, 207–12, 220–1, 117; *see* France; Liberal nationalists
Rothschild bankers, 208
Rouchefoucauld, Duc de la, 192
Russell, Lady William (Odo Russell's mother), 43, 48, 51, 55, 201
Russell, Lord John (Foreign Minister of Great Britain, 1859–65), 3, 9, 29, 30–1, 46, 48, 50, 107–10, 113, 114–15, 117, 132, 179–88, 195–200, 206, 209–12, 212–21, 224–5; policy and views toward the papacy and the Papal States, 20–1, 52–3, 55, 80–7, 118–23, 124–8, 131–8, 141, 147–52, 153, 159–62, 163–9, 170–1, 175–8, 186–7, 189–91, 193, 198–200, 203–5, 210–12, 212–21, 222–7; *see* Palmerston, Lord; Liberals; Nonintervention
Russell, Odo (British unofficial representative in Rome, 1858–70), 9, 17, 40–65, 66–9, 125, 128, 147, 153–4, 175, 189, 195–6, 209–12, 212–21, 227; status, 9, 46–50, 185, 220, 224; and Pius IX, 9, 22–3, 27, 46, 51, 55–6, 66, 71–2, 74, 78, 162, 198–9, 200, 201–4, 214, 219–20; and Antonelli, 9, 24, 46, 48–9, 51, 56, 66, 72, 80, 90–2, 98–101, 104–6, 130, 139, 147, 156–7, 160–1, 173–4, 191, 196–7, 201–2, 208; and Malmesbury, 40, 47–8, 52–3, 83–5, 91, 97–101, 105–6, 107–11; and Lord John Russell, 46, 48, 52–3, 57, 118–23, 134–5, 144, 151, 153, 158–9, 173, 192, 202, 219; and Whiggism, 50–7, 144, 160; anti-Catholic views of, 50–7, 224
Russia, 6, 20, 94, 145, 154, 170, 183, 212, 215, 217

Sacconi, Monsignor Carlo (papal nuncio in Paris), 22, 79, 103, 117, 134, 143–4, 154–6, 161, 175, 179, 183, 187, 206; and England, 49, 69–70, 72, 79,

Index

81, 85, 90, 92, 134, 154, 158–9, 164–5, 172, 210–11, 213
Sackville West, L.S. (British *chargé d'affairs* in Turin), 64, 147
Saffi, Aurelio, 32
Sardinia, *see* Piedmont–Sardinia
Savoy and Nice, 178–81, 183–4, 187–8, 189–90, 193, 225
Scarlett, Peter (British Minister at Florence), 61
Schismatics (Russian Orthodox), 6, 130, 144
Secularization, 11–12, 14n, 29, 35, 127, 226–7
Settembrini, Luigi, 71
Severn, Joseph (British consul in Rome, 1861–72), 45
Seymour, Hamilton (British representative in Florence), 47
Shaftesbury, Lord, 67, 72
Sicily, *see* Naples, Kingdom of
Simpson, Richard, 27n
Socio-cultural visions, 3–6, 224–5
Spain, 6, 24, 41, 59, 132, 145, 153–4, 156, 183, 186, 201, 210, 212, 213, 214; Spanish troops, 20, 86, 131–4, 142, 169, 206, 215–17, 225; *see* Isabella II, Queen
Standard, The (London), 146
Stratford de Redcliffe, Lord, 41, 55
Styles, Captain Edward, 202
Sullivan, A.M. (editor of The *Nation*, Dublin), 202
Sweden, 145, 154

Tablet, The (Catholic newspaper, London), 26, 43, 74, 76n–7, 110, 112, 146–7, 172–3, 185
Talbot, George (private chamberlain of Pius IX), 43, 50, 54n, 77, 171n, 214, 219
Thouvenel, Edouard-Antoine (French Foreign Minister from January 1860), 164, 167–8, 171, 176, 178–82, 186, 197–8, 200, 206, 208, 209, 213–14
Taylor, Brook, 20
Times, The (London), 32, 42–3, 77, 111, 146–7, 157n, 172, 191
Tories, Tory government (1858–59), 2, 3, 23, 29, 52, 66–87, 88–113, 222; as opposition, 128, 166, 172–3, 176–7, 220; and Roman Catholics, 29–31, 106–13, 146–7, 172–3, 176–7, 183–4, 224–5; *see* Malmesbury; Derby
Trade, British and papal, 3, 7, 46, 57–65, 118, 137, 149–50, 164, 212, 219, 224–5; *see* material prosperity
Tuscany, Parma, Modena, the Duchies of, 2, 13, 17, 47, 64, 89–92, 93–4, 96–7, 102–4, 106, 115–17, 120, 124, 131, 132–3, 137–8, 142, 145, 147–52, 154–5, 159, 166, 167–8, 176–7, 179–82, 184–8, 194, 214, 220–1

Ullathorne, Bishop (Bishop of Birmingham), 41, 172
Umbria, *see* Marches and Umbria
Univers, Le (French Catholic newspaper), 109–10
Universe, The (British Catholic newspaper), 26

Venetia and Lombardy, 2, 6, 18, 106, 120, 124, 129, 165, 166n, 176, 196–7, 200, 205–6, 208, 210, 212, 217, 220–1
Victor Emmanuel, King of Piedmont–Sardinia, 1, 3, 5–6, 57, 106, 116, 124, 125–6, 139, 141, 142–3, 150–2, 153, 159, 178–80, 186, 190, 209–12, 214, 221; and England, 36, 75–8, 125–6, 209–12, 218–21; and Garibaldi, 199, 205, 207–8, 218; *see* Piedmont–Sardinia; Cavour
Victoria, Queen of Great Britain and Ireland, 2, 4, 7, 36, 57, 173, 205; and the Tories, 2, 17, 18, 103–4; and the Liberals, 2, 113, 114, 119, 120, 125, 127, 128–9n, 136, 137n, 138, 149, 150, 155, 159, 160n, 164, 165–6, 179, 193, 195, 203, 216, 217–18, 220; and Pius IX, 70, 73–9
Vienna, Treaty of (1815), 6, 13, 18–21, 94, 145, 169, 183, 217, 222, 225
Views of history, interpretation of history, 3–6, 25–6, 29, 37–9, 57, 126–7, 157, 165, 169–70, 188, 189, 195–6, 200, 216–17, 219, 224–5
Villafranca, Peace of (1859), 123–9, 132, 144; *see* Austro-Sardinian War (1859)

Walewski, Count Alexander (French Foreign Minister until January 1860), 69, 89, 93, 101, 121, 125, 129, 133–5, 141, 144, 148, 159, 165

Index

Whigs, *see* Liberals
Williams, Penry, 42
Wiseman, Nicholas, Cardinal
   (Archbishop of Westminster), 7, 24–5
   26n, 30–1, 36, 41–3, 50, 108–11,
   146–7, 172–3, 201, 214
Wood, Shakespeare, 42
Woodward, Rev. F.B. (Anglican
   Chaplain in Rome), 43

Wreford, Henry (*The Times*
   correspondent in Italy), 44
Zambianchi, General, 194–5
Zurich, Treaty of (1859), 127–9, 133,
   140, 143, 148, 151–2, 154–5, 168

DATE DUE

DEC 1 6 1999			

HIGHSMITH #45230